MEDIA CULTURE

In this thorough update of one of the classic texts of media and cultural studies, Douglas Kellner argues that media culture is now the dominant form of culture that socializes us and provides and plays major roles in the economy, polity, and social and cultural life.

The book includes a series of lively studies that both illuminate contemporary culture and society, while providing methods of analysis, interpretation, and critique to engage contemporary U.S. culture. Many people today talk about cultural studies, but Kellner actually does it, carrying through a unique mixture of theoretical analysis and concrete discussions of some of the most popular and influential forms of contemporary media culture. Studies cover a wide range of topics including: Reagan and *Rambo*; horror and youth films; women's films, the TV series *Orange Is the New Black* and Hulu's TV series based on Margaret Atwood's *The Handmaid's Tale*; the films of Spike Lee and African American culture; Latino films and cinematic narratives on migration; female pop icons Madonna, Beyoncé, and Lady Gaga; fashion and celebrity; television news, documentary films, and the recent work of Michael Moore; fantasy and science fiction, with focus on the cinematic version of *Lord of the Rings*, Philip K. Dick and the *Blade Runner* films, and the work of David Cronenberg.

Situating the works of media culture in their social context, within political struggles, and the system of cultural production and reception, Kellner develops a multidimensional approach to cultural studies that broadens the field and opens it to a variety of disciplines. He also provides new approaches to the vexed question of the effects of culture and offers new perspectives for cultural studies. Anyone interested in the nature and effects of contemporary society and culture should read this book.

Douglas Kellner is George Kneller Chair in the Philosophy of Education at UCLA, U.S.A., and is author of many books on social theory, politics, history, and culture, including *American Nightmare: Donald Trump, Media Spectacle, and Authoritarian Populism* (2016) and *American Horror Show: Election 2016 and the Ascent of Donald J. Trump* (2017).

MEDIA CULTURE

Cultural Studies, Identity, and Politics in the Contemporary Moment

Second Edition
25th Anniversary Edition

Douglas Kellner

Routledge
Taylor & Francis Group

LONDON AND NEW YORK

Second edition published 2020
by Routledge
2 Park Square, Milton Park, Abingdon, Oxon OX14 4RN

and by Routledge
52 Vanderbilt Avenue, New York, NY 10017

Routledge is an imprint of the Taylor & Francis Group, an informa business

First edition published by Routledge 1995

British Library Cataloguing-in-Publication Data
A catalogue record for this book is available from the British Library

Library of Congress Cataloging-in-Publication Data
Names: Kellner, Douglas, 1943- author.
Title: Media culture : cultural studies, identity, and politics in the
contemporary moment / Douglas Kellner.
Description: Second edition. | London ; New York : Routledge, 2020. |
Includes bibliographical references and index.
Identifiers: LCCN 2019057990 (print) | LCCN 2019057991 (ebook) |
ISBN 9780367199333 (hardback) | ISBN 9780367199340 (paperback) |
ISBN 9780429244230 (ebook)
Subjects: LCSH: Mass media–United States. | Popular culture–United
States.
Classification: LCC P92.U5 K38 2020 (print) | LCC P92.U5 (ebook) |
DDC 302.230973–dc23
LC record available at https://lccn.loc.gov/2019057990
LC ebook record available at https://lccn.loc.gov/2019057991

ISBN: 978-0-367-19933-3 (hbk)
ISBN: 978-0-367-19934-0 (pbk)
ISBN: 978-0-429-24423-0 (ebk)

Typeset in Bembo
by Swales & Willis, Exeter, Devon, UK

Printed in the United Kingdom
by Henry Ling Limited

CONTENTS

Introduction to *Media Culture* 2020   **1**
Media culture and society 3
Batman *and social corruption 6*
Media/cultural studies, social theory, and critical media literacy 8

**1   Theory wars, ideology critique, and media/cultural
     studies**   **15**
Theory wars 18
Ideology and media culture: critical methods 21
Rambo *as global media spectacle 23*
Approaches to media/cultural studies 28
         The Frankfurt School 29
         British cultural studies and its legacy 31
Components of a critical media/cultural studies 36
Notes 47

2   For a critical media/cultural studies   **52**
For a critical intersectional multiculturalism 53
Toward a multiperspectival cultural studies 58
The Handmaid's Tale *as dystopia and ecological/political critique 62*
Superheroes from Wonder Woman to Black Panther 69
Notes 77

3   Social anxiety, horror, and American nightmares   **80**
Hollywood and horror 81
Poltergeist, *the occult, and anxieties of the middle class 84*

American Horror Story *and the crisis of the family and patriarchy 89*
Extreme horror, violence, and American nightmares 91
    Halloween, slasher films, and the last girl standing 92
    Racial and class angst in the Trump Era: *Get Out, Us,*
    and *Sorry to Bother You* 98
Notes 104

4   **Race, resistance, and representation**   **107**
   The films of Spike Lee 108
      Do the Right Thing as a Brechtian morality tale 109
      From *Malcolm X* to *BlacKkKlansman* 116
   Ava DuVernay and female empowerment 120
   Latino, immigration, and the American dream 126
   Immigration to the promised land 139
   Notes 142

5   **Gender and sexuality wars**   **147**
   Women's films, female resistance, and empowerment 148
   Epic of intersectionality: Orange Is the New Black *153*
   Men's films and crises of masculinity and patriarchy 159
      Dude flicks and the renegotiation of masculinity 167
   The LGBTQ+ movement and Hollywood's exploration of gays,
    lesbians, transsexuals, and multiple forms of queer identity 169
   Notes 176

6   **Youth, identities, and fashion**   **179**
   Youth films from Alan Freed to Slacker *181*
      Richard Linklater: auteur of youth 183
      The *Slacker* effect 184
      Social anxiety and class: Mike Judge from *Beavis and*
      Butt-Head to *Silicon Valley* 187
   Buffy the Vampire Slayer *as spectacular allegory:*
   a diagnostic critique 192
   Fashion and identity 200
   Pop culture icons from Madonna to Beyoncé and Lady Gaga 203
   Notes 208

7   **News, entertainment, and documentary as political**
   spectacle   **211**
   Presidential politics: the movie 212
   News and infotainment as contested terrain 227
   The Barack Obama media spectacle 229

The Donald Trump reality show presidency 236
Political documentary: Michael Moore vs. Corporate America and
  the conservative political establishment 245
Notes 249

8   **Fantasy, technoculture, and dystopia**   255
Fantasy entertainment as political allegory: reading LOTR *256*
David Cronenberg, the technoculture, and the new flesh 269
Blade runners, dystopia, and social apocalypse 277
    The apocalyptic vision of Philip K. Dick 279
    Androids, humans, and entropy in the *Blade Runner* films 281
Notes 286

**Conclusion: technologies, literacies, and the future
of media culture**   289
From the future back to the present 289
Critical media pedagogy 294
Media and cultural activism 296
Media, cultural policy,and cultural politics 298
Notes 302

Bibliography   *303*
Index   *317*

INTRODUCTION TO *MEDIA CULTURE* 2020

A media culture emerged in the twentieth century in which images, sounds, stories, and spectacles helped produce the fabric of everyday life, dominating leisure time, shaping political views and social behavior, and providing the materials out of which people forge their very identities. Radio, television, film, popular music, newspapers and magazines, the Internet and social networking, accompanied by the rise and dissemination of new media platforms like Facebook, YouTube, and Google, help construct our notion of what it means to be male or female, and our conception of class, of ethnicity and race, of nationality, of sexuality. Media culture divides the world into categories of "us" and "them" and tell us who are our friends and enemies, who we should love and hate, and who we are and should be.

Media images, narratives and spectacles thus help shape our view of the world and our deepest values: what we consider good or bad, positive or negative, moral or evil. Media stories provide the symbols, myths, and resources through which we constitute a common culture and through the appropriation of which we insert ourselves into this culture. Media spectacles demonstrate who has power and who is powerless, who is allowed to exercise force and violence, and who is not. They dramatize and legitimate the power of the powers that be and show the powerless that they must stay in their places.

Media culture encompasses radio and the commercial reproduction of sound disseminated by the music industry in ever-changing formats from albums to CDs to digital devices. It consists of the mutating film, television, and video industries with their theatrical spectacles and cable channels that show everything from movies to TV news and entertainment to sports to pornography. Significantly, media culture has been absorbed into the Internet and social networking that transforms the products of media culture into digital artifacts and pleasures.

Media culture was initially industrial culture, organized on the model of mass production and consumption, and for decades was produced largely for mass audiences according to genre and formula, producing products that would attract consumers, fans, and dollars. It has been a form of commercial culture and its products are commodities that attempt to attract private profit produced by giant corporations interested in the accumulation of capital. Since media culture in the United States and other countries that privilege media corporations over state media must attract large audiences, it must resonate with current themes and concerns, popular tastes and pleasures, and thus is highly topical, providing hieroglyphics of contemporary social life. Yet media culture is increasingly a high-tech culture, deploying the most advanced technologies and new forms of media. It is a vibrant sector of the economy, one of the most profitable sectors and one that is attaining global prominence. Media culture is thus a form of technoculture that merges culture and technology in new forms and configurations, producing novel types of societies in which media and technology become organizing principles.

Since, we are immersed from cradle to grave in a media culture and society, it is important to learn how to understand, interpret, and criticize its meanings and messages. The media are a profound and often misperceived source of cultural pedagogy: They contribute to educating us how to behave and what to think, feel, believe, fear, and desire – and what not to. The media are forms of pedagogy that teach us how to be men and women. They show us how to dress, look, and consume; how to react to members of different social groups; how to be popular and successful and how to avoid failure; and how to conform to the dominant system of norms, values, practices, and institutions. Consequently, learning how to read, criticize, and resist sociocultural manipulation can help empower oneself in relation to dominant forms of media and culture. It can enhance individual sovereignty vis-à-vis media culture and give people more power over their cultural environment and the necessary forms of literacy necessary to empower us in our contemporary media environment and to participate in a society that increasingly demands new forms of literacy.

Hence, the realities of twenty-first-century life, and the technological and information revolutions that characterize it, demand that all citizens become media literate. And, in fact, many universities are expanding and opening up their cinema/television courses to the university at large, due to rising demands for these kinds of analytical and practical skills, which are hardly restricted anymore to those looking for careers in the entertainment industry. In particular, the pedagogy of critical media literacy should be an essential part of education (Kellner and Share 2019). Unfortunately, too many educational forums ignore or undervalue the significance of critical media literacy as a crucial dimension of knowledge.

Living in a media culture, it is the responsibility of everyone to become media literate and to learn to read, interpret, critique, contextualize, and even produce media culture. In today's media-and-technology-saturated world, everyone can contribute to discussion, critique, and media creation through social media and new technologies and platforms. Individuals can not only participate in critical discussions of their media culture, society, and politics, but increasingly can even create their own narratives, images, analyses and media artifacts as the tools of media production become part of the digital devices of everyday life.

Indeed, it is one of the aims of this book to provide a practical guide to learning to become media literate and to be able to read, analyze, interpret, and criticize the images, narratives, and messages of the major multiple forms of media culture. This edition of *Media Culture* is designed for undergraduate and graduate students, as well as a general audience who are interested in critical media studies and practices. It will provide an introductory framework for understanding and decoding major forms of media culture from a critical media literacy perspective. Rather than separating different forms of media into generic categories, this text will introduce students to critical theories and practices that are applicable to dominant media forms and artifacts, and will emphasize the underlying similarities in seemingly disparate media, as well as differences in industries, genres, and forms of media culture.

Media culture and society

In this Introduction, I discuss the potential contributions of a media/cultural studies perspective to empower individuals to engage in media critique and to gain critical media literacy. The following chapters help provide understandings of contemporary media culture and suggests ways that it can be understood, used, and appreciated. I want to provide each reader with resources to learn to study, analyze, interpret, and criticize the texts of media culture and to appraise their impact. I examine some of the ways that media culture intersects with political and social struggles and helps shape everyday life, influencing how people think and behave, how they see themselves and other people, and how they construct their identities.

Accordingly, the following studies will explore some of the ways that contemporary media culture provides forms of ideological domination that help to reproduce the current relations of power, while also providing resources for the construction of identities and for empowerment, resistance, and struggle. I argue that media culture is a *contested terrain* across which key social groups and competing political ideologies struggle for dominance in ever-changing conflicts, and that individuals live through these struggles through the images, discourses, myths, and spectacles of media culture. Indeed, individuals construct their subjectivities, identities, and their place in the world in part through their engagement with media culture.

Culture in the broadest sense is a form of highly participatory activities in which people create and reproduce their societies and identities. Culture shapes individuals, drawing out and cultivating their potentialities and capacities for speech, action, and creativity. Media culture is also involved in these processes, yet it is something new in the human adventure. Our culture *is* a media culture in which individuals spend tremendous amounts of time listening to the radio, watching television, going to see films, experiencing music, going shopping, reading magazines and newspapers, or doing all these things and more on their digital devices.

Thus media culture has come to dominate everyday life, serving as the ubiquitous background and often the highly seductive foreground of our attention and activity, which many argue is undermining human potentiality and creativity. This book will explore some of the consequences for a society and culture dominated by media culture. It will probe the nature and influences of the ways in which this form of culture is deeply influencing many aspects of our everyday life. A major theme of this book concerns how the forms of media culture position individuals to identify with dominant social and political ideologies, positions, representations, and figures, and how the dynamics of race, gender, sexuality, class, and other key dimensions of social and political struggle play out in media culture.

In general, media culture in the twenty-first-century United States is not a system of rigid ideological indoctrination that induces consent to existing capitalist–patriarchal societies, but enables individuals to participate in the pleasure of the media, cyber, and consumer culture. Media entertainment is often highly pleasurable and uses images, sounds, stories, and spectacle to enjoin individuals to participate in a system of commercial gratification and pleasures, including consuming various forms of media culture for hours on end, day after day, year after year.

In advanced capitalist societies, media and consumer culture work hand in hand to generate thought and behavior that conform to existing values, institutions, beliefs, and practices, and certain forms of media culture may influence individuals to accept dominant political ideologies, attitudes, parties, and figures. Yet audiences are not simply, or solely brainwashed, and may resist dominant meanings, values, and messages, and create their own readings and appropriations of mass-produced culture, and thus use their culture as resources to empower themselves and to invent their own meanings, identities, forms of life, and even forms of media culture themselves through social networking and emerging modes of media production and distribution.

Hence, media culture itself provides resources that individuals can emulate and modify, or reject, in forming their own identities against dominant models. Media culture thus induces individuals to conform in some ways to the established organization of society, but it also provides resources that can empower individuals to rebel against existing society and culture. Exploring these contradictory functions and effects will be one of the goals of this book.

Media culture is highly complex and so far has resisted any generally accepted theorizations, although there have been many attempts. Most general theories, as I'll indicate in the following pages, appear one-sided and blind to important aspects of media culture. Most theories of media manipulation and domination that were highly popular in the 1960s, and continued to resonate in succeeding decades to the present, assumed that the media were all-powerful forces of social control and that they imposed a monolithic dominant ideology on their victims. Reacting against this model, many theories in recent years emphasized the power of audiences to resist media manipulation, to create their own meanings and uses, and to empower themselves with materials from media culture. As we shall see in the following studies, these and other current theories of the media are one-sided, limited, and should give way to more comprehensive and multi-dimensional critical approaches that theorize the contradictory nature and effects of media culture.

Theories of the media and culture are, I believe, best developed through specific studies of concrete phenomena contextualized within the vicissitudes of contemporary society and history. Thus, to interrogate contemporary media culture critically involves carrying out studies of how the culture industries produce specific artifacts that reproduce the social discourses and ideas that are embedded in key conflicts and struggles of the day. This involves seeing how popular texts like the *Star Wars*, *Lord of the Rings*, *Avatar*, and other blockbuster franchises, rap music or punk, key genres of television entertainment such as reality TV, advertising, news, and discussion shows all articulate specific ideological positions and help reproduce dominant forms of social power, serving the interests of societal elites or dominant social groups – or, by contrast, represent resistance to the dominant forms of culture and society. Yet I also argue that we should recognize that specific cultural texts may have contradictory messages and effects, and are always interpreted by individuals who have their own subject positions according to their class, gender, race, sexual orientation, region, religion, or other forms of identity.

Accordingly, in the studies that follow, I attempt to demonstrate how some of the most popular cultural texts and forms of the past decades are involved in and mediated by specific political and cultural struggles. The study of popular and mass-mediated culture has been influenced by various forms of "cultural studies," which I'll describe in the following chapter. In this book, I provide some models of a media/cultural studies that is critical, multicultural, and multi-perspectival. A critical media/cultural studies conceptualizes society as a terrain of domination and resistance, and engages in a critique of domination and of the ways that media culture engages in reproducing relationships of domination and oppression.

A critical media/cultural studies is concerned with advancing the democratic project, conceptualizing both how media culture can be a tremendous impediment for democratizing society, but can also be an ally, advancing the cause of freedom, democracy, and social justice. Media culture can be an impediment to democracy to the extent that it reproduces reactionary discourses, promoting racism, sexism, classism, ageism, and other forms of prejudice. Yet media culture can also advance the interests of oppressed and subordinate groups if it attacks oppressive forms like racism or sexism, or at least undermines them with more empowering representations and narratives of race and gender.

I argue throughout this book that media culture is highly political, and is involved in the key political struggles of its era that involve such things as race, gender, class, sexuality, political ideologies, religion, and topics like the environment, state, corporation, police, or military. Its representations, narratives, and spectacles often reproduce or support specific political positions like celebrating macho males and patriarchy, while promoting or opposing phenomena like sexism, racism, classism, or ageism.

Batman and social corruption

To illustrate the complex politics of contemporary Hollywood film in the 2000s I shall offer a reading of two of the popular Batman franchise films directed by Christopher Nolan, *Batman Begins* (2004) and *The Dark Knight*, the highest grossing film of 2008.[1] Hollywood film in the 2000s thrives on franchises like Batman that provide material for highly popular cinematic spectacles yet they arguably can provide illuminating insights into the period from which they arise. Christopher Nolan's two Batman films arguably present a critical allegory about the corruption, violence, and nihilism of the Bush/Cheney era.

In an earlier era, *Superman* I (1978) and II (1980) and other superhero films of the late 1970s and 1980s showed the yearning in the American popular imagination for a Savior/Redeemer who would save us from the morass of confusion coming out of the 1960s and 1970s and restore an older America, helping to fuel Reaganite conservatism (see Kellner and Ryan 1988: 217ff.). Some of the superhero films of the last years of the Bush/Cheney regime, by contrast, can be read as a critique of the failed conservative regime. The Batman films of the late Bush/Cheney era show the polity to be utterly corrupt and the economic, political and legal system in paralysis, approximately the case by the end of the failed Bush/Cheney era.

The theme of police, military, and government corruption and failure to solve social problems is on display throughout Christopher Nolan's *Batman Begins* (2004). His Batman (Christian Bale) is a human-all-too-human figure who must overpower his fears (of bats) and remorse over the murder of his parents after bat-figures in an opera frightened the young lad and he maneuvered his parents to leave early, leading them to a mugging and murder. Grown up, he is devastated with remorse and guilt, but learns the martial arts disciplines and gains the technology necessary to be a crusader against evil.

The evil in *Batman Begins* involves the deranged scientist Dr. Jonathan Crane, a.k.a. Scarecrow, plotting to poison Gotham's water supply – a barely disguised figure for Weapons of Mass Destruction unleashing mass murder. Other villains involve the League of Shadows and its sinister and mysterious leader Ra Al Guhl, a figure for the threat of China as a potential strategic enemy; these villains have a gas extracted from a rare flower to decimate the populace, another WMD figure, evoking fears of biological weapons.

However, it is Earle (Rutger Hauer), the ruthless CEO of Bruce Wayne's (a.k.a. Batman) family corporation, who is producing, among other things, WMDs, who aids the villains. Further, the film presents an almost totally corrupt legal system, dominated by corporate and criminal powers, an analogue to the Bush/Cheney administration partisan evisceration of the political and legal system, just as the malfeasance of corporate criminals in the film is an analogue to corporate corruption in the contemporary era.

In Nolan's follow-up *The Dark Knight* (2008), the vision is darker, the corruption and chaos is more pervasive, and the film overlaps with recent social apocalypse films that portray the system under crisis and careening toward collapse (see Chapter 8). Crime is on the rise again in Gotham, but tabloid newspapers are questioning Batman's vigilante tactics with headlines screaming: "Batman: Crusader or Menace?" Bruce Wayne/Batman's longtime love Rachel (Maggie Gyllenhaal) is involved with Gotham's charismatic and committed D.A. Harvey Dent (Aaron Eckhart), who is presented as the squeaky-clean Good Knight. Despite Dent's involvement with his beloved Rachel, Batman, questioning his own tactics and outside-the-law status, comes to believe that Gotham needs a completely honest and competent D.A. to clean up crime and replace Batman as the center of law enforcement, and strongly supports Dent.

It appears that the Joker (Heath Ledger) is behind the recent crime outbreak in Gotham, which includes hits on a mob bank, unleashing retaliatory crime by the town's criminal elements. The Joker, frighteningly inhabited by Heath Ledger, is presented as the spirit of anarchy and chaos, of a particularly destructive and nihilistic nature. In the contemporary context, Joker represents the spirit of terrorism and the film is full of iconography related to 9/11, with dark whirling clouds of smoke and explosions of sound in the opening frame suggesting a city under attack. As the convoluted plot unfolds, the succeeding spectacle portrays a series of attacks on the inner city, targeting corporations, banks, the police, and the legal system. In this desperate situation, Batman goes after the Joker, employing surveillance of the telephone system, putting civil rights and the constitution aside, and torturing the Joker once he is caught. This appears to legitimate Bush/Cheney politics against terrorism and going over the Dark Side: if our enemy, the logic runs, is absolutely evil, anything we do to destroy him is good, including going over to the Dark Side.[2] In fact, a columnist for Rupert Murdoch's *Wall Street Journal* claimed that Batman was a figure for George W. Bush himself, who went over to the Dark Side to fight terror and took criticisms from liberals for pursuing his unpopular but supposedly necessary policies like torture and surveillance.[3]

The film, however, sharply criticizes the tactics of the Dark Side, as it appears that the Joker manipulated Batman, Dent, and the police to get them to carry out his evil agenda. Police surveillance helps capture the Joker who, when submitted to torture, lies, leading Rachel to be kidnapped. The previously upright Dent is drawn into the abyss by the Joker, killing one person a day to keep

Rachel alive and when she is killed he goes over the edge and into the Dark Side himself, symbolized by his disfigurement and transformation into Two-Face. Like the villain Chirgurh in *No Country For Old Men* (2007), Dent sacrifices morality and choice for a flip of the coin, deciding people's fates, a plunge into a completely meaningless existence of pure contingency and nihilism.

Thus, *The Dark Knight* portrays the deep morass and abyss of the Bush/Cheney era. Together, the Batman films of the 2000s articulate the dark, deep pessimism of a populace plagued by its own economic and political elites and deadly enemies that want to destroy them. The dark and murky political allegory suggests that going over to the dark side twists and corrupts individuals and a society, and that, paraphrasing Nietzsche, if you look into the face of a monster long enough you become the monster.

Media/cultural studies, social theory, and critical media literacy

Since political struggles and ideologies unfold in a specific social and historical context, a critical media/cultural studies involves critical social theory of the historical context in which media culture in a specific place and era in which it is produced and consumed. Hence, throughout this book I employ social theory to properly contextualize, interpret, and analyze the nature and effects of specific artifacts of media culture. It is my conviction that cultural studies cannot be done without social theory, and that we need to understand the structure and dynamics of a given society to understand and interpret its culture. I am also assuming that media cultural texts are neither merely vehicles of a dominant ideology, nor pure and innocent entertainment. Rather, they are complex artifacts that embody social and political discourses whose analysis and interpretations require methods of reading and critique that articulate their embeddedness in the political economy, social relations, and the political environment within which they are produced, circulated, and received.

The following studies take this comprehensive approach to the study of media culture and use the resources of history, social theory, communications research, and cultural studies to elucidate some of the meanings and effects of popular cultural forms. Examples range from films that reproduce or contest conservative ideologies from the Age of Reagan to the Trump Era. Politics also involves the dynamics of race, gender, class, and sexuality, and so I explore African American culture from the films of Spike Lee and rap music, and other forms of popular music, while discussing how rebellions of various cultural types circulate through the music of Madonna, Lady Gaga, rap, and punk. I engage popular films including the films of Spike Lee and Michael Moore, youth films like *Slacker*, and a film and a TV series presenting Margaret Atwood's *Handmaid's Tale*. I will also critically dissect news and information, and how infotainment and propaganda entered political media spectacles. I discuss the transition from the Bush/Cheney to the the Obama and Trump presidencies in terms of the emergence of more diverse and liberal TV entertainment and news and how Donald Trump used techniques of propaganda and disinformation to help win the 2016 presidential election and to (mis)govern during his administration. As I write in 2020, the relationship between Donald Trump's reality TV series *The Apprentice* and his reality TV presidency is widely discussed and will also be engaged in this book.

I assume that society and culture are contested terrains and that cultural artifacts are produced and have their effects within determinate contexts. It is my conviction that the analysis of media culture within its matrix of production and reception helps illuminate its artifacts and their possible effects and uses, as well as the contours and trends within their broader socio-political context. Since the forms of culture produced by giant media and entertainment conglomerates are an immediate and pervasive aspect of contemporary life, and since media culture is both constituted by and constitutive of larger social and political dynamics, it is an excellent optic to illuminate the nature of contemporary society, politics, and everyday life. Indeed, I will argue that understanding popular Hollywood films, TV series, musical forms and performers, and news and infotainment can help us to understand our contemporary societies. That is, understanding why certain artifacts are popular can illuminate the social environment in which they arise and are circulated, and can thus provide insight into what is going on in established societies and cultures.

My focus is on media culture in the United States from the 1980s to the contemporary moment, but since U.S. culture is increasingly exported to the entire world, this study should illuminate dominant forms of globalized consumer and media culture elsewhere as well. U.S. media culture has invaded cultures all over the world, producing new forms of what I call the *global popular*. Such phenomena of U.S. media culture as the *Batman, Jurassic Park,* or *Star Wars* films; pop entertainers like Madonna, Michael Jackson, Lady Gaga, Beyoncé, Jennifer Lopez, and rap music; CNN and the documentaries of Michael Moore; and U.S. TV series, advertising, fashion, and consumer culture are popular throughout the world, thus the studies collected here should be of global and not merely regional interest.

My media/cultural studies were conceived and begun during a specific historical moment, that of the triumph of conservativism in the United States and other Western capitalist democracies in the 1980s. Accordingly, I begin in Chapter 1 by setting out my concept of the types of media/cultural studies and social theory needed to understand contemporary media culture. I discuss the theory and cultural wars of recent decades, and review some of the key models of cultural studies and social theory that I will deploy in this book, including the Frankfurt School, British Cultural Studies, postmodern and poststructuralist theories, and an array of critical theories focusing on race, gender, sexuality, and other major components of media culture.

I use the term *media/cultural studies* since the topic of my research is media culture, which itself points to the dimensions of mass media of communications and the terrain of culture. There has been a binary division of the study of media culture since the 1960s between a humanities and text-based literary and cultural approach to media culture opposed to a social science-based empirical and media-based approach, as in the dominant models of communications studies (Kellner 1997). Overcoming this divide, I will use history, political economy, social and theory, and myriad methods of textual interpretation and critical theory to engage the high complex terrain of media culture. Hence, my perspective is transdisciplinary and will use multiple theories to the contested terrain of contemporary media culture.

I will explicate more fully the concept of media/cultural studies in Chapter 1 where I will explicate the main sources of my analyses of media culture and articulate the model, methods, and metatheory of media/cultural studies that I deploy, which I illustrate through reading a reading of "*Rambo* as global media spectacle." In Chapter 2, I begin delineating my model of a critical and multicultural media/cultural studies, and argue that to critically engage the texts of media culture we need to critique the intersection of class, gender, race, sexuality, and other key determinants of culture and identity in order to more fully conceptualize the ideological dimensions of cultural texts and to appraise the full range of their effects. This claim is illustrated in a discussion of how the 2017–2019 Hulu TV version of Margaret Atwood's *The Handmaid's Tale* can be mobilized to provide radical critiques of the patriarchy and conservative politics in the contemporary moment.

I further delineate my model of a cultural studies that is critical, multicultural, and multiperspectivist, and explicate key concepts of ideology critique, diagnostic critique, and intersectionality. I indicate as well the need to read media culture against its ideological grain, to ferret out critical and subversive moments in conservative or liberal texts, and to analyze how the ideological projects of media texts often fail. I also explicate a concept of diagnostic critique that uses media culture to diagnose social trends and tendencies, reading through the texts to the fantasies, fears, hopes, desire, and political discourses that they articulate, which I illustrate through a reading of "Superheroes from *Wonder Woman* to *Black Panther*."

A diagnostic critique also analyzes how media culture provides the resources of producing identities and advances either reactionary or progressive politics – or provides ambiguous texts and effects that can be appropriated in various ways, sometimes contradictory. Next, in Chapter 3, I take on "Social anxiety, horror, and American nightmares" by, first, engaging "*Poltergeist*, the occult, and anxieties of the middle class." I follow with examination of "*American Horror Story* and the crisis of the family and patriarchy," and conclude the chapter with studies of "Extreme horror, violence, and American nightmares," with a section on "*Halloween*, slasher films, and the last girl standing" followed by a study of "Racial and class angst in the Trump era: *Get Out*, *Us*, and *Sorry to Bother You*."

Thus, whereas Chapter 2 showed how Hollywood films transcoded dominant conservative political discourses of their era, Chapter 3 indicates how the desires, anxieties, and insecurities of individuals in a specific historical epoch find expression in media culture, allowing the depiction of crisis tendencies beneath the ideological façade of a happy, secure consumer society. Appraising the politics of media culture thus ranges from ideological critique of the way that popular texts embody dominant political discourses concerning the major political issues and conflicts of the day to analyzing texts that encode the politics of everyday life and the anxieties and tensions concerning class, race, gender, youth, and the hopes and yearnings of different groups of people in a specific society at a particular time.

Succeeding chapters go into specific fields of the politics of representation with Chapter 4 focusing on "Race, resistance, and representation" in media culture with, first, a study of the films of Spike Lee, which provide an exemplary instance of the cinematic exploration of key issues of race, gender, and class in the contemporary moment. Drawing on Black feminist and political criticism of his films, I examine Lee's work and the contributions and limitations of his style, texts, and politics. I also engage the topics of the work of "Ava DuVernay and female empowerment" and "Latinos, immigration, and the American dream" with deals with some exemplary Latino/a filmmakers followed by a study of "Immigration to the promised land" – a theme that has become explosively central to U.S. politics and culture in the Trump era that is mutating daily as I conclude this book in winter 2019.

Chapter 4 as a whole examines some of the ways that radical cultural producers of color are pushing beyond the previously established limits of mainstream culture to articulate their experiences of oppression, rage, and rebellion while Chapter 5 engages "Gender and sexuality wars." Indeed, intense struggles in contemporary U.S. society have been taking place for decades on the terrain of gender and sexuality. From the 1960s to the present #MeToo movement, feminist and gay and lesbian movements challenged representations of gender and sexuality, and media culture of the era exhibit the gender wars with films that are anti-feminist and present negative and conventional images of women contrasted to films with stars such as Jane Fonda, Meryl Streep, Oprah Winfrey, Jennifer Lawrence, and Penélope Cruz, which present more empowering representations and narratives concerning women. I illustrate the gender wars with studies of "Women's Films, Female Resistance, and Empowerment" and a look at "Epic of Intersectionality: *Orange Is the New Black*" that takes on a popular TV series of the contemporary era.

The other side of the gender wars involves contested representations of masculinity involving contrasting representations of men that exhibit crises of masculinity, bromance between male characters, and the continuation of hard toxic masculinity that characterized much previous Hollywood film that I discuss through study of "Men's films and crises of masculinity and patriarchy." I then turn to sexuality wars with studies of "The LGBTQ+ movement and Hollywood's exploration of gays, lesbians, transsexuals, and multiple forms of queer sexuality." This study engages wars over sexuality with the contest of representations contrasting homophobic images and narratives with more positive images of gay, lesbian, and transgender characters. This discussion provides an opportunity to deflate the myth of binaries that operative with problematic contrasts of masculine and feminine, or straight vs gay sexuality, while many people combine character traits and behavior associated with one or the other side of the binaries that establish conventional gender roles and sexuality.

The book as a whole is concerned with media culture and identities, politics, and the need for critical media literacies to empower audiences, producers, and consumers of media culture. In Chapter 6, I engage "Youth, identities, and fashion" through, first, a study of "Youth films from Alan Freed to *Slacker*" and then studies of the work of Richard Linklater as an "Auteur of youth" followed by engaging "Social anxiety and class" in the work of "Mike Judge from *Beavis and Butthead* to *Silicon Valley*." I then move to "*Buffy the Vampire Slayer* as spectacular allegory: a diagnostic critique." This is followed by study of "Fashion and identity" illustrated by a section on "Pop culture icons from Madonna to Beyoncé and Lady Gaga." This section engages the role of popular music, stars and celebrities, and fashion in contemporary media culture. I argue that Madonna's shifts in image and identity articulate transformations in values and politics of the epoch, as well as reflecting stages of her life and career, while Lady Gaga, Beyoncé, and subsequent superstar performers represent further changes in style, fashion, identity, and gender politics.

Chapter 7 focuses on "News, entertainment, and documentary as entertainment" opening with a discussion of how media narratives depicted shifts from the conservative Reagan regime to Clinton's liberal presidency to the Bush/ Cheney regime, followed by Obama's liberal presidency and Trump's rightwing "shitstorm in a dumpster fire" reign of error – to cite the colorful phrase of George Conway, the husband of Trump advisor Kelly Anne Conway who popularized the equally revealing term "alternative facts."[4] I then engage documentaries of Michael Moore who has critically dissected major events in contemporary U.S. society for decades, and I will discuss some of his films taking on corporate America, the conservative political establishment, and the presidency of Donald Trump. In a separate section on Trump I take on his emergence as a national figure of media culture celebrity in his hit TV series *The Apprentice* to his 2016 election campaign and his reality show media presidency, focusing on Trump and his exploitation of media culture. I also offer a notion of news and information as a contested terrain, while defending notions of truth and fact against the attack on "fake news" launched by Donald Trump and other authoritarians throughout the world in recent times.

In Chapter 8, I discuss the popular genres of science fiction and fantasy to show how representations of the future in these genres can illuminate the present, as well as anticipate future trends. I first engage "Fantasy entertainment as political allegory: reading *Lord of the Rings*" providing readings of director Peter Jackson's cinematic version of J.R.R. Tolkien's popular fantasy novels. I then turn to "David Cronenberg, the technoculture, and the new flesh" as a critical and pessimistic mediation on contemporary technoculture, followed by studies of "Blade runners, dystopia, and social apocalypse" in analysis of "The apocalyptic vision of Philip K. Dick" and "Androids, humans, and entropy in the *Blade Runner* films."

This chapter illustrates how optimistic utopian visions of the future in a certain type of traditional science fiction have been largely supplanted by more negative dystopic visions of the future in the *Blade Runner* films and other popular dystopic films of the era, as well as cyberpunk literature and films. I argue that these visions of the future often involve contemporary debates over race, gender, class, the environment, and politics.

In conclusion, I indicate some remaining tasks for media/cultural studies, and some of the issues that media/cultural studies should address in the future. My studies ultimately propose developing syntheses of social theory, cultural criticism, and media pedagogy to illuminate our contemporary society, culture, and politics. Combining philosophy, social theory, cultural critique, and political analysis, I present some perspectives on society and culture, methods of cultural criticism, and make some proposals for the reconstruction of media/cultural studies and critical social theory. Yet the following studies were not only written for an academic audience. Although they respond to academic debates over the proper method and forms of social theory and cultural criticism to engage contemporary society and culture, I also address urgent social and political issues of the day, and attempt to write for a popular audience. I aspire to clearly explain complex theoretical terms when they emerge in my arguments and to amply illustrate my key methodological and theoretical positions in concrete studies.

I also note in the conclusion how the media culture that became a global popular in the last decades of the twentieth century was absorbed into the cyber and digital culture of the twenty-first century, and so the critical media literacies that largely focused on broadcast media need to be supplemented by new digital literacies. The problematic election of Donald Trump in 2016, that haunts the contemporary mediascape and this book and author, requires a rethinking of so-called "social media" and how they have assumed a sinister and (a)social dimension as more is continually revealed concerning how the Russians, members of the Trump campaign, and Donald Trump himself manipulated Twitter, Facebook, and other (a)social media, which have become instruments of fake news, propaganda, bullying, and a culture of narcissism, as well as forms of expression and communication.

Media culture and new media are constantly evolving, producing exciting and sometimes disturbing effects and impacts, yet they constitute the culture in which more and more people live, interact, and act out. Nonetheless, I would argue that the "old media" of broadcasting, film, popular music, and other forms of media culture that have long been with us continue to be of interest and importance, although we need to be aware of how they are constantly changing and developing in a highly complex and contested mediascape. This new edition of *Media Culture* recognizes changes and continuities in the culture and politics of the past decades and that novelties and surprises continue to delight and appall us. Media culture is our common culture and thus we need to be constantly aware of its shifting and evolving nature, impacts, and multiple effects.

Notes

1 As of January 19, 2009, *The Dark Knight* grossed $997,033,655 worldwide (see www. boxofficemojo.com/movies/?id=darkknight.htm).
2 Ron Suskind's book *The Two Percent Solution* (2006) quoted Dick Cheney as saying that even if there was a 2 percent chance that a specific group or individual was going to launch a terrorist attack, their arrest, violation of rights, and even torture was totally justified. Later, journalist Jane Mayer titled her book on the lawless and vicious nature of Bush/Cheney administration policy *The Dark Side* (2008), describing, again in Dick Cheney's own terms, where the administration went in order to fight terror.
3 See Andrew Klavans, "What Bush and Batman Have in Common," *Wall Street Journal,* July 25, 2008, A15.
4 Melissa Quinn, "George Conway: Trump Administration Like a 'S–t Show in a Dumpster Fire.'" *Washington Examiner,* November 16, 2018 at www.washingtonexa miner.com/news/george-conway-trump-administration-like-a-s-t-show-in-a-dump ster-fire (accessed November 18, 2018).

1

THEORY WARS, IDEOLOGY CRITIQUE, AND MEDIA/ CULTURAL STUDIES

Media culture in the United States and most capitalist countries is a largely commercial form of culture, produced for profit, and disseminated in the form of commodities. The commercialization and commodification of culture has many important consequences. First of all, production for profit means that the managers of the culture industries attempt to create products that will be popular, that will sell or, in the case of radio and television, that will attract mass audiences. In many cases, this means production of lowest common denominator products that will not offend mass audiences and that will attract a maximum of consumers. Yet precisely the need to sell their productions means that the programming of the culture industries must resonate with social experience, must attract large audiences, and must thus offer enticing products, which may shock, break with conventions, contain social critique, or articulate current ideas that may be influenced by progressive social movements or creators.

Thus, while media culture largely advances the interests of the class that owns and controls the large media conglomerates, its products are also involved in social conflict between competing groups and articulate positions of opposing groups, sometimes advancing forces of resistance and progress. Consequently, media culture cannot be simply dismissed as banal instruments of the dominant ideology, but must be interpreted and contextualized within the matrix of the competing social discourses and forces which constitute it – as I attempt to do in this book.

In fact, in a certain sense, media culture *is* the dominant culture today, it has replaced the forms of high culture as the center of cultural attention and impact for large numbers of people. Furthermore, visual, oral, and digital forms of media culture are supplanting forms of book culture, requiring new types of critical media literacy to decode and properly interpret the emerging forms of media culture (Kellner-Share 2019). Moreover, media culture has become a dominant force of socialization, with media images, celebrities, and social media "influencers" replacing families, schools, and churches as arbitrators of taste, value, thought, and behavior, producing new models of identification and resonant images of style, fashion, and behavior.

Whatever the effects, individuals today are subjected to an unprecedented flow of sights and sounds into one's own home and digital device, and new virtual worlds of entertainment, information, sex, and politics are reordering perceptions of space and time, erasing distinctions between reality and media spectacle, while producing novel modes of experience and subjectivity – much of which is monitored by corporations and governments. Big Data collects, stores, analyzes and sells consumer information to the highest bidders (Noble 2018).

Such emergent challenges and proliferating problems require innovative theories and political responses to interpret our current social situation and to illuminate our contemporary problems, conflicts, challenges, and possibilities. In the conjuncture in which we find ourselves today, media/cultural studies can play an important role in elucidating the significant transformations that have taken place in our culture and society. We are surrounded by new technologies, novel modes of cultural production, and ever-emerging forms of social and political life. Moreover, media culture is playing an ever more significant role in every realm of contemporary society, ranging from its multifarious functions in arenas from the economic to the social.

In the economy, seductive cultural forms shape consumer demand, produce needs, and mold a commodity self with consumerist values. In the political sphere, media images have produced an ever-changing mediascape of sound-bite politics and spectacle that places the media at the center of political life. In our social interactions, mass-produced images guide our presentation of the self in everyday life, our ways of relating to others, and the creation of our social values and goals. As work declines in importance, leisure and culture become more and more the focus of everyday life and the locus of value and importance. Of course, one must work to earn the benefits of the consumer society (or inherit sufficient wealth), but work is arguably declining in importance in the proliferating consumer societies in which individuals allegedly gain primary gratification from consuming goods and leisure activities, rather than their labor activity.[1]

There have also been discussions of how labor is changing into a "gig economy" where workers take temporary positions for short-term engagements, shifting from one "gig" to another.[2] Thus, contemporary society and culture is in a state of ferment and change and competing theories strive to make sense of these new developments. The contested terrain of theory is accompanied by culture wars between conservatives, liberals, and progressives, with conservatives attempting to roll back the advances of the 1960s and 1970s in order to impose more traditional values and forms of culture. Throughout the Western world, from the 1980s to the present, conservatives have been aggressively attempting to gain hegemony by seizing political power and using it to carry through their economic, political, social, and cultural agendas. They have been using their political and economic power to carry through an agenda of cultural transformation, attempting to turn back the clock to an earlier era of conservative rule.

Yet there are also countervailing trends. The progressive social movements of the 1960s and 1970s are still alive and well, and struggles for human rights, the civil liberties of oppressed people, peace and justice, ecology, and a more humane organization of society are everywhere visible. In 2011, democratic movements surged through North Africa, Europe, and the United States (see Kellner 2012) with the Arab Spring and Occupy movements throughout the Western world, followed by Black Lives Matter, the #MeToo movement, the Dreamers, and the Trump Resistance. Yet many of the democratizing regimes of the Arab Spring were overthrown by reactionary forces and progressive movements in the West are countered by fierce conservative movements, making the present era a highly contested moment throughout the world. Yet, the very instability, motility, flux, and uncertainty of the present creates openings for more positive futures and possibilities for the creation of a better world out of the nightmares of the present moment. On the other hand, the penchant for micropolitics and/or identity politics fragments the progressive movements and renders many blind to the necessary linkages and interconnections with others in opposition or in counter-hegemonic struggles.

Within this context, it is therefore of vital importance to understand the role of media culture in a wide range of current social struggles, trends, and developments. It is the conviction of the studies in this book that our current local, national, and global situations are articulated through the texts of media culture, which is a contested terrain that competing social groups attempt to use to push their agendas and ideologies. Not just news and information, but entertainment and fiction articulate the conflicts, fears, hopes, and dreams of individuals and groups confronting a turbulent and uncertain world. The concrete struggles of each society are played out on the screens of media culture, especially in the commercial media of the culture industries which produce texts that must resonate with people's concerns if they are to be popular and profitable. Culture has never been more important and never before has there been such a need for serious scrutiny of contemporary media culture and its effects.

Consequently, to understand what is going on in society and everyday life today, we need theories that will help us make sense of the changes and conflicts of the present age. Throughout this book, I will thus delineate theoretical perspectives that I find useful in grasping the vicissitudes of contemporary society and culture.[3] Yet the fortunes of theory are related to their historical matrices, which shape and structure them and which in turn they attempt to illuminate. Therefore, in the following study, I will sketch the emergence and effects of some critical theories that I will make use of in this work.

Theory wars

The past decades of intense cultural, social, and political struggle since the 1960s also saw the rise of many new theories and approaches to culture and society. It is as if the tumultuous struggles of the era sought expression and replication in the realm of theory. Political passions and energies seemed to be sublimated into the discourse of theory and new theories were appropriated with the intensity that marked the absorption and use of radical political ideas and practices in the 1960s. The proliferation of new theoretical discourses first took the form of theory fever, in which each new, or newly discovered, theoretical discourse produced feverish excitement, as if a new theory virus totally took over and possessed its host. Then the proliferating theory fever took on the form of theory wars between the competing theoretical discourses.

In the United States, where forms of what Herbert Marcuse called "one-dimensional thought" reigned in the 1950s and early 1960s, Marxism and feminism were the first forms of theory fever to circulate. Experiences of the Vietnam War in the 1960s drove many in the New Left and anti-war movement to Marxist theory, tabooed during the Cold War and driven underground.[4] Marxist discourse proliferated and a stunning variety of neo-Marxist theories from Europe and non-Western countries were imported to the United States, producing a wide range of new radical theories.

Feminism quickly became part of the new theoretical discourses throughout the world. In the late 1960s, women began revolting against what they considered oppressive practices of both contemporary patriarchal societies and their male comrades in the radical movements. The wave of feminism in the 1960s and 1970s discovered classics like Mary Wollstonecraft's *Declaration of the Rights of Women*, Simone de Beauvoir's *The Second Sex*, and other feminist classics, as well as a rich women's history and the importance of women's experience and culture for the radical project.[5] Many, often unhappy, marriages between Marxism and feminism took place, while other varieties of feminist theory found important resources in psychoanalysis to analyze women's oppression and experiences, and to provide for the reconstruction of more nurturing, feeling, and loving subjects. Thus, as with Marxism, a tremendous range of feminist theories emerged, that often warred with each other, as well as with other theoretical discourses (see Hammer 2001).

Previously marginalized groups sought their own voices and discourses, and in the United States, new African American, Native American, Chicano, Asian-American, and other people of color produced oppositional social movements and new theories, discourses and academic studies. Gay and lesbian movements and studies problematized sexuality and provided new perspectives on gender, culture, and society, developing what became known as "queer studies," with evolving terminology such as LGBTQ+ studies, a term I'll use in this book.[6] Theorists whose national origin was outside the West generated new subaltern studies, attacking Western colonization, while studies of the "post-colonial

subject" and voices from newly emerged nations produced some exciting theoretical innovations and greatly expanded the terrain of critical discourses.[7] Cumulatively, these discourses have contributed to some of the most challenging social
theory and cultural criticism of the past decades and in the following studies
I draw on these new oppositional studies and discourses.

Although the tumult of the 1960s passed into the more quiescent 1970s, the
explosion of theories continued and theory wars intensified. An accelerating globalization of theory erupted with proliferating theoretical discourses being rapidly disseminated across borders and national cultures. Theorists throughout the
world appropriated European discourses, and the resulting new critical theories
were circulated in turn throughout the globalizing theory world. Discourses of
race, class, ethnicity, sexual preference, and nationality challenged theoretical discourses to take account of phenomena previously ignored or underplayed.
Theory wars broke out between those that privileged class with those that privileged such things as race, gender, and sexuality.

Over the past decades, it is to feminist, LGBTQ+ studies, critical race theories, and multiculturalist theories of gender, sexuality, race, ethnicity, class,
nationality, ability, subalterneity, and other oppositional groups and identities
that we can turn for specific critiques of oppression and theories of resistance,
and these groups have made important contributions to media/cultural studies.[8]
Their discourses and theories have resonated with the struggles of oppressed
people, and thus politicize theory and critique with passion and perspectives
from existing political struggles. Such perspectives enlarge the field of media/
cultural studies and political struggle, expanding, for instance, the concept of
ideology critique to include dimensions of race, gender, sexuality, ethnicity, religion, and other factors, as well as class – a topic that I take up in this chapter
and the following ones. These oppositional political discourses also infuse
media/cultural studies with political passion and intensity, breathing new life
into its projects.

Building on this work, I argue in this chapter for the need to deploy Marxian
theories of class, feminist concepts of gender, critical race theories, LGBTQ+
theories of sexuality, and multicultural and social theories to articulate the full
range of representations of domination and resistance that one finds structuring
the terrain of media culture. The forms of media culture are intensely political
and ideological, and thus those who wish to discern how it embodies political
positions and has political effects should learn to read media culture politically.
This means not only reading media culture in a socio-political-historical and
economic context, but seeing how the internal constituents of its texts either
encode relations of power and domination, serving to advance the interests of
dominant groups at the expense of others, or oppose hegemonic ideologies,
institutions, and practices, sometimes presenting progressive alternatives. Thus,
reading media culture politically involves situating it in its historical conjuncture
and analyzing how its generic codes, its positioning of viewers, its dominant

images, its discourses, and its formal-aesthetic elements all embody certain political and ideological positions.

Reading culture politically also involves seeing how media culture artifacts reproduce the existing social struggles in their images, spectacle, and narrative. In *Camera Politica: The Politics and Ideology of Contemporary Hollywood Film* (1988), Michael Ryan and I indicate how struggles within everyday life and the broader world of social and political struggles are articulated within popular film, which in turn are appropriated and have their effects within these contexts. We indicated how some of the most popular Hollywood films and genres from the 1960s to the late 1980s *transcode* contending social and political discourses and represent specific political positions within debates over the Vietnam war and the 1960s, gender and the family, class and race, the corporation and the state, U.S. foreign and domestic policy, and other issues which preoccupied U.S. society over the past decades.

The process of transcoding describes how social discourses are translated into media texts, as when *Easy Rider* transcodes 1960s countercultural discourses of freedom, individualism, and community in cinematic images and scenes, when, for instance, the bikers drive through nature with the soundtrack playing "Born to be Wild," or "Wasn't Born to Follow." And during the highly contested Vietnam war in the 1960s and 1970s, some U.S. films transcoded critical discourses that advanced the positions of the anti-Vietnam war movement (e.g. *Vietnam: Year of the Pig* and *Hearts and Minds*), while others, like *The Green Berets* (1967) transcoded positive representations of the U.S. intervention in Vietnam and attacked the counterculture and anti-war movement. In the contemporary era, liberal TV series like *The West Wing* (1999–2006), *Madame Secretary* (2014–2020), *The Good Fight* (2017–2019), and *Blunt City Law* (2019) present the state, politics, and the law in a favorable light in accordance with liberal political discourses, while more radical TV shows like *Our Cartoon President* (2018–2019), or late night talk shows like *The Late Show with Stephen Colbert* (2015–2019), present the current presidency of Donald Trump in a completely negative light.

From the 1960s to the present, media culture in the United States has thus been a battleground between competing social groups and discourses with some texts advancing liberal or more progressive positions, while others transcode conservative or reactionary ones. Likewise, some texts of media culture advance progressive positions and representations of such things as gender, sexual preference, class, race, or ethnicity, while others articulate reactionary forms of racism, sexism, homophobia, classism, and other forms of discrimination – although often there are contradictions and ambiguities in the texts of media culture.

On this view, media culture is a *contested terrain* that reproduces existing social struggles and transcodes the political discourses of the era. Furthermore, media/cultural studies examines the effects of media cultural texts, the ways that audiences appropriate and use media culture, and the ways that media images, figures, and discourses function within the culture. In the following pages, I accordingly articulate some theoretical perspectives on media culture, politics, and ideology, which I believe are of use in doing media/cultural studies, including concepts of ideology, hegemony, intersectionality, and multiculturalism. In these analyses, I defend the centrality of ideology critique within media/cultural studies, yet specify problems with the classical Marxian conceptions of ideology and propose some perspectives, methods, and a model of media/cultural studies that I find useful in critically engaging media culture in the contemporary moment.

Ideology and media culture: critical methods

Within the Marxian tradition, Marx and Engels characterized ideology as the ideas of the ruling class that achieved dominance in a specific historical era. The concept of ideology set out in *The German Ideology* (Marx 1975: 59ff) was primarily denunciatory, and attacked ideas that legitimated ruling class hegemony, which disguised particular interests as general ones, which mystified or covered over class rule, and which thus served the interests of class domination. In this view, ideology critique consisted of the analysis and demystification of ruling class ideas, and the critic of ideology was to ferret out and attack all those ideas which furthered class domination.[9]

The classical Marxism of Marx and Engels, the Second International, and the Third International tended to focus on the primacy of economics and politics and to defocus attention on culture and ideology. However, during the 1920s, Lukàcs, Korsch, Bloch, and Gramsci focused on the central importance of culture and ideology and the Frankfurt School and other versions of Western Marxism also took up the importance of the critique of ideology as an important component of the critique of domination.[10] British media/cultural studies too, in its formative period, made the concept of ideology central to the study of culture and society and one of their early collection of texts was titled *On Ideology*.[11]

Yet there were problems within the Marxian tradition of ideology critique that needed to be overcome. Some Marxian traditions, including orthodox Leninism, the Frankfurt School, Althusser, and others, tended to presuppose both a monolithic concept of ideology and of the ruling class, which unambiguously and without contradiction articulates its class interests in a dominant ideology. This concept reduces ideology to defense of class interests and is thus predominantly economistic with ideology referring primarily, and in some cases solely, to those ideas that legitimate the class rule of the capitalist ruling class. Thus, in this conception, "ideology" is confined to those sets of ideas that promote the capitalist class's economic interests.

Since the civil rights, feminist, gay and lesbian, and other movements of the 1960s, however, this model has been contested by a multiple of individuals and tendencies who have argued that such a concept of ideology is reductionist because it equates ideology solely with those ideas that serve class, or economic interests, and thus leaves out such significant phenomena as gender, race, sexuality, and other forms of ideological and political domination. Reducing ideology to class interests makes it appear that the only significant domination going on in society is class, or economic, domination, whereas many theorists argue that gender, sexuality, and race oppression are also of fundamental importance and, some would argue, are entwined in integral ways with class and economic oppression (see Cox 1948; Rowbotham 1972; Robinson 1978; Said 1978; Sargent 1981; Marable 1982; Lorde 1984; Kellner and Ryan 1988; Spivak 1988; Fraser 1989; hooks 1992; Gilroy 1991; Crenshaw 1991).

A critical media/cultural studies deploys a variety of theories and perspectives to engage a full range of the politics of representation in which media texts present constructs of class, race, gender, sexuality, and other constituents of identity in ways that promote oppression and perpetuate classism, racism, sexism, heterosexism and other forms of discrimination. The concept of *theory* derives from the Greek word *theoria* and denotes *a way of seeing* phenomena in the world. Each theory has its specific focuses, so that a Marxist theory will focus on class, capitalism, economic themes, and ideology critique, while a Weberian analysis focuses on state, bureaucracy, and more political-institutional issues and processes. Feminist theory will focus intensely on gender and gender relations, critiquing sexist and patriarchal representations and narratives. Critical race theory engages constructions of race and ethnicity, and critiques racism and racial stereotypes, while seeking representations that break with conventional limited and biased representations. LGBTQ+ theories take on issues of sexuality, critiquing homophobia and seeking more positive and diverse images of sexuality. All of these theories thus have strong focuses and emphases, but in some cases can be reductive. Taken together, these theories and others constitute a powerful repertoire to engage the politics of representation as a contested terrain.

The concept of *intersectionality* articulated by Kimberly Crenshaw (1991) calls for the importance of mapping the intersections of oppression and domination across the lines of race, gender, sexuality, class, and other forms of oppression. The concept suggests that forms of oppression intersect and work together, and critical theorists have used intersectionality to explore how cultural representations interact to provide racist, sexist, classist, and other forms of representation and texts that promote oppression. A critical media/cultural studies, however, is also concerned with delineating representations and texts that counter forms of oppression and that depict forms of struggle and emancipation in the contested terrain of contemporary media culture and society.

Thus many critics have proposed that ideology be extended to cover theories, ideas, texts, and representations that legitimate interests of ruling gender and race, heteronormative, and class domination. From this perspective, doing ideology critique involves criticizing sexist, heterosexist, and racist ideology as well as bour-geois-capitalist class ideology. Such ideology critique is multicultural, discerning a range of forms of oppression of people of different races, ethnicities, gender, and sexual preference and tracing the ways that ideological cultural forms and discourses perpetuate oppression. Multicultural ideological critique involves taking seriously struggles between men and women, feminists and anti-feminists, racists and anti-racists, people of diverse sexualities and those heterosexualists who attack members of the LGBTQ+ communities. It also engages many other conflicts, which are seen to be as important and worthy of attention as class conflicts by Marxian theory. It assumes that society is a field of struggle and that the heterogeneous struggles are played out on the screens and texts of media culture and are the proper terrain of a critical media media/cultural studies.

To carry out a multicultural and ideology critique of the first wave of *Rambo* films (1982, 1985, 1988), for instance, it would not be enough simply to attack its militarist or imperialist ideology, and the ways that the militarism and imperialism of the films serve imperialist interests by legitimating intervention in such places as Southeast Asia, the Middle East, Central America, or wherever. While this is an important dimension of the ideology critique of the films, it is also crucial to criticize the discourses and figures that construct the text's gender, racial, and national prob-lematics to carry out a full ideology critique, showing how representations of women, men, the Vietnamese, the Russians, and so on are a fundamental part of the *Rambo* films, and that a key element of the texts is remasculinization and re-establishment of white male power after defeat in Vietnam and assaults on male power by feminist and civil rights movements. Consequently, reading the ideological text of the *Rambo* films requires interrogation of its images and figures as well as its discourse and language across a range of problematics and inscribing these problem-atics within the context of existing political struggles and history. Such an analysis, as I will argue below, suggests that the figure of Rambo represents a specific set of images of male power, American innocence and strength, and warrior heroism, which serve as vehicles of masculist and patriotic ideologies that were resurrected during the Reagan era when the films appeared and continued into the Trump era. I illustrate these arguments with a brief interrogation of the production and thematics of the Rambo films, and will discuss their cultural effects later in the chapter.

Rambo as global media spectacle

The *Rambo* films appeared in the 1980s during the presidency of Ronald Reagan and articulated its patriarchal conservativism, militarism, and anti-communism during the final era of the Cold War. *Rambo: First Blood* was based on a 1972 novel by David Morrell, which was sold first to Columbia pictures, then to Warner Brothers and passed through three companies and 18 screen plays before the film finally appeared a decade after the book's publication.[12] *First Blood* was directed by Ted Kotcheff and produced by Buzz Feitshans and the production team of Carolco Pictures, which specialized in male-oriented actions pictures.

Unlike Morrell's novel, which shows Rambo as an angry Vietnam vet who is violent and threatening, the film, *First Blood* (1982) presented its Vietnam veteran hero as a victim who was mistreated by the public after his return from the unpopular war, a common theme of rightwing discourse at the time. Rambo's return to the U.S. merged an uneasy set of images that ascribed responsibility for his victimization to societal forces and that showed them driving him to violence. In the plot, Special Forces veteran John Rambo (Sylvester Stallone) is searching for the final member of his unit, who he discovers died of Agent Orange contamination, thus situating the Vietnam vets as victims of their government. Unable to hitch a ride, Rambo walks into the small town of Hope, and is arrested by the sheriff who complains that he needs a haircut and bath. Mistreated by the sheriff and his deputies, Rambo escapes and wages war against the local and National Guard law enforcement agencies, being positioned as a victim of oppressive authority and power. At the end, he surrenders to his former Special Forces Commander Col. Trautman (Richard Crenna) and breaks down, complaining that although he was a hero in Vietnam, he cannot even hold a job and is a figure of contempt and hatred, thus blaming society for making him an outcast.

In the second *Rambo* film (1985), Rambo is transformed into a superhuman warrior who rescues U.S. POWs still being held in Vietnam, thus transcoding the paranoia concerning missing POWs in Vietnam.[13] The film is but one of a whole series of return-to-Vietnam films that began with the success of *Uncommon Valor* in 1983 and continued with the three Chuck Norris *Missing in Action* films of 1984–1986. All follow the same formula of representing the return to Vietnam of a team of former vets, or a superhuman, superhero vet like Rambo, to rescue a group of American soldiers "missing in action" who are still imprisoned by the Vietnamese and their evil Soviet allies.

The film *Rambo* synthesizes this "return to Vietnam" cycle with another cycle that shows returning vets transforming themselves from wounded and confused misfits to super warriors (e.g. *Rolling Thunder, Firefox, First Blood*). All of these cinematic attempts to overcome the "Vietnam syndrome" show the U.S. and the American warrior hero victorious this time and thus exhibit a symptom of inability to accept defeat. They also provide symbolic compensation for loss, shame, and guilt by depicting the U.S. as "good" and this time victorious, while its communist enemies are represented as the incarnation of "evil" who this time receive a well-deserved defeat. In these cinematic fantasies, it is always the "enemy" that performs vicious and evil acts, while the Americans are always virtuous and heroic. Cumulatively, the return-to-Vietnam films therefore exhibit a defensive and compensatory response to military defeat in Vietnam and, I would argue, an inability to learn the lessons of the limitations of U.S. power and the complex mixture of "good" and "evil" involved in almost all military undertakings.

On the other hand, *Rambo* and the other Stallone–Norris macho hero films can be read as expressions of white male paranoia that present white males as victims of foreign enemies, other races, the government, and society at large – a syndrome exploited by rightwing politicians from Ronald Reagan to Donald Trump. The return to Vietnam films also exhibit an attempt at remasculinization, in which highly masculist male behavior is celebrated, as a response to feminism and other attacks on male power. In *The Remasculinization of America*, Susan Jeffords (1989) argues that Vietnam was a terrible blow to masculine pride, for which American males experienced great guilt and shame. A vast number of Vietnam films and literature deals with this problem, she claims, attempting to heal the wounds and to reconstruct a damaged male psyche.

Yet the films can also be read diagnostically as symptoms of the victimization of the working class. Both the Stallone and Norris figures are resentful, remarkably inarticulate, brutal, and thus indicative of the way many American working class youth are educationally deprived and offered the military as the only way of affirming themselves. Rambo's neurotic resentment is less his own fault than that of those who run the social system in such a way that it denies his class access to the institutions of articulate thought and mental health. Denied self-esteem through creative work, they seek surrogate worth in metaphoric substitutes like sports (Rocky) and war (Rambo). It is symptomatic that Stallone plays both Rocky and Rambo during a time when economic recession was driving the Rockys of the world to join the military where they became Rambos for Reagan's and two Bushes' interventionist foreign policies.

The Rocky–Rambo syndrome, however, puts on display the raw masculinism that is at the bottom of conservative socialization and ideology. One way that the Rockys and Rambos of the world can gain recognition and self-affirmation is through violent and aggressive self-display. And Rambo's pathetic demand for love at the end of the first two Rambo films is an indication that the society is not providing adequate structures of mutual and communal support to provide healthy structures of interpersonal relationships and ego ideals for men in the culture. Unfortunately, the Stallone character intensifies this pathology precisely in its celebration of violent masculism and militarist self-assertion.

The film machine also mobilizes images and displays of gender and race to do its ideological work. In regard to gender, one might note that Rambo instantiates a masculinist image that defines masculinity in terms of the male warrior with the features of great strength, effective use of force, and military heroism as the highest expression of life. Symptomatically, the women characters in the film are either whores, or, in the case of a Vietnamese rebel, a handmaiden to Rambo's exploits who functions primarily as a seductive and destructive force. Her main actions are to seduce Vietnamese guards – a figure also central to the image of woman in the conservative John Wayne film *The Green Berets* (1968) which promoted U.S. intervention in Vietnam – and to become a woman warrior, a female version of Rambo, who helps Rambo fight the bad guys. Significantly, the only (brief and chaste) moment of eroticism in the film comes when Rambo and his woman agent kiss after great warrior feats, and seconds after the kiss (of death) the woman is herself shot and killed. This renunciation of women and sexuality highlights the theme that the male warrior must go it alone and must thus renounce erotic pleasure. This theme obviously fits into the militarist and masculinist theme of the film, as well as the genre of ascetic male heroes who must rise above sexual temptation in order to become maximally effective saviors or warriors.[14]

The representations and thematics of race also contribute fundamentally to the militarist theme. The Vietnamese and Russians are presented as alien Others, as the embodiment of evil, in a typically Hollywood Manichean scenario that presents the Other, the Enemy, and "Them," as the embodiment of evil, and "Us," the good guys, as the incarnation of virtue, heroism, goodness, innocence, and so on. *Rambo* appropriates stereotypes of the evil Japanese and Germans from World War II movies in its representations of the Vietnamese and the Russians, thus continuing a Manichean Hollywood tradition with past icons of evil standing in for – from the Right's point of view – contemporary villains. The Vietnamese are portrayed as duplicitous bandits, ineffectual dupes of the evil Soviets, and cannon fodder for Rambo's exploits, while the Soviets are presented as sadistic torturers and inhuman, mechanistic bureaucrats.

And yet reflections on the representations of gender and race in the film make clear that these phenomena are socially constructed stereotypes that are reproduced in films and media culture in a specific historical moment such as our warriors are good and our enemies are evil, as in the representations of the communists in the *Rambo* films. The stereotypes of race and gender in *Rambo* are so exaggerated, so crude, that they point to the artificial and socially constructed nature of all ideals of masculinity, femininity, race, ethnicity, and other subject positions. These representations are presented in cinematic terms that celebrate the white male power of Rambo against women and other races. Thus, to fully explicate filmic ideology and the ways that film advances specific political positions, one must also attend to cinematic form and narrative structure, to the ways that the cinema apparatus transcodes social discourses and reproduces ideological effects.

Rambo's rightwing ideology is transmitted through images, scenes, generic codes, and the narrative as a whole. Camera positioning and lighting help frame Sylvester Stallone as a mythic hero; an abundance of lower camera angles present Rambo as a mythic warrior, and frequent close-ups present him as a larger-than-life human being. Focus on his glistening biceps, his sculptured body, and powerful physique presents him as a sexual icon, as a figure of virility, which promotes both female admiration for male strength and perhaps homo-erotic fascination with the male warrior. Slow-motion travelling shots code Rambo as a force of nature, effortlessly gliding through the jungle, while triumphant music codes his accomplishments as super heroic. His regeneration into superhero are presented in shots where he magically leaps out of the water, purified and potent, poised to avenge and triumph.[15]

The action shots center on Rambo's body as the instrument of mythic heroism, while the fast editing creates an impression of dynamism that infuses Rambo with energy and superhuman power and vitality, just as slow motion shots and lengthy takes which center on Rambo for long stretches of action tend to deify the character. When, by contrast, Rambo is tortured by villainous communists, the images are framed in the iconography of crucifixion shots with strong lighting on his head producing halo effects, as in medieval paintings, and the redder-than-red blood producing a hyperrealization, if I may borrow a Baudrillardian term (1983a), of heroic suffering. Close-ups on the communist villains focus on their sneering and sadistic pleasure in torturing Rambo, while the battle scenes depict the communists predominantly in long shots as insignificant and incompetent pawns in Rambo's redemptive heroism. And in one incredible scene, Rambo bites off the head of the snake, evoking the myth of Adam and Eden, in which Adam cannot tame the serpent and must leave the Garden of Eden, whereby Rambo conquers it, demonstrating his power to rule the jungle.

Furthermore, the "happy ending" closure situates the film as a return to the conservative Hollywood adventure tradition,[16] and the victory over the evil communists codes *Rambo* as a mythic redemption of U.S. defeat in Vietnam by heroic action – a trope reproduced in the films of Stallone, Chuck Norris, and countless other films, pulp novels, and television shows. Such mythic redemption was carried out politically during the era in the actions of Ronald Reagan, Oliver North, and other "cowboys," who supported violence to resolve political conflict (Jewett and Lawrence 1988: 248f). Not by accident did both the Hollywood heroes and the Hollywood president Reagan and his cronies act outside the law to carry out "heroic" actions constrained by the legal and political order.

Consequently, although the U.S. was denied victory in Vietnam, it attempted to achieve it in media culture. This phenomenon shows some of the political functions of media culture, which include providing compensations for irredeemable loss while offering reassurances that all is well in the American body politic – reassurance denied in more socially critical films such as Oliver Stone's *Salvador, Platoon, Wall Street, Talk Radio, Born on the Fourth of July, Heaven and Earth*, and *Natural Born* Killers, which provide an instructive counter-cycle to the Stallone Rocky/Rambo cycles and which also testify to the conflictual nature of cinematic ideology in the contemporary period. For the Stone films demonstrate the pain of defeat and depict powerful institutions and social forces overshadowing individual ability to control the course of events. The conservative films, by contrast, celebrate the triumph of the will over adversity.

Thus, such variables as race, class, gender, sexual preference, and ideology are articulated in media culture to reproduce and reinforce dominant ideologies, and to promote hierarchies of domination and subordination – or to oppose and resist domination and forms of inequality. At stake is developing a media/cultural studies that can analyze, first, how media culture transcodes positions of domination and resistance within existing political struggles and, in turn, provides representations that mobilize consent to specific political positions through images, spectacle, discourse, narrative, and the other forms of media culture. And then the actual social effects of the phenomena should be traced through examination of the social impact of key media culture texts on certain societies at specific times in history. In the following chapters, I will undertake this inquiry through a close reading of media texts and analysis of their possible range of political effects, in order to provide some examples of the nature, functions, and effectivity of media culture within contemporary society, and in this chapter illustrate my methods, theories, and models of media/cultural studies through analysis of the *Rambo* films and cultural phenomena, while in the next chapter I will use Margaret Atwood's novel and the Hulu TV series of *The Handmaid's Tale* to illustrate my approach to media culture. The following chapters will illustrate the impact of media culture on contemporary U.S. society through reading specific genres, key popular texts, and key creators of media culture. Next, however, I want to delineate key traditions of media/cultural studies that I have drawn upon and will set forth my three-part model.

Approaches to media/cultural studies

The metatheory for and models of social theory and cultural criticism that I am proposing here have been especially influenced by the Frankfurt School, British cultural studies, and a range of critical theories that have emerged from social movements and struggles. As I indicate below, the Frankfurt School inaugurated critical studies of mass communication and culture and developed an early model of cultural studies. There are many traditions and models of cultural studies, ranging from neo-Marxist models developed by Lukàcs, Gramsci, Bloch, and the Frankfurt School in the 1930s to feminist and psychoanalytic cultural studies. In Britain and the United States, there is a long tradition of media/cultural studies that preceded the Birmingham School.[17] The major traditions combine – at their best – social theory, media/cultural analysis, history, philosophical speculation, and specific political interventions, thus overcoming the standard academic division of labor by surmounting specialization which bifurcates the field of study of the media, culture, and communications. Media/cultural studies thus operates with a *transdisciplinary* conception that draws on social theory, economics, politics, history, communication studies, literary and cultural theory, philosophy, and other theoretical disciplines.

A transdisciplinary media-cultural studies thus draws on a disparate range of fields to theorize the complexity and contradictions of the multiple effects of a vast range of forms of media culture in our lives and demonstrate how these forces serve as instruments of domination, but also offer resources for resistance and change. In the following sketch, I first indicate how the Frankfurt School developed an early conception of cultural studies still worth attending to, although I also point to its limitations. I next discuss British cultural studies, which has been growing in recent decades in popularity and influence as a critical approach to the study of culture and society, indicating its contributions, but also some limitations.

Interestingly, in the 1980s and 1990s when I conceived and developed the first edition of *Media Culture*, postmodern theories were a new and controversial and hotly debated theoretical matrix (see Best and Kellner 2001), while today postmodern theories have been "normalized" as an accepted, although still controversial and debated, type of theory. In the following discussions, I will focus primarily on aspects of these traditions that I believe are useful today for media/cultural studies and some limitations of these traditions that have vitiated some forms of contemporary media/cultural studies.

The Frankfurt School

The Frankfurt School inaugurated critical communications studies in the 1930s and combined the political economy of the media, cultural analysis of texts, and audience reception studies of the social and ideological effects of mass culture and communications.[18] The group emigrated from Germany had created a multidisciplinary research institute in Frankfurt when the rise of Hitler and fascism drove Jews, radicals, and others threatened by the Nazis to leave the country. The Frankfurt group arrived in the mid-1930s at Columbia University where they revived their research projects and had the opportunity to observe the role of media culture in the United States, as they did in Germany. They coined the term "cultural industry" to signify the process of the industrialization of mass-produced culture and the commercial imperatives that drove the system. The critical theorists analyzed all mass-mediated cultural texts within the context of industrial production, in which the commodities of the culture industry exhibited the same features as other products of mass production: commodification, standardization, and massification. The products of the culture industry had the specific function, however, of providing ideological legitimation of the existing capitalist societies and of integrating individuals into the framework of mass culture and society.

Adorno's analyses of popular music, Lowenthal's studies of popular literature and magazines, Herzog's studies of radio soap operas, and the perspectives and critiques of mass culture developed in Horkheimer and Adorno's famous study of the culture industry provided many examples of the usefulness of the Frankfurt School approach. Moreover, in their theories of the culture industry and critiques of mass culture, they were the first to systematically analyze and criticize mass-mediated culture and communications within critical social theory. They were the first social theorists to see the importance of what they called the "culture industry" in the reproduction of contemporary societies, in which so-called mass culture and communications stand in the center of leisure activity, are important agents of socialization, mediators of political reality, and should thus be seen as major institutions of contemporary societies with a variety of economic, political, cultural and social effects.

Yet there are serious flaws in the original program of critical theory, which requires a radical reconstruction of the classical model of the culture industries (Kellner 1989a). Overcoming the limitations of the classical model would include: more concrete and empirical analysis of the political economy of the media and the processes of the production of culture; more empirical and historical research into the construction of media industries and their interaction with other social institutions; more empirical studies of audience reception and media effects; and the incorporation of new cultural theories and methods into a reconstructed critical theory of culture and the media. Cumulatively, such a reconstruction of the classical Frankfurt School project would update the critical theory of society and its activity of cultural criticism by incorporating contemporary developments in social and cultural theory into the enterprise of critical theory.

In addition, the Frankfurt School dichotomy between high culture and low culture is problematical and should be superseded by a more unified model that takes culture as a spectrum and applies similar critical methods to all cultural productions ranging from high cultural forms like opera to popular music, from modernist literature to soap operas. In particular, the Frankfurt School model of a monolithic mass culture contrasted with an ideal of "authentic art," which limits critical, subversive, and emancipatory moments to certain privileged texts of high culture, is highly problematic. The Frankfurt School position that all mass culture is ideological and debased, having the effects of duping a passive mass of consumers, is also objectionable. Instead, one should see critical and ideological moments in the full range of culture, and not limit critical moments to high culture and identify all of low culture as ideological. One should also allow for the possibility that critical and subversive moments could be found in the products of the cultural industry, as well as the canonized classics of high modernist culture that the Frankfurt School seemed to privilege as the site of artistic opposition and emancipation.[19]

It is precisely the critical focus on media culture from the perspectives of ideology and domination that provides a perspective useful as a corrective to more populist and uncritical approaches to media culture that surrender critical perspectives. Although the Frankfurt School approach is partial and one-sided, it does provide theories to criticize the ideological and debased forms of media culture and the ways that it provides ideologies that legitimate forms of oppression. As I argue throughout the book, ideology critique is a fundamental constituent of cultural studies and the Frankfurt School is valuable for inaugurating systematic and sustained critiques of ideology within the cultural industries. Further, the Frankfurt School approach is valuable because it provides an integral model that transcends divisions in the study of media, culture, and communications between text and humanities-based cultural studies and empirical social science-based communication studies.[20] The Frankfurt School carried out their analysis within the framework of critical social theory, thus integrating communication and cultural studies within the context of study of capitalist society and the ways that communications and culture were produced within this order and the roles and functions that they assumed. Thus with the Frankfurt School, the study of communication and culture was integrated within critical social theory and became an important part of a theory of contemporary society, in which culture and communication were playing ever more significant roles.[21]

British cultural studies and its legacy

The Frankfurt School developed their model of the culture industry in the decades from the 1930s through the 1950s, and then turned more to focus on philosophy, social theory, aesthetics, and politics (Kellner 1989a). British cultural studies emerged in the 1960s as a project of approaching culture from critical and multidisciplinary perspectives, which was instituted in England by the Birmingham Centre for Contemporary Cultural Studies and others.[22] British cultural studies situates culture within a theory of social production and reproduction, specifying the ways that cultural forms served either to further social domination, or to enable people to resist and struggle against domination. Society is conceived as a hierarchical and antagonistic set of social relations characterized by the oppression of subordinate class, gender, race, ethnic, and national strata. Building on the Italian Marxist thinker Antonio Gramsci's model of hegemony and counter-hegemony, cultural studies analyze "hegemonic," or ruling, social and cultural forces of domination, and seek "counterhegemonic" forces of resistance and struggle.[23]

For Gramsci, societies maintained their stability through a combination of force and hegemony, with some institutions and groups violently exerting power to maintain social boundaries (e.g. the police, military, and vigilante groups, etc.), while other institutions (like religion, schooling, or the media) serve to induce consent to the dominant order through the establishing the hegemony, or ideological dominance, of a specific type of social order (e.g. liberal capitalism, fascism, white supremacy, democratic socialism, communism, or other modes of socio-political domination).

Hegemony theory involved both analysis of current forces of domination and the ways that specific political forces achieved hegemonic power (e.g. Mussolini and fascism in Gramsci's classic theory, or Thatcherism or Reaganism in 1980s British cultural studies texts). Yet hegemony theory also involved the delineation of counterhegemonic forces, groups, and ideas that could contest and overturn the existing hegemony. British cultural studies was thus connected with a political project of social transformation in which location of forces of domination and resistance would aid the process of political struggle against the hegemonic social formation.

My analysis of contemporary media culture will suggest that ideological hegemony in U.S. society today is complex, contested, and constantly being put into question. Hegemony is negotiated and renegotiated, and is vulnerable to attack and subversion. In past decades, for instance, the New Right political hegemony of the Reagan years passed over to a more centrist conservatism of the George H.W. Bush regime that in turn became increasingly militarist in the wake of the Panama invasion and Persian Gulf war. Yet, despite the seeming popularity of the Gulf war, Bush's hegemony turned out to be vulnerable, shaky, and subject to overthrow and reversal – as happened in the 1992 presidential election that led to eight years of centrist Democratic Party rule (1992–2000) in the Clinton administrations before the return of the Bush dynasty (2000–2008), followed by eight years of the liberal Obama presidency (2009–2016), before the return to conservative Republican hardright politics in the Trump administration, complicated by his erratic political behavior and intense political contestation (2016–).

British cultural studies thus situates culture within a socio-historical context in which culture promotes domination or resistance, and criticizes forms of culture that promote domination. In this way, culture studies can be distinguished from idealist, textualist, and extreme discourse theories that only recognize linguistic forms as constitutive of culture and subjectivity. Cultural studies by contrast is materialist in that it focuses on the material origins and effects of culture and the ways that culture is imbricated in process of domination or resistance.

A critical media/cultural studies thus requires a social theory that analyzes the system and structure of domination and forces of resistance. Since capital and economic forces have played a key role in structuring contemporary societies (often referred to as "capitalist" or "democratic capitalist") societies, Marxism has played an important role from the beginning of media/cultural studies, though there have been fierce battles concerning *which* forms of Marxist theory and there has been some sharp rejection of Marxist perspectives (see Fiske 1993).[24] Classically, however, media/cultural studies has conceptualized society as a system of domination in which institutions like the family, schooling, workplace, media, and the state control individuals and provide structures of domination in which individuals struggling for more freedom and power must struggle against.

British cultural studies, therefore, like the critical theory of the Frankfurt School, developed theoretical models of the relationship between the economy, state, society, culture, and everyday life, grounded in the problematics of contemporary social theory. Yet British cultural studies also draws significantly on theories of culture. Crucially, British cultural studies subverts the high and low culture distinction – like postmodern theory and unlike the Frankfurt School –

and thus valorizes cultural forms like film, television, and popular music dismissed by previous approaches to culture, which tended to utilize literary theory to analyze cultural forms, or to focus primarily, or even solely, on the creations of high culture.

A question of terminology

One important innovation of British cultural studies, then, was to see the importance of mass-mediated culture and how it is involved in processes of domination and resistance. Yet there is some debate concerning the proper terminology to describe the objects of those forms of culture that permeate everyday life in the familiar form of such things as radio or television. Raymond Williams and the members of the Birmingham School were responsible for the rejection of the term "mass culture," which they argue, properly I believe, tends to be elitist, erecting a binary opposition between high and low, that is contemptuous of "the masses" and its culture. The concept of "mass culture" is also monolithic and homogeneous, and thus covers over cultural contradictions and dissolves oppositional practices and groups into a neutral concept of "mass."

There are also problems with the term "popular culture," which John Fiske (1989a, 1989b) and other practitioners of cultural studies have uncritically adopted (e.g. Grossberg 1982; Grossberg et al. 1992; Storey 2015). The term "popular" suggests that mass-mediated culture arises from the people and covers over that it is a top-down form of culture that often reduces the audience to a passive receiver of predigested meanings. As used by Fiske, Grossberg, and others, "popular culture" collapses the distinction between culture produced by the people, or "popular classes," contrasted to mass-produced media culture, thus reveling in a "cultural populism" (McGuigan 1992) that often uncritically celebrates media and consumer culture.

Hence, while widely used, the term "popular culture" risks blunting the critical edge of media/cultural studies, and arguably it is simply better to avoid ideologically loaded terms like "mass culture" and "popular culture." A possible move within media/cultural studies would therefore simply be to take culture itself as the field of one's studies without divisions into the high and the low, the popular and the elite – though, of course, these distinctions can be strategically deployed in certain contexts. Thus, I believe that instead of using ideological labels like "mass" and "popular," one could simply talk of culture and communication and develop a "media/cultural studies" cutting across the full range of media and culture.

In this book, I am adopting the terms "media culture" and "media/cultural studies" to delineate the subject matter of my investigations. The term "media culture" has the advantage of signifying both the nature and form of the products of the culture industries (i.e. culture) and their mode of production and distribution (i.e. the media). It avoids ideological terms like "mass culture" and "popular culture" and calls attention to the circuit of production, distribution, and reception through which media culture is produced, distributed, and consumed. The term breaks down artificial barriers between the fields of cultural, media, and communications studies and calls attention to the interconnection of culture and communications media in the constitution of media culture, thus undercutting reified distinctions between "culture" and "communication."[25]

In fact, the distinction between "culture" and "communications" is arbitrary and rigid, and should be deconstructed. Whether one takes "culture" as the artifacts of high culture, the ways in which people live their lives, the context of human behavior, or deploys other models of "culture," it is intimately bound up with communication. All culture, to become a social artifact, and thus properly "culture," is both a mediator of and mediated by communication, and is thus communicational by nature. Yet "communication," in turn, is mediated by culture, it is a mode through which culture is disseminated and rendered actual and effective. There is no communication without culture and no culture without communication, so drawing a rigid distinction between them, and claiming that one side is a legitimate object of a disciplinary study, while the other term is relegated to a different discipline is an excellent example of the myopia and futility of arbitrary academic divisions of labor.[26]

In any case, British cultural studies presents an approach that allows us to avoid cutting up the field of media/culture/communications into high and low, popular vs. elite, and to see all forms of media culture and communication as worthy of scrutiny and criticism. It allows approaches to culture and communication that force us to appraise their politics and to make political discriminations between different types of media texts that have different political effects. Like other multicultural approaches, it brings the study of race, gender, class, and sexuality, into the center of the study of media culture and communication.[27] It also adopts a critical approach that, like the Frankfurt School, but without some of its flaws, interprets culture within society and situates the study of culture within the field of contemporary social theory and oppositional politics.

Yet some who operate within the tradition of British cultural studies not only reify the concept of "the popular" but ignore theorizing and do not even use the term "media." John Storey, for instance, in his introductory text *Cultural Studies and the Study of Popular Culture* (1996/2003) and his text book *Cultural Theory and Popular Culture* (2019; fifth edition) privileges without theorizing or presenting critical perspectives the term "popular culture." Storey does not use the concept of "media," analyzing its political economy, or the economic-technological-material base of "popular culture." The concept of media, which I deploy, signifies, with McLuhan (1964), the technological infrastructure, forms, and political imaginary of "media culture," as well as its institutional structure and how media industries fit into a specific socio-economic and political system.

In this book, I am using the term media/cultural studies to describe the approach I have been using for some decades to signal that media/culture/

communications/society/politics are a matrix grounded in political economy and society, and that culture is not independent of media and communications which are also a highly important field of study.[28] The term "media culture" also has the advantage of signifying that our culture *is* a media culture, that the media have colonized culture, that they are the primary vehicle for the distribution and dissemination of culture, that the dominant media of communications have supplanted previous modes of culture like the book or spoken word, that we live in a world in which media dominate leisure and culture, and that media culture is thus the dominant form and site of culture in contemporary societies.

A question of politics

Media culture is also the site where battles are fought for the control of society. Feminists and anti-feminists, critical race theorists and racists, liberals and conservatives, radicals and defenders of the status quo struggle for cultural power not only in the medium of news and information, but also in the domain of entertainment, as I shall demonstrate throughout this book. The media are intimately connected with power and open the study of culture to the vicissitudes of politics and the slaughterhouse of history. Media help shape our view of the world, public opinion, values and behavior, and are thus an important forum of social power and struggle.

From the beginning, the work of the Birmingham School was oriented toward the crucial political problems of their age and milieu and focused intently on the politics of culture. Some of the first studies that defined British cultural studies, such as Richard Hoggart's *The Uses of Literacy* (Hoggart 1958), indicated how individuals created their identities and lives through their cultural resources. The first half of Hoggart's book details how working class communities in Britain traditionally created oppositional cultures to the mainstream, and then described how they were being eroded by the development of a national culture and processes of cultural homogenization directed by the state, schooling, and the media. This was also a theme of such major early influences on British cultural studies as Raymond Williams and E.P. Thompson.

From the 1960s, British cultural studies began to indicate how media culture was producing identities and ways of seeing and acting that integrated individuals into the mainstream culture (Hall and Whannel 1964). The Birmingham group's early focus on class and ideology thus derived from their acute sense of the oppressive and systemic effects of class in British society and the struggles of the 1960s against class inequality and oppression. Studies of subcultures in Britain sought to search for new agents of social change when it appeared that sectors of the working class were being integrated into the existing system and conservative ideologies and parties. Attempts to reconstruct Marxism for use of British cultural studies were influenced as well by 1960s struggles and political movements. The turn toward feminism, often conflicted, was directly influenced by the feminist movement, while the turn toward race as a significant factor of study was fueled by the anti-racist struggles of the day. The move in British cultural studies toward focus on education was related to political concern with the continuing bourgeois hegemony despite the struggles of the 1960s. The right turn in British politics with Thatcher's victory led in the late 1970s to concern with understanding the authoritarian populism of the new conservative hegemony.

In other words, the focus of British cultural studies at any given moment was determined by the struggles in the present political conjuncture and their major work was thus conceived as political interventions. Their studies of ideology, domination and resistance, and the politics of culture, directed cultural studies toward analyzing cultural texts, practices, and institutions within existing networks of power and of showing how culture both provided instruments and forces of domination and resources for resistance and struggle. This political focus intensified emphasis on the effects of culture and audience use of cultural texts, which provided an extremely productive focus on audiences and reception, topics that had been neglected in most previous text-based approaches to culture.[29]

In the following section, I will therefore indicate some of the chief components of the type of media/cultural studies that I find most useful for understanding and critically engaging contemporary society, culture, and politics, building on the approaches of media/cultural studies developed by the Frankfurt School, British cultural studies, and other contemporary critical theories.

Components of a critical media/cultural studies

As a theoretical apparatus, media/cultural studies contains a threefold project of analyzing the production and political economy of culture, cultural texts, and the audience reception of those texts and their effects in a concrete socio-historical context. This comprehensive approach avoids too narrowly focusing on one dimension of the project to the exclusion of others. To avoid such limitations, I propose a multiperspectival approach that (a) discusses production and political economy, (b) engages in textual analysis, and (c) studies the reception and use of cultural texts.

Production and political economy

Since cultural production has been neglected in many modes of contemporary cultural studies, it is important to stress the importance of analyzing cultural texts within their system of production and distribution, often referred to as the political economy of culture.[30] Inserting texts into the system of culture within which they are produced and distributed can help elucidate features and effects of the texts that textual analysis alone might miss or downplay. Rather than being an antithetical approach to culture, political economy can actually contribute to textual analysis and critique. The system of production often determines in part what sort of media texts will be produced, what structural limits there will be as to what can and cannot be said and shown, and what sort of audience effects the text may generate.

Study of the codes of television, film, or popular music, for instance, is enhanced by studying the formulas and conventions of production, which are shaped by economic and technical, as well as aesthetic and cultural considerations. Dominant cultural forms are structured by well-defined rules and conventions, and the study of the production of culture can help elucidate the codes actually in play. Because of the demands of the format of radio or music television, for instance, most popular songs are three to five minutes, fitting into the format of the distribution system, just as the length of YouTube or Twitter has technical constraints.

From the early years of the Internet up to the present, there have been legal and political conflicts concerning file-sharing of music and other forms of media culture and information, situating media culture in a force-field of political conflict. Because of their control by giant corporations oriented primarily toward profit, television production in the United States is dominated by specific genres such as talk and game shows, soap operas, situation comedies, action/adventure series, reality TV, and so on, which are familiar and popular with audiences. This economic factor explains why there are cycles of certain genres and subgenres, sequelmania in the film industry, crossovers of popular films into television series, and a certain homogeneity in products constituted within systems of production marked by relatively rigid generic codes, formulaic conventions, and well-defined ideological boundaries.

Political economy can also illuminate generic codes or cultural forms and ideological and cultural codes that help structure texts. Media industries follow production codes that delimit the types or genres of media texts, their technical codes, and they limits within which they can safely critique dominant institutions or go outside of the boundaries of dominant ideologies. For example, corporate owned media corporations rarely allow radical critiques of capitalism, while state-controlled media rarely allow radical critiques of a specific states that regulates media.

Another school of production studies has been developed by John Caldwell and his colleagues, which combines "Production Studies" as a subfield within Media Industries Research with "Creative Theory/Practice Research." Moving from work as a filmmaker and video artist, Caldwell turned to academic research with a focus on the production and creative practices in cinema and media. Indeed, his industry experience, interaction, and research is fully evident in the major books he has contributed to the field such as *Production Culture: Industrial Reflexivity and Critical Practice in Film/Television* (2008; 2nd edition, 2013), which established Caldwell as a major scholar of media production culture in film and television.[31]

Likewise, study of political economy can help determine the limits and range of political and ideological discourses and effects. My study of television in the

United States, for instance, disclosed that the takeover of the television networks by major transnational corporations and communications conglomerates in the 1980s was part of a "right turn" within U.S. society whereby powerful corporate groups won control of the state and the mainstream media (Kellner 1990a). For example, during the 1980s, all three networks were taken over by major corporate conglomerates: ABC was taken over in 1985 by Capital Cities, NBC was taken over by GE, and CBS was taken over by the Tisch Financial Group. Both ABC and NBC sought corporate mergers, and this motivation, along with other benefits derived from Reaganism, might well have influenced them to downplay criticisms of Reagan and to generally support his conservative programs, military adventures, and simulated presidency.

The infrastructure of broadcasting shifted in the 1990s with the proliferation of global cable and satellite television, which emerged in an era of neoliberalism and deregulation, and increased both media monopoly and competition between different media corporations and media technologies. The period marks the rise of cable news networks that broadcast news 24/7 and used media spectacle to capture viewers. In the 1990s in the United States, new media and politicized forms of media proliferated including Talk Radio, *Fox News*, and other highly partisan and explosive talk shows, in conjunction with the emergence and the diversity and contentiousness of Internet news, opinion, and multitudinous new media and forms of expression. In the 2000s, the explosion of social networking and Facebook, YouTube, Twitter, and the like intensified diversity but also created partisan tribes and intense cultural wars over every conceivable issue, a mediascape manipulated by Donald Trump as we will see below.

Highly politicized mainstream media continue to heat up and expand today in the U.S., illustrated by the battles between *Fox News* on the right and *MSNBC* on the left, with CNN becoming more highly politicized in the Trump era. In addition, the Internet, different forms of digital media, and social networking have become an ever-more contested terrain used by left, right, and everyone in-between. Further, after the 2016 election of Donald Trump, Facebook, Twitter, Google, and other digital media powerhouses have themselves become contested and under attack in the light of exposure of their role in Trump's election and presidency (see Kellner 2017), as well as their data-harvesting, threats to privacy, and other scandals (see Noble 2018).

Looking toward entertainment, female pop music stars, such as Madonna, Britney Spears, Beyoncé, or Lady Gaga, deploy the tools of the glamour industry and media spectacle to become icons of fashion, beauty, style, and sexuality, as well as purveyors of music. Furthermore, in an era of globalization, one must be aware of the global networks that produce and distribute culture in the interests of profit and corporate hegemony (Flew 2014). The Internet and new media link the globe and distribute more culture to more people than at any time in history, while giant media conglomerates and institutions like the state continue to be major forces of cultural hegemony (see McChesney 2013; Galloway

2017). Thus, to fully grasp the nature and effects of media culture, one needs to develop methods to analyze the full range of its meanings and effects that are sensitive to the always mutating terrain of media culture and technology and political economy.

Textual analysis

The products of media culture require multidimensional close textual readings to analyze their various forms of discourses, ideological positions, narrative strategies, image construction, and effects. "Reading" a text of media culture involves interpreting the forms and meanings of elements in a music video or television advertising, as one previously read and interpreted books. There have been a wide range of types of textual criticism of media culture, ranging from quantitative content analysis that dissects the number of, say, episodes of violence in a text to qualitative study that examines representations of women, Blacks, or other groups or that applies various critical theories to unpack the meanings of the texts or to explicate how texts function to produce meaning. Traditionally, the qualitative analysis of texts attended to the formal artistic properties of imaginative literature – e.g. style, verbal imagery, characterization, narrative structure and point of view. From the 1960s on, however, literary–formalist textual analysis has been enhanced by methods derived from semiotics, a system for investigating the creation of meaning not only in written languages but also in other, nonverbal codes, such as the visual and auditory languages of film and TV.

Semiotics analyzes how linguistic and nonlinguistic cultural "signs" form systems of meanings, as when giving someone a rose is interpreted as a sign of love, or getting an A on a college paper is a sign of mastery of the rules of the specific assignment. Semiotic analysis can be connected with genre criticism (the study of conventions governing long-established types of cultural forms, such as soap operas) to reveal how the codes and forms of particular genres construct certain meanings. TV situation comedies, for instance, classically follow a conflict/resolution model that demonstrates how to solve certain social problems by correct actions and values and thus provide morality tales of proper and improper behavior. Soap operas, by contrast, proliferate problems and provide messages concerning the endurance and suffering needed to get through life's endless miseries, while generating positive and negative models of social behavior. And advertising shows how commodity solutions solve problems of popularity, acceptance, success, and the like.

A semiotic and genre analysis of James Cameron's *Avatar* (2009), for instance, would reveal how the images in the film present an anti-militarist and pro-ecological agenda, although the narrative form celebrates a White Male Savior, replicating more conservative narratives. *Avatar* also demonstrates how fantasy spectacles can project a wealth of political and ideological meanings, often ambiguous or contradictory. Discussions of *Avatar* have also generated heated debates in the politics of representation, concerning how the film has represented gender, sexuality, race, the military, and the environment, as well as other themes and dimensions of the film.[32]

The textual analysis of cultural studies thus combines formalist analysis with critique of how cultural meanings convey specific ideologies of gender, race, class, sexuality, nation, and other ideological dimensions. Ideologies refer to ideas or images that construct a superiority of one class or group over others (i.e. men over women, whites over people of color, ruling elites over working class people, and so on), and thus reproduce and legitimate different forms of social domination. Ideological textual analysis should deploy a wide range of methods to fully explicate each dimension of ideological domination across domains of representations of class, race, gender, sexuality, and other forms of domination and subordination, and to show how specific narratives serve interests of domination and oppression, contest it, or are ambiguous (as with many examples of media culture). Each critical method focuses on certain features of a text from a specific perspective: The perspective spotlights, or illuminates, some features of a text while ignoring others. Marxist methods tend to focus on class, for instance, while feminist approaches will highlight gender, critical race theory spotlights race and ethnicity, and gay and lesbian theories explicate sexuality. Yet today, the concept of "intersectionality" is often used and many feminists, Marxists, critical race scholars, and other forms of media/cultural studies depict how gender, class, race, sexuality, and other components intersect and co-construct each other in complex cultural ways (see Crenshaw 1991).

Various critical methods have their own strengths and limitations, their optics and blind spots, as noted above. Traditionally, Marxian ideology critiques have been strong on class and historical contextualization and weak on formal analysis, while some versions are highly "reductionist," reducing textual analysis to denunciation of ruling class ideology. Feminism excels in gender analysis and in some versions is formally sophisticated, drawing on such methods as psychoanalysis and semiotics, although some versions are reductive, and early feminism often limited itself to analysis of images of gender. Psychoanalysis in turn calls for the interpretation of unconscious contents and meaning, which can articulate latent meanings in a text, as when Alfred Hitchcock's dream sequences project cinematic symbols that provide insight into his characters' dilemmas, or when the image of the female character in *Bonnie and Clyde* (1967), framed against the bar of her bed, suggests her sexual frustration, imprisonment in middle-class family life, and need for revolt and emancipation.

Of course, each reading of a text is only one possible reading from one critic's subject position, no matter how multiperspectival, and may or may not be the reading preferred by audiences (which themselves will be significantly different according to their class, race, gender, ethnicity, ideologies, and so on). Because there is a split between textual encoding and audience decoding, there is always the possibility of a multiplicity of readings of any text of media culture (Hall et al. 1980). There are limits to the openness or polysemic nature of any text, of course, and textual analysis can explicate the parameters of possible readings and delineate perspectives that aim at illuminating the text and its cultural and ideological effects. Such analysis also provides the materials for criticizing misreadings, or readings that are one-sided and incomplete. Yet to further carry through a media/cultural studies analysis, one must also examine how diverse audiences actually read media texts and attempt to determine what impact or influence they have on audience thought and behavior.

Audience reception and uses of media culture

All texts are subject to multiple readings depending on the perspectives and subject positions of the reader. Members of distinct genders, classes, races, nations, regions, sexual preferences, and political ideologies are going to read texts differently, and cultural studies can illuminate why diverse audiences interpret texts in various, sometimes conflicting, ways. Media culture provides materials for individuals and communities to create identities and meanings, and cultural studies work on audiences detects a variety of potentially empowering uses of cultural forms.

It is one of the merits of cultural studies to have focused on audience reception and fan appropriation, and this focus provides one of its major contributions, although there are also limitations and problems with some of the audience reception approaches to media/cultural studies.[33] In his classical article "Encoding/Decoding," Stuart Hall distinguished between the "encoding" of media texts in the production process through which the creators of texts communicate meaning through cultural, formal, generic and ideological codes, and the "decoding" of cultural texts through which audiences interpret the text and create their own meanings. In Hall's analysis, a "dominant" reading follows the codes of the producers and the dominant cultural meaning of the images, codes and messages of the texts. A "resistant" reading, by contrast, resists a dominant encoding of the text by, for instance, reading images of a minstrel show with white actors in blackface, as an example of a racist past rather than a humorous and harmless form of entertainment.[34] Finally, a "negotiated" reading may accept some aspects of a text's encoding representations and meanings, but resist others, as when, for example, a white woman may accept racist representations or narratives yet be offended and critical of gender representations in the same text. One should also distinguish between the encoding and decoding of media texts, and recognize that an active audience often produces its own meanings and use for products of the cultural industry.

Dominant meanings are encoded into cultural texts such as *Game of Thrones*, which encode relations of power and domination into its fantasy stories. Audiences decode the text to interpret who possesses power and is dominant and who is subordinate. The dominant reading of *Game of Thrones* would be in line with the intentions of the novelist George R. R. Martin or the TV series producers who present some characters as more powerful and others as less powerful. A negotiated reading could recognize, for instance, some male characters as most powerful but see their power as illegitimate and unstable and identify other characters in a negotiated reading as more formidable. An oppositional reading would offer, say, feminist readings of the obviously quite male and patriarchal series – or would negotiate to what extent the series, or specific seasons or episodes, are or are not patriarchal and sexist or their opposite. Decoding of cultural texts is thus highly contested and sometimes contentious and each individual will decode texts according to their own subject positions, level of media literacy, or overall views and knowledge.

Ethnographic research studies people and their groups and cultures and is frequently used in an attempt to determine how media texts affect specific audiences and shape their beliefs and behavior. Ethnographic cultural studies have indicated some of the various ways that audiences use and appropriate texts, often to empower themselves. For example, teenagers use video games and music television as an escape from the demands of a disciplinary society. Males use sports media events as a terrain of fantasy identification, in which they feel empowered as "their" team or star triumphs. Such sports events also generate a form of community that is currently being lost in the privatized media and consumer culture of our time. In fact, fandoms of all sorts help produce identities and communities, ranging from *Star Trek* fans ("Trekkies"/"Trekkers") to devotees of various soap operas, reality shows, or current highly popular TV series, like *Game of Thrones*. These fan cultures often form communities that enable people to relate to others who share their interests and hobbies. Some fans, in fact, actively re-create their favorite cultural forms (see examples in Jenkins 2012). Other studies have shown that audiences can subvert the intentions of the producers or managers of the cultural industries that supply them, as when astute young media users laugh at obvious attempts to hype certain characters, shows, or products (see de Certeau 1984 and Livingstone 2017 for more examples of audiences constructing meaning and engaging in practices in critical and subversive ways).

Further, social media such as Facebook, YouTube, Twitter, and other social networking sites produce forums for more active audiences, as well as sites for audience research. As audiences critically discuss or celebrate their preferred products of media culture and, in some cases, produce their own versions, disseminated to audiences throughout the Internet and new digital technologies, media culture expands its reach and power while audiences can feel that they are part of their preferred cultural texts and phenomena. Studies are proliferating in this field of how Facebook, YouTube, Twitter, and other new media are used by individuals and groups in diverse ways ranging from sharing pictures and media content through social networking through political expression and organizing and pedagogical purposes (see Noble 2018).

The emphasis on active audience reception and appropriation, then, has helped media/cultural studies overcome the previous one-sided textualist orientations to culture and also has directed focus on the actual political effects that texts may have. By combining quantitative and qualitative research, audience reception and fandom studies are providing important contributions to how people actually interact with cultural texts.

Thus, while emphasis on the audience and reception was an excellent correction to the one-sidedness of purely textual analysis, I believe that in past years, media/cultural studies has overemphasized audience reception and textual analysis while underemphasizing the production of culture and its political economy. This type of cultural studies fetishizes audience reception studies and neglects both production and textual analysis, thus producing populist celebrations of the text and audience pleasure in its use of cultural artifacts. This approach, taken to an extreme, would lose its critical perspective and would lead to a positive gloss on audience experience of whatever is being studied. Such studies also might lose sight of the manipulative and conservative effects of certain types of media culture and thus serve the interests of the cultural industries as they are presently constituted.

No doubt, media effects are complex and controversial, and it is the merit of media/cultural studies to make their study an important part of its agenda. Previous studies of the audience and the reception of media privileged ethnographic studies that selected slices of the vast media audiences, usually from the site where researchers themselves lived. Such studies are invariably limited, and broader effects research can indicate how the most popular products of media culture have a wide range of effects. One new way to research media effects is to use Google, or databases that collect media texts, to trace certain effects of media texts through analysis of references to them in the media or internet and social networking sites. Likewise, there is an expanding terrain of Internet audience research that studies how fans act in chat rooms or fan-sites devoted to their favorite products of media culture (see Noble 2018).

In fact, when I published the first edition of *Media Culture* in 1995, I noted how new computer data bases, like Dialog and Lexis/Nexis, made it possible to do a new type of reception studies, such as I did at that time. One could type in code words like "Rambo" and "Reagan" to see some of the ways that the figure of Rambo was articulated within dominant political discourses. The result was literally hundreds of references, which I drew upon in the previous chapter in my study of "the Rambo effect," and I did similar data bases searches concerning all the films that I am analyzed at that time, as well as the Gulf war, rap music and hip hop culture, *Beavis and Butt-Head*, *Miami Vice*, MTV, cigarette advertising, Madonna, and cyberpunk fiction (Kellner 1995). One found in the 1990s literally thousands of references to specific media texts, which enables one to trace the effects of texts that enter into media culture through a wide range of social discourses that articulate a variety of diverse effects.

Of course, with the explosion of the Internet, social networking sites like Wikipedia and Google, and many other forms of digital information, the amount of material one can gain from researching popular films, TV shows, music, and the like is now overwhelming. We are in a Golden Age of research for media culture where one can discover surprising references to the artifacts of media culture in all arenas of life, as well as information on production, reception, and the impact of specific films, TV shows, or artists.

Although figures like Rambo, Beyoncé, Lady Gaga, or successful TV shows like *Game of Thrones*, can generate powerful direct effects, it is rare that single films, popular songs, television programs, media figures, and so on directly influence their audiences. Yet some examples of the *global popular* attain the status of directly influencing thought and behavior by producing models of gender, style, or action. Such powerful images are emulated throughout the world and often directly impact their audiences. Yet for the most part, it is the cumulative effects of 1960s films, music, and other forms of media culture that articulate countercultural ideologies that serve to promote 1960s countercultural movements that influenced the ways that people see, talk, and behave in a specific historical epoch (see Roszak 1968). Or perhaps it is the cumulative effects of racist images of Arabs in Hollywood movies and television news and entertainment that makes it possible to mobilize anti-Arab or anti-immigrant discourses in political events like the 1991 Gulf war, the September 11, 2001 terror attacks, the 2003 Iraq war, or Donald Trump's (2016–) war on immigrants.[35]

And so while the very figure of Rambo may have a massive range of effects, some of which I documented, it is the cumulative impact of all of the anti-Arab, or anti-Latino/a, images of film and television that negatively constituted images of Arabs, Asians, or Latinos, rather than a single film or artifact alone. Thus, on one hand, a critical media/cultural studies is concerned with analyzing certain *resonant images* (Kellner 1990a), which is one of the keys to ferreting out media effects. Memorable images resonate to our experiences and stick in the mind, moving us to later thought and action. Sometimes pop figures like a Rambo, a Madonna, a Lady Gaga, or hip hop artist, become highly resonant, mobilizing thought and behavior, so that one wants to be a Beyoncé or Lady Gaga, imitating her style of dress and changes of image; or one wants to be a Rambo or a Bruce Willis, imitating his macho behavior. Wonder Woman has been given multiple iterations as a comic book character over the years, was the subject of a popular TV series, the figure in an animated film, and was introduced in her current form in *The Justice League* in which Superman, Batman, Wonder Woman and a pantheon of DC comics superheroes band to fight a phalanx of evildoers who threaten the existence of earth.[36] In the 1970s, Gloria Steinem highlighted the feminist dimension of the heroine by putting her on the first cover of *Ms. Magazine* and providing an article in the issue that highlighted Wonder Woman's feminist credentials.

In the 1950s, resonant images of non-conformist rebels and bikers (Marlon Brando, Elvis Presley, and James Dean), or beatnik writers like Jack Kerouac and his novels, became highly influential, modelling style, thought, and behavior. Occasionally, a resonant image might be detached in affect and memory from its narrative structure, and while the narrative message may be "crime does not pay," or "adultery brings unhappiness," it is the memory of the attractive criminal or the sexual transgression that remains in one's mind, that could influence transgressive thought and behavior, hence negating the ideological message. This was possibly true of 1930s crime dramas in which the energy and power of a Cagney or Bogart might have been what stuck in one's mind, producing rebellious or criminal behavior, rather than their getting caught or murdered and any message that "crime does not pay." Likewise Mario van Peeble's *New Jack City* (1991) might attempt to convey an anti-drug message and develop a narrative in which crime is punished and does not pay, yet perhaps the images of the drug dealers leading the high life are what resonates and what influences later behavior.

In addition, paleosymbolic scenes (Kellner 1979) may be vehicles of powerful media effects, as scenes of communal fun in films like *Easy Rider* or *Woodstock* might promote the ideologies and lifestyle of the counterculture with their images of nude swimming, easy sex, getting high, and participating in social ritual. The preface "paleo" signifies a sort of "before symbolism" or "underneath symbolism." Paleosymbols are tied to particular scenes that are charged with drama and emotion. Freud found that certain scenic images, such as a child being beaten for masturbation, or discovering his parents having sex, have profound impact on subsequent behavior. The images of these scenes remain as paleosymbols that control behavior, for instance, producing guilt accompanying masturbation, or infusing sex with great fascination and attraction, or fear and repulsion. Paleosymbols are not subject to conscious scrutiny or control; they are often repressed, closed off from reflection, and can produce compulsive behavior. Thus Freud believed that scenic understanding was necessary to master scenic images, and, in turn, this mastery could help to understand what the scenic images signified and how they influenced behavior.

Paleosymbolic scenes may deeply influence one's perception of members of opposite genders, races, and classes, and deeply influence gender behavior and style. Media representations of Blacks as violent and threatening may produce negative images of members of this race. Such images are often presented in gripping and dramatic scenes and the images are likely to stay in the viewer's mind. Likewise, images of violence as the way to solve problems and to exert power may create powerful paleosymbolic residues that shape violent attitudes and behavior. Or the paleosymbolic scenes of *Rambo* may stick in one's mind, leading one to engage in body-building, arms training, and perhaps violent action, as with the examples noted in my discussion of the Rambo-effect.

Further, paleosymbolic symbolic images of predatory and destructive women, such as the vampire-like predators of *Fatal Attraction* and *Basic Instinct*, or the monstrous women of horror films, might produce fear of women. Or pornography or scenes that degrade, brutalize, or mutilate women may produce male violence toward women and treating women as objects of abuse. On the other hand, a multitude of media images featuring beautiful white, thin, and sexually attractive women may produce inferiority attitudes with some audiences.

Media culture thus provides powerful images and scenes for identification that may directly influence behavior, providing models of action, morality, style, and identity. There is also an anticipatory dimension to media culture that I might note. Media culture anticipated the election of a Black president by having prominent Black actors like Denzel Washington and Morgan Freeman playing African American presidents or political leaders in film, or portrayals of a Black president in TV series like *The West Wing*. Such anticipations of Black presidents in major products of media culture made it possible for U.S. audiences/electorate to imagine a Black president so when Barack Obama undertook his startling and successful campaign for the presidency in 2008 it was possible to actually envisage that the U.S. could have a Black chief of state.[37]

In appraising the effects of media culture, one must avoid the extreme of either romanticizing the audiences of media culture, or of reducing them to a homogeneous mass incapable of critical thought or action. One needs to grasp the contradiction that the media do manipulate people and yet people also manipulate and use the media. British cultural studies tries to capture this contradiction in the distinction between *encoding* and *decoding*, whereby the texts of media culture may be encoded as the most crass, ideological and banal artifacts, and yet audiences can produce their own meanings and pleasures out of this material. Yet it is a mistake to go too far toward the active audience, as some have done, and to exaggerate the power of audiences against media culture. The media are tremendously powerful forces and underestimating their power does not benefit critical projects of social transformation.

In any case, the effects of media culture are complex and highly mediated, and require study of the origin and production of media culture texts, their distribution and reception by audiences, and the ways that individuals use cultural texts to produce meaning, discourses, and identities. Such effects can best be discerned by concrete studies of how popular cultural artifacts like *Rambo*, *Avatar*, rap music, or major TV series like *Game of Thrones* or *The Handmaid's Tale*,[38] circulate and gain effectivity within media culture and everyday life. I will engage in such concrete studies later in the following chapters, but in conclusion and in the next chapter also want to introduce additional theoretical concepts and methods concerning some of the ways that one can learn to read media culture critically and thus increase one's critical media literacy.

To avoid the one-sidedness of textual analysis approaches or audience and reception studies, I propose that cultural studies itself be *multiperspectival*, getting at culture from the perspectives of political economy, text analysis, and audience reception, as outlined above. Textual analysis should use a multiplicity of perspectives and critical methods, and audience reception studies should delineate the wide range of subject positions, or perspectives, through which audiences appropriate culture. This requires a multicultural approach that sees the importance of analyzing the dimensions of class, race and ethnicity, and gender and sexual preference within the texts of media culture, while studying as well their impact on how audiences read and interpret media culture.

In addition, a critical cultural studies attacks sexism, hetrosexualism, racism, or bias against specific social groups (e.g. gays, intellectuals, seniors, etc.), and criticizes texts that promote any kind of domination or oppression. To understand the range of meanings of specific texts of media culture, one needs to contextualize the topic of inquiry within its matrix of cultural production and reception to discern the dominant meanings and effects, an operation I will illustrate through a critical reading of dominant genres and products of media culture throughout this book.

Notes

1   Studies show that the amount of hours devoted to work in the United States is at an all-time high; see Schorr's study of *The Overworked American* (1992) and G.E. Miller, "The U.S. is the Most Overworked Developed Nation in the World," *20somethingfinance*, January 2, 2018 at https://20somethingfinance.com/american-hours-worked-productivity-vacation/ (accessed October 20, 2019). Yet there are also technological trends that might lead to diminution of the length of the workday. See Gorz 1982, 1985 and an article in the *New York Times* (November 24, 1993: A1) that indicated that there was a serious movement abroad in Europe to limit the workday to four days a week. For a website that documents "The Decline of Working Hours per Year after the Industrial Revolution," see https://ourworldindata.org/working-hours#the-decline-of-working-hours-per-year-after-the-industrial-revolution (accessed October 10, 2018).
2   Indicating that the gig economy is growing, "(a) study by Intuit predicted that by 2020, 40% of American workers would be independent contractors." See the discussion of the gig economy at www.google.com/search?source=hp&ei=hszxW4iLBtHJ_wSxzo-QBw&q=gig+economy&oq=gig+econo&gs_l=psy-ab.1.0.0l10.1714.3982.6739..0.0. 0.109.876.8j2...0..1.gws-wiz...0.0i131j0i10.4cxcbNNrG1M (accessed November 18, 2018).
3   Convinced against those who argue "against theory" (e.g. Rorty et al.) that theories are of use in illuminating our social world, throughout this book I shall reflect on the nature and function of social theories, for it is not at all agreed upon, or evident, what social theories are, what they do, and what are their value and limitations. The theoretical perspectives that I'll sketch out are perhaps most influenced by the critical theory of the Frankfurt School (see Kellner 1989a; Bronner and Kellner 1989) and British cultural studies (see Grossberg, Nelson and Treichler 1992; Hall et al. 1980), although I also draw heavily on feminism, critical race theory, queer and multicultural theory, and attempt to synthesize these theories into my own critical theoretical perspectives to illuminate our present moment. I explicate the concept of "theory" and "perspective" that I am using later in the chapter.
4   See Howard and Klare 1972. In Europe, by contrast, Marxism was part of the standard intellectual discourse, though it tended to be monopolized by the Marxist

parties. On the impact of Marxism on a diverse range of academic fields in the United States, see Ollman and Vernoff, 1982. For Britain, see Anderson 1980; Davies 1996.

5   On the successive waves of feminism that appeared beginning in the United States during the 1960s, see the accounts in Willis 1984; Faludi 1991; Brenner 1993; Hammer 2002. On the unhappy marriage between Marxism and feminism, see Hartmann 1981. For an example of psychoanalytic feminism, see Mitchell 1974. For feminism in Britain, see Barrett 1980 and Caine, ed. 1997.

6   See, for example, Hall 2012; Henderson 2019. LGBTQ+ refers to lesbian/gay/bisexual/transgender/queer studies and people who have these orientations; the + enables other individuals and groups to identify with this orientation. Many more terms of this nature are used and "correct" usage is often changing in use.

7   See Said 1978; Spivak 1990, 1999.

8   On multiculturalism and multicultural theories, see the work collected in Taylor and Gutmann, 1994. I further explicate multicultural perspectives on cultural studies in the following pages of this chapter and in later analyses.

9   John Thompson (1984, 1990) examines classical and contemporary theories of ideology and finds that many of them sever the link between ideology and domination, and therefore rob ideology of the critical edge that it had in Marx and other neo-Marxists. I would therefore agree with Thompson on the need to link the concept of ideology with theories of hegemony and domination, and thus to delimit its application to ideas and positions that serve functions of legitimation, mystification, and domination that assure the domination of the ruling class over other classes and groups within society, rather than equating *all* ideas or political positions with ideology – although as I argue in this chapter, the concept of ideology should be expanded to encompass domains of race, gender, sexuality, and other fields of hierarchal oppression.

10 Attempts within media/cultural studies to downplay the importance of ideology critique, such as Fiske (1993), play into the hands of an establishment that has for decades attempted to abolish the concept of ideology as too political and politicizing. The "end of ideology" debate within the social sciences and apolitical approaches to literature, philosophy, and the other humanities have all attempted to banish the concept of ideology. Given the centrality of the concept of ideology to earlier traditions of media/cultural studies, it is ironic that some of those identifying with media/cultural studies are now trying to banish one of its central and defining concepts.

11 The collection was first published as part of the series of *Working Papers on Cultural Studies* 10 (1977).

12 David Morrell tells the history of the transformation of *First Blood* from novel to film in the 2017 Hatchette paperback of his novel that includes an opening essay "Rambo and Me" and "A Conversion with David Morrell" at the end of the novel. On Morrell and Rambo, see also Faludi 1999 who interviews Morrell, places the novels and film in the context of returning Vietnam veterans and also spells out the differences between the novel and film versions of the Rambo epic.

13 As late as 1992, a disinformation campaign took place alleging that a KGB file contained documents indicating that Vietnam was purposively holding U.S. POWs hostage after the war, a myth perpetuated for decades by Ross Perot, and those who wanted to block normalization of relations with Vietnam as revenge for U.S. military defeat in the region. For exposure of the 1992 disinformation campaign, see Bruce Franklin's article in *The Nation* (May 10, 1992: 616).

14 Jeffords notes that *Missing in Action* (1984) also shows the hero renouncing women and sexuality, inscribing the hero in the fascist scenario of sexual purity, subliminally identifying his efficacy with asceticism (1989: 132f). Such representations point to parallels in Theweleit's analysis of male fascist warriors in Nazi Germany (1987).

15 Jeffords (1989: 130ff) points out that there are four scenes where Rambo emerges from water to accomplish heroic action, thus enacting mythic purification rites, primal images also present in the slow-motion climax of *Missing in Action*, when Chuck Norris emerges from water, machine-gun blasting, to destroy his enemies.

16 Interestingly, the novel *First Blood*, early versions of the screenplay, and even one filmed version of the ending showed the Sheriff shooting and killing Rambo, but reportedly audiences, Stallone, and other members of the cast and production team argued successfully for the happy Hollywood triumphant ending; see the discussions in Faludi 1999; Morrell 2017.

17 On earlier traditions of cultural studies in the U.S., see Aronowitz 1993 and for Britain, see Davies 1996.

18 On the Frankfurt School theory of the cultural industries, see Horkheimer and Adorno 1972; the anthology edited by Rosenberg and White 1957; the reader edited by Bronner and Kellner 1989; and the discussion of the Frankfurt School approach in Kellner 1989a.

19 There were, to be sure, some exceptions and qualifications to this "classical" model: Adorno would occasionally note a critical or utopian moment within mass culture and the possibility of audience reception against the grain; see the examples in Kellner 1989a. But although one can find moments that put in question the more bifurcated division between high and low culture and the model of mass culture as consisting of nothing except ideology and modes of manipulation which incorporate individuals into the existing society and culture, generally, the Frankfurt School model is overly reductive and monolithic, and thus needs radical reconstruction — which I have attempted to do in work over the past decades.

20 The field of communications was initially bifurcated into a division, described by Lazarsfeld (1941) in an issue edited by the Frankfurt School on mass communications, between the critical school associated with the Institute for Social Research contrasted to administrative research, which Lazarsfeld defined as research carried out within the parameters of established media and social institutions and that would provide material that was of use to these institutions — research with which Lazarsfeld himself would be identified. Hence, it was the Frankfurt School that inaugurated critical communications research in the United States, and I am suggesting that a return to a reconstructed version of the original model would be useful for media and cultural studies today.

21 In the 1930s model of critical theory, theory was conceptualized as an instrument of political practice. Yet the formulation of the theory of the culture industries by Horkheimer and Adorno (1992 [1947]) in the 1940s was part of their turn toward a more pessimistic phase in which they eschewed concrete politics and generally located resistance within critical individuals, like themselves, rather than within social groups, movements, or oppositional practices. Thus, the classical Frankfurt School analysis ultimately is weak on the formulation of oppositional practices and counterhegemonic cultural strategies.

22 I have been immersed in the problematic of British cultural studies since 1975, when I was involved in a study group in Austin, Texas, and wrote Stuart Hall of the Birmingham Centre for Contemporary Cultural Studies. He responded with a long letter describing the history of the Centre and sent me a set of their stenciled papers, which our group carefully studied. We read all of their studies, journal articles, and books, and thus the first U.S. cultural studies group emerged in Austin, Texas. See my review of the earlier stages of the Birmingham project in *Theory, Culture, and Society*, I, 1 (1980).

23 Gramsci 1971; 1992; Hall 1986. I further elucidate and illustrate the concept of hegemony in the following chapters.

24 Many of Stuart Hall's programmatic pieces discuss the appropriation of Marxism in British cultural studies, and especially the Marxism of Gramsci and Althusser; see (Hall et al. 1980, 1986, 1987, 1992).

25 For some years, there has been a bifurcation in the field of the study of media culture between approaches that adopt the methods of the humanities to interpret media culture as cultural texts opposed to the approach of communication studies which utilize more empirical methods of the social sciences to analyze the production, nature, and effects of media culture. I am arguing for the need of combining these approaches and overcoming the current division in the field between the approaches of "cultural studies" and "communication studies."

26 Although he works in a department of communications, Lawrence Grossberg (1992) begins his meta-theoretical presentation of cultural studies by attacking the concept of communication and effectively removing it from the conceptual field (37ff), drawing upon an earlier attempt to deconstruct the concept of communication (Grossberg 1982). I would prefer, however, to dissolve binary oppositions between culture and communication, to refuse privileging one over the other, and to show how contemporary media culture and mass-mediated communications are interconnected in the products of the cultural industries. I would also argue that methods drawn from the humanities to study "culture" and methods from the social sciences that investigate "communication" are both valuable for media/cultural studies. Finally, it is also curious that some departments and disciplinarians use the term "communication" to describe the objective of their study, while other departments and individuals use the plural "communications." There are obviously different types and levels of communication/s in our culture, thus the plural has its uses and validity, though the singular also serves to note that the many varieties are all forms of communication; consequently, I will use both terms in different contexts to denote plurality or singularity.

27 The early focus in Birmingham studies was on class and subcultures, but the influence of feminism forced a focus on gender and sexuality, and the influence of people of color within the Centre forced focus on race and ethnicity (see the narrative in Hall 1986; Gilroy 1991; Brunson, Hall et al. 1996). In any case, by the 1980s cultural studies generally had a multicultural agenda, though the earlier focus on class has been displaced in some versions, a neglect that I shall attempt to avoid in my studies.

28 For earlier attempts to delineate a model of a media/cultural studies see the readers that I have edited with colleagues who share this approach in Durham and Kellner 2001, 2012; Hammer and Kellner 2009.

29 Textualism was especially one-sided in North American "new criticism" and other literary approaches which for some decades in the post-World War II conjuncture defined the dominant approach to textual analysis in the United States. The post-structuralist approaches that developed in France in the 1970s and quickly disseminated throughout the world were also highly textualist. The British cultural studies focus on audience and reception, however, was anticipated by the Frankfurt School: Walter Benjamin focused on the importance of reception studies as early as the 1930s, while Adorno, Lowenthal, and others in the Frankfurt School carried out reception studies in the same era. See the discussion in Kellner 1989a: 121ff. Except for some exceptions, however, the Frankfurt School tended to conceive of the audience as primarily passive, thus the Birmingham emphasis on the active audience is a genuine advance, though, as I argue below, there have been some exaggerations on this issue and qualifications to the notion of the active audience are now needed.

30 The term *political economy* calls attention to the fact that production and distribution of culture take place within a specific economic system, constituted by relations between the state and economy. For instance, in the United States, a capitalist economy dictates that cultural production is governed by laws of the market, but the democratic imperatives of the system mean that there is some regulation of culture

by the state. There are often tensions within a given society concerning how many activities should be governed by the imperatives of the market, or economics, alone and how much state regulation or intervention is desirable, to ensure a wider diversity of broadcast programming, for instance, or the prohibition of phenomena agreed to be harmful, such as cigarette advertising or pornography (see Kellner, 1990; McChesney, 2007).

31 Caldwell continued to ground his work in industry and production analysis in his book *Production Studies: Cultural Studies of Media Industries* (2009), co-edited with Vicki Mayer, and Miranda Banks. He has also published *Televisuality* (1995); *New Media: Theories and Practices of Digitextuality*, edited by Caldwell and Anna Everett (2003); *Theories of the New Media: A Historical Perspective*, (2000), and edited *Electronic Media and Technoculture*, (2000).

32 For the Vatican critique of *Avatar* see the discussion in Nic Squires, "Vatican calls 'Avatar' bland," (January 11, 2010 at www.telegraph.co.uk/news/worldnews/europe/vaticancityandholysee/6963399/Vatican-calls-Avatar-bland.html (accessed April 13, 2010). *Telegraph.co.uk* also published articles the same week on "Avatar hit by accusations of racism" and by claims of plagarism. Slavoj Zizek decried as well the "brutal racist undertones" of *Avatar* in "Return of the natives," *New Statesman*, March 4, 2010 at www.newstatesman.com/film/2010/03/avatar-reality-love-couple-sex (accessed April 13, 2010).

33 Influential cultural studies approaches that have focused on audience reception include (Brunsdon and Morley 1978; Radway 1983; Ang 1985, 1996; Morley 1986; Fiske 1989a; 1989b; Jenkins 1992; Lewis 1992). On "fandom," see Gray, Sandvoss, and Harrington, (Eds) (2007) and Duffett 2013.

34 Talk show host Megyn Kelly lost a job in the fall of 2018 by not being able to grasp that the "dominant" reading of minstrel shows had shifted from harmless entertainment to seeing them as residues of noxious racism. See Jacob Shamsian, "Megyn Kelly defended blackface on the 'Today' show, but here's the racist history behind it," *Insider News*, October 24, 2018 at www.thisisinsider.com/megyn-kelly-blackface-controversy-racist-history-2018-10 (accessed November 24, 2018). During the same period, Southern politicians in the U.S. were shamed by pictures of them appearing in blackface, sending the message that this longtime racist practice is no longer acceptable.

35 On representations of Arabs in films and television, see (Shaheen 1984, 2012a, 2012b).

36 For an excellent analysis of representations of Wonder Woman in DC comics from the 1940s to the 2000s, see Cocca 2016.

37 On how media culture anticipated a Black U.S. president and thus made it imaginable that Barack Obama could be president and that the U.S. could have a Black president, see the analysis in Kellner 2009.

38 I discuss the impact of the TV series *Miami Vice* in the 1980s in the first edition of *Media Culture* (Kellner 1995: 238ff) and discuss *The Handmaid's Tale* in the next chapter.

2

FOR A CRITICAL MEDIA/CULTURAL STUDIES

The artifacts of media culture are thus not innocent entertainment, but are thoroughly ideological products bound up with political rhetoric, struggles, agendas, and policies. Given their political significance and effects, it is important to learn to read media culture politically in order to decode its ideological messages and meanings, which are often multiple and contested. As I have argued so far, reading media culture politically requires expanding ideological criticism to include the intersection of gender, sexuality, race, and class, and to see that ideology is presented in the forms of images, figures, generic codes, myth, and the technical apparatus of film, television, music, and other media forms, as well as in ideas or theoretical positions.

Yet cultural texts are not intrinsically "conservative" or "liberal." Rather, many texts try to go both ways to maximize their audiences, while others advance specific ideological positions, which are often undercut by other aspects of the text. The texts of media culture incorporate a variety of discourses, ideological positions, narrative strategies, image construction, and codes (e.g. cinematic, televisual, musical, and so on), which rarely coalesce into a pure and coherent ideological position. They attempt to provide something for everyone to attract as large an audience as possible and thus often incorporate a wide range of ideological positions, although in some contexts specific demographics guide media production, as when the film industry gears megablockbuster spectacles to teenage boys. Still, as I have argued, certain media cultural texts advance specific ideological positions that can be ascertained by relating the texts to the political discourses and debates of its era, to other artifacts concerned with similar themes, and to ideological motifs in the culture that are active in the text.

In this chapter, I will explicate my approach to cultural studies, the need for a contextual cultural studies, and the notion of diagnostic critique. I will first present my conception of a critical intersectional multiculturalism as a basis for cultural studies and then discuss my model of a multiperspectival cultural studies, which I will illustrate through a reading of the 2015–2019 TV mini-series version of Margaret Atwood's *A Handmaid's Tale*. After setting forth my critical and contextual approach, I indicate why it is important to utilize a dialectical optic that ferrets out both ideological and utopian moments from media culture. I also explicate my conception of a diagnostic critique which I illustrate with a reading of "Superheroes From *Wonder Woman* to *Black Panther*."

For a critical intersectional multiculturalism

I aim at developing a cultural studies that is *critical* in that it probes forms of oppression and domination and how media culture reproduces forms of inequality, subordination, and injustice. To develop a critical perspective requires articulating the social representations in specific media texts of gender, class, race, ethnicity, sexuality, age, and other categories that involve forms of conformity to dominant social norms and involve subordination and oppression, and analyzing how individuals in these categories are represented. It also involves critically engaging the ways that representations of gender, race, class, and so on produce identities in contemporary societies, as well as how alternative representations produce models of new and different identities. Maintaining a critical perspective also requires interpreting culture and society in terms of relations of power, domination, and resistance, as well as articulating the various forms of oppression in a given society via multicultural perspectives. Moreover, critical social theory and media cultural studies involves developing perspectives from which one can critically engage cultural texts. This requires spelling out specific values, norms, and ideals and validating them in concrete contexts, such as how representations of race, gender, or other forms of identity promote oppression and subordination.

Critical perspectives toward culture and society have long attacked domination and oppression while positively valorizing resistance and struggle that attempts to overturn these forces. This is true of British cultural studies, the Frankfurt School, feminism, critical race theory, and critical multiculturalism. Thus, values of resistance, empowerment, democracy, and freedom are adopted as positive norms, used to criticize forms of oppression and domination. Yet such values are adopted as normative standards through which one can criticize specific examples of domination, oppression, and the ideologies that further multiple forms of oppression, rather than as absolute moral principles. A broad range of contemporary theory thus renounces foundationalism, seeing concepts and norms as critical standards adopted to critique specific forms of domination in particular socio-historical contexts.

A critical media/cultural studies thus adopts norms and values with which it criticizes texts, artifacts, and conditions that promote oppression and domination. It positively affirms phenomena that promote human freedom, democracy, individuality, and other values that the project adopts and defends in concrete studies and situations. Yet a critical media/cultural studies also intends to relate its theories to practice, to develop an oppositional politics aimed at producing a progressive turn in contemporary culture and society through contributing to development of emancipatory alternatives to the conservative hegemony of the past years. A critical perspective sees culture as inherently political and as, in many cases, promoting specific political positions and as aiding forces of domination or resistance, progress or regression. Such a perspective perceives existing culture and society as a *contested terrain*, and chooses to ally itself with the forms of resistance and counterhegemony against the forces of domination. Grounding its politics in existing struggles and social forces, it places social theory and cultural studies in the service of socio-cultural criticism and political change.

Furthermore, a critical media/cultural studies must be constantly critical of its own methods, positions, assumptions, and interventions, constantly putting them in question and revising and developing them. Critical social and cultural theories are thus open, flexible, non-dogmatic, and without guarantees. Recognizing that contemporary society and culture is a contested terrain, critical theories engage opposing, sometimes conflicting, theories and are not afraid to appropriate material from them and to reject aspects of its own theories shown to be problematic, or to question its own assumptions or values if they are shown to be questionable in changing historical situations.

Both the Frankfurt School and the Birmingham School of cultural studies were constantly renegotiating their positions in relation to new historical conditions and theoretical developments, and this self-reflexivity and flexibility is an epistemological strength that other versions of cultural studies and social theory should emulate. The Birmingham School was constantly appropriating new perspectives, such as feminism and multiculturalist theories of race and nationality, as a result of criticisms of their previous positions (see Chapter 1). There was also constant reflection and debate over the methods and goals of cultural studies. This reflexivity and flexibility was also characteristic of certain stages of development of the Frankfurt School, though some of its positions hardened into an orthodoxy, resistant to new theoretical developments and unable to deal with new social conditions, while later generations of the Frankfurt School developed its theories to engage new social conditions and challenges (see Chapter 1 and Kellner 1989a). There is always the danger that a powerful theory and method can degenerate and harden into an orthodoxy and only vigilant critique, openness, flexibility, and a commitment to revision and development can prevent such rigidity and dogmatism.

Maintaining a critical perspective also involves developing a *critical theory of society* to ground one's cultural analysis and critique. Critical social theory carries out a critique of existing systems of domination and points to forces of resistance and possibilities for radical social transformation (Kellner 1989a). It reads media culture texts in the context of how they relate to structures of domination and forces of resistance and which ideological positions they advance within the context of current debates and social struggles. Thus, a critical media/cultural studies is not merely interested in providing clever readings of cultural texts, but is also interested in advancing a critique of structures and practices of domination and advancing forces of resistance struggling for a more democratic and egalitarian society.

A critical social theory and media/cultural studies that attacks oppression and strives for social equality is necessarily *multicultural* and seeks to attend to cultural diversity, plurality, and social justice. I am using the term "multicultural" here as a cover-concept for those diverse interventions in media/cultural studies that insist on the importance of scrutinizing representations of class, gender, sexuality, ethnicity, subalterneity, abilities, and other phenomena in media cultural texts.[1] A multicultural approach, in my conceptualization, involves analysis of relationships of domination and oppression in regards to specific social groups, to the ways that stereotyping works, and forms of resistance on the part of stigmatized groups to dominant representations, and practices, as well as the struggle of subordinate groups to represent themselves, to counter dominant and distorting representations and narratives, and to produce more positive ones.

Relationships of domination and oppressional are *intersectional* and Kimberly Crenshaw (1991) signals the importance of mapping the intersections of oppression and domination across the lines of race, gender, sexuality, class, and other forms of oppression (see Chapter 1). The concept of intersectionality suggests that forms of oppression intersect and work together, and critical theorists have used intersectionality to explore how cultural representations interact to provide racist, sexist, classist, and other forms of representation and texts that promote oppression. A critical media/cultural studies, however, is also concerned with delineating representations and texts that counter forms of oppression and that depict forms of struggle and emancipation in the contested terrain of contemporary media culture and society and indeed resistance and social movements often intersect in struggles in the domain of state politics, over the environment, for civil and human rights, and struggles against forms of domination rooted in classism, patriarchy, racism and other forms of domination.

A "Critical Multiculturalism" here thus functions as a description for all those attempts to resist the stereotyping, distortions, and stigmatizing by the dominant culture and to recognize a multiplicity of cultures within media culture and society. A critical multiculturalism also works to open cultural studies to analysis of the differential relations of force and domination in society and the ways that these are covered over and/or legitimated in dominant ideological representations.

From the 1980s to the present, there have been a diverse range of types of multiculturalism such as corporate/conservative, liberal and neo-liberal statist positions, and more oppositional insurgent multicultural projects associated with oppressed groups who affirm their cultural identities against oppression.[2] The United States is grounded in a statist multicultural project in which the melting pot ideology has affirmed U.S. democracy as a haven for oppressed immigrants throughout the world and held that ethnic differences would "melt" as immigrants became "Americans" – although the Trump administration has been pushing a white nationalist agenda that is in opposition to previous American liberal and egalitarian ideologies, which are still alive in the fervent opposition to Trump and his white nationalist agenda. A liberal multiculturalism associates itself with diversity, tolerance, and societal and cultural integration of various groups and ethnicities. A critical and insurgent multiculturalism, such as I am affirming, supports critiques of oppression of different racial, ethnic, and social groups and supports resistance, struggle, and the affirmation of difference and multiple identities.

A critical and insurgent multicultural perspective takes seriously the conjunction and intersection of class, race, ethnicity, gender, sexual preference, age, and other determinants of identity as important constituents of culture that should be carefully scrutinized and analyzed in order to detect sexism, racism, classism, homophobia, agism, and other tendencies that promote domination and oppression. Insurgent multiculturalism recognizes that there are many cultural constituents of identity, and cultural studies indicates how culture provides material and resources for identities and how cultural artifacts are appropriated and used to produce individual identities in everyday life.

The critical multicultural project also validates the positive contributions to culture and society of diverse races, genders and sexual identities, ethnicities, and social classes and groups. It is often noted that the most exciting work in recent years comes from feminist theory and those multiculturalists analyzing race, gender, nationality, and alternative sexualities. These critical cultural theories gain inspiration from insurgent social movements and have forced a sea change in how we look at and respond to texts. The canons of white male European culture have been challenged and a wide range of new voices and individuals have emerged. In addition, the perspectives of oppressed groups present critical insights into mainstream culture, allowing us to see oppressive elements that we might overlook from our more privileged perspectives.

An insurgent multiculturalism and media/cultural studies does not just register differences (although this activity can be important), but analyzes relations of inequality and oppression that generates struggles. Moreover, it also positively valorizes media representations and narratives that help promote the struggle of the oppressed against domination, while attacking representations and narratives that legitimate, naturalize, or cover over domination. An insurgent multiculturalism is thus part of the "pedagogy of the oppressed" (Freire 1972) that helps the oppressed see their oppression, name their oppressors, and articulate the goals and practices of liberation.

The theories of interpretation, approaches to culture and society, and political interventions of a wide range of oppressed and multicultural groups have thus produced radical and critical perspectives, concepts, and methods of criticism. Marginalized groups have used cultural studies as a way of challenging canons and orthodoxies, legitimating the texts and voices of subordinate groups, and politicizing culture and education. Yet multiculturalism as a movement and ideology (in a broader sense than I am using the term) can easily be coopted by statist and corporate forces that promote the term as a new front for melting pot neo-liberalism that helps individuals work and get along together through the promotion of toleration and acceptance of difference. Multiculturalism can also lead to in-group separatism and the various forms of identity politics, through which individuals identify with single-interest groups and construct their identities through identification with specific groups and categories and exclusion of others. Such single-interest politics fragment or block development of progressive blocs and alliances, and thus weaken the possibility of progressive social transformation.

Against such attempts to coopt the discourse of multiculturalism, or to use it as a badge of separatism that promotes special interests, I am using the term to describe attempts to resist exclusion of specific issues and perspectives from the terrain of cultural studies. Indeed, multiculturalism, as I am using the term, demands openness to the discourses of all oppressed or subordinate groups and to perceive the importance of engaging a broader range of types of representation in order to produce fuller and more critical readings of texts. Yet a critical multiculturalism does not entail affirming that there are nothing but differences; rather it points out that there are common forces and patterns of oppression, common strategies of exclusion, stereotyping, and stigmatizing of oppressed groups, and thus common enemies and targets of attacks. A critical multiculturalism thus stresses commonalties as well as differences and insists on the articulation of how representations of such things as race, gender, and class are intertwined and function as vehicles for ideologies of domination which naturalize, legitimate, or cover over social inequalities, injustice, and oppression.

Critical multiculturalism also sees differences in terms of contradictions between unequal forces, theorizing oppositions between the more powerful and subordinate groups in terms of relationships of domination, which creates the possibility of resistance against all forms of oppression. It also articulates common goals in struggle whereby dominant representations, or other forms of social oppression, are resisted and struggled against. A critical multiculturalism thus allies itself with the struggles for emancipation and for the creation of a more free, just, and egalitarian social order.

A multiculturalist focus on the diversity of forms of oppression and resistance is connected to development of a multiperspectival social theory and media/cultural studies that draws on the wide range of work done in the field in recent years.[3] A multiperspectival media/cultural studies attempts to avoid one-sidedness, orthodoxy, and cultural separatism by stressing the need to adopt a wide range of perspectives to understand and interpret cultural phenomena. As I have been arguing, the politics of representation of gender, race, class, and other key cultural constructs are interconnected and are reproduced in cultural texts. To get a fuller picture of media culture, one must therefore grasp a wide range of constituents elements of cultural texts and practices. To properly do this, one needs to draw on a spectrum of critical methods and theories, as some are better able to grasp class, others to conceptualize gender and sexuality, and yet others to articulate race, nationality, and global dimensions of culture, or cultural differences and specificity.

Toward a multiperspectival cultural studies

The cultural studies that is critical and multicultural that I am delineating should therefore also be "multiperspectival." This is a cumbersome and unattractive term, but remains the best concept that I have found to describe the sort of media/cultural studies that I am trying to develop. I shall elucidate this concept with some theoretical and practical analyses in this and in following chapters. Simply put, a multiperspectival media/cultural studies draws on a range of textual and critical strategies to analyze, interpret, and criticize the artifact under scrutiny. The concept builds on Nietzsche's perspectivism, which holds that all interpretation is necessarily mediated by one's perspectives and is thus inevitably laden with presuppositions, values, biases, and limitations. To avoid one-sidedness and partial vision one should learn "how to employ a *variety* of perspectives and interpretations in the service of knowledge" (Nietzsche 1969: 119). For Nietzsche: "There is only a perspective seeing, *only* a perspective 'knowing'; and the *more* affects we allow to speak about one thing, the more complete will our 'concept' of this thing, our 'objectivity,' be" (ibid.). Expanding this call for multiperspectival interpretation in later aphorisms collected in *The Will to Power*, Nietzsche argues: "every elevation of man brings with it the overcoming of narrower interpretations; that every strengthening and increase of power opens up new perspectives and means believing in new horizons" (1968: 330).

Applying these notions to cultural interpretation, one could argue that the more interpretive perspectives one can bring to a cultural artifact, the more comprehensive and stronger one's reading may be. To provide a robust reading of the popular TV series *Game of Thrones* (2011–2019) would require engaging how George R. R. Martin's popular novel was taken up by HBO and made into a blockbuster TV series that earned a major fan base and global audience. It would analyze how the constraints of series television structured the saga and how the producers and writers presented each season, highlighting key characters, events, and ongoing conflicts in the series. Reading *Game of Thrones* critically would involve engaging its representations of gender, race, sexuality, and the social classes of the different characters in the mythological universe. It would require engaging dominant ideologies in the series around war, power, sexual politics, and individual characters. Depending on the scope of the reading, it could critically engage the entire series as emerging from the original novel, or just discuss one season or even one episode.

Hence, to capture the full political and ideological dimensions of the texts of media culture, one needs to view them from the perspectives of gender, race, sexuality class, and other identity markers. This multiperspectival approach would, in my version of critical cultural studies, combine Marxist, feminist, queer studies, critical race, and other critical perspectives in order to provide fuller, more complete, and potentially stronger readings. Combining, for instance, ideology critique and genre criticism with semiotic analysis allows one to discern how the generic forms of media culture, or their semiotic codes, are permeated with ideology. The conflict/resolution code of most television entertainment, for example, provides an ideological notion that all problems can be resolved within the existing society by following conventional behavior and norms. Advertising often deploys a similar model, showing a problem and that the product advertised provides the solution.

A perspective, in this analysis, is an optic, a way of seeing, and critical methods can be interpreted as perspectives that enable one to see characteristic features of cultural artifacts. Each critical method focuses on specific features of an object from a distinctive perspective: the perspective spotlights, or illuminates, some features of a text while ignoring others. The more perspectives one focuses on a text to do ideological analysis and critique – generic, structural, formal, feminist, Marxist, and so on – the better one can grasp the full range of a text's ideological dimensions and ramifications. It therefore follows that a multiperspectival approach will provide an arsenal of weapons of critique, a full range of perspectives to dissect, interpret, and critique cultural artifacts.

Some qualifications to this position should be made, however. Obviously, a single reading – Marxist, feminist, semiotic, or whatever – may yield more brilliant insights than combining various perspectival readings; more is not necessarily better. Yet a variety of critical perspectives utilized in a proficient and revelatory fashion provides the potential for stronger (i.e. more many-sided, multidimensional, illuminating, and critical) readings. Second, a multiperspectival approach may not be particularly illuminating unless it adequately situates its text in its historical context. A text is constituted by its internal relations and its relations to its socio-historical situation, and the more relations articulated in a critical reading, the better grasp of a text one may have. A multiperspectival method must necessarily be socio-historical and should read its text in terms of its constitutive context and may also choose to read the society and culture in which it is produced, distributed, consumed, and interpreted in the light of the text.

Certain methodological strategies are, of course, incompatible, and a multiperspectival approach must choose between competing perspectives in terms of what specific task is at hand and what specific goals one has. For some purposes, it may be useful to engage in a focused feminist reading, while for other purposes one might carry through multivalent readings, getting at a text from a variety of perspectives. A multiperspectival position, however, that is not a mere liberal eclecticism, or merely a hodge-podge of different points of view, should allow its various perspectives to inform and modify each other. For instance, a Marxism that is informed by feminism will be different from a one-dimensional Marxism innocent of feminism (and vice-versa). A Marxist–feminist position that is informed by poststructuralism will be different from a dogmatic

Marxist–feminist perspective that reduces media culture solely to class and gender problematics. For poststructuralism eschews methodological dogmatism, champions a multiplicity of perspectives, focuses attention on features ignored by some Marxist or feminist perspectives, and undermines naive beliefs that one specific interpretation is certain and true.[4] Yet a poststructuralist perspective like deconstruction can itself become predictable and one-sided if it does not utilize other perspectives such as Marxism and feminism (see Ryan 1982; Spivak 1988).

Each critical method has its own strengths and limitations, its optics and blind spots. Marxian ideology critiques have traditionally been strong on class and historical contextualization and weak on formal analysis, as well as gender and race; feminism excels in gender analysis but sometimes ignores class, race, and other determinants; semiotics is useful for narrative analysis but tends to be overly formal; and psychoanalysis calls for depth hermeneutics and the articulation of unconscious contents and meaning, but sometimes ignores sociological determination of texts and individuals. Thus, the more of these critical methods one has at one's disposal, the better chance one has of producing reflexive and many-sided critical readings.

Of course, a reading of a text is only a reading from a critic's subject position, no matter how multiperspectival. Any critic's specific reading is only their own reading and may or may not be the reading preferred by audiences (which themselves will be significantly different according to class, race, gender, region, ethnicity, sexual preferences, ideologies, and their individual perspectives). There is thus a division between textual *encoding* and audience *decoding* and always the possibility of a multiplicity of readings and meanings of specific texts (Hall et al. 1980). One way to discover how audiences read texts is to engage in ethnographic surveys (see the Appendix to Kellner and Ryan 1988), but even then one is not sure how audiences consume texts and shape their beliefs and behavior. Thus, one needs to study which images, figures, and discourses of media culture become culturally resonant in a given era, and to trace their impact in a variety of historical contexts, as I will do in the chapters that follow.

Although all texts are polysemic and subject to multivalent readings depending on the standpoint of the reader,[5] I am not advocating an "anything goes" liberal pluralism. All of the methods that I have mentioned are deployed by a critical media/cultural studies to interpret the text and its effects within the existing system of domination and oppression and uses critical social theory to contextualize the artifact and the reading in relation to existing social struggles. The critical cultural studies that I am envisaging takes the side of progressive groups struggling against domination and attacks structures, practices, and ideologies of domination and oppression. Thus, the various critical methods are deployed within a critical social theory that attacks a system of domination and that struggles for a more democratic and egalitarian social order.

A multiperspectival approach thus multiplies both theoretical perspectives and methods from which specific cultural phenomena can be viewed and interpreted. Within the history of cultural studies, the project has been driven to

appropriate new weapons in its theoretical arsenal, as new socio-political movements produce new theories and discourses. Media/cultural studies is now genuinely international and multicultural, and this has greatly expanded the
perspectives from which we can view and appraise dominant, marginal, and
oppositional cultures. And, as noted in Chapter 1, the struggles and turbulence
of the past decades have also generated a proliferation of theories and methods
that we can deploy as instruments and weapons in developing more multiperspectival visions and methods. Each theory and perspective is to some degree
a product of a social struggle and can be adopted as a weapon of critique in the
struggle for a better society. It is the project of cultural studies to adopt such
weapons and to employ them in specific projects and domains.

Consequently, I am deploying media/cultural studies and critical social theory
both to analyze hegemonic forces of domination and counterhegemonic forces of
resistance in the U.S. from the 1980s to the present. There are always controlling
forces in society that form a hegemonic project, as well as groups and individuals
struggling against this hegemony. During the conservative hegemony in the
United States of Reagan, two Bush presidencies and Trump, for example, conservative forces dominated the economy, polity, society, and culture, but there were
always forces in struggle against this hegemony, ranging from liberals fighting for
political power to immigrants fighting for their rights. The forces of domination
find articulation in media cultural texts, as do forces of resistance and individuals
oppressed by the existing social system.

As I argued in the last chapter, films like *Rambo* and other militarist films like
American Sniper (2014) mobilize desire into subject positions congruent with the
Reaganite military-buildup and interventionist foreign policy, while male hero
films mobilize desire and fantasy into a remasculinized male subject that was part
of a backlash against feminism (see Faludi 1991; Jeffords 1994). Yet films like
Catch-22 (1970 and 2019) *Casualties of War* (1989), *A Few Good Men* (1992), or
Why We Fight (2005) summoned their audiences against the sort of military heroism celebrated in the conservative films and positively valorized individuals with
a conscience who would stand up to conservative authority to "do the right
thing." These liberal or radical individuals with a conscience were also more sensitive than the hard-bodied heroes of the Stallone–Norris–Willis–Schwarzenegger
conservative films. In the cultural wars between liberals and conservatives of the
era, media culture thus intervened on different sides, producing opposing visions
of war, male identities and models of masculinity, and values for its audiences.

A critical media/cultural studies thus demonstrates how cultural texts produce
social identities and subject-positions and thus impacts its audiences. It attempts
to show how certain figures, models, and values undermine the values and ethos
of a pluralistic, egalitarian, democratic, and multicultural society, whereas other
figures and models may promote the creation of a more egalitarian and democratic society. A cultural studies that is critical and multicultural thus intervenes
in the cultural wars of the period and uses its analyses of media culture to promote social change toward a more democratic society, fighting forms of media

culture that promote oppression while linking more progressive media culture with political movements struggling for freedom, democracy, and social justice. In the next section, I will present the TV series of Margaret Atwood's "*The Handmaid's Tale* as Dystopia and Ecological/Political Critique" as a political intervention in the early days of the Trump administration that transcodes women's and other forms of critical resistance to an oppressive society.

The Handmaid's Tale as dystopia and ecological/political critique

Margaret Atwood's novel *The Handmaid's Tale* was first published in 1985 as a critique of what she saw as disturbing conservative trends in U.S. politics during the Reagan era, embodied in groups like the Moral Majority, rightwing segments of the Republican Party, and evangelical religious groups, who all attacked women's freedoms and rights. Having taught at Harvard and lived in Boston and the Cambridge, Massachusetts, area during this time, Atwood set her novel in a Northeastern U.S. urban area in a near future time frame.

Atwood's father was an environmentalist and she spent much time in the north of Canada and thus became involved in the ecology movement of the era. It is often overlooked that Atwood's dystopic novel is also an ecological parable showing a U.S. society some few decades further along than our own that has poisoned the environment, caused infertility in most women and many men, and had thrown modern industrial–technological societies into crisis.

The Handmaid's Tale envisages a small rightwing U.S. male cabal carrying out a revolution, murdering the previous power elite, and establishing a religious patriarchal theocracy called Gilead in which women are reduced to child-bearing and reproduction or oppressive forms of servitude. In Atwood's dystopic vision of Gilead, women have no rights and are the property of their husbands. Women are either the wives of the dominant male caste, Marthas who serve in households as servants, Handmaids whose sole task is production of children, or Jezebels who are condemned to serve in houses of prostitution for the male elite, or are sent to the colonies to engage in slave labor in a nuclear-polluted area where their lives are nasty, brutal, and short.

In 2017, shortly after Trump's election, the Hulu channel inaugurated a TV limited series of Atwood's novel and *The Handmaid's Tale* became a global sensation, as women throughout the world donned the white hat, cloak, and modest uniform of the handmaids as symbols of resistance to the attack on women's rights in the Trump administration and elsewhere, while debates raged whether Trump's America was coming to embody feature of Atwood's dystopia.[6] The first season of the Hulu broadcast focused on the events told in Atwood's novel, whereas the second and third seasons went beyond Atwood's text, envisaging the main character Offred/June (Elizabeth Moss) escaping from bondage, encountering a resistance movement, then returning to her bondage as a Handmaid to try to save her daughter who had been taken away from her, yet increasingly attempting to resist and help cultivate a movement to overthrow the fascist theocratic state of Gilead.

The proliferation of cable channels in the 2000s and growth of streaming channels like Netflix, Amazon, Hulu, and others has proliferated TV production to previously unimaginable levels, and allowed for the production of more radical series and movies like *The Handmaid's Tale* (2017–2019), Joseph Heller's anti-war novel *Catch-22* (2019), Armistead Maupin's gay drama *Tales of the City* (2019), and countless other series or films that embody a diversity or productions by different races, creators, and individuals previously kept out of conservative white male dominated TV production. The Hulu TV series was created by Bruce Miller, who is also an executive producer and became showrunner as the show proceeded. Margaret Atwood served as consulting producer, giving feedback on some of the areas, especially where the series expands upon and goes beyond the narrative of the book. In June 2016, Reed Morano was announced as director of the series and the series was cast and began filming in Canada from September 2016 to February 2017. The series premiered on April 26, 2017, received a positive reception, and on May 3, 2017, *The Handmaid's Tale* was renewed for a second season to premiere in 2018.

The Hulu *Handmaid's Tale* opens with June Osborne attempting to escape to Canada with her husband, Luke, and daughter, Hannah. June is captured and due to her fertility, she is made a Handmaid to Commander Fred Waterford and his wife, Serena Joy, and is now known as "Offred." The Handmaid's names are created by the addition of the prefix Of- to the first name of the man who owns them, so Offred is Of-Fred, the property and reproductive handmaid of Fred and his family. When handmaids are transferred, their names are changed, and at the end of the first episode and throughout the series, Offred keeps reminding herself and the viewers that she is really "June."

The Waterfords are part of the Gilead elite as Fred Waterford is a high-ranking government official and his wife, Serena Joy, was a former conservative activist, writer, and celebrity. Serena has accepted her new role in Gilead, despite losing her fame and cultural power. Infertile herself, she yearns to have a child and willingly participates in the bizarre sexual "ceremony," whereby Serena folds Offred in her arms as the latter copulates with Fred, attempting to impregnate Offred and have her much desired child.

Aunt Lydia (Ann Dowd) is in charge of the training of the Handmaids and is a major figure in the plot, and in early episodes she indoctrinates the Handmaids into their role as child bearer, and stresses their importance to the survival of the society. Aunt Lydia uses a fundamentalist version of Christianity to indoctrinate the Handmaids into performing their roles as bearers of children and submissive underlings. While Lydia appears to be deeply religious, she is capable of great cruelty and embodies an authoritarian personality who serves to discipline and control the young women.

Early episodes depict Offred/June and other Handmaids going shopping and meeting on the street and in various stores where they are doing errands, which also affords the opportunity to present the oppressive features of Gilead such as a wall where men are hanged for being gay, or not conforming in some way. The Handmaids also observe "Savagings" where rebels are hung to death or executed in public ceremonies. The Handmaids wear long red dresses, heavy boots and white coifs, with a larger white coif to be worn outside, concealing their facial figures from public view and restricting their own vision. Indeed, the women of different castes wear different clothing, with Marthas who are house-keepers and cooks, wearing long, loose-fitting dull green garments and covering their hair with headwraps. The upper class Wives wear elegant, tailored dresses in blue and turquoise, cut in styles evoking the 1950s, while Jezebels who work in brothels to service the male elite dress in provocative lowcut blouses, tight skirts, and clothing to show off their bodies.

Flashbacks show June and other women losing their jobs, having their bank accounts frozen, and forfeiting all their rights, in cautionary warnings that oppressive patriarchy can return women to second class citizenship and worse. Throughout, there are also flashbacks to June's past pre-Gilead life, her relation with her husband, Luke, her child, Hannah, her feminist mother, and her friend Moira, creating contrasts between the former human life and the inhuman life of Gilead. In many images in the series, the camera tightly focuses on June's face and depicts the story from her point-of-view, showing the misery etched on her facial expressions and the indignities and oppression forced on her and the other Handmaids – although on occasion June's face expresses flashes of anger and resolute resistance, while the final episodes of season 3 depict June as relentlessly focused on freeing the oppressed women and children.

The first season that follows the storyline of Atwood's novel focuses on June's relations with the other Handmaids, depicting their shared oppression and moments of solidarity, and June's increasingly complex relations with the Water-ford family. Seeking to humanize the nonhuman relations, the Commander Fred invites June/Offred to his private study where they play Scrabble and eventually talk like normal people; he also takes her to a brothel, meant for the entertainment of the male elite, where she meets her friend Moira and begins forging relations of resistance. Serena, jealous of Offred's relation with Fred and afraid he may be infertile, encourages Offred to have sexual relations with Fred's driver, Nick, which she does and begins to have a relation with him that will eventually yield Serena's much desired child.

At the end of the first season, Moira escapes to Canada where a Gilead resistance movement is forming, and Offred is arrested and taken away in a black van. In the second season, Offred escapes her imprisonment, but decides to stay in Gilead to unite with her first daughter, Hannah. She ultimately hopes to go to Canada with Hannah to join her husband, Luke, and second daughter who is stolen from Serena near the end of the second season and who Moira spirits to Canada.

The second and third season of *The Handmaid's Tale*, produced during the Trump era, depict the growing resistance to Gilead, parallel to growing resist-ance to Trump, and *The Handmaid's Tale* is widely discussed as a critique of

Trump's America, although Trump's defenders attack the interpretation making the series one of the most contested and debated TV series of all time.[7] As states from Georgia and Alabama to Missouri have been banning abortion rights for women, protestors often show up with the Handmaid's uniforms and hats, and Atwood's novel has periodically jumped to the top of the *New York Times'* best seller's list, decades after its initial publication in 1985.

The final episode of season 3 "Mayday" (August 14, 2019) opens with a flashback depicting June, after being captured, witnessing women being rounded up and presumably executed, a scene transcoding the brutality of Gilead that has led June to become a leader of the resistance. In this episode, June is organizing a flight from Gilead for the children and the Marthas, creating a network of resistance that will lead the oppressed women and children to a transport plane that will fly them to safety. The Guardians learn of the escape plan and send out patrols to the woods to apprehend the rebels. A determined June ambushes a Guardian, seizes his gun, and forces him to declare "All Clear," allowing the group to escape to the plane and freedom. In a triumphant scene, the children disembark in Canada, are greeted by the Handmaids who have escaped, and in some cases are reunited with their families. June, however, was left behind, as she and some other handmaids and Marthas threw stones at soldiers in order to allow the children to board the airplane. June is shot in a scuffle with a soldier, but in the closing scene is found alive by some of her fellow Handmaids who carry her to an indeterminate future as she closes her eyes and recites scripture.

The popularity of the series and contested reception shows a divided country between those seeking to defend women's rights and democracy and those who deny they are under attack or are happy to attack women along with Trump, his most rabid defenders, and rightwing media. Perhaps never before has media culture become so politicized and, as I argue later in this chapter, blockbuster hits like *Wonder Woman* and *Black Panther* show the resistance of women and people of color to rightwing oppression and how new superheroes have entered the pantheon of major Hollywood icons, showing a desire to diversify media culture and its heroes and ideals.

Hegemony, ideology critique, and utopia

Because of the closeness of popular media texts to their social conditions, they provide privileged access to the social realities of their era and can thus be read to gain insight into what is actually going on in a particular society at a given moment. Consequently, the ideologies of media culture should be analyzed within the context of the social struggles and political debates within which the texts of media culture emerge, rather than seeing them simply as purveyors of false consciousness whose falsity is exposed and denounced by ideology critique. Although demystification is part of ideology critique, simply exposing mystification and domination isn't enough; we need to look behind the ideological

surface to see the social and historical forces and struggles which generate ideological discourses and to examine the media apparatus and strategies which make
ideologies attractive.

Hence, on this model, ideology criticism is not solely denunciatory and
should seek socially critical and oppositional moments within all ideological
texts – including conservative ones. As feminists and others have argued, one
should learn to read texts "against the grain," yielding progressive insights even
from reactionary texts. One can also attend to the possibility of using more liberal or progressive moments or aspects of a film against less progressive moments
as when Jameson (1979, 1990) extracts the socially critical elements from films
like *Dog Day Afternoon* or *Jaws*, which are contrasted with more conservative
positions and used to criticize aspects of the existing society.

Furthermore, radical cultural criticism should seek out those utopian
moments, those projections of a better world, that are found in a wide range of
texts (Bloch 1986). Extending this argument, one could claim that since ideology contains rhetorical constructs that attempt to persuade and to convince, they
must have a relatively rational and attractive core and thus often contain emancipatory promises or moments. Specification of utopian moments within the most
seemingly ideological artifacts was the project of Ernst Bloch whose great work
The Principle of Hope was translated into English in 1986.[8] Bloch provides
a systematic examination of the ways that daydreams, popular culture, great literature, political and social utopias, philosophy and religion – often dismissed
tout court as ideology by some Marxist ideological critique – contain emancipatory moments that project visions of a better life that put in question the organization and structure of life under capitalism (or state socialism).

Throughout his life, Bloch argued that Marxism was vitiated by a one-sided,
inadequate, and merely negative approach to ideology. For Bloch, ideology is
"Janus-faced," two-sided: it contains errors, mystifications, and techniques of
manipulation and domination, but it also contains a utopian residue or surplus
that can be used for social critique and to advance political emancipation. Bloch
believed that even ideological artifacts contain expressions of desire and articulations of needs that socialist theory and politics should heed to in order to provide programs and discourses that appeal to the deep-seated desires for a better
life within everyone. Ideologies thus provide clues to possibilities for future
development and contain a "surplus" or "excess" that is not exhausted in mystification or legitimation. And ideologies may contain normative ideals whereby
the existing society can be criticized, as well as models of an alternative society.

Utopias can be conservative or reactionary, however. The pro-military *Top
Gun* (1986) provides a conservative utopia that uses the military as a scene for
resonant images of community, romance, male heroism, and self-affirmation.
Films like *Jaws* (1975), however, might use utopian images to provide a critique
of the loss of community, and its destruction by commercial interests. Popular
texts may thus also contain social criticism in their ideological scenarios and one
of the tasks of radical cultural criticism is to specify utopian, critical, subversive,

or oppositional meanings, even within the texts of media culture (see Kellner 1979). For these artifacts may contain implicit and even explicit critiques of capitalism, sexism, or racism, or visions of freedom and happiness that can provide critical perspectives on the unhappiness and unfreedom in the existing society. *The Deer Hunter* (1978), for instance, though an arguably reactionary text (Kellner and Ryan 1988), contains utopian images of community, working class and ethnic solidarity, and personal friendship that provides critical perspectives on the atomism, alienation, and loss of community in everyday life under contemporary capitalism.

The utopian images of getting high and horsing around in the drug hootch in Oliver Stone's progressive Vietnam film *Platoon* (1986) provides visions of racial harmony and individual and social happiness, which provide a critical perspective on the harrowing war scenes and which code war as a disgusting and destructive human activity. The images of racial solidarity and transcendence in the dance numbers of Luis Valdez's *Zoot Suit* (1981) provide a utopian and critical contrast to the oppression of people of color found in the scenes of everyday and prison life in the film. And the transformation of life in the musical numbers of Herbert Ross's *Pennies From Heaven* (1981) provide critical perspectives on the degradation of everyday life due to the constraints of an unjust and irrational economic system that informs the realist sections of the film, while *La La Land* (2016) uses a frothy celebration of Hollywood and romance to present LA as a utopia.

In addition, Hollywood films, even conservative ones, can put on display hopes and fears that contest dominant hegemonic and hierarchal relations of power. Ideological texts thus put on display both the significant dreams and nightmares of a culture and the ways that the culture is attempting to channel them to maintain its present relations of power and domination. *Top Gun*, for example, puts on display the need for individual achievement, recognition, community, and love. It presents the (dubious) argument that these needs can be satisfied by military life. Other films show that the present society cannot satisfy existing needs, or assuage existing fears, as when *Thelma and Louise* (1991) suggests that women must take radical action to maintain their autonomy in existing patriarchal society. And a documentary like *Roger and Me* (1990) shows the destruction of working class communities, as multinational corporations close down their plants, while Michael Moore's later documentary *Fahrenheit 11/19* (2018) shows how political neglect bordering on criminality destroyed the water supply of his home town Flint Michigan.

From this perspective, a critical cultural studies should not only critique dominant ideologies, but should also specify any utopian, oppositional, subversive, and, emancipatory moments within ideological constructs that are then turned against existing forms of domination. This procedure draws on the sort of immanent critique practiced by the Frankfurt School in the 1930s, when they turned earlier forms of democratic bourgeois ideology against current, more reactionary, forms in fascist society. An immanent critique of contemporary society thus turns its own values against current social forms and practices that deny or contradict widely recognized values such as freedom, individualism, or justice (see Kellner 1984, 1989a). Thus, while bourgeois ideologies of freedom, individualism, and rights are to some extent ideologies that cover over class rule and domination, they also contain critical and emancipatory moments that can be used to criticize the suppression or curtailment of rights and freedom under capitalist society. The practice of what the Frankfurt School called "immanent critique" thus turns ideology against ideology, using more rational and progressive ideologies against more repressive and reactionary ones (i.e. turning liberalism against fascism or new right conservativism). The Frankfurt School critical theorists, however, never engaged in such an immanent critique of media culture and I am proposing here that such a project could be of use to media/cultural studies today, replacing earlier denunciatory models.

Consequently, sharp distinctions between ideology and science or theory, or ideology and utopia, should be deconstructed.[9] Ideology has to have some cognitive and utopian features in order to appeal to individuals. If ideology were nothing more than lies and mystification, it would have no hold on an individual's experience of life, and if it had no attractive features it would not appeal to people. Thus, ideological texts often have some cognitive content and utopian moments that cultural studies should examine and discuss. Yet ideology critique is also interested in how ideology tricks individuals into accepting contemporary social conditions and ways of life. Ideology presents historically constructed conditions as natural, as common sense and the way things are, as if it were natural for Rambo to slaughter hundreds of individuals and then to turn on the state and its computers.

Ideology also presents the specific interests of groups or political factions as universal, as if it was in everyone's interests to intervene in foreign countries and to kill communist or Arab "enemies," or to stigmatize immigrants a la Trump. Ideology also transforms negative conditions and forces into positive ones, as if it were good that the U.S. employs mercenaries and undercover agents to carry out its dirty work. Ideology thus represents the world upside down, with culture and the historically contingent appearing as nature and the eternal; with particular class interests appearing as universal; with highly political images, myths, and stories appearing as apolitical.

Ideology is thus a rhetoric that attempts to seduce individuals into identifying with the dominant system of values, beliefs, and behavior. Ideology replicates their actual conditions of existence, but in a mystified form in which people fail to recognize the negative, historically constructed and thus modifiable nature of their societies. Ideology has utopian elements that attract individuals to certain values, behavior, and ways of life promising happiness, freedom, community and other popular values. The dialectic of ideology and utopia thus must deal with contemporary conditions of domination and resistance, and thus helps illustrate which forces and media representations and texts are promoting domination and which are promoting resistance and liberation.

A *diagnostic critique*, such as I will illustrate and develop in the following studies, uses history to read texts and texts to read history. Such a dual optic allows
insight into the multiple relations between texts and contexts, between films,
ideologies, and history. A diagnostic critique can use media culture to gain critical historical knowledge of the past and present, constructing readings that tell
us what media cultural texts indicate about the historical period they represent
and the period in which they are produced and appear. Diagnostic critique also
engages the politics of representation and how media culture presents relations
of domination and subordination around the axes of gender, race, class, and
sexuality, as well as embodying in story, image, and discourse various ideological
problematics and conflicts of ideas in a particular period.[10]

From my diagnostic perspective, media culture thus provide important insights
into the psychological, socio-political, and ideological make-up of a society and
culture at a given point in history. Reading media culture diagnostically allows
one to gain insights into social problems and conflicts, and to appraise the dominant ideologies and emergent oppositional forces. Moreover, diagnostic critique
enables one to perceive the limitations and pathologies of mainstream conservative
and liberal ideologies and politics, as well as oppositional ones.[11] This approach
involves a dialectic of text and context, using texts to read social realities and context to help situate and interpret key media of the epoch.

While corporations, the state, and media are major institutions of contemporary U.S. society, politics, however, pervades everyday life, as well as the great
political battles that dominate media news and information. A diagnostic critique
thus also probes the politics of everyday life and its struggles around issues like
race, gender, sexuality, and class. From this perspective, media cultural texts
articulate the fears and hopes, the dreams and nightmares, of a culture and thus
are a source of novel and important socio-psychological insights, displaying what
audiences are feeling and thinking at a given moment. This explains why psychoanalysis continues to be of importance for cultural studies. Against the
notion of depthlessness and surface of cultural texts claimed by postmodern
theory, I would argue that cultural texts continue to be bearers of meaning and
to require depth-hermeneutical models to ferret out their meanings and the
range of their possible effects. The studies in the next section will pursue these
topics, showing how cultural studies can contribute to presenting insight into
the struggles of everyday life, as well as the major political and media events of
the era.

Superheroes from *Wonder Woman* to *Black Panther*

In this section, I will illustrate diagnostic critique with a reading of the significance of the immense popularity of recent superhero films *Wonder Woman*
and *Black Panther* and how they expanded the pantheon of popular cinematic
superheroes. A diagnostic critique reads the texts of media culture politically
in order to analyze what the popular texts of media culture tell us about

contending forces and opposing political struggles and positions in the contemporary era. It attempts to discern how media culture mobilizes desire, sentiment, affect, belief, and vision into various subject positions, and how these support one political position, such as liberalism, feminism, racial justice, and so on, or opposing political positions like conservativism, sexism, or racism. A diagnostic critique thus indicates how the texts of media culture help to produce political identities and practices, and criticizes those identifies and representations that are counter to democracy and that support the forces of domination and oppression.

Likewise, film, TV series, and other forms of media culture can either glorify and legitimate corporate capitalist society and its culture and values, or present critiques. While many TV series like *Dallas*, *Dynasty*, and *Succession* appear to glorify capitalist culture, some TV series like *Succession* present a thinly veiled critical views of the Murdoch media dynasty, while the *Wall Street* films of Oliver Stone (1987 and 2010) provide critical visions of the institutions of corporate capitalism. Obviously, corporate media are an important tool of contemporary capitalism and while film and TV traditionally celebrated capitalist culture, wealth, and corporations, the TV series *Succession* (2018–) presents a more critical vision. *Succession* deploys a fictional family, the Roys, who own a media empire and fight over succession as the family patriarch prepares to retire. The series presents dramatic exposes of family dynamics like the Murdoch dynasty, which is facing succession battles for its empire as the patriarch Rupert prepares to retire.

Superhero films and TV series have been a major form of media culture throughout its history and superheroes are usually defenders of the status quo and dominant society (see Kellner and Ryan 1988). In this section, I argue that the popularity of *Wonder Woman* (2017) and *Black Panther* (2018) provides insight into oppositional forces to mainstream political culture during the Trump era that exhibited virulent racism and sexism confronted by powerful forces of struggle and resistance by women and people of color.

The dominant superheroes of an era exhibit fantasies of power and traditionally embody dominant values of masculinity and white male power (see Kellner and Ryan 1988). While they tend to reproduce dominant gender, racial, and political ideologies, they can be encoded to represent more complex and critical media texts. In an earlier era, *Superman I* and *II* (1978) and other superhero films of the late 1970s and 1980s showed the yearning in the American popular imagination for a savior/redeemer who would save its audiences from the morass of confusion coming out of the 1960s and 1970s and restore an older America, helping to fuel Reaganite conservatism (see Kellner and Ryan 1988: 217ff). Some of the superhero films of the last years of the Bush–Cheney regime, by contrast, can be read as a critique of the failed conservative regime. The Batman films of the late Bush–Cheney era show the polity to be utterly corrupt and the economic, political, and legal system in paralysis, approximately the case by the end of the failed Bush–Cheney administrations (Kellner 2010: 9ff).

An American Nightmare took place in 2016 with the election of Donald Trump as President of the United States followed by the Horror Show of his presidency (Kellner 2016; 2017). Trump's presidency was resisted from the beginning starting with the Woman's March in Washington the day after his inauguration that was one of the largest demonstrations in history, accompanied by anti-Trump demonstrations throughout the world. Hollywood noted, and in some cases participated in, the Trump resistance, and *Wonder Woman*, the most popular film of 2017, can be read as a monument to female empowerment in an era in which a conservative regimes threaten women's rights. Likewise, *Black Panther*, the most popular film of 2018, can be read as an allegory of Black empowerment in a time in which people of color in the United States faced unprecedented hostility and repression from the Trump regime and its allies.

Wonder Woman (2017) presents a breakthrough model of a female superhero film and became one of the highest grossing and most popular films of the year. For a diagnostic critique, the film's popularity showed that mass audiences were ready for a female superhero and that Wonder Woman represented a powerful feminist fantasy figure.

The character of Wonder Woman was created by William Moulton Marston for a new DC *Wonder Women* comic in the early 1940s, and throughout its long comic book run, Marston gave it a feminist inflection, providing a range of super powers for the heroine and grounding her in a realistic figure.[12] Gloria Steinem celebrated the feminist inflection of Wonder Woman by putting her on the first cover of *Ms. Magazine* and repeating the gesture in later covers.[13] In fact, Wonder Woman is the most mythical and marvelous of the DC comics superhero(ine)s. While Superman's alter ego, Clark Kent, grew up in a modest home in Kansas and Batman's Bruce Wayne was raised in a fading mansion in a crime-infested urban metropolis in their contemporary twentieth century eras, Wonder Woman is a mythical creature created by the gods 2500 years ago in a fantasy island utopia where she is cultivated by her fellow Amazons to be a warrior and discovers her superpowers. While Clark Kent is somewhat insecure and never able to properly romance Lois Lane, and Bruce Wayne has a dark side, Wonder Woman is truly wonderful in every way revealing wonder, awe, and curiosity at the marvels of the world and growing as she experiences its challenges. Wonder Woman has wondrous superpowers and is dedicated to peace and ending war, love and protecting humanity, empathy for others, and awesome abilities to fight and defeat evil of every sort.

Directed by Patty Jenkins and starring Gal Gadot as the titular superheroine, *Wonder Woman* introduces Princess Diana as a child who matures into a young woman growing up in a utopian culture where she is love, nurtured, and taught the arts of survival and living on the Amazon island of Themyscira.[14] The film opens in present-day Paris with Diana Prince (Gadot) receiving a photographic plate of herself and four men taken during World War I, prompting her to recall her past. Daughter of Queen Hippolyta, Diana was raised on the hidden island of Themyscira, home to the Amazonian warrior women created by Zeus to protect mankind. Hippolyta shares the Amazonian history with Diana, including how Ares, Zeus's son, became jealous of humanity and orchestrated its destruction. When the other gods attempted to stop him, Ares killed all but Zeus, who used the last of his power to wound Ares and force his retreat (thus dying in the process). Zeus left the Amazons the island and a weapon, the "Godkiller," to prepare them for Ares' return.

The plot device is triggered by American pilot Steve Trevor crashing offshore and being rescued by Diana, reversing the usual trope of leading man saving the woman. Learning that there is a World War going on, Diana chooses to accompany Steve back to the war and uses her superpowers to turn the tide of a battle and save a Belgium village. Armed with her "Godkiller" sword, a magic lasso, and her fighting armor, Diana perceives her mission as a mandate to kill Ares, god of war, and thus to end the World War and to bring peace to the humans.

In London, Steve and Diana deliver the notebook of Dr. Maru, the chief chemist associated with the German General Ludendorff who specializes in chemistry and poisons, to the British Supreme War Council, where Sir Patrick Morgan is trying to negotiate an armistice with Germany. Diana translates Maru's notes and reveals that the Germans plan to release the deadly gas at the Western Front, and that her gas weapon must be destroyed before there can be an armistice. While not publicly recognizing the danger, Steve and Diana are sent on a secret mission to find and destroy the gas and assemble a multi-cultural and talented team of spy Sameer, marksman Charlie, and smuggler Chief to save humanity from the destructive gas.

The London scenes reveal the modern world to be unfolding as an industrial society with masses of workers, pollution, an expanding consumer society for the wealthier classes, and the emergence of mass warfare, with deadly weapons that could destroy humanity, thus situating the fantasy with the socio-historical matrix of the early twentieth century and World War I. Steve, Diana, and the team enter a crowded railroad station and travel to Europe, reaching the front in Belgium. We see Diana/Wonder Woman's superpowers in action and she goes alone through No Man's Land and captures an enemy trench, allowing the Allied forces to help her liberate the village of Veld.

After celebrating the liberation of the village with the townspeople, the team learns that a gala festivity will be held at a nearby German High Command castle. Steve and Diana separately infiltrate the party, with Steve intending to locate the gas and destroy it, while Diana intends to kill the German General Ludendorff, believing that he is Ares and thus killing him will end the war. The rest of the plot involves a murky mythology with the British diplomat Sir Patrick revealing himself as Ares, explaining how he creates chaos and war through giving humans ideas and inspirations, and by using the military, politicians, and military scientists like Maru as pawns in the process. Yet the cynical representative of British imperialism, Sir Patrick, insists that it is ultimately human beings' own decisions to resort to violence, as humans are inherently corrupt. During a high-tech special effects battle with Sir Patrick/Ares and Diana, Wonder

Woman wins, and the film concludes on a Beatlesque note, with Diana proclaiming that "only love can truly save the world."

Wonder Woman cuts to the present day, with a still youthful Diana sending an email to Bruce Wayne thanking him for the photographic plate of the photo of her, Steve, and the other team members, and she reaffirms her new mission to continue fighting to save the world and create more super profitable films for the DC superhero franchise that rivals the Marvel comic superhero franchise as the most lucrative Hollywood property. Indeed, in 2018 Marvel's *Black Panther* would be the most successful film of the year and one of the most profitable in history,[15] demonstrating that a mass audience would go see a superhero of color, just as they flocked to see a female superheroine in *Wonder Woman* the year before.

Hence, Patty Jenkins was the first woman to direct a successful blockbuster superhero[ine] film and showed the female audiences were also keen for redemptive heroes and that women could provide the goods. Similarly, the success of *Black Panther*, directed by an upcoming Black director Ryan Coogler, also showed that Black themes and production teams could create blockbusters in the Age of Trump, where the culture was extremely divided but yearning for more positive heroes and heroines.

Black Panther was produced by Marvel Studios and distributed by Walt Disney Studios as the eighteenth film in the Marvel Cinematic Universe (MCU). Directed by Ryan Coogler, *Black Panther* stars Chadwick Boseman as T'Challa/ Black Panther, who is crowned king of Wakanda following his father's death, but his sovereignty is challenged by an adversary who plans to abandon the country's isolationist policies and begin a global revolution.

Influenced by a tradition of comic books of *Black Panther*,[16] including a 2016–2018 series by Ta Nehisi Coates that updates the older Marvel comic series, the plot of the film is organized around Wakanda's possession of a meteorite containing vibranium. The magical metal enables Wakanda to develop a superior high-tech civilization and its King to obtain supernatural powers through ingesting a "heart-shaped herb" affected by the metal, becoming the first "Black Panther." The King unites all of the tribes in the region, except the mountain Jabari Tribe, to form the nation of Wakanda. Over centuries, the Wakandans isolate themselves from the world by posing as a Third World country to hide their advanced civilization and avoid theft and conflict. Informed by the aesthetic of Afrofuturism, the mise-en-scène of *Black Panther* contrasts a high-tech and highly colorful civilization with the beauty of nature in Africa and its traditional tribalist culture, creating a synthesis of old and new and a classy Afrofuturist look for the film.[17]

After expository opening sequences establishing the world of Wakanda and its dominant tribe and leaders, the story shifts to a scene in the present. It portrays Wakanda's King T'Chaka visiting his brother N'Jobu in 1992, who is working undercover in Oakland, California (director Ryan Coogler's hometown). T'Chaka accuses N'Jobu of assisting black-market arms dealer Ulysses Klaue (Andy Serkis) with stealing vibranium from Wakanda. Klaue, a villainous Germanic type ("klauen" means to steal in German) is one of the bad guys in *Black Panther*, who seeks to rob Wakandan technology and use it to gain wealth and power for himself, a figure who represents colonialist imperialism and the looting of Africa's resources.

Black Panther then shifts to the present day, showing that following the King T'Chaka's death, his son T'Challa returns to Wakanda to assume the throne. Rival tribes initially do not challenge T'Challa's claim for the throne and he prepares for his coronation, hoping that his ex-lover Nakia (Lupita Nyong'o) will become his queen; Nakia is now a spy who has T'Challa and Okoye, the leader of the Dora Milaje regiment,[18] extracted from an undercover assignment so she can attend his coronation ceremony with his mother, Ramonda, and younger sister, Shuri, highlighting the importance of family. However, at the ceremony, the Jabari Tribe's leader M'Baku challenges T'Challa for the crown in ritual combat, and following the script of the hero who must vanquish rivals, T'Challa defeats M'Baku and persuades him to yield rather than die, displaying his pro-life and peaceful values.[19]

The plot then goes global when Klaue and an accomplice Erik Stevens steal a Wakandan artifact from a London museum, and T'Challa, Nakia, and others travel to Busan, South Korea, where Klaue plans to sell the artifact to CIA agent Everett K. Ross (Martin Short). This scene allegorically represents the global nature of imperialism and how white colonialists and thieves loot developing world continents like Africa.

A firefight erupts and Klaue attempts to flee but is caught by T'Challa, who reluctantly releases him to Ross' custody. Klaue tells Ross that Wakanda's international image is a front to cover its technologically advanced civilization. Klaue escapes and good CIA guy Ross is gravely injured protecting Nakia. Rather than pursue Klaue, T'Challa takes Ross to Wakanda, where their technology can save him.

While Shuri heals Ross, T'Challa confronts the tribe's shaman Zuri (Forest Whittaker) about N'Jobu, a Wakandan noble who appears to be involved in the black market theft of vibranium. Zuri explains that N'Jobu planned to share Wakanda's technology with people of African descent around the world to help them conquer their oppressors, a figure of Africans and Black revolutionaries creating a world revolution that was popular in the 1960s. T'Challa learns that his father had killed N'Jobu and left behind N'Jobu's American son who believes his father had disappeared. This boy grew up to be Stevens, a U.S. black ops soldier who adopted the name "Killmonger" (Michael P. Jordan). Killmonger has scarred ritualistic tribal markings on his chest, wears dreadlocks, and has the style of the hood, as opposed to T'Challa's more aristocratic African demeanor. Killmonger returns to Wakanda and comes before the tribal elders, revealing his identity and claim to the throne. Killmonger challenges T'Challa to ritual combat, and the usurper kills Zuri, defeats T'Challa, and hurls him over a waterfall to his presumed death. Killmonger then ingests the heart-shaped herb to presumably gain superpowers to lead a world revolution and/or rule the world. While she orders the rest of the herb incinerated, Nakia extracts part of it and eventually administers it to T'Challa so that he can recover and fight again for his throne and kingdom.

Meanwhile Killmonger prepares to distribute shipments of Wakandan weapons to operatives around the world. Healed by the powerful herb, T'Challa returns to fight Killmonger, who dons his own Afrofuturist designed Black Panther suit. Both sides have their African and Western allies and the screen erupts in high-tech battle spectacle. Killinger's army is defeated by T'Challa's warriors, including Shuri, Nakia, and the female Dora Milaje brigade, again positively valorizing the female characters. The battle ends in generic one-to-one combat between T'Challa and Killmonger in Wakanda's vibranium mine, where T'Challa pierces Killmonger's Black Panther suit and stabs him. Refusing an offer to be healed, Killmonger chooses to die a free man rather than be incarcerated.

In a concluding modern day sequence, T'Challa establishes an outreach center at the building where N'Jobu died, to be run by Nakia and Shuri. In a mid-credits scene, T'Challa appears before the United Nations to reveal Wakanda's true highly developed nature to the world and proclaims that they plan to share their technology to try to build a better world. In a speech that can be read as a rebuke to Donald Trump, T'Challa states that wise men build bridges and share their knowledge and tools, while the unwise erect barriers and create divisions,[20] certainly the project of Trump and his followers who chant at rallies "build that wall!" and "send her home," referring to a Congresswoman of African descent who is a critic of Trump.

As I write this analysis in early August 2019, the U.S. has suffered one of its worst weeks of mass shootings in history with an attack on a Garlic Festival in California, a shopping district in El Paso, Texas, and an entertainment center in Dayton, Ohio. For the first time, the mainstream media and public recognized that White Nationalism and the divisive rhetoric of Trump and his administration was becoming a factor in many mass shootings in the U.S. and around the world. In this conjuncture, the concluding sequence of *Black Panther* calling for unity rather than division, sharing rather than competing, and building bridges rather than barriers is a progressive intervention in contemporary media and political culture. The film's popularity shows that millions will respond to a more progressive and racially and culturally inclusive message than offered by Trump and his allies.

Yet the reception of *Black Panther* was quite controversial, with some critics seeing it as a progressive and empowering popular representation of Africans, African Americans, and the continent of Africa that has been badly represented historically in media and other cultural forms. Yet some critics said that *Black Panther* revitalized old stereotypes and is problematic in its representations. Patrick Gathara described the film as offering a "regressive, neocolonial vision of Africa", which – rather than a "redemptive counter-mythology" – offers "the same destructive myths." Gathara argued that Africa is still portrayed in *Black*

Panther in European terms, as being divided and tribalized, with Wakanda run by a wealthy and feuding elite that despite its advanced technical abilities does not have a means of succession beyond lethal combat. The Wakandans "still cleanly fit into the Western molds [of] a dark people in a dark continent" according to Gathara, and they

> remain so remarkably unsophisticated that a "returning" American can basically stroll in and take over … [The film] should not be mistaken for an attempt at liberating Africa from Europe. Quite the opposite. Its "redemptive counter-mythology" entrenches the tropes that have been used to dehumanize Africans for centuries.[21]

Hence, there is sharp criticism of *Black Panther*, as well as praise by its defenders, and like most blockbuster films dealing with race or gender, the film is highly contested. However, for a diagnostic critique, the great success of *Wonder Woman* and *Black Panther* shows that mass audiences are receptive to women superheroines and superheroes of color, as these films are of now among the most popular and successful superhero films in history.[22] Their popularity suggests that while Trump, sexists, racists, and white nationalists carry out a war on women, people of color, and immigrants, the public responds positively to narratives that take a non-sexist, non-racist, and more inclusive view of culture, society, and humanity.

Reading media culture diagnostically thus presents insights into the current political situation, into the strengths and vulnerabilities of the contending political forces, and into the hopes and fears of the population. From this perspective, the texts of media culture provide important insights into the psychological, socio-political, and ideological make-up of a specific society at a given point in history. Reading media culture diagnostically also allows one to detect what ideological solutions to various problems are being offered, and thus to anticipate certain trends, to gain insights into social problems and conflicts, and to appraise the dominant ideologies and emergent oppositional forces. Consequently, diagnostic political critique enables one to perceive the rise of more progressive ideologies, movements, and trends, as well as the limitations of mainstream conservative and liberal political ideologies, while also helping to decipher their continuing appeal. It enables one to grasp the utopian yearnings in a given society and challenges progressives to develop cultural representations, political alternatives, and practices and movements which address these predispositions.

Such diagnostic reading thus helps with the formulation of progressive political practices which speak to salient hopes, fears, and desires, and the construction of social alternatives that are grounded in existing psychological, social, and cultural matrixes. Consequently, diagnostic film critique does not merely offer another clever method of reading films but provides tools for understanding contemporary society, as well as weapons of critique for those interested in producing a better one.

Notes

1   On multiculturalism and multicultural discourses, see the works collected in Taylor and Gutmann, 1994.

2   On "Insurgent Multiculturalism" see Giroux 1993; Macedo and Bartolomé 1999.

3   For some of my earlier work in developing multiperspectival theory, see Kellner 1991, 1992a, and Kellner 1991.

4   For my take on poststructuralist and postmodern perspectives, see the trilogy I co-authored with Steven Best (Kellner 1991, 1997, 2001).

5   Following Harding (2003), I am using *standpoint* to describe the critic's class, gender, race, and other identity markers *and* the theories and methods used to analyze, interpret, and critique media culture, or other artifacts. Hence, my standpoint is that of a white straight male retiring professor who has taught and written on media culture for over 50 years and who uses a variety of critical theories to interpret media culture. This standpoint, or "subject position," requires me to attempt to be self-critical of what might be my own class, gender, racial, or other biases and to engage representations of those other than my own standpoint carefully and reflectively, while drawing upon literature and interpretations of members of the groups represented in the texts under interrogation to help me interpret, contextualize, and critique the texts of media culture.

6   Adi Robertson, "In Trump's America, *The Handmaid's Tale* matters more than ever. Nolite te bastardes carborundorum," *The Verge*," November 9, 2016 at www.theverge.com/2014/12/20/7424951/does-the-handmaids-tale-hold-up-dystopia-feminism-fiction (accessed August 21, 2019), and Tom Engelhardt, "Trump's America Is Worse Than Orwell's '1984.' As global warming intensifies, our world is becoming bleaker than one of the darkest dystopias ever imagined." *The Nation*, August 12, 2019 at www.thenation.com/article/donald-trump-george-orwell-1984/ (accessed August 21, 2019).

7   The previous note documents some articles that sees parallels between *The Handmaid's Tale* and Trump's American while one feminist critic warns against too fast analogies; see Jessa Crispin, "*The Handmaid's Tale* is just like Trump's America? Not so fast. Many women are comparing their lives with that of the characters in the new Hulu series based on Margaret Atwood's novel. That is problematic," *The Guardian*, May 2, 2017 at www.theguardian.com/commentisfree/2017/may/02/handmaids-tale-donald-trump-america (accessed August 21, 2019). For a pro-Trump conservative who denies the analogies between Gilead and Trump's America, see Rich Lowry, "Conflating 'Handmaid's Tale' is lunacy," *Lacrosse Tribune* September 20, 2017 at https://lacrossetribune.com/opinion/columnists/rich-lowry-conflating-handmaid-s-tale-is-lunacy/article_5e4bd2b2-a9c0-5503-95a2-e77a41cba684.html (accessed August 21, 2019).

8   Ernst Bloch was a German-Jewish refugee from fascist Germany who emigrated to the United States in the 1930s and returned to Germany after the war, eventually becoming a Professor of Philosophy at the University of Tubingen, where I studied, sitting in on Bloch's seminars from 1969–1971. I returned to Tubingen to interview him in the mid-1970s and drew on the interview in Kellner-O'Hara 1972 and Kellner 1997.

9   Althusser wants to contrast science to ideology, as its radical other, whereas Mannheim, Bloch, Ricoeur, and others oppose ideology to utopia. I would suggest that one should not make such tight distinctions, and that ideology and science, as well as ideology and utopia, are interconnected. Yet I see the concept of culture as wider than ideology and believe that one can, on an analytical level, counterpoise various critical discourses to ideology. One can also contrast ideological discourses and criticize one ideology from the standpoint of another, as when one attacks fascism from the standpoint of liberal humanism. Theories that might be ideological, in the sense of legitimating a dominant social order, in one context, can be critical and subversive in another, as when Marxism provided conservative social functions in legitimating the former Soviet Union, while presenting radical critical perspectives on actually existing capitalist societies. Thus, all discourse and critique is contextual, using norms in specific contexts, rather than positing absolute standards of critique.

10 On diagnostic critique and my views on reading film politically, see Kellner and Ryan 1988, and the discussion below and in succeeding chapters.
11 See, 1988; Kellner 1995, pp. 116–117.
12 Marston made his Wonder Woman comic figure very sexy, had her raised in an all-woman environment, puts her in bondage situations in the stories, and allegedly grounded Wonder Woman's sexuality in a *menage à trois* in which he lived with two women who themselves cohabited for many years after Marston died. See Noah Berlatsky, "The crucial thing the new Wonder Woman movie gets right about the character's history. Historians are reluctant to admit how a long-term polyamorous relationship formed Wonder Woman, but *Professor Marston and the Wonder Women* dives in without shame," *The Verge*, October 16, 2017 at www.theverge.com/2017/10/16/16481692/wonder-woman-professor-marston-homophobia-history-sexuality-real-life-vs-fiction (accessed on November 13, 2019). The cited reference to "new Wonder Woman movie" obviously is referring to the Marston biopic *Professor Marston and the Wonder Women*, which tells the story of Marston and his two female life-time companions and how their experience and experiments in psychology contributed to producing the Wonder Women comics as a feminist intervention in U.S. culture.
13 "How Gloria Steinem Saved Wonder Woman For her new film *Professor Marston and the Wonder Women,* director Angela Robinson spoke to the feminist icon about the true story behind the superheroine." *Vanity Fair*, October 10, 2017 www.vanityfair.com/hollywood/2017/10/gloria-steinem-wonder-woman (accessed November 13, 2019).
14 On the background of the *Wonder Woman* story from comic book into movie, see Cocca 2018 and for an illustrated history of *Wonder Woman* with many illustrations and much documentation on its creator William Moulton Marston, see Daniels 2000.
15 Mary Elizabeth Williams reports: "Director Ryan Coogler's 'Black Panther' has been all but unstoppable since its late January opening, and this past weekend it soared past the one billion dollar mark in grosses. Domestically, it's already the seventh highest grossing film of all time and biggest single superhero release of all time (surpassing 'The Dark Knight'). A month ago, Deadline called the film's juggernaut 'insane' – and its reign seems likely to stay unbroken for some time to come. Box Office." See Mary Elizabeth Williams, "The box office made history this weekend," *Salon,* March 12, 2018 at www.salon.com/2018/03/12/the-box-office-made-history-this-weekend/ (accessed August 6, 2019).
16 On the history of the *Black Panther* comic books tradition, Anna Deavere Smith writes:

> The Black Panther character has a long, rich history. Seeing an opportunity to bring a black superhero into the almost entirely white comic book world, Jack Kirby, a Jewish artist, introduced the Black Panther into the world of the Fantastic Four in 1966. Stan Lee, the former publisher and chairman of Marvel Comics and who had a cameo in the movie, was cocreator. The Black Panther comic book character predated the Black Panther Party by a few months. Not wanting to carry the baggage of the controversial BPP, Marvel at one point changed the character's name to the Black Leopard, but the original name prevailed.
>
> The Black Panther had many permutations. Christopher Priest in the late 1990s and early 2000s and Reginald Hudlin in the mid-2000s, both African-American, wrote comics in the series. They are said to have given the character a more Africa-centered, self-determining ethos. Most recently, Ta-Nehisi Coates, following the extraordinary success of his *Between the World and Me* (2015), was approached by Marvel to write a Black Panther series with the illustrator Brian Stelfreeze, and another chapter in the life of the superhero was born.

See Anna Deavere Smith, "Wakanda Forever!," *The New York Review of Books,* May 24, 2018 at www.nybooks.com/articles/2018/05/24/black-panther-wakanda-forever/ (accessed August 6, 2019).

17 On Afrofuturism, see Jamie Broadnax, "What The Heck Is Afrofuturism?" *HuffPost,* February 16, 2018 at www.huffpost.com/entry/opinion-broadnax-afrofuturism-black-panther_n_5a85f1b9e4b004fc31903b95 (accessed August 21, 2019).
18 The Dora Milaje regiment is an all-women organization that serves as both spies and warriors, producing a strong female component to the nation of Wakanda.
19 T'Challa's narrative follows the pattern of the hero myth outlined in Joseph Campbell's *Hero With a Thousand Faces.* New York: New World Library, 2008.
20 Director Ryan Coogler claims that *Black Panther* was written and in progress before Trump's election and that the concluding scene was not intended as a commentary on Trump, but as the days go by, the concluding sequence offers a prescient critique of Trump and his white nationalist and separatist supporters. For Coogler's initial response to whether the film sequence was intended as a critique of Trump, see the CBS video of February 8, 2018 at www.cbsnews.com/video/director-ryan-coogler-discusses-blockbuster-hit-black-panther/ (accessed August 6, 2019).
21 Patrick Gathara, "'Black Panther' offers a regressive, neocolonial vision of Africa." *The Washington Post* (February 26, 2018) at www.washingtonpost.com/news/global-opinions/wp/2018/02/26/black-panther-offers-a-regressive-neocolonial-vision-of-africa/ (accessed August 6, 2019).
22 See the analysis at Box Office Mojo where *Wonder Woman* has grossed domestic $412,563,408 and foreign $409,283,604 as of August 6, 2019 at www.boxoffice mojo.com/movies/?id=wonderwoman.htm (accessed August 6, 2019), while *Black Panther* has grossed domestic $700,059,566 and foreign $646,853,595, breaking at the time many box office records; see www.boxofficemojo.com/movies/?id=marvel2017b.htm (accessed August 6, 2019).

3

SOCIAL ANXIETY, HORROR, AND AMERICAN NIGHTMARES

In the previous chapters, I delineated aspects of my method and model of media/ cultural studies and in the rest of the book will apply it to concrete studies of popular genres and films dealing with gender, race, class, sexuality, and other salient themes. In the last chapter, I introduced the concept of diagnostic critique, which I will illustrate in the following studies. Diagnostic critique uses history and social theory to analyze cultural texts and cultural texts to illuminate historical trends, conflicts, possibilities, and anxieties.[1] My conceptions of a contextual media/cultural studies and the notion of diagnostic critique will be illustrated, first, by study of some horror and fantasy films that articulate the social anxieties of working and middle class people in an era of economic insecurity in the United States and elsewhere. In Chapter 2, I interrogated how Hollywood films transcoded the political discourses of the era, while the studies in this chapter will probe the anxieties of ordinary people in the terrain of everyday life during the same period. Contemporary Hollywood horror films are also spectacles of intersectionality as the films engaged in this chapter all have class and gender problematics, and many have racial themes, while sexuality has always been an undercurrent to many horror films throughout history.

Media/cultural studies can thus use its methods to interrogate events, discourses, and social trends on both the macro- and micro-level, engaging both the defining social and political trends and events of the era, as well as the texture and travails of everyday life. I have focused on the politics of representation in previous chapters and have analyzed the thematics and images of race, gender, sexuality, and class in a variety of popular films of the era, as well as how they articulated with conservative, liberal, or more radical ideologies and discourses of the era. I also analyzed films in terms of genre, or type of film, reading, for instance, *Rambo* as a war film that transcoded Reaganite militarism.

I will analyze films as well in terms of their auteurs, or creators. Successful directors attain the status of auteur, or distinctive author of a certain type, style, and often theme of film, as Steven Spielberg and James Cameron have emerged as auteurs of Hollywood blockbuster films, while John Carpenter and Wes Craven have emerged as masters of horror, and Oliver Stone is perceived as an auteur of corporate and political films that are critical of U.S. institutions and values.[2] I will continue to study some dominant contemporary Hollywood film genres and auteurs throughout the book and will highlight how they deal with key issues and problems of the era.

On the whole, Hollywood films fit into categories of genre, and in this chapter I will look at some representative horror films that display key fears, conflicts, and hopes of the era. Genre films like the Western, war film, women's melodrama, musical and other popular Hollywood genres deal with the dreams, hopes, and fantasies, and in some genres like the horror film, the nightmares and fears, of individuals in a specific culture at a certain historical moment.

I open by arguing that *Poltergeist* (1982) and other haunted house horror films articulate fears of downward mobility in the working and middles classes and provide allegories concerning social anxiety over losing one's job, home, and family. Next, I interrogate a TV horror series *American Horror Story* (2011) that articulates some of the same themes some decades later. Then, I interrogate *Halloween* and slasher films as articulating fears of sexual violence and assault from unknown strangers and in some cases a dangerous underclass. Often the young woman targets of the slasher films survive and Carl Clover's theme of "the Last Girl Standing" (1992) points to a neo-feminist subtext in many of these films, especially some of the vengeance films in the cycle when the victims get their revenge by violently assaulting and often castrating the perpetrators.

I then turn to analysis of "Racial and Class Angst in the Trump Era" through a diagnostic reading of the popular horror films by Jordan Peele *Get Out* (2018), and *Us* (2019), and Brooks Riley's horror/SF/social satire *Sorry to Bother You*, which articulate fears of people of color in aggressively conservative and racist eras and put on display white liberal racism. Brooks Riley's *Sorry to Bother You* uses horror and science fiction motifs to express anxieties about labor and social oppression, while signaling tendencies toward social revolt.

Throughout this chapter, I will suggest that media culture provides social allegories that articulate class and social group fears, yearnings, and hopes in specific political eras.[3] Decoding these social allegories thus provides a diagnostic critique with insight into the situation of individuals within various social classes, races, and social groups and their underlying fears, hopes, and fantasies. Thus, horror and fantasy films may be the vehicle of deadly serious diagnoses of the contemporary era which media/cultural studies should engage and interpret.

Hollywood and horror

During the past several decades, the horror–occult genre was one of the most popular and successful Hollywood genres.[4] Horror films have traditionally dealt with universal and primal fears (i.e. fears of dying, aging, bodily decay, violence, sexuality, etc.). Horror films also put on display archetypal monsters that represent deeply rooted fears of the modern era, such as the *Frankenstein* films that reveal fears of science and technology getting out of control; *The Mummy*, *King Kong*, and zombie films that express fears of destructive monsters who will terrorize modern civilization, unleashing horrors found in exotic and premodern cultures; *Dracula* and vampire films that articulate fears of sexual domination and control by ancient cultures; and the ghoulish Living Dead monsters that have had a resurrection in post-1960s U.S. culture.

However, some of the most interesting contemporary Hollywood horror films (*The Exorcist*, *The Texas Chainsaw Massacre*, *Carrie*, *Alien*, *The Shining*, and so on have presented, often in symbolic-allegorical form, both universal fears and the deepest anxieties and hostilities of contemporary U.S. society (see Kellner and Ryan 1988). The subtext of these films is the confusion and fright of the population in the face of economic crisis, accelerating social and cultural change, a near epidemic of cancer, industrial diseases, AIDS and other deadly diseases, political instability, and fear of nuclear annihilation. The wide range and popularity of post-1970s Hollywood horror films suggests that something is profoundly wrong with U.S. society and a probing of these films may help reveal something about the source of contemporary fears and inchoate anxieties.

The 1980s was a boom period for horror films and the social anxieties of the era will be related in the following analysis to the conservative hegemony of the Reagan and Bush I regimes (1980–1992). I argue as well that the conservative hegemony of the later eras of the Bush–Cheney presidency (2000–2008) and Trump nightmare (2016–) have also been fertile periods for horror films to resonate. In this chapter, I will thus relate significant cycles and examples of the horror film to the effects of rightwing political regimes, politics, and ideologies and the real horrors they create, as well as resistance by forces of rebellion and revolt. The post-1980s United States has experienced an unprecedented era of class warfare with massive re-distribution of wealth from working and middle class sectors to the rich and an era of high fear of unemployment, downward mobility, and crisis for the working classes, as well as social divisions between the races, conflicts over sexuality and gender, and conflicting values and politics in different areas of the country.[5]

While the 1970s saw a wave of popular films dealing with the working class (Kellner and Ryan 1988), it was rarely featured in mainstream Hollywood films from the 1980s to the present which have focused more on middle and upper class families and individuals. Yet working class, rural, and underclass individuals were sometimes featured as threatening others to middle class life, especially in horror films, and, as I attempt to demonstrate below, were often negatively stigmatized in certain cycles of the contemporary horror film.

The broad panorama of popular Hollywood horror films also attests to a resurgence of the occult and irrationalism in U.S. society over the past decades which suggests that individuals are no longer in control of everyday life. When individuals perceive that they do not have control over their lives and that they are dominated by powerful forces outside themselves, people are attracted to occultism and the irrational. Consequently, during eras of socio-economic crisis when individuals have difficulty coping with social reality, the occult and horror become efficacious ideological modes that helps explain unpleasant circumstances or incomprehensible events, sometimes with the aid of religious or supernatural mythologies.

In the crisis of German society after World War I, for instance, there was a proliferation of horror films (see Kracauer 1947) and the first great wave of American horror films appeared in the midst of the 1930s depression. After the explosion of the atomic bomb and with the heating up of the Cold War and arms race in the 1950s, another wave of occult horror films appeared, featuring visions of mutant animals and humans, alien invasions, or apocalyptic holocausts (see Biskind 1983). Over the years, American popular culture has accumulated a rich treasure house of occultist lore to draw upon, and from the 1970s into the twenty-first century, Americans turned to horror motifs and the occult for experiences and ideas which helped them cope with economic crisis, political turmoil and cultural malaise. In this resurgence of horror and the occult, repressed fears and irrational forces sought symbolic expression, which often served as vehicles for reactionary ideologies in contemporary film (i.e. *The Exorcist* trilogy, *The Omen* trilogy, and a variety of monster films, demonic possession films, haunted house films, and other occult thrillers (Kellner and Ryan 1988).

Whereas conservative horror films provide fantasies of reassurance that existing authorities and institutions can eliminate evil, many contemporary horror films do not provide reassurance that historically specific or universal evils can be suppressed and contained. Instead, they reveal a society in crisis, where evil is rampant and conventional authorities and values are incapable of defeating and eliminating evil. Consequently, these films often do not legitimate contemporary American institutions and values, but show evil and horror to be ubiquitous and powerful forces in the contemporary social order. This is true to some extent of films that rely on religious institutions to defeat evil (i.e. *The Exorcist* and to a greater extent the more nihilistic films of George Romero, Tobe Hooper, Wes Craven, Larry Cohen, and others that show contemporary institutions and ways of life to be the source of evil).[6]

In the following discussion, I shall first disclose how the original *Poltergeist* film (1982) negotiates middle-class fears and insecurities concerning race, gender, and class in the contemporary era. I'll interpret the film allegorically as articulating deep-rooted fears that are often explored in genres like the horror film rather than realist films, where they might be too painful to confront and deal with. Horror films can be a reactionary genre to the extent that they blame occult forces for societal disintegration and a life out of control, thus deflecting attention from the real sources of social suffering. Yet they also offer the possibility of radical critique by presenting suffering and oppression as caused by institutions, values, and behavior that needs to be reconstructed, or overcome.

Hence, the metaphorical and allegorical modes of horror films can be used both as vehicles for conservative ideology and radical critiques, and I will show examples of both in this chapter. The horror films of the 1970s, for example, saw monsters being produced by families, and thus could be taken as socially critical, cinematically articulating the critiques of the family in 1960s political movements. Films like *The Texas Chain Saw Massacre*, *The Hills Have Eyes*, *Motel Hell*, and so on presented the family as monstrous, as the source of monsters, thus replicating feminist critiques of the patriarchal family (Wood 2018). Yet films like *Poltergeist* show harmonious families being attacked by monsters, and thus serve as ideological defenses of the middle-class family, which transcode cinematically the conservative pro-family discourses of the 1980s. Read diagnostically, even conservative horror films reveal contemporary anxieties concerning the family, downward mobility, and homelessness in an uncertain economy and deteriorating social order.

Contemporary tensions and conflicts in the family that reproduce wider social issues and anxieties are also found in the 2011 season of the popular TV-show *American Horror Story*, which I shall engage to show how the horror genre can illuminate contemporary issues of significant importance. Finally, turning from the fears of white middle class families, I examine how Jordan Peele's horror films *Get Out* and *Us*, and Brooks Riley's horror/SF/social satire *Sorry to Bother You*, articulate fears of people of color in the aggressively conservative and racist context of the Trump presidency.

Poltergeist, the occult, and anxieties of the middle class

Among the wave of 1980s occult-horror films, *Poltergeist* (1982), directed by Tobe Hooper and co-authored and produced by Steven Spielberg,[7] is especially interesting because it articulates the underlying anxieties of the middle class in the age of Reagan. The 1982 film *Poltergeist*, its sequels, and a 2015 remake of the original also deal with the crisis of patriarchy and the family, and in the following diagnostic reading, I accordingly discuss the *Poltergeist* films as indicators of social anxiety and crises of the family and patriarchy in contemporary U.S. society.

Poltergeist, along with Spielberg's *E.T., The Extra-Terrestrial* (1982), explores with sympathy and even affection the environment and life-style of the new affluent, suburban middle class and presents symbolic projections of its insecurities and fears. While *E.T.* presents an optimistic and charming allegory of suburban middle class life, *Poltergeist* presents its shadow-side and nightmares in a story where the Other, the Alien, is not a friendly extra-terrestrial who comes from outside the society to help it, but threateningly emerges from *within* the socio-economic system and social subconscious to terrorize the ordinary middle class people who are the subject of the film. Thus, whereas *E.T.* is Spielberg's childlike fantasy of hope, *Poltergeist* is a symbolic probing of universal and specifically American fears that takes the form of an allegorical nightmare, the decoding of which should tell us something about everyday life during the 1980s era of Reaganite conservatism.

Poltergeist features the adventures with the occult of the Freeling family, which discovers that its house is built upon top of a Native American graveyard whose spirits seek revenge against the intruding family.[8] In another plot twist, evil spirits attempt to seduce the clairvoyant five-year-old daughter, Carol Anne, into the spirit world. Her parents try to rescue her and are forced to turn to parapsychologists and a diminutive woman medium for help.

The family unit in *Poltergeist* contains a father, Steve Freeling (Craig T. Nelson), his wife, Diane (Jobeth Williams), a teenage daughter, Dana (Dominique Dunne), a young boy, Robbie (Oliver Robins), and little Carol Anne (Heather O'Rourke), who is the first to make contact with the poltergeists. The Freelings live in one of the first houses built in Phase One of a housing project called Cuesta Vista. The father is a successful real estate agent who has sold 42% of the housing units in the area – which his boss tells him represents over seventy million dollars' worth of property. As a reward for his heroic efforts, he has all the commodities desired by the new affluent middle class. Depiction of this class and its fears of losing their home, family, and property is a central focus of the *Poltergeist* films.

The name "Freeling" evokes the dominant ideology of freedom and from this perspective a "freeling" is a free being, a member of a class and society free from basic worries and cares, free to celebrate and live the American middle-class dream. "The Star-Spangled Banner," referring to the "land of the free," plays in an opening segment and refrains later in the film, which presents iconic images of American flags throughout. Yet *Poltergeist* deals with the threats to freedom and loss of sovereignty in contemporary middle-class life, and the all-too-real prospects of downward mobility in an American dream gone sour and become a nightmare.

Moreover, unlike typical horror films where individuals frequently blunder into disaster, in *Poltergeist* the individuals act rationally, cooperatively, and courageously. The father goes to Stanford and summons a group of parapsychologists who come to investigate the phenomena and they in turn call in a diminutive woman spiritualist, Tangina (Zelda Rubinstein), who tells the family how to deal with the poltergeists and how to get their daughter back. With the spiritualist's guidance, the mother enters the spirit world to retrieve her daughter – revealing the depth of her love and concern for her child. Significantly, it is the women who play the key role in rescuing Carol Anne – reinforcing traditional images of women as protectors and nurturers of children.

In addition to representing fears of the family being torn apart, *Poltergeist* deals with anxieties about losing one's home, or watching it fall apart. The American dream has traditionally focused on buying and owning one's own home and in an era of accelerating unemployment, a weak economy, and diminishing discretionary income, fear of losing one's home, or not being able to maintain it, accelerated during the 1980s. Stephen King, author of such popular books as

Carrie, The Shining, The Stand, It, and many others – which themselves are a fertile source of symbolic allegories about contemporary American anxieties – writes of *The Amityville Horror,* a gothic, occult precursor to *Poltergeist:*

> the picture's subtext is one of economic unease … Little by little, it is ruining the Lutz family financially. The movie might as well have been subtitled 'The Horror of the Shrinking Bank Account' … *The Amityville Horror,* beneath its ghost-story exterior, is really a financial demolition derby.[9]

Poltergeist, too, shows a house gradually but inexorably falling apart. Rooms become uninhabitable, machines and technology either do not work or operate out of the family's control, commodities and toys fall apart. Finally, the house literally collapses and the family must flee. This allegory of the home under siege is part of the reason that the film was so effective in manipulating its audience: viewers can identify with this very average middle-class family in a house that constantly gives them troubles and is eventually taken away from them. This *is* a contemporary horror story for current and would be home owners, many of whom lost their homes during the age of Reagan and Bush, and succeeding eras.

As it turns out, the source of the poltergeist disturbance is the result of a decision of the land developing company, for which the father works, to build their project on top of a graveyard after removing the headstones, but without removing the corpses. In zombie scenes reminiscent of the horror classic *Night of the Living Dead,* the dead arise from the earth and terrorize the neighborhood. The film thus plays on fears that land developers will destroy the environment and upset delicate ecological balance – another contemporary worry that is the site of current struggles to limit growth and urban and suburban development.

Yet the poltergeists also represent fear of racial otherness, and the films can be read as fear of racial invasion and destruction of suburban middle-class utopia. The monsters in *Poltergeist* are connected with native peoples and they appear as dark-skinned monstrosities, and otherness to white middle class "normality." Fears of racial Others are linked to fears of working class Others in *Poltergeist.* Some workers appear early in the plot to toil on a family swimming pool, itself a symbol of middle-class affluence. The workers are slightly dark-skinned ethnic types, and somewhat uncouth and uncivilized. Two male workers leer at the teenage daughter who responds with obscene gestures to the mother's amusement. Soon after, one worker opens the window to drink the mother's coffee and snack on some food laying on the drainboard. The mother catches him and good-humoredly chastises the vaguely-threatening worker who she calls "Bluto" (an odd name, perhaps after the menacing working-class character in *Popeye*).

Horror films thus mobilize fear of the Other and draw lines between normality and abnormality, good and evil. Goodness resides in middle-class familial normality and Otherness resides in the working class and racial Others like Native Americans in the *Poltergeist* films, or people of color in many genres of film. Popular Hollywood film is made from the standpoint of the white male upper/middle class subject from whom people of color, working and under class people, and often people of queer sexualities, are seen and discriminated against as the Other. From this perspective, the threatening monsters in many horror films stand in allegorically for race and class forces threatening middle class stability. Such cinematic representations transcode the conservative, yet anxious, pro-family discourses of the era in their celebration of the family and negative stigmatizing of Otherness.

Another major subtext of the film is fear of television, which stands in for a more generalized fear of new technologies which appears frequently in later horror films. Carol Anne first comes under the spell of the poltergeists through the TV set and then disappears – indeed, how many American children have disappeared into the TV set! The poltergeists and the disembodied voice of the little girl after she is spirited away communicates through the TV set just as so many Americans receive their communication from the outside world through TV. As noted, television static is an iconic image of disturbance throughout the film, and the television is on constantly. During the scenes in which the parapsychologists attempt to analyze the situation, state of the art video cameras and recorders are placed throughout the house. The poltergeists are actually recorded and played back on a video-recorder demonstrating the mechanical reproducibility of everything in media society and the possibility of instant replay.

The images of video surveillance may also articulate fears that Big Brother is watching, that new technologies will invade privacy, that a new technological panopticon is emerging in which we are all under surveillance.[10] We see here, symbolically portrayed, the power of television to captivate audiences, spy on people, and become an organizing center of leisure and social power. The fear that television might eventually totally replace cinema has been one of Hollywood's greatest fears and perhaps a concern of Spielberg and his collaborators. In the final scene, when the family has left their ill-fated house and checks into the Holiday Inn, we see them taking out the TV set and putting it on the balcony. The audience laughs and claps and the filmmakers grin and everyone goes home, and sooner or later, probably sooner, turns on the TV.[11]

Poltergeist thus presents a panorama of symbolic images of contemporary American nightmares. It achieves its power by drawing on real fears, which it presents in symbolic form that allows people to experience their subconscious anxieties in the safe medium of film in an ideology machine that smooths over and tranquilizes their fears by showing the family pulling through. *Poltergeist* presents the landscape of contemporary consciousness more powerfully than the fairy tale *E.T.*, revealing the contours of American consciousness in the age of Reagan to be fearful, consumer and family oriented, and ready to believe and do anything in order to survive.

Although *Poltergeist* hints that corporate capitalism is rapacious, destroying the earth, exploiting people, and even threatening human survival, the real source of contemporary anxieties is displaced onto the occult. Hence, while *Poltergeist* and other recent horror films contain allegories about contemporary anxieties, the audience is directed by the film toward spectacles of occult horror rather than the horror show of contemporary life in the United States. The irrationalist–occultist metaphysics in films like *E.T.* and *Poltergeist* therefore weaken the social insights present in the films and strengthen the rampant irrationalism in U.S. society manifest in religious revivalism, cults, new age spiritualism, and the search for salvation through false prophets, and so on.

In fact, several of Spielberg's major 1980s and 1990s films are permeated with the fuzzy-minded occultism that T.W. Adorno shrewdly characterized as "the metaphysics of dopes" (1974: 24). Although Spielberg and company's excursions into the supernatural allow individuals to experiences anxieties in a symbolic form that they might not be able to face in a more realist narrative form, his occult films tend to project real fears onto threats by evil spirits, and focus hope on deliverance by some beneficent extra-terrestrials (*Close Encounters of the Third Kind, E.T.*, or superheroes like Indiana Jones in *Raiders of the Lost Ark*). Spielberg's ideology machines all too often summon the audience to escapist fantasies, conservative affirmation of middle class values, traditional mythic heroes, and the forms of traditional popular culture. Unlike the more critical Hollywood filmmakers who dissect dominant myths and question dominant values (i.e. Altman, Scorsese, Redford, Spike Lee, and so on), Spielberg is a story teller and mythmaker who affirms both the opposing poles of middle class values and life-styles as well as a transcendent occultism.

The turn to the occult in post-*Exorcist* (1973) Hollywood film represents an ideological crisis in American society by presenting a society in crisis whose institutions are under attack by a variety of forces. Some of the most popular horror–occult films of the post-1970s era (*The Exorcist, The Omen, Carrie, The Amityville Horror, The Shining*, and an industry of Stephen King novels and films) portray a disintegrating society incapable of dealing with the evils presented in the films. If there is any salvation, or a solution to the problems depicted, in most of these and other Hollywood "blockbuster" films, it appears transcendentally in the form of aliens or extra-terrestrials, the church or the spirit world, or superheroes from other worlds or other times like Superman, Batman, Wonder Woman, or Spiderman. The appeal to the past, or to the transcendental, for heroes, values, and legitimation does not, however, effectively legitimate the institutions of the existing society, and points to a legitimation crisis in contemporary American society (Habermas 1975).

Poltergeist, it is true, does attempt to positively portray the family and middle class life styles, but there are ideological contradictions in Spielberg's work between attempts to celebrate existing middle class institutions and values in contrast with the search for salvation from extra-terrestrials, or spiritualism. There are also hints in his films that existing institutions and values lack vitality. In *Close Encounters*, the husband abandons his family to pursue his fantasy of making contact with the aliens in the U.F.O.'s; in *E.T.* the absence of the father (separated from the mother and in Mexico with a new girlfriend) can be seen as a psychological reason for the boy to turn for friendship and love to the extra-terrestrial; and while in *Poltergeist*, we have a particularly strong portrait of the family as a viable institution, the rest of the dominant institutions, and especially the corporation, are presented in a critical light.

Indeed, whatever one thinks of Spielberg's occultism, or his affirmation of middle class values, his work is valuable for shedding light on contemporary U.S. society and revealing the fears, hopes, and fantasies of the new affluent, suburban middle class. In Steven Spielberg, the new middle class has found its story teller and ideologue. His fantasies are permeated with ideologies that should be probed, decoded and criticized by those interested in understanding U.S. society and culture in the contemporary era.[12]

American Horror Story and the crisis of the family and patriarchy

Television has featured many TV horror series and the popular and acclaimed *American Horror Story* has run from 2011–2018, with at least two more seasons in production. This creepy and sometimes campy anthology horror series was created by Ryan Murphy and Brad Falchuk for the cable network FX, following their success with the series *Nip/Tuck* (2003–2010) and *Glee* (2009–2015). Each season of *American Horror Story* is conceived as a self-contained miniseries, following a different set of characters, settings, and thematic, and a storyline with its own "beginning, middle, and end."

The first season *Murder House* takes place in Los Angeles, California, during the year 2011, and centers on a family that moves into a house haunted by ghosts of previous occupants. The *Murder House* season of *American Horror Story* uses the format of the haunted house story to probe the conflicts, anxieties, and crises of the family in contemporary society and culture.

In the plot line of "Murder House," a family moves from Boston to Los Angeles to escape the trauma of the mother Vivien's (Connie Britton) miscarriage, after discovery that her husband, Ben (Dylan McDermott), was having an affair with one of his students. The Harmons, who we learn are far from harmonious, buy an old LA restored mansion that is creepy, but much larger than they could afford elsewhere in the area. Their teenage daughter, Violet (Taissa Farmiga), is resentful of the move, and is alienated from both of her parents, presenting a classic case of a dysfunctional family trying to start over with a new home and life.

As they move into the old mansion, the camera lingers on a bone sculpture of the sort found in *The Texas Chain Saw Massacre* and a strange-looking young girl tells them that "You are going to die here." The weird girl's mother, their bothersome neighbor Constance (Jessica Lange), picks up her daughter Adelaide (Jamie Brewer) who keeps breaking into the Harmon's house, portraying annoying neighbors. The Harmons soon encounter the residence's housekeeper, Moira O'Hara (Frances Conroy), who has been living in the house for decades and knows all its secrets and the family is pressured to hire her.

Ben encounters the old and dead-eyed Moira as a beautiful seductress, and we quickly learn that Ben is unable to distinguish between fantasy and reality, and indeed the house is haunted by ghosts of former inhabitants that slowly make themselves known to the family. Ben suffers an increasing breakdown embodying the theme of a crisis of patriarchy in which a father loses control of his family and himself, much like the plot in Stephen King's *The Shining*, which influenced *American Horror Story*. Like *The Shining*, the LA house is haunted by ghosts of the past in the Harmons' well-known "Murder House," which has witnessed a series of brutal murders, that are replayed in flashbacks during episodes of the series.

The wife, Vivien, learns on an "Eternal Darkness" bus tour that the house was built by a doctor Charles Montgomery in the 1920s, who became addicted to drugs and performed Frankenstein-like experiments in the basement. His socialite wife, Nora, insisted that the doctor earn money to support the family, and led her husband, Charles, to begin performing abortions on young women in the basement, thus producing, in the mythology of the TV-series, a legacy of evil in the house.

A major plot-line deals with Ben's affair with his student in Boston, Hayden (Kate Mara), who is herself pregnant, and Ben travels to Boston to try to get her to have an abortion; she refuses, telling him that she wants to be with him and that he must assume his responsibilities as a father. Hayden shows up in Los Angles, but a ghost who calls himself Larry, who Ben met jogging near Silver Lake, kills her and buries her in the Harmon's backyard, helping to build a gazebo over the dead body. Hayden's ghost, like other murdered ghosts in the house, keeps appearing to create explosive tension in Ben's fragile marriage to Vivien.

Meanwhile, their teenage daughter, Violet, is bullied at school, but gains the protection and friendship of a teen ghost, Tate, who lives in their cellar and who has fallen for Violet. It turns out that Tate (Evan Peters) murdered several students at Westfield High in a school shooting whose bloody ghosts turn up to confront him on Halloween on his first date with Violet. The convoluted plot serves to highlight themes of the crisis of patriarchy as Ben continues to unravel as his past in the form of his affair with Hayden and infatuation with a younger specter of their maid, Moira, continually erupts as he tries to mend his relation with his wife, Vivien.

Thus, while Ben appears at first the ideal father, we quickly learn he had cheated on his wife, and guilt from this transgression and the stresses of playing the father role lead him to progressively unravel. Likewise, the mother, Vivien, is increasingly unable to serve the traditional role of wife and parent, and eventually snaps, shooting Ben with a gun kept in the house; Ben reports the shooting, which leads her to be incarcerated in a mental institution. The daughter too cuts herself off from her family, stops going to school after being bullied, and ends up in a fantasy relation with the ghost Tate, himself a school shooter.

Indeed, the danger of guns is a series motif as the plot comes back frequently to Tate's school shooting rampage, Vivien's shooting Ben and her incarceration, while references to Trump and/or the NRA are put in for laughs. As the season and subsequent seasons unfold, the plot and thematics become increasingly gothic providing critical and often satirical views of the contemporary family, teen life, schooling, and the travails of men, women, and teens in the present age. *American Horror Story* makes frequent references to popular culture and previous horror movies and cleverly satirizes contemporary business and real estate culture, teen culture, school, and U.S. popular culture. It also engages sexual politics in an intelligent way, not only dealing with conflicts between men and women and romantic issues with teen romantic relations, but the series also has a lot of gay and sexually ambiguous characters, showing sexuality and sexual relations to be a potential Horror Show in the contemporary moment.

By the end of the first season, the ghosts have taken over the house as Vivien gives birth to twins and the surviving one is fought over by the Harmons, their neighbor Constance, and the ghosts. The Harmons' marriage has unraveled and the ghost of his student lover, Hayden, kills Ben, providing a cautionary warning to married men not to get involved with a young lover. Their now dead daughter Violet who has committed suicide, rejects the ghost/killer Tate's declaration of eternal love, and the younger daughter ghost remains in the house and attempts to chase away potential home buyers to protect them from the fate of the families that have lived in the murder house. The episode ends with a cut to three years later when Vivien comes home and finds her young child covered with blood and holding a knife with which he has apparently carved up his babysitter.

The continuing success of *American Horror Story* and numerous cycles of horror films suggests that the horror genre is especially relevant in contemporary U.S. society marked by accelerating violence and multiple nightmares which the horror genre deals with in symbolic and often allegorical forms.

Extreme horror, violence, and American nightmares

The so-called "slasher films" have been one of the one most controversial contemporary Hollywood subgenres. The films on a crude level represent male fantasies of violence against women, yet we'll see the genre is considerably more complex and has complicated relations to feminism and male/female relations since the sexual, gay, and women's liberation movements of the 1960s and 1970s, which have continued to develop into the present.

John Carpenter's *Halloween* (1978) is often said to have launched the cycle of stalk and slash films, but in retrospect, the genealogy is more complex. Carpenter and his collaborators turned a $300,000 budget into a multi-million-dollar profit and led to a rash of spinoff, sequels, and imitations. The film establishes a template for a certain dominant formula of the cycle: young teens, especially girls, are shown engaging in "immoral" activities like sex and drugs, are pursued by a psycho killer, and many are killed, although often there is a "last girl standing" who survives and sometimes extracts revenge (Clover 1992).

Yet before *Halloween*, Wes Craven's The *Last House on the Left* (1972) begins a slaughter/revenge cycle that will mark many later horror films and create a new subgenre cycle that include Craven's *The Hills Have Eyes I* (1977) and *II* (1985) and Tobe Hooper's *The Texas Chainsaw Massacre I* (1974) and *II* (1986). These films feature young urban teens accosted in rural areas by underclass, frequently subhuman, families or groups who murder the teens who sometimes fight back and avenge themselves. Another distinct variant on this subgenre of the slasher film *I Spit On Your Grave* (1977) and (2010) feature an urban woman who is violently assaulted and raped by rural or working class thugs, and the woman acts out highly clever, violent, castrating murders of the perpetrators in what some see as revenge dramas, although more conventional critics dismiss the entire cycle as misogynist and perverted.

Whereas the slasher films put on display violence against women, and represent gender politics and wars in contemporary U.S. society, the Wes Craven/Tobe Hooper/et al. slaughter/revenge films display a dichotomy between middle class families vs. rural and underclass families, or groups, and constitute a kind of class war, putting on display the violence in U.S. society that permeates rural, suburban and urban areas and all classes. In the following discussion, I will engage some of the key thematic films of the slasher film cycles, including some recent remakes or new entries to see how the cycle has evolved and takes on different meanings in diverse historical epochs. I begin with one of the most influential slasher films in the cycle, *Halloween*, which has been remade more than ten times, including an entry from 2018 that brings the genre into the Trump era that has featured fierce debate about violence against women and the "Me Too" movement.

Halloween, *slasher films, and the last girl standing*

John McCarty's *Splatter Movies* traces the origins and development of a troubling subgenre of horror with such labels as "stalk and slash," "slash and gash," "slice and dice," or simply slasher films.[13] The original *Halloween* (1978) was directed and scored by John Carpenter, co-written with producer Debra Hill, and starred Jamie Lee Curtis in her film debut as the "last girl" who survives an onslaught of small town killings of young attractive and sexually active women. Curtis is the daughter of actors Tony Curtis and Janet Leigh, who herself played the lead role in Alfred Hitchcock's *Psycho* (1960), which can be seen as a key precursor of the later slasher genre with its iconic shower knife murder of the Leigh character.

The villain of *Halloween* is eventually revealed to be Michael Myers, who was committed to a sanitarium for murdering his teenage sister, Judith Myers, on Halloween night. Fifteen years later, Myers escapes and returns to the fictional town of Haddonfield, Illinois, where he stalks teenage babysitter Laurie Strode (Curtis) and her friends, while being pursued by his psychiatrist Samuel Loomis

(Donald Pleasance). Dr. Loomis is an ambiguous and slightly sinister character in the cycle, embodying fears of psychiatry and doctors. *Halloween* was shot on a $300,000 initial budget and grossed over $47 million at the box office in the United States and $23 million internationally for a total of $70 million worldwide,[14] making John Carpenter one of the most popular young filmmakers in the country at the time.

The success of *Halloween* generated a cycles of sequels and a proliferation of other low-budget horror film franchises that could turn over a high profit. The original 1978 *Halloween* focuses on three teenage girls, Laurie, Annie, and Lynda; the latter two are sexually active and are killed; Laurie (Jamie Lee Curtis) is virginal and is saved. Each of the killings immediately follows scenes of sexual activity and/or innuendo. Indeed, it is possible to predict the next victim in these films by observing the behavior of the characters: those who engage in behavior objectionable to conservative morality will be harshly punished. Hence, on this level, slasher films are an exemplar of conservative and puritan-ical morality, although feminist and other critics find more progressive moments in the subgenre.

The narrative of the *Halloween* franchise opens in Haddonfield, Illinois, on Halloween evening, where Judith Myers is alone with her boyfriend. We see them kiss and go upstairs to her bedroom; the boy leaves and Judith combs her hair in the mirror with a mussed up bed behind in the background: the mirror and bed point to narcissism and sexual activity. The audience is then positioned into the point-of-view of the killer who views the young woman through the slits in his Halloween mask and slashes the sexually transgressive teenager to death. The film and its sequels feature point-of-view tracking shots, using the then-new Steadycam cameras, which critics say leads the audience to identify with the killers who are stalking and slashing their victims.[15]

Next, we see a confused and frightened six-year-old boy, Michael Myers, stand in front of his house with a bloody knife in his hand; we never learn what motivated him to kill his sister and I shall note below the ambiguity concerning the nature and motivation of the killer in the franchise as a whole. The story of *Halloween* concerns Myers' escape from a mental institution and his return to his hometown 15 years later on Halloween to repeat his ghastly murders. *Halloween* vacillates narratively as to whether the killer should be seen as a psychologically disturbed young boy/man, or as an impersonal, supernatural embodiment of pure evil, with emphasis on the latter. The style of the film is naturalistic and the initial images presents him as a disturbed young boy upset by his sister's sexual activity while their parents were out.

However, we learn from his psychiatrist Dr. Loomis (Donald Pleasance) that Michael has not spoken for the entire period during which he was incarcerated in the mental institution; yet he is able to escape, steal, and drive a car; rob a hardware store to procure the instruments of his killings; find and remove his sister's headstone in the grave yard, which he later places over the bed of one of his victims; and effectively stalk and kill his victims. These activities suggest a supernatural interpretation of the killer, an interpretation given credence by a series of comments from the psychiatrist who tried to cure him, Dr. Loomis, that Myers is "not a man"; he has "the devil's eyes"; and is "purely and simply evil."

Moreover, the killer is repeatedly referred to as the "Bogeyman," the mythic Other of fairy tales. And during the fateful Halloween evening, the victims and the children that they are babysitting are watching *The Thing From Another World* on television, a 1951 alien invasion horror movie produced by Howard Hawks that Carpenter later remade (1982). This suggests that Michael Myers, referred to as "the Shape" in the titles of *Halloween II* and in interviews with Carpenter and producer Debra Hill in a 2000 featurette in a DVD release of the film, is a pure Thing, an indeterminate entity who appears and kills for no particular reason.

Not only is there a narrative muddle between psychological and supernatural interpretation of the Shape/Michael Myers, but there is clichéd conservative presentation of characters and small town environment. Two teenage girls, Annie and Laurie, are shown together in a couple of scenes and Annie brags about her sexual escapades, while Laurie states that she doesn't date because "boys think I'm too smart." In another scene, Laurie and Annie smoke a marijuana joint: Laurie chokes while Annie competently and deeply inhales. These scenes cue us to Annie's "immorality," and indeed she is the killer's first victim, murdered after we see her talking to her boyfriend on the phone in a conversation full of sexual innuendo. And, of course, Laurie, the "good girl," is able to save herself and survive the serial killing.

The narrative muddle between psychological and supernatural presentations of the Shape/Michael Myers is reproduced in *Halloween II* where, on one hand, we learn that Laurie is Michael's other sister and that he has returned to kill her, to complete the cycle of sibling extermination (though we are given no clues as to why he might want to kill Laurie or her sister, Judith). The ambiguity allows the *Halloween* films to exploit conventions of both the psychological thriller/ psychotic killer genre and the horror/occult genre. Many of the films in the stalk and slash cycle opt for the psychological and naturalistic interpretations for the motivation of the killer, although some of the films have an occultist subtext like *Halloween*.

The narrative ambiguity is still evident in the 2018 sequel and reboot of *Halloween* directed by David Gordon Green in which Jamie Lee Curtis returns to play Laurie Strode 40 years after the initial carnage. Laurie has never gotten over the trauma of the confrontation and gore of the Michael Myers rampage, and is given her chance to confront the killer when he escapes on October 29, 2018, from the sanitarium where he has been held for the last 40 years. Michael breaks loose as he was being transferred to a new facility, and his first victims are obnoxious "True-crime podcasters" Aaron Korey and Dana Haines who seek to interview Michael's psychiatrist Dr. Ranbir Sartain who, following his mentor Dr. Loomis, is interested in studying "pure evil." The quick dispatch of these creepy media hounds and the hyperintellectual doctor no doubt provided a charge to Donald Trump's fans who see the media as "the enemy of the people" and intellectuals as highly suspect.

Meanwhile, Laurie Strode has been living an isolated life in Haddonville in a heavily fortified house, full of weapons with which she will ultimately confront Michael Meyers in an anticipated showdown with Evil. Still traumatized by the 1978 events, Laurie has been divorced twice, has a strained relationship with her daughter Karen putting on display a crisis of the family that is a motif of many popular horror films, and has prepared for Michael's potential return through combat training.

Subplots involve Laurie's daughter Karen, who is concerned about her mother's obsession with Michael Meyers, Karen's daughter Allyson, and Allison's problems with her boyfriend who has a wandering eye. Michael Myers begins a murder spree by stealing a kitchen knife, killing an elderly woman, a young lady living next door, and then murders Allyson's best friend, Vicky, who is babysitting, repeating the trope of the first and all successive *Halloween* slaughterfests with the killer assaulting baby-sitters.

Laurie arms herself and goes after Michael, who continues murdering all the townspeople who have revealed some moral or intellectual flaw that makes them prey to the avenging angel who appears as a faceless man in a mask. In a final showdown, Laurie severely injures Michael and severs two of his fingers, but he pushes her over a balcony. She gamely arises and attacks him again, trapping Michael inside a basement safe room. Laurie, her daughter Karen, and granddaughter Allyson unite and set the house on fire, hoping to burn the monster from hell. This purifying image provides a nice feminist ending where three generations of Strode women come together to kill the monster, although the success of the movie makes it more than likely that Michael will escape to do battle again and generate more megaprofits for the gory franchise.

Following the success of the Halloween franchise in 1978, for the next decades up to the present, countless stalk and slash films appeared and were shown on network television and pay cable as well. Many of the films took celebrations like prom night, Valentine's day, birthday parties, and teen parties, and turned them into settings for rites of slaughter. No space inhabited by teenage America was safe from attacks by the psychotic killers of these films. The films were parodied in *Student Bodies* (1981), which numbered the body count across the screen after each bizarre murder; in *The Slumber Party Massacre* (1982), which consisted largely of satirical citations of other slasher films; and in *Pandemonium* (1982), which flashes victim numbers across the screen as the characters are introduced and then parodies recent stalk and slash and other horror films. The parodies reveal that the formulas of the stalk and slash films have become a cliché readily perceivable by both filmmakers and at least some of the audience.

The entire stalk and slash cycle singles out women as victims. Although some of the teen films distribute violence more equally among boys and girls, focus tends to be on the stalking and slashing of women victims. Some feminists criticized these films for terrorizing women in order to keep them in their place; for allowing males to feel more powerful and superior to women; and for feeding male fantasies of power and violence by presenting women under the control of men who are able to do whatever they want to them. There has also been frequent criticism of the increasing number of murders and explicitness of violence as the cycle develops (see Clover 1992; Kerswell 2012).

A subgenre of these slasher films features women avenging themselves and might be seen as women revenge fantasies. In *Lipstick* (1976) a model avenges herself for the rape of herself and her sister by shooting the male rapist. *I Spit On Your Grave* (1980) shows a woman writer brutally killing four local males who had raped her. The feminist TV personality in *Visiting Hours* (1982) stabs the psychopathic killer herself. And in *The Slumber Party Massacre* (1982, 1987, 1990), the surviving girls repeatedly stab the killer who has murdered their friends, in a satire of the revenge film. Although these films might provide pleasure to those wishing to see victims avenging themselves against their victimizers, they tend to stereotype women as vengeful killers and provide revenge fantasies which do not reach to the roots of the problems of male violence. If anything, they are part of the problem by promoting distrust and hostility among the sexes.

Revenge fantasies also reveal hypocrisy concerning sexuality because despite the ultra-moralistic punishment of sexually active women and teenagers, it is doubtful that either the filmmakers or audience for the films believes in their implicitly ultra-conservative morality. In fact, slasher films employ a combination of sex and violence to excite the audience with violation of moral standards which is then punished. The use of sex and violence to attack eroticism thus produces a contradiction between the explicitly sexual scenes and the puritanical messages. Does the popularity of slasher films point to sexual and moral confusion in contemporary U.S. society which is obsessed with sex yet still continues to associate sexual activity with guilt and transgression? The explicit violence in the films against members of the opposite sex seems to articulate worrying hostility among the sexes in contemporary U.S. society. The dismaying popularity of the genre suggests that the sexual revolution of the 1960's and 1970's was not an overwhelming success.

Although new birth control devices, liberalized abortion laws, and sexual permissiveness led to increased sexual activity, it also led to increased sexual tensions, guilt, and confusion. Teen pregnancies, increased sexual pressure and competition, and classical and new venereal diseases all removed sexual activity from the sphere of healthy pleasure, and introduced fear, competition, guilt, and hostilities. Does the rising body count in splatter films correspond to a rise in sexual tensions and hostilities among the film's audiences? Do the killers in the stalk and slash films carry out secret desires of the audience to attack violently members of the opposite sex to avenge or expiate whatever pain, guilt, jealousy, or rejection they have experienced in their sexual relations or fantasies? If these films express new sexual tensions and hostilities, then it is unlikely that they will go away until the conflicts are healed which helped produce them.

There are a couple of final objections to stalk and slash films that I note in conclusion. David Thompson (1981: 184) has suggested that portrayal of the psychopathic killer in the splatter films fosters intolerant attitudes toward the "mentally ill and criminally deviant," and supports the most reactionary theories of criminality and law enforcement. Indeed, most of the killers are thoroughly evil and appear incapable of change or any rational behavior. They are the kind of people that conservatives want to lock up forever or execute. Moreover, the multitude of psychotic killers in splatter films may generate fears in the population of crime and violence, as well as supporting reactionary calls for "law and order" and severe treatment of criminals. The films show a society threatened at every minute by criminal violence with no safe haven from penetration by criminal elements. The attacks on the domestic sphere in these films helps breed fear and insecurity and project the "mean world" syndrome, which George Gerbner and his colleagues found to be a distinctive feature of American television, which they claimed produced fears in the audience that could be manipulated by right-wing politicians (see Gerbner and Gross 1976).

Interestingly, the slasher films display killers who use axes and primitive objects in their mayhem and not guns, whereas extreme gun violence in everyday life over the past decades in every site of U.S. society from schools to malls to movie houses and even churches and synagogues has been one of the one horrifying and appalling features of contemporary U.S. society (Kellner 2008). Whether horror films promote this sort of societal violence or provide a cathartic release of tensions that diminishes propensities for gun violence is an open question, and provides challenges to filmmakers, students and scholars, and all citizens, to try to understand U.S. propensities toward gun violence and to contain an out of control gun culture.

In any case, the stalk and slash films are a problematic subgenre in the contemporary Hollywood cinema. They and other horror films were so popular, however, that their thematics, iconography, and style were borrowed by other genres such as adventure films, disaster films, science-fiction films, and fantasy films in the broadest sense. Although some of the horror films and cycles that I have examined in this chapter are morally and politically objectionable, I believe that they should be taken seriously because they frequently reveal the hidden underside of U.S. society, and suppressed psychic and social tensions. In fact, the horror films deal symbolically with tensions in sexual relationships, fears about the disintegration of the family, and anxieties about the growing social and sexual power of women before more "realistic" genres such as the women's, family and romance film dealt with these themes (see the discussion in Chapter 5). It is as if people could best confront their deep fears and gnawing anxieties concerning the family and sexually in the mode of allegory and horror. Consequently, horror films became a bell weather genre that anticipate the problematics of later Hollywood films. The horror film therefore became a battleground for sexual politics and a genre that symbolically presented attacks on women and feminism, as well as fears concerning sexuality and the family. Horror films also represent fears concerns race and concerns about class and the urban/rural divide that has become especially apparent during the Trump era.

Racial and class angst in the Trump Era: Get Out, Us, and Sorry to Bother You

While a cycle of films by Tobe Hooper, Wes Craven, and others featured rural, working, or underclass families terrorizing white middle class families, during the Trump era, Jordan Peele's *Get Out* (2017) featured whites terrorizing African Americans dramatizing the racial tensions and escalating racial violence in the Trump era. Further, Peele's subsequent film *Us* (2018) deploys the extreme horror format to dramatize an African American family surviving nightmare assaults and pulling together in situations of existential crisis. Both films mix surrealism and horror with realistic depictions of the nightmare of racism in U.S. society.

Get Out (2017) reverses the codes of traditional horror films by making a white middle class family monsters terrorizing an African American photographer. In the DVD commentary, Peele noted that he conceived of the film during the Obama era to counter a "post-racial lie" that maintained that racism has been transcended in U.S. society by the election of an African American President. To counter this myth, Peele wanted to make a horror film that showed racism is alive and virulent in the depths of the American psyche and in social relations between Blacks and whites. With some understatement, Peele added that *Get Out* is highly relevant in the Trump era by depicting racism as deeply embedded in white Americans' psyches.

Get Out presents a dissection of white liberal racism and how virulent racism can terrorize African Americans. The plot depicts a young African American photographer Chris (Daniel Kaluuya) traveling with his white girlfriend Rose (Allison Williams) to meet her parents for the first time. In the initial signal that the film is a horror spectacle, the couple hit a deer in the woods as they are approaching the parents' home. The deer symbolizes innocence destroyed and may refer to the death of Chris' mother in a hit-and-run accident, which becomes a major plot point later in the film. Although the white girlfriend, Rose, is driving, a policeman stops them and harasses the African American demanding to see his papers. Rose sharply rebukes the policeman who lets them drive on, seeming to signal she's a good liberal, but quickly the viewer will discover otherwise.

Initially, Chris must suffer the liberal platitudes of his girlfriend's parents and the subservient behavior of an African American couple working for the white family, but when Rose's brother, Jeremy, arrives for dinner, Chris must undergo aggressive racist taunts, and becomes unnerved as well by the strange robotic behavior from the estate's Black workers, housekeeper Georgina and grounds-keeper Walter. Unable to sleep, Chris goes outside to smoke a cigarette and is almost knocked over by Walter sprinting through the grounds and he is frightened as well by observing Georgina prowl through the house in robotic fashion.

The horror intensifies when the wife, Missy, pressures Chris into a hypnotherapy session to cure his smoking addiction, and he finds himself in a trance, unable to move, as he stares at a coffee cup and silver spoon, which he fixates on. Perhaps the silver spoon is a symbol of the family's wealth that attracts Chris, but it is also a symbol of the unbreachable class and race differences. Missy prompts Chris to recount the painful death of his mother in an auto accident when he was a child, evoking guilt and loss at his mother's demise, and Chris sinks into a dark void that the wife calls the "sunken place," a dark hole that evokes the unconscious and the repressed memories of such horrors as slavery which becomes a literal theme of the film.

The next morning, Chris and Rose awaken and while he thinks that the encounter with Rose's mother during the night was a dream, Chris discovers that cigarettes now repulse him. The horror show intensifies as the couple descend to a house full of visitors for the Armitage family's annual party. The mostly white visitors gush over Chris's physique, fondle him, and express admiration for Black figures such as Tiger Woods. One guest notes that while for centuries pale-faced individuals ruled and were the norm, that now Blacks have become the physical ideal.

Unnerved by the condescending and strange behavior of the guests, Chris ventures outside to take photos, where he encounters an odd-looking Black man, Logan King, who is married to a much older white woman and acts robotish and peculiar. Seeking contact with his previous world, Chris calls his Black buddy, TSA agent Rod Williams, and complains about the strange people and behavior at the house. When he attempts to photograph Logan with his phone, the flash goes off accidentally, and Logan becomes hysterical, yelling at Chris to "get out."

Taking this advice, Chris tells Rose that they should leave, and sends a photo of Logan to his buddy Rod, who recognizes Logan as Andre Hayworth, a man they once knew who had been missing for months. Suspecting a conspiracy, Rod goes to the police, but they deride him. While this is going on, Rose's father, Dean, holds an auction with a photo of Chris, which one of the older guests Hudson, a blind art dealer, wins. While Chris packs to leave, he finds photos of Rose in prior relationships with Black men, contradicting her previous claim that Chris is her first Black boyfriend. The collection also includes pictures of Rose with Walter and Georgina. Chris tries to leave the house, but is blocked by the Armitage family and subsequently hypnotized, later awakening strapped to a chair in the basement. A video presentation featuring Rose's grandfather Roman explains that the family transplants the brains of white people into Black bodies; the consciousness of the host remains in the "sunken place," conscious but powerless. The blind art dealer Hudson, over a video-call, tells Chris he wants his body so he can gain Chris's sight and artistic talents.

Chris plugs his ears with cotton stuffing pulled from the chair padding, obstructing the hypnosis. When the brother, Jeremy, comes to fetch him for the surgery, Chris knocks him unconscious, and impales the father Dean on the antlers of a mounted deer. Dying, Dean stumbles and knocks over a candle which sets fire to the operating room with Hudson inside. After killing Missy and Jeremy as well, Chris drives away in Jeremy's car, but he hits Georgina. Remembering his mother's death, Chris carries Georgina into the car. However, she is possessed by Rose's grandmother Marianne who attacks Chris and he crashes the car, killing her. Rose's family continues to attack and try to overpower Chris, but his TSA worker friend Rod arrives in an airport police car and rescues Chris, leaving Rose in the road as she dies from her gunshot wound.

Get Out was extremely successful, grossing $255 million worldwide on a - $4.5 million budget, making it the tenth most profitable film of 2017.[16] Jordan Peele became extremely busy in the following months producing and narrating ten episodes of a remake of the popular TV series *The Twilight Zone,* and in 2019 released another racially charged and socially critical horror film *Us* (2019). The film opens in Santa Cruz, California, in 1986 with a young African American Girl wearing a Michael Jackson "Thriller" T-shirt wandering in a fun house in an amusement park, who recoils after seeing a double of herself. When her parents find her, she will not speak of the event.

The scene cuts to the present with the Wilsons, an African American nuclear family, led by the strong mother, Adelaide (Lupita Nyong'o), the good natured father, Gabe (Winston Duke), their teenage daughter, Zora (Shahadi Wright Joseph), and a bright and offbeat young son, Jason (Evan Alex). After some debate, the family drives to stay for the summer in their lake house in Santa Cruz, and hang out with their white friends Josh and Kitty Tyler at the beach. The son, Jason, wanders off by himself and sees a man standing with blood dripping from his hands, and when the family finally finds Jason after a frantic search, they leave the beach and return home.

That night, the Wilsons hear thumping noises and look out of the window to see four people who look like the figures in their own family all dressed in red and standing mysteriously in the driveway. The horror of home invasion follows as the mysterious family breaks into the Wilsons' home and attacks them, taking control of the house. The Wilsons quickly perceive that the intruders are doubles of themselves.

As the story unfolds, we learn that The Wilsons' doubles, called "the Tethered," were produced in an underground lab by the U.S. government to create clones to control the public, but that the Tethered were abandoned underground where they lived for years, presumably feeding on rabbits who had overrun the facility. However, Adelaide/Red led them to revolt and they are now on a rampage killing the humans who they double. The red clothes that the Tethered wear with their leader, Red, points to fears of socialism and that the Reds (i.e. commies) will invade and wreak havoc. TV images of rampaging doubles dressed in red evokes images of a revolutionary zombie apocalypse in which the repressed red doubles are now taking over the world.

Thus *Us* evokes images of an intractable racist and class society that blocks escape and rising to a higher class. The structuring mythology of the under-ground Tethered factory evokes the fate of the working class trapped in jobs and unable to rise to the world above that is depicted in the Santa Cruz scenes that evoke wealth and privilege. Yet the images of the Reds revolting against their tethered condition and emerging above in a state of rampage evokes threats of revolution, as the enslaved revolt against their oppressors.

Playing on George Romero's "Living Dead" mythology, Jordan Peele thus produces a frightening allegory of the "return of the repressed," when individ-uals release their violent and destructive herd instincts and form groups of unleashed "Tethereds," who now are able to express their long forbidden and repressed instincts, similar to Trump's followers at his mass rallies who never seem to tire of chanting "lock her up," "CNN sucks," "build the wall!", and other Trump rallying cries. Hence, the images of the Tethered unleashed in Peele's film can be read as either the emergence of a revolutionary force or a destructive mob. Ironically, TV images earlier in *Us* of the 1986 "Hands Across America" spectacle, a movement created to dramatize the problem of poverty, and the concluding images of the red zombies forming a human chain winding through the landscape, evoke a fantasy of Trump's followers linked in an expanding chain, becoming the protective wall that he maniacally evokes. *Us* ultimately thus fits into a social apocalypse genre that has become a major genre in contemporary Hollywood cinema over the past years.

While Jordan Peele's *Get Out* and *Us* deploy the horror genre to depict deep anxieties of people of color in the Trump era, Boots Riley's *Sorry to Bother You* (2018) uses comedic satire with overtones of horror to present the story of an African American Everyman struggling for survival in an ultra-competitive high tech capitalist society, which mutates into a dark satire of how a corporation planned to enslave workers and create a workforce of human–animal hybrids.

In his directorial debut, music artist Boots Riley uses his hometown of Oak-land, California, to show how African Americans struggle for survival in corpor-ate America. Riley describes his first major film as "an absurdist dark comedy with aspects of magical realism and science fiction inspired by the world of telemarketing,"[17] and, indeed, *Sorry to Bother You* uses satire, absurdist comedy, and fantasy to critique corporate and consumer capitalism. The film follows an unemployed young African American Cassius "Cash" Green (Lakeith Stanfield), who is told by his landlord/Uncle that he must get a job to pay his rent to avoid conviction. Opening scenes show Cash waking up in his uncle's garage, greeting friends from the neighborhood and hanging with his girlfriend, Detroit (Tessa Thompson), a performance artist, who spends her days twirling a sign on Oakland street corners and preparing for the opening of her art show.

Cash sets off to go for a job interview and we see him travelling through the streets of Oakland passing through his downscale neighborhood into wealthier sections of the city to the downtown area of high rise corporate affluence, highlighting the class divisions in the city. Cash shows up for an interview with a counterfeit trophy and a phony employee-of-the-month plaque to impress the manager that he is highly qualified for the position. His employer sees through the con (that evokes the Con Man in Chief, Donald Trump), and hires him anyway as a telemarketer on the lower levels of the RegalView company, where he is assigned a cubicle, surrounded by hundreds of other workers all engaging in telemarketing. A sign on the wall proclaims STTS ("Stick to the Script"), and indeed he is admonished by bosses continually to maximize calls, stick to the company script, and sign up customers, highlighting the alienation of labor under capitalism.

Cash has trouble selling anything to customers until an older co-worker, Langston (Danny Glover), advises him to use a "white voice" that makes its pitch in a self-confident, aggressive form, moving quickly to "seal the deal" and make the sale. Cash finds that he is indeed able to increase sales dramatically with his "white voice," and his manager suggests Cash will soon be promoted to the coveted position of "Power Caller," where on the floor above, the real money is made.

Cash's co-worker Squeeze organizes a union to lobby for raises among the telemarketing staff, and his friend Sal and girlfriend, Detroit, strongly support the struggle. Cash, however, is promoted to Power Caller, and in his rich and self-assured white voice, Cash seems to be on his way to success. However, he finds he is leaving his previous friends behind and is selling problematic items like weapons, and that, moreover, RegalView is also selling human labor from a mysterious company WorryFree to other companies and governments, producing a form of slave labor.

Although Cash finds himself increasingly uncomfortable with the work, he is able to afford a new car and apartment, to pay off his uncle's mortgage, and to buy tokens of affluence for himself and his girlfriend. Cash also stops participating in the union, claiming he still supports them from the sidelines, and his relationship with Detroit starts to deteriorate as a result of his new life-style and behavior, especially as Cash continues to work while his friends picket RegalView outside in the streets.

After making more sales, Cash is invited to a party with Steve Lift (Armie Hammer), the CEO of WorryFree. After the party, Lift has a one-on-one meeting with Cash and offers him a powdered substance to snort, which he does. Looking for the bathroom, Cash wanders through many hallways of the mansion, opens a door and finds a half-horse, half-human hybrid begging for help. He flees and bumps into Lift, who tries to calm him down by explaining how WorryFree is planning to make their workers stronger and more obedient by transforming them into half-horse, half-human hybrids, referred to as "Equisapiens." The transformation takes place when a human snorts a gene-modifying powder similar to cocaine.

The underground laboratory where humans are converted into human/animal hybrids evokes the site in Jordan Peele's *Us* where "the Tethered" were produced by the U.S. government to create clones to control the public. In both cases we see the horrors of imagined resurrections of slavery and the converting of human beings into mere instruments of labor. Lift explains he wants Cash to become an Equisapien and act as a false revolutionary figure among them to keep them in line with WorryFree's goals, offering Cash $100 million for five years. When the five years are up, Lift says Cash will be able to take a "defusing powder" and return to his normal self.

After leaving in a panic, Cash becomes worried he was tricked into snorting the gene powder and visits his artist girlfriend, Detroit, who tells him she received a video message from his missing phone, which turns out to be a cry for help from the Equisapiens and Lift threatening to turn them into glue. To make the video viral, Cash goes on a reality show called "I Got the S#*@ Kicked Out of Me!", enduring a variety of physical punishments in order to get the video played at the end at the show, so that he can reach a mass audience and publicize WorryFree's noxious plan.

However, Cash's stunt backfires, and Lift's project is hailed as a groundbreaking scientific advancement, leading WorryFree's stock to reach an all-time high. This sequence satirizes an immoral capitalism, interested only in profit and shows how capital uses the media to promote its ventures and products.

Cash apologizes to Squeeze, Sal, and Detroit for abandoning them and selling out to the corporation. The union decides to make one last stand in the picket line, now joined once again by Cash. The next day, Cash copies the code he saw in the Equisapiens' video to break into Lift's home before heading to the picket line where the workers and police clash and create a riot. Cash is knocked out by an officer just after he blows a whistle into a phone that summons the Equisapien, half-horse/half humans. Later that night, Cash wakes up in a police wagon and witnesses the Equisapiens that he called with the whistle fighting back against the police, who they easily overpower with their superior strength. The Equisapiens then free Cash, Squeeze, Sal, and Detroit, and run off to keep fighting, providing a fantasy of revolutionary solidarity.

With everything seemingly returning back to normal, Cash suddenly grows massive nostrils on his face signaling his transformation into an Equisapien. Later a fully transformed Cash leads a mob of Equisapiens to Lift's house to confront their capitalist oppressor. Cash calls over the intercom and remarks "sorry to bother you," before leading the mob to break down the door and attack Lift in another fantasy of revolutionary insurrection against the capitalist class.

Boots Riley has suggested that his film offers a radical class analysis of capitalism,[18] rather than a specific analysis of America under President Trump, clarifying that he wrote the initial screenplay during the Obama administration, and that the target was never any specific elected official or movement,[19] but rather a broader look at "the puppetmasters behind the puppets."[20] While the majority of the final script remained the same, minimal changes were made prior to shooting in order to avoid the film appearing to be a critique of Trump specifically, including removing a line where a character says "Worry Free is making America great again,"[21] written before Trump would use the line in his 2016 presidential campaign.

The title of the film *Sorry to Bother You* has a double meaning, referencing both the phrase's use by telemarketers and its general usage when telling a person something you know they might not like to hear, such as the anti-capitalist themes present in the film. According to Boots Riley,

> ... the other side of it is, is that often when you're telling someone something that is different from how they view things, different from how they view the world, it feels like an annoyance or a bother. And that's where that comes from.[22]

The theme of the strike was used to reflect the need to "organize people in the workplace" and for workers to recognize their power.[23]

As we have seen in this chapter, the horror genre deals with key social issues like race, gender, class, and sexuality. In the next chapter on "Race, Resistance and Representation" I focus on race and the contested terrain of representation of racial identities and politics. In Chapter 5, I turn to "Gender and Sexuality Wars," so will continue with my interrogations of the politics of representation in contemporary U.S. media culture presented in this chapter through the medium of the horror genre.

Notes

1 This dual optic of reading history through texts and using history and theory to read texts was that of T.W. Adorno and Walter Benjamin and other members of the Frankfurt school; see Kellner 1989b.
2 While a graduate student of philosophy in the 1960s at Columbia University, I was influenced by the writings of Susan Sontag and Andrew Sarris who developed the auteur theory to analyze major directors of Hollywood films and to review contemporary films in his job as film critic for *The Village Voice*, seeing the director as the major creative force of quality film in terms of style, vision, and thematics. I regularly read Sontag's and Sarris's film reviews at the time and was strongly influence by auteur theory, an inclination strengthened in my year in Paris as a graduate student in 1971–1972. During my years of teaching at the University of Texas from 1973 to the mid-1990s, I was influenced by genre theory that was popular in film studies circles in Austin, where many budding film scholars championed the horror genre.
3 I should acknowledge here the influence of Fredric Jameson. For his use of allegory, that I draw upon here, see Jameson 1979, 1981, 1990, 1991 and on Jameson see my study of Jameson's methodology for reading cultural texts in Kellner 1989c.
4 *Variety* claimed that in 1980 horror and sci-fi films would generate more than one-third of all box-office rentals and predicted that by 1981, the figures would reach 50%. See "Horror Sci-Fi Pix Earn 37% of Rentals–Big Rise During 10-Year Period" (January 3, 1981). *Cinefantastique* reported in a decade re-cap that half of the top ten money making films of all time are horror and science fiction films. Vol. 9, Nos. 3–4 (1980): 72. Horror films continued in popularity through the following years with

waves of slasher films, remakes of the "classics" of the multiple subgenres of horror, and new variations on the most popular horror films and subgenres.

5 As Ferguson and Rogers argue: "The combination of social-spending cuts, other budget initiatives, and the massively regressive tax bill produced a huge upward distribution of American income. Over the 1983–1985 period the policies reduced the incomes of households making less than $20,000 a year by $20 billion, while increasing the incomes of households making more than $80,000 by $35 billion. For those at the very bottom of the income pyramid, making under $10,000 per year, the policies produced an average loss of $1,100 over 1983–85. For those at the top making more than $200,000, the average gain was $60,000. By the end of Reagan's first term, U.S. income distribution was more unequal than at any time since 1947, the year the Census Bureau first began collecting data on the subject. In 1983, the top 40% of the population received a larger share of income than at any time since 1947" (1986: 130). A similar redistribution of wealth upwards (i.e. reverse Robin Hoodism, robbing from the poor and middle classes to enrich the wealthiest 1%) occurred during the Bush-Cheney and Trump eras marking Trump and the Republicans the party of the 1%. See Robert Costa and Mike DeBonis, "With Social Program Fights, Some Republicans Fear Being Seen as the Party of the 1%," *The Washington Post*, March 29 at www.washingtonpost.com/politics/with-social-program-fights-some-republicans-fear-being-seen-as-the-party-of-the-1-percent/2019/03/29/9cfc3232-516b-11e9-a3f7-78b7525a8d5f_story.html (accessed November 15, 2019).

6 On "subversive" and "critical" moments in these and other contemporary horror filmmakers' works, see the studies in Britton et al. 1979; Wood 2018; Kellner and Ryan 1988.

7 *Poltergeist* is credited as a Tobe Hooper film and Hooper is credited as director, while Spielberg is credited as producer, source of the story, and one of the writers. There have been many discussions concerning alleged tensions between Hooper and Spielberg during the filming, as well as debate over whose film it really is – as if a collective enterprise "belonged" to one person or another. In fact, the film itself is an amalgam of the cinematic styles and concerns of Hooper and Spielberg. This film exhibits Hooper's flair for the suspenseful, odd and horrific, and Spielberg's affection for the middle class, fuzzy minded occultism, and nose for the Market.

8 Guilt over Native American genocide and the systematic mistreatment of Native Americans is also present in more realist films like *Tell Them Willie Boy is Here* (1969), *Soldier Blue* (1970), *Little Big Man* (1970), and *I Will Fight No More Forever* (1975 TV-movie). *The Manitou* (1978) uses the horror film genre to present a story about the reincarnation of an evil Native American medicine man in the back of a San Francisco woman; a "good" Native American helps defeat the evil spirit and the film could be seen as an allegory of the transcendence of threatening Native American customs and their domestication within contemporary U.S. culture, whereas Larry Cohen's *Q* (1983) uses a story about the reincarnation of the Aztec god Quetzalcoatl to present a sly critique of contemporary U.S. society.

9 Stephen King, "Why We Crave Horror Movies," *Playboy* (Jan. 1981): 237.

10 In *Discipline and Punish*, French theorist Michel Foucault analyzed the apparatus of surveillance developed in the early nineteenth century by Jeremy Bentham, which he called a "panopticon," describing an architectural structure whereby prisoners, students, workers, or others could be constantly monitored. New technologies present the possibilities that high-tech surveillance could create a frightening panopticon society, à la Orwell's *1984*.

11 Fear of television has been an obsession of Spielberg's in his 1980s suburban films. Early in *Poltergeist*, the children are told not to play so roughly and Carol Anne is directed to watch TV: she flicks it on and a violent Western is playing! In *E.T.*, when the alien watches television for the first time, he communicates his thoughts and feelings to the young boy at school (they have apparently achieved a "mind-meld," to use *Star*

Trek lingo, sharing each other's minds). When E.T. watches a violent scene on TV, the boy is then violent at school; E.T. watches John Wayne kiss Maureen O'Hara and the boy kisses a little girl at school. The fear that children will imitate what they see on TV is widespread in U.S. society today, and is symbolically portrayed in *Poltergeist* and *E.T.* – the concern has emerged in contemporary discussions of media violence and the impact of shows like *Beavis and Butt-Head* on the young. Not accidently, when the little boy in *E.T.* succeeds in his ploy to stay home from school to be with his new companion, the mother warns: "And no TV!".

12 To be sure, Spielberg is also responsible for a series of historical dramas dealing with oppression such as *The Color Purple, Empire of the Sun, Schindler's List, Amistad, The Post*, and others, thus bifurcating his work into serious socially-conscious films and popular entertainment films.

13 John McCarty, *Splatter Movies: Breaking the Last Taboo of the Screen.* New York: St Martin's Press, 1984.

14 See *Halloween* at www.boxofficemojo.com/movies/?id=halloween.htm (accessed September 2, 2019).

15 *Halloween* received generally favorable initial reviews and was even praised by critics like Gene Siskel and Roger Ebert on their TV show and writings, who had been carrying out a mini-crusade against gore and slasher movies. *Halloween* is praised as well-crafted and suspenseful with superior lighting, camera-work and music. See Roger Ebert, "Why Movie Audiences Aren't Safe Anymore," *American Film* (March 1981): 54–55. Splatter movie buff McCarty correctly notes the inconsistency of their praise of *Halloween* and criticism of its progeny; he also has refreshingly critical comments to make on *Halloween*; see pp. 134–138. Other critical perceptions of *Halloween* are found in Jonathan Rosenbaum's review in *Take One* (January 1979, pp. 8–9; in scattered references in *American Nightmare*; and in David Thompson, *Overexposures* (New York: William Morrow, 1981), especially 183–187.

16 See *Get Out* in Box Office Mojo that indicates that as of June 25, 2019 the film had a worldwide gross of $255,407,663; see www.boxofficemojo.com/movies/?id=blumhouse2.htm (accessed June 25, 2019).

17 "How Boots Riley Infiltrated Hollywood," *The New York Times*, May 22, 2018 at www.nytimes.com/2018/05/22/magazine/how-boots-riley-infiltrated-hollywood.html (accessed July 11, 2019).

18 "Boots Riley on How His Hit Movie *Sorry to Bother You* Slams Capitalism & Offers Solutions". *Democracy Now!*, July 17, 2018 at www.democracynow.org/2018/7/17/boots_riley_on_how_his_hit (accessed July 11, 2019).

19 Riley, Boots [@@BootsRiley] (July 20, 2018). "Wrote it and published it during Obama presidency. We're in the same economic system, which is why it was relevant then and is now" *(Tweet);* Accessed July 26, 2018 – via Twitter.

20 Morrison, Patt, "Boots Riley on power, organizing and who really runs the country. (Hint: It's not Trump)". *Los Angeles* Times, July 18, 2018 at www.latimes.com/opinion/op-ed/la-ol-patt-morrison-boots-riley-sorry-to-bother-20180718-htmlstory.html (accessed July 11, 2019).

21 Morrison, op. cit.

22 Mark Maynard, "Boots Riley of The Coup … on Communism, Corporatism, hip-hop, and the need to beat down scabs" at http://markmaynard.com/2012/11/boots-riley-of-the-coup-on-communism-corporatism-hip-hop-and-the-need-to-beat-down-scabs/ (accessed July 11, 2019).

23 "Sorry to Bother You," *WikiMili,* Updated June 21, 2019, *at* https://wikimili.com/en/Sorry_to_Bother_You (accessed July 11, 2019).

4

RACE, RESISTANCE, AND REPRESENTATION

During the 1980s, Hollywood joined Ronald Reagan and his administration in neglecting African American issues and concerns.[1] Few serious films during the decade featured Blacks, who were generally stereotypically portrayed in comedies, often with comics like Richard Pryor or Eddie Murphy playing against a white buddy (Guerrero 1993a: 113ff.). In this context, Spike Lee's films constitute a significant intervention into the Hollywood film system (see Reid 1993; Kellner 1995). Addressing issues of race, gender, and class from a resolutely African American perspective, Lee's films provide insights into the explosive problematics of race missing from mainstream cinema. By the 2000s, there were, however, many more African American filmmakers at work and in the mainstream and independent film movement there has been a flowering of films dealing with race and the African American experience, including a continuing series of significant films by Spike Lee and the rise of new types of African American films by directors like John Singleton, Tyler Perry, Lee Daniels, Ryan Coogler, Jordan Peele, and Ava DuVernay.

By the 2000s, there was also an active Latino, Asian American, and multiculturally diverse independent film movement, which gave voice to stories and experiences neglected by the Hollywood mainstream. Occasionally, these films broke into cinematic release, but with DVD and streaming digital video, it is now possible to access films that provide a panoramic kaleidoscope of multicultural life in contemporary U.S. society. In addition, television is increasingly open to multicultural voices and controversial issues engaging race and resistance.

In this chapter, I engage the problematics of race, representation, and resistance, showing how some key writers, filmmakers, and TV creators of color have used media culture to represent racism and in many case resistance. I begin with analysis of the cinema of Spike Lee and its importance for centering on the themes of race and resistance in contemporary Hollywood cinema. I follow with discussion of the increasingly important work of Ava DuVernay and the themes of Black and female empowerment, followed by analysis of George Tillman Jr.'s *The Hate U Give*, a study of police violence and a young Black woman coming of age. In the next section, I discuss some examples of contemporary Latino cinema. Common to many ethnic groups is the problem, often traumatic, of immigration, and so I conclude the chapter by discussing some attempts at representation of immigration and depiction of the contemporary immigrant experience, showing that media culture today provides a wealth of representations of a multicultural United States in analyses of race, resistance, and the experiences of people of color in the United State over the past decades, which has been and continues to be a nation of immigrants.

The films of Spike Lee

Despite the continued oppression of Blacks and people of color and growing violence against African Americans, Black culture has produced extremely important works in the last decades in the fields of literature, film, music, theater, and a full range of arts. Cultural expression has always been a way of resisting oppression and articulating experiences of resistance and struggle. Gospel, blues, jazz, R&B, and other forms of music have traditionally articulated African American struggle and resistance. Black literature has also been a rich source of original voices, articulating the vicissitudes of the African American experience and their culture of resistance. During the past decade, new African American voices have appeared in the realms of film, hip-hop culture, and rap music, and these Black incursions into media culture will be the focus of this chapter.

Addressing issues of race, gender, and class from a resolutely Black perspective, Spike Lee's films provide insights into these explosive problematics missing from mainstream white cinema. Starting with low-budget independent pictures like *Joe's Bed-Stuy Barbershop: We Cut Heads* (a 1983 student film) and *She's Gotta Have It* (1986), Lee moved to Hollywood financing of his films starting with *School Daze* (1988), a focus on Black college life that spoofed the college film genre and the musical. His next film, *Do the Right Thing* (1989), was immediately recognized as an important cinematic statements concerning the situation of Blacks in contemporary U.S. society and the films that followed (*Mo' Better Blues, Jungle Fever, Malcolm X*, and a series of outstanding films that continue to appear) won Lee recognition as one of the most important cineastes at work in the United States today.

Moreover, the financial success of Lee's films helped open the door to financing of a wide range of other films by young Blacks in the decades to come. The profits made by Lee's films produced on a low-budget showed that there was an audience for Black films dealing with contemporary realities. Estimates suggest that from 25 to 30% of the U.S. film audience are Black Americans (over-representing their 13% of the population), and Hollywood calculated that there was a significant audience for Black-oriented films (Guerrero 1993b).[23] Moreover, the profits that Spike Lee made on his early films, produced on a low budget, procured continued financing of his own films and opened the door for a renaissance of films by, usually young male, African Americans during the 1990s and succeeding decades.

In the following study, I examine Spike Lee's aesthetics, vision of morality, and politics, arguing that his aesthetic strategies draw on Brechtian modernism and that his films can be read as morality tales that convey ethical images and messages to their audiences. I also discuss Lee's politics, focusing on the figure of Malcolm X in Lee's work and his sometimes contradictory identity politics, in which politics is subordinate to creating one's identity and identity is defined primarily in terms of cultural style. I argue that Lee's films push key buttons of race, gender, sexuality, class, and Black politics and provide a compelling cinematic exploration of the situation of Blacks in contemporary U.S. society and the limited political options that they have at their disposal in the current organization of society. I begin with a reading of *Do the Right Thing* (hereafter *DRT*), turn to *Malcolm X* (1992), and follow with comments on Lee's later work and his gender politics, his identity politics, and his aesthetic strategies.[4]

Do the Right Thing *as a Brechtian morality tale*

DRT (1989) takes place in a Brooklyn ghetto on the hottest day of the year. Mookie, a young Black man (played by Spike Lee), gets up and goes to work at Sal's Pizzeria on a Saturday morning. Various neighborhood characters appear as Lee paints a tableau of the interactions between Blacks and Italians, and the Hispanic and Korean residents of the Brooklyn ghetto of "Bed Stuy." Conflicts between the Blacks and Italians erupt and when a Black youth is killed by the police, the crowd destroys the pizzeria.

Lee set out to make a film about Black urban experience from a Black perspective and his film transcodes the discourses, style, and conventions of African American culture, with an emphasis on Black nationalism that affirms the specificity of Black experience and its cultural differences from mainstream white culture. Lee presents Black ways of speaking, walking, dressing, and acting, drawing on Black slang, music, images, and style. His films are richly textured ethnographies of urban Blacks negotiating the allures of the consumer and media society, and the dangers of racism and an oppressive urban environment. The result is a body of work that articulates uniquely Black perspectives, voices, styles, and politics.

Yet Lee also draws on the techniques of modernism and produces original innovative films that articulate his own individual vision and aesthetic style. In particular, like the German artist Bertolt Brecht, Spike Lee produces a cinema that dramatizes the necessity of making moral and political choices.[5] Both Brecht and Lee produce "epic drama" that paints a wide tableau of typical social characters, shows examples of social and asocial behavior, and conveys didactic messages to the audience. Both Brecht and Lee utilize music, comedy, drama, vignettes of typical behavior, and figures who articulate the messages desired by the author. Both present didactic learning plays, which strive to teach people to discover and then do "the right thing," while criticizing improper and anti-social behavior. Brecht's theater (as well as his film *Kuhle Wampe* and his radio plays) present character types in situations that force one to observe the consequences of typical behavior. Lee, I would argue, does the same thing in *DRT* (and most of his other films), depicting typical work, familial, and street scenes and behavior. In particular, the three street corner philosophers, who offer comic commentary throughout, are very Brechtian, as is the radio DJ, Mister Señor Love Daddy, who tells the audience not only to do the right thing throughout the movie ("and that's the truth, Ruth"), but he repeatedly specifies "the right thing," insisting that the ghetto population: "Wake Up!," "Love one another," and "Chill!"

DRT posits the question of political and social morality for its audience in the contemporary era: what is "the right thing" politically and morally for oppressed groups like urban Blacks? The film is arguably modernist in that the question of the political "right thing" is left open in the film. By "modernist," I refer, first, to aesthetic strategies of producing texts that are open and polyvocal; that disseminate a wealth of meanings without a central univocal meaning or message; and that require an active reader to produce the meanings.[6] Second, I take modernism to be an aesthetic tendency dedicated to the production of unique works of art that bear the vision and stylistic imprint of their creator. Third, the type of modernism associated with what Peter Burger calls the "historical avant garde" attempts to produce serious works that change individuals' perceptions and lives and strive to promote social transformation. Movements like futurism, expressionism, Dada, and surrealism meet these criteria, as do the works of Brecht and Lee, though I ultimately argue that Lee's films contain a unique mixture of American popular cultural forms and modernism, inflected through Lee's African American experience.[7]

Thus, I am claiming that in a formal sense the works of Spike Lee are in accord with these modernist criteria and that his aesthetic strategies are especially close to those of Brecht. Lee's texts tend to be open, to elicit divergent readings, and to generate a wealth of often divergent responses. He is, in this sense, an "auteur" whose films project a distinctive style and vision which cumulatively exhibit a coherent body of work with distinctive features and effects. His work is highly serious and strives for specific transformative moral and political effects. Yet there are also ambiguities in Lee's work. While the disk jockey, Mister Señor Love Daddy, serves as a voice of social morality (Sittlichkeit, how to treat others) in *DRT*, it is an open question what, if any, political position Lee is affirming. Does he agree with the politics of Malcolm X or MLK? Is he advocating reform or revolution, integration or Black nationalism, or a synthesis of the two?

Throughout the film, Public Enemy's powerful rap song "Fight the Power" resonates, but it is not clear from the film how one is supposed to fight the power, or what political strategies should be employed to carry out the struggle. Indeed, one could read *DRT* as a postmodern evacuation of viable political options for Blacks and people of color in the present age.[8] That is, one can read the film as demonstrating that, politically, there is no "right thing" to do in the situation of hopeless ghetto poverty, virulent racism, and the lack of viable polit-ical options and movements. In this postmodern reading, the film projects a bleak, nihilistic view of the future, marked by hopelessness and the collapse of modern Black politics. In this context, political reformism and Martin Luther King's non-violence appear questionable as viable instruments of change. But it is not clear that violence is an attractive option and one could even read the film as questioning social violence, demonstrating that it ultimately hurts the people in the neighborhoods in which it explodes. (One could read the events in Los Angeles, which Lee's film uncannily anticipates, in a similar light).

On this reading, it is not clear what the power is that one is supposed to fight, what instruments one is supposed to use, and what one's goals are sup-posed to be. This nihilistic postmodern reading suggests that modern politics as a whole are bankrupt,[9] that neither reform or revolution can work, that Blacks in the U.S. are condemned to hopeless poverty and the subordinate position of an oppressed underclass without the faintest possibility of improving their situ-ation by any means whatsoever. Yet one could also read DRT as a modernist film that forces the viewer to compare the different politics of Malcolm X and Martin Luther King and to decide for his or her self what the "right thing" is for Blacks and oppressed groups in the contemporary era. In the following ana-lysis, I'll interrogate whether *DRT* is a modernist or postmodernist film in both its style and politics, and whether Lee privileges Malcolm X or Martin Luther King in the film. But first I want to interrogate the cultural politics of DRT.

The characters in *DRT* are portraits of distinctive neighborhood African, His-panic, Italian, Anglo, and Korean American individuals and Lee depicts typical modes of their behavior and their conflicts with one another. Race for Lee is presented in *DRT* in terms of cultural identity and image, especially cultural style. As Denzin points out (1991: 125, 130ff.), the characters wear T-shirts that identify their cultural politics and style. Mookie, the Black worker in Sal's Piz-zeria, wears a Jackie Robinson baseball jersey, symbolizing the position of a Black who breaks the colorline in the white man's world (as Lee himself has done!). While working, Mookie also wears a shirt with his name on it and the logo of "Sal's Pizzeria," signifying his position between the two worlds. Radio Raheem, whose radio blasts out "Fight the Power," which provokes the con-frontation with Sal, wears a T-shirt proclaiming "Bed-Stuy or Die." This mes-sage identifies him as a figure who asserts Black solidarity and rebellion to preserve the community.

Lee also deploys color-coding symbolism in the wearing of T-shirts, with Pino, Sal's racist son, wearing white, while Vito, his son who gets along with

Blacks, wears a black T-shirt. Sal's clothes codes him as the boss/worker who drives up to his pizzeria in a Cadillac, but he dons an apron to make the pizzas, presenting him as a petit-bourgeois small businessman. Other shirts identify the wearer with white or Black cultural heroes. A young white man who has just purchased a ghetto apartment wears a Larry Bird Boston Celtics' jersey, while a young Black man wears the L.A. Lakers' jersey of Magic Johnson. The Hispanics wear sleeveless colored T-shirts, while the older Black men wear sleeveless white T-shirts, conventional single-colored shirts, or go topless. Most of the young women wear tube tops, though Mookie's sister Jade sports designer clothes.

Clothes and fashion accoutrements depict the various characters styles and identity. Buggin' Out, an angry young Black youth, wears a yellow African kente shirt with a gold chain around his neck and a gold tooth. He also wears Nike Air Jordan shoes (that Lee does commercials for!), and explodes with anger when the Celtic fan accidentally soils them. Radio Raheem wears the same type of shoes himself and his ghetto-blaster and rap music establishes his cultural identity (he only plays Public Enemy). He also displays a set of gold brass knuckle rings, engraved with "love" and "hate": supposedly the two sides of the sometimes gentle and sometimes violent Raheem.[10] Mookie too sports a gold tooth and earring, marking him as a participant in Black urban cultural conventions.[11] The three Black street-corner philosophers, discoursing on the current situation of Blacks, are casually dressed, while the alcoholic Da Mayor (Ossie Davis) wears old and dirty clothes, coding him as an example of failed Black manhood. Mother Sister (Ruby Dee) dresses conventionally and represents traditional matriarchal Black values, disapproving of Da Mayor and "shiftless" young Blacks.

In fact, *DRT* influenced fashion trends of the time: "the summer of 1989 saw millions of young people wearing Mookie-style surfer baggies over lycra bike shorts" (Patterson 1992: 125). In fact, Spike Lee himself opened a fashion store in Brooklyn, designing his own T-shirts and clothes, and he produced and acted in commercials for Nike Air Jordan shoes. He thus depicts a society in which cultural identity is produced through style and consumption and himself contributes to this trend in his films and commercial activity.[12]

The ways that mass cultural images pervade style and fashion suggest that cultural identity is constituted in part by iconic images of ethnic cultural heroes, which are badges of identity and forces of division between the races. Sal has pictures of famous Italian Americans (his "Hall of Fame") on the wall of his pizzeria, and Buggin' Out's demand to put pictures of Blacks on the wall and Sal's vehement refusal to do so precipitates the attempted boycott and the subsequent violence. A stuttering and perhaps mentally retarded young Black teen, Smiley, is selling pictures of Malcolm and Martin,[13] who appear as icons of Black politics, and references to Jessie Jackson and Al Sharpton appear in graffiti, constituting Black political leaders as cultural heroes, along with sports and music stars.

These scenes suggest how media culture provides the material for identity and how different subcultures appropriate different images and style to provide identities. Identity is thus formed on a terrain of struggle in which individuals choose their own cultural meanings and style in a differential system that always involves the affirmation of some tokens of identity and rejection of other ones. Social institutions individuate people with social security numbers, voting registration, consumer lists, data bases, police and academic records, and so on, but producing one's individual identity means refusing to be defined by these determinations and choosing other forms of identity. More and more, it is the case that media culture provides resources that are appropriated by audiences to make meanings, to create identities, as when teenage girls use Madonna as a model, or Blacks emulate African American cultural heroes, or aspiring Yuppies look to professionals on TV shows like for patterns of identity.

Identity is thus mediated by mass-produced images in the contemporary media society, while image and cultural style is becoming ever more central to the construction of individual identities – as I am indicating in this discussion and will take up again in the following chapters. Media culture provides a powerful source of new identities, replacing nationalism, religion, the family, and education as sources of identity. As Benedict Anderson argued (1983), nationalism provided a powerful imaginary community and identities, and the forms of media culture provide surrogates for both individuals and groups who are able to participate in imaginary communities through cultural style and consumption and who can produce individual and group identities through the appropriation of media cultural images.[14]

Media culture also provides modern morality tales that demonstrate right and wrong behavior, that show what to do and what not to do, that indicate what is or is not "the right thing." Media culture is thus an important new force of socialization and it is one of the merits of *DRT* to put this process of the creation of identity through image and cultural style on display in a fashion that shows as well how different identities are produced in opposition to each other and represent a terrain in which social conflicts are played out.

DRT shows how cultural identity is also articulated through music and expressive styles. The Black DJ and Radio Raheem play exclusively Black music, while the Puerto Rican street teens play Spanish-inflected music. A scene where Radio Raheem and the Puerto Ricans duel each other with loud playing radios signifies the cultural clash and divisions in the ghetto community. In addition, Sal provokes Radio Raheem by ordering him to "turn that jungle music off. We ain't in Africa," while Buggin' Out replies: "Why it gotta be about jungle music and Africa."

Thus, different cultures use popular music to establish their cultural identities and different styles of music divide the community. But it is the racial epithets that most pungently articulate the contemporary social conflicts and tensions between racial groups. At a key juncture in the film, in modernist and Brechtian fashion, Lee interrupts his narrative and has the characters look into the camera and spit out vicious racial slurs, with Mookie attacking the Italians ("Dago, Wop, guinea, garlic breath, pizza slingin', spaghetti bender," etc.). Pino, the racist son, replies to the camera, assaulting Blacks: "Gold chain wearin' fried chicken and biscuit eatin' monkey, ape, baboon, fast runnin', high jumpin', spear chuckin', basket ball dunkin' titso spade, take your fuckin' pizza and go back to Africa."

A Puerto Rican attacks Koreans in similar racial terms and the Korean grocer attacks Jews. This scene, thoroughly Brechtian, brilliantly shows the racial differences encoded in language, but tends to equate all modes of racism as logically equivalent, whereas one could argue that the institutional racism against Blacks is far more virulent than the variegated cultural racisms articulated here, and one could argue that Lee's earliest work does not really catch the reality of racism as part of a structural and hierarchical system of oppression.[15] On this structuralist view, the existing society especially oppresses people of color: it is, then, not just the case that there is racism, and racial hatred, among all the races and ethnicities, but there is an unequal distribution of power and wealth in contemporary U.S. society, in which Blacks and people of color tend to suffer disproportionately from systemic racial and class oppression, bolstered by an ideology of white supremacy, which the Trump era has shown continues to be alive and still destructive in the U.S.A. today. Put otherwise, Lee's DRT does present capitalism as a system of oppression, which especially exploits and oppresses its underclass, particularly people of color.

Thus, DRT has its insights, as well as its limitations, and a diagnostic critique can read the film as articulating some of the conditions that produce violence in the ghettoes. The film is particularly strong in depicting the ghetto explosion that erupts after Radio Raheem is killed by white policemen when he and Sal start fighting. Lee has his own character Mookie throw a garbage can through the window of Sal's Pizzeria and violence breaks out that destroys the establishment. A close viewing of Mookie's action suggests that it was a conscious, deliberate act and that Lee was presenting it as "the right thing." The camera zooms in on Mookie deliberating about what to do after the police have accidentally choked Radio Raheem to death, in a fight that began when Sal smashed his beloved radio. Lee then pans a long and slow shot of Mookie studiedly walking away to pick up a garbage can and then return to throw it through the window of the pizzeria, starting the riot that ends in its destruction. It is clear that he is doing it because of rage over Radio Raheem's death and that Lee is depicting the act as a conscious, deliberate act on Mookie's part.[16]

On this reading, Lee is privileging human life over property and is suggesting that violence against property is a legitimate act of retaliation. One could also argue that Mookie is directing the mob's violence against the pizzeria and away from Sal and his sons, thus ultimately protecting them against the mob's wrath.[17] It is, of course, debatable whether the act of violence was "the right thing," as it is a rejection of King's philosophy of non-violence. Yet it is not clear that this act produces anything positive for Mookie or the Black community; one could indeed argue the opposite.[18] Smiley puts the picture of Malcolm X and Martin Luther King standing side by side on the wall, thus fulfilling Raheem's desire to have Black images in the pizzeria. But they are shown burning in the wall, raising the question of whether this can be read as a sign of the futility of Black politics in the present age, allegorically enacting the fading away of the relevance of Malcolm and Martin in the current moment.

In any case, the (white conservative) critique that *DRT* was "bad" because it was likely to produce violence and increase race hatred is misplaced. Rather, Lee's film reveals the living conditions and the racial tensions and conflicts that are likely to produce racial and other forms of urban violence. That is, DRT explores the social environment that produces violence and urban explosions. In interviews after the film, Lee protested that he was only depicting certain situations and not offering solutions, and this position seems wholly reasonable.

Yet there have been readings of his work that criticize Lee for deconstructing modern politics as futile or irrelevant, thus giving voice to a postmodern nihilism.[19] However, certain aspects of the film counter this reading of *DRT* as an expression of a bleak, postmodern pessimism that would affirm the obsolescence of a modern Black politics of the sort typified by Malcolm and Martin. Lee himself later claimed that he is affirming a politics that would embrace aspects of both King and Malcolm, that would use both men's philosophies and strategies for social change in different contexts. He calls attention to the still picture put on the wall of the pizzeria as it burns:

> Malcolm X and Dr. King are shaking hands and smiling. So when I put those two quotes there, it was not a question of either/or, not for me, anyway, just a choice of tactics. I think they were men who chose different paths trying to reach the same destination against a common opponent.
>
> *(Lee and Wiley 1992: 5)*

Thus, the seemingly opposing quotes of King and Malcolm X that close *DRT* both, on this view, articulate valid positions and it would thus be a question of context concerning which view was most appropriate. Yet the scenario of the film itself seems to privilege Malcolm X, who would eventually be the topic of Lee's major film epic to date. Indeed, the vision of *DRT* is in some ways consistent with Malcolm X's Black nationalist teachings and thus does affirm certain modern political positions. One of the street corner philosophers expresses wonder and chagrin that the Korean grocer can turn a boarded-up building into a successful business, while Blacks cannot. Surely this is a nod toward Malcolm X's views on Black self-sufficiency and economic independence, and certainly Spike Lee has enacted this philosophy as successfully as anyone in the Black community. It is clear that Mookie is going to get nowhere working in Sal's Pizzeria and the other home-boys in the movie are also rapidly going nowhere.

"Time to wake up, brothers, and get your shit together," following the examples of brothers Malcolm and Spike, is an arguable message of the film.

Likewise, Malcolm X put a heavy emphasis on Black manhood, standing up to the white power structure, fighting back, and acting decisively to maintain one's self-respect. In that sense, Mookie's violent action instantiated certain of Malcolm's teachings, though one could raise the question whether this was in fact "the right thing." One could also raise some questions concerning whether Malcolm X did or advocated the "right thing" politically at various phases of his life and what his legacy is for us today. I will interrogate Spike Lee's *Malcolm X* from these perspectives, arguing that the film, like *Do the Right Thing*, is ultimately a morality tale and that Lee's can neither be pinned down to specific modern positions (i.e. Martin or Malcolm), nor to postmodern nihilism as some critics claimed of his early work in the 1990s.

From Malcolm X *to* BlacKkKlansman

From the perspective of my reading of *DRT*, one could argue that *Malcolm X* (1992) can be read as a morality tale interrogating what is the "right thing" for Blacks in contemporary U.S. society in both the individual and the political sense. In this reading, it is the figure of Malcolm X that is the center of the film and the key transitions involve his transforming himself from criminal to dedicated Black nationalist working for the Nation of Islam, and then transforming himself again into a more secular internationalist. The key, then, is Malcolm X as moral ideal, as a model of a Black transforming making something of himself, becoming self-sovereign, rather than any specific political position or message that Malcolm X taught.

Although Lee strongly affirms Malcolm X's politics, he is not, I believe, an uncritical sycophant and hagiographer, and puts in question many of Malcolm X's views, while forcing the audience to decide whether the actions of Malcolm or other characters in his films are indeed "the right thing." I thus see *X* and *DRT* as political morality plays and believe that Spike Lee was perfectly justified to tell Black and other children to skip school to see the film *X*. Not only does one learn a great deal about one of the most important figures of our time, but one is forced to reflect upon what is the "right thing" for individual and political morality. Yet I would argue that Lee's film on Malcolm X focuses more on Malcolm as a role model for Blacks and is more of a morality tale than a political drama. The life of Malcolm X is certainly exemplary as an example of a figure able to undergo profound self-transformation and to forge his own individual identity under difficult circumstances (the delineation of such righteous models is also congruent with Brechtian strategy).

The first part of *Malcolm X*, arguably, shows what the wrong thing is for Blacks today, that is, to engage in a life of crime, drugs, and shallow materialism.[20] Yet Lee invests so much time and energy to this phase of Malcolm's life that it makes the one-time criminal Malcolm Little almost attractive and certainly sympathetic. Malcolm X himself in his autobiography presents Malcolm Little as a very bad dude and negative figure (Haley and X 1965), though it does not seem that this image emerges from Lee's film. Denzel Washington creates an engaging character and Lee's use of comedy and melodrama invests the Malcolm Little character with positive energies. So although he is caught in criminal activity and goes to jail, the film tends to glorify his early life, full of high times with white women, drugs, exciting high jinks, and good buddies.[21]

Lee uses the strategy of epic realist historical tableaux in this sequence, heavily seasoned with comedy, satire, and music. As always, music is extremely important in Lee's films and X can be seen and heard as a history of Black music over the decades and how it was an integral part of the texture of everyday life. Once again, parallels with Brecht are obvious, as Brecht used music to capture the ethos and style of an age and as a way of making, or highlighting, certain didactic points. Moreover, it is clear that Lee is presenting certain forms of Black behavior, such as "conking" hair, as negative, and the early sequences contain the obvious moral that a life of crime leads to jail. The message concerning Black men involving themselves with white women is less clear, though Lee tends to present interracial relationships negatively in X and his other films like *Jungle Fever*.[22]

The prison sequence shows Malcolm Little refusing to submit to the humiliations of prison life and then being broken by solitary punishment. Yet he is also shown coming to accept Black Muslim teaching and bettering himself through study. It is one of Lee's pervasive messages that education is the way to "Uplift the Race" (one of the mottos of Lee's film *School Daze* [1988], and the title of the book on that film), and certainly Malcolm X embodies a positive model of this philosophy, as he is shown learning to study and to gain knowledge. Indeed, Malcolm X emerges from prison a totally changed man and an exemplar of an individual who undertakes to transform himself successfully.

So far, the aesthetic strategies of X can be read as a Brechtian epic drama, as a Brechtian morality tale which embodies specific lessons for Blacks and others through showing tableaux of social and asocial behavior contrasting positive and negative values and behavior. Lee deploys a variety of genres and styles, and mixes in music, comedy, and dramatic flashbacks into key episodes of Malcolm X's early life (the mixing of genres is also Brechtian). The last third of the film continues this strategy, though it is too dense and compressed to present adequately Malcolm X's teaching and the complexity of his later positions. The key episode is the shift from Malcolm X's adherence to the teachings of Elijah Muhammad and the Nation of Islam to his radical activist social philosophy. Yet there was, arguably, too much of the religious and dubious racial teachings of the Nation of Islam and not enough of Malcolm X's late social philosophy, which many believe is his most valuable radical legacy.[23]

In Lee's defense, he does spend much energy trying to make clear the reasons for Malcolm X's break with the Nation of Islam and shows that Malcolm underwent a very significant transition to a radically new position, thus again making the point concerning the importance of radical self-transformation. Lee also dealt with the complexity of Malcolm X's assassination and the strong possibility that both the Nation of Islam and U.S. government agencies were involved in his murder – as opposed to just pinning it on the Nation of Islam. He also strongly emphasized that the "mature" Malcolm saw that all colors were equal in his experiences in Mecca. In fact, I am bracketing the question of historical accuracy in my discussion (upon which much of the critique of the film has focused, both from Lee's friends and enemies) and am focusing instead on the issue of aesthetic strategy and the politics of the film.[24]

Spike Lee continued to make a series of political films, documentaries, and a TV series based on his film *She's Gotta Have It* (2017–2019) critically engaging race, representations, and the African American experience. Indeed, since his early work in the 1980s Spike Lee has been one of the most productive and outstanding filmmakers of his generation making significant fictional films following *X* like *Crooklyn* (1994); *Clockers* (1995); *Girl 6* (1996); *Get on the Bus* (1996); *He Got Game* (1998); *Summer of Sam* (1999); *Bamboozled* (2000); *25th Hour* (2002); *She Hate Me* (2004); *Inside Man* (2006); *Miracle at St. Anna* (2008); *Red Hook Summer* (2012); *Oldboy* (2013); *Da Sweet Blood of Jesus* (2014); *Chi-Raq* (2015; and *BlacKkKlansman* (2018). Lee has also made a highly impressive and underappreciated series of documentaries including *4 Little Girls* (1997); *Freak* (1998); *The Original Kings of Comedy* (2000); *A Huey P. Newton Story* (2001); *The Concert for New York City* (2001); "Come Rain or Come Shine" (2001); *Jim Brown: All-American* (2002); *When the Levees Broke* (2006); *Kobe Doin' Work* (2009); *Passing Strange* (2009); *If God Is Willing and da Creek Don't Rise* (2010); *Bad 25* (2012); and *Michael Jackson's Journey from Motown to Off the Wall* (2016). This astonishing body of work certainly qualifies Spike Lee to be appreciated as one of the greatest filmmakers of his generation.

Lee's 2018 film *BlacKkKlansman* is based on the 2014 memoir *Black Klansman* by Ron Stallworth, starring John David Washington as Stallworth, a Black policeman who went uncover to investigate the Ku Klux Klan in the 1970s. Set in Colorado Springs, the plot follows the first African American detective in the city's police department as he sets out to infiltrate and expose the local Ku Klux Klan chapter.

BlacKkKlansman opens with footage of wounded Confederate soldiers lying in the streets of Atlanta, Georgia, from *Gone with the Wind* in 1939, which evokes the history of Hollywood celebrating the South and promoting racism. Lee's film cuts to a Black-and-white PSA, where a Dr. Kennebrew Beauregard (Alec Baldwin) spews and botches a contemporary racist diatribe, signally that racism is alive and well. We are then introduced to Ron Stallworth, an African American interviewing for, and getting, a job on the Colorado Springs Police Department, the first African American to do so. "Re-elect Nixon" signs on the wall suggest that the story takes place in the mid-1970s, and during Stallworth's interview we see that the Police Department is blatantly racist on many levels.

Ron Stallworth's book, and Lee's film, describes how he infiltrated the Ku Klux Klan, when after seeing an ad for the local chapter of the KKK in the local newspaper, he calls the telephone number and is invited to interview to join the "Organization," as the Klan members refer to their outfit. Of course, Stallworth cannot himself go to the interview so he recruits his Jewish co-worker, Flip Zimmerman (Adam Driver), to act as him to meet the Klan members. Zimmerman meets local Klan members who show off their guns and talk about an upcoming attack on Blacks.

Stallworth calls Klan headquarters in Louisiana to expedite his membership, and begins regular phone conversations with Klan "Grand Wizard" David Duke. Using the mode of comedic satire, Lee makes the Klan members and David Duke ludicrous but dangerous. David Duke is presented as a precursor of Donald Trump shouting out slogans like "Make America great again!", and using the phrase "America first," showing the connections between racism of the 1970s and the Trump era; the posters of Nixon also evoke the lineage.

A powerful montage sequence features Harry Belafonte as a veteran activist addressing his audience about the 1916 lynching of a Black man Jessie Turner in Texas, accused of raping a white woman, while another sequence in which the KKK hold a sinister initiation ceremony to induct new members concludes with explicitly juxtaposing cries of "White power!" with "Black power!" evoking the racial divisions that have intensified under Donald Trump and the normalization of White Supremacy during the Trump era.

After several plot complications, Stallworth stops the Klan from a murderous bomb attack by the bumbling wife of a local Klan leader, and is able to tape a drunken police officer bragging about his assault on a local Black Student Union member, thus providing happy endings and tying up the plot threads. The Happy Ending effect is soon shattered, however, when the police see a flaming cross on a hillside surrounded by Klan members, followed by footage from the 2017 far-right Unite the Right rally in Charlottesville, Virginia. The footage depicts the car-ramming attack by James Alex Fields killing Heather Heyer, Trump's speech about good people on all sides, and David Duke praising Trump. The montage concludes with a shot of an upside-down American flag fading into Black and white, signaling that racism is alive and as virulent as ever.

Spike Lee's *BlacKkKlansman* was one of many 2018 films dealing with race. In a controversial call, it lost the Academy Award to *Green Book* (2018), a buddy/white savior film that depicted African American entertainer Don Cherry's white driver teaching him about the harsh realities of racism, an awareness that friends and relatives claimed Cherry possessed without the help of his white driver. *Green Book* did depict a shameful era of racism in U.S. history in which intense segregation forced people of color to use a Green Book, to see which hotels, restaurants, and other places in the South were safe for African Americans.

Yet as a reaction to the public expression of virulent racism by the president and his supporters, there have been many films in the Trump era featuring

African American directors and themes, depicting racism and Black and female empowerment, and in the next section I will discuss some of these works, while a later section will take up Latino filmmakers over the past decade and how a variety of filmmakers of color have depicted immigration to the promised land, which has been under assault since the first day of the Trump (mis) Administration.

Ava DuVernay and female empowerment

As the films of Spike Lee attest, media culture provides opportunities for people of color to express their experience, vision, and politics. Other filmmakers of color have also used film, television, and new media to address race and their lives and experience in multiple forms in significant works of contemporary media culture. In the following sections I discuss the recent work of Ava DuVernay and the themes of Black and female empowerment, followed by analysis of *The Hate You Give*, a study of police violence and a young Black woman coming of age. In the concluding sections, I discuss some examples of contemporary media culture that engage Latinos, Asians and Asian Americans, and the theme of immigration.

Media culture has traditionally been – and to a significant sense still is – a bastion of white male power, although people of color, women, gays and lesbians, and members of other groups excluded from mainstream culture have intervened in recent decades and have increasingly constituted media culture as a contested terrain over race, gender, sexuality, class and representation.

Ava Marie DuVernay had a double major in English literature and African American studies at UCLA and sees herself as part of the LA rebellion film movement including Charles Burnett (*Killer of Sheep*, 1978; *My Brother's Wedding*, 1983; *To Sleep with Anger*, 1990; *The Glass Shield*, 1994; and *Namibia: The Struggle for Liberation*, 2007); Julie Dash (*Daughters of the Dust*), and Haile Gerima (*Sankofa*, *Ashes and Embers*), who attended UCLA film school between the 1970s and 1990s. Her second feature film *Middle of Nowhere* won the 2012 Sundance Film Festival directing award in the U.S. dramatic competition. For her work on *Selma* (2014), DuVernay became the first Black woman to be nominated for a Golden Globe Award for Best Director, and to have her film nominated for the Academy Award for Best Picture. In 2017, she was nominated for the Academy Award for Best Documentary Feature for her film on race and the criminal justice system in the U.S. *13th* (2016), and has won acclaim for the 2019 Netflix drama miniseries *When They See Us*, based on the 1989 Central Park jogger case, which she created, directed, and co-wrote, producing as well a TV series, *Queen Sugar* (2017–present).

DuVerany's *Selma* is based on the 1965 Selma to Montgomery voting rights marches led by Martin Luther King, Jr., John Lewis, and others. The film opens with Martin Luther King, Jr. (David Oyelowo) accepting his Nobel Peace Prize in 1964 juxtaposed with four Black girls walking down the stairs in the

Birmingham, Alabama, 16th Street Baptist Church who are killed by a bomb set by the Ku Klux Klan, followed by images of a young Black woman Annie Lee Cooper (Oprah Winfrey) attempting to register to vote in Selma, Alabama, who is prevented from registering by an obnoxious racist white registrar.

A major narrative strand of *Selma* shows King meeting with President Lyndon B. Johnson (Tom Wilkinson) and asking for federal legislation to allow Black citizens to register to vote through removing traditional barriers, while Johnson explains that his priority is the war on poverty that he argues will help Black and white citizens. Eventually, King's persistence pays off, but it takes dramatic marches in Selma for the right to vote, southern racist mass arrests and the murder of Blacks, and eventually intense media focus on the civil rights movement to drive Johnson to address voting rights and civil rights.

DuVernay creates a detailed portrait of King and his relations with Black civil rights activists Ralph Abernathy, Andrew Young, James Orange, and Diane Nash, and depicts tensions between King's liberal and non-violent Southern leadership Conference organization and more radical Student Nonviolent Coordinating Committee (SNCC) activists. She also depicts FBI director J. Edgar Hoover's (Tim Roth) attempts to destroy King by attempting to disrupt his marriage to Coretta Scott King (Carmen Ejogo), although the film does not depict Hoover's campaign to smear King as a communist.

A key focus of *Selma* involves the efforts of King and other SCLC leaders leading Black Selma residents to march to the registration office to register to vote, and then organizing a major nationally impactful march after initial attempts to demonstrate and register are met by harsh police brutality and the arrest of King and other leaders. *Selma* also shows Alabama Governor George Wallace speaking out against the movement and using state troopers to assault the demonstrators. Another major theme involves Coretta Scott King Coretta meeting with Malcolm X, who says he will drive whites to ally with King by advocating a more extreme position, and King's relations with SNCC, which included future major Black leaders like Jon Lewis and Stokely Carmichael. King's discussions with these various civil rights leaders enables the viewer to get insight into King's specific philosophy of non-violence and the position of other African American activists of the period.

Eventually, Gov. George Wallace chooses to use force at an upcoming night march in Marion, Alabama, deploying state troopers to assault the marchers. Intense and powerful scenes depict the violence that King and other civil rights activists experienced, and highlight King persisting in the struggle but always insisting on non-violent protest. Meanwhile, the Kings receive harassing phone calls, including a recording of sexual activity implied to be MLK and another woman, leading to an argument with Coretta, who nonetheless chooses to stand by him and the movement.

A significant part of *Selma* deals with the difficulties in organizing the Selma to Montgomery march, and pressures to cancel it, with King himself having misgivings. The narrative leads, however, to the march eventually taking place as King, John Lewis of SNCC, Hosea Williams of SCLC, and an army of Selma activists cross the Edmund Pettus Bridge and approach a line of state troopers armed and with gas masks. The troopers order the marchers to turn back, and when they hold their ground the troopers attack with clubs, horses, tear gas, and other weapons. The attack is shown on national television and pressures mount for Johnson to send federal troops to protect the marchers, while Johnson himself tries to persuade King to postpone a second planned march.

King receives permission from a federal judge to march, but after praying, turns around and leads the group away as another march begins, and King comes under sharp criticism from SNCC activists. Further, a white supporter of the march is killed by local thugs, and it looks like King's movement is unravelling. Yet King rallies and the largest march to date takes place from Selma to Montgomery. Concluding scenes of *Selma* show how King and his fellow activists' persistence paid off, as Lyndon Johnson calls on Congress to carry out a quick passage of a civil rights act, and praises the courage of Dr. King and his other activists. The film concludes with a long montage of the march on the highway from Selma to Montgomery with focus on the faces of the marchers, Black and white, young and older, followed by a rousing speech by King on the steps of the Alabama State Capitol.

In 2016, DuVernay produced a documentary *13th* that explores the intersection of racism, injustice, and mass incarceration in the United States. *13th* begins with an audio clip of former President Barack Obama stating that the U.S. had 5% of the world's population but 25% of the world's prisoners. *13th* explores the economic history of slavery and post-Civil War racist legislation and practices that replaced a plantation slave economy with "systems of racial control" and forced labor from chain gangs and prison farms

13th is titled after the Thirteenth Amendment to the United States Constitution, adopted in 1865, which abolished slavery throughout the United States and ended involuntary servitude except as a punishment for conviction of a crime. Yet DuVernay's documentary contends that slavery has been perpetuated since the end of the American Civil War through criminalizing behavior and enabling police to arrest poor freed Blacks, forcing them to work for the state under convict leasing, which is a form of slavery. The documentary also engages the suppression of African Americans by disenfranchisement, lynchings, and Jim Crow segregation laws.

13th suggests that the criminalization of minor offenses, not only forced Blacks into new forms of slave labor, but also disenfranchised many Blacks across the South, excluding them from the political system (including juries), at the same time that lynching of Blacks by white mobs reached a peak. In addition, Jim Crow legislation was passed to legalize segregation and suppress minorities, forcing them into second-class status.

13th features major activists, academics, political figures from both major U.S. political parties, and public figures, such as Angela Davis, Van Jones, Newt Gingrich, Cory Booker, Henry Louis Gates Jr., and other figures. Experts interviewed note that law and order political campaigns, the so-called war on drugs, and criminal justice "reform," that calls for harsher penalties and longer sentences, impact more heavily on minority communities and had created, by the late twentieth century, mass incarceration of people of color in the United States.

DuVernay's *13th* thus examines both the emergence of the prison-industrial complex and current forms of the detention-industrial complex, discussing how much money is being made by corporations from such incarcerations. Scholars note how mass incarceration has steadily increased since the 1970s and that today one out of four Americans have been imprisoned, making the U.S. the industrial nation with the highest rates of incarceration.[25]

In depicting this deplorable situation, *13th* explores the role of the American Legislative Exchange Council (ALEC), backed by major corporations, rightwing think tanks, and the Republican Party that has provided Republican state and federal legislators with draft legislation to support the prison-industrial complex. The film contends that only after some of the relationships were revealed did corporations like Wal-Mart and others receive criticism and drop out of the organization, although ALEC continues to be an influential force continuing mass incarceration and the oppression of Blacks.

13th ends with graphic videos of fatal shootings of Blacks by police, evoking the Black Lives Matter Movement and the need to curtail police violence against Blacks, that is reaching epidemic proportions. *13th* was funded by Netflix and garnered acclaim from a number of film critics, receiving a nomination for the Academy Award for Best Documentary Feature at the 89th Academy Awards, and it won the Primetime Emmy Award for Outstanding Documentary or Nonfiction Special at the 69th Primetime Emmy Awards. Netflix also produced an interview with Oprah Winfrey and DuVernay that reveals a highly progressive Oprah and a highly articulate DuVernay who acknowledges that she learned much on the art of interviewing from Oprah. DuVernay noted that each of the many conservative and progressive figures interviewed for the film agreed to a two-hour interview, which she drew on to document the arguments embodied in the film.

DuVernay has also produced a powerful TV mini-series for Netflix, *When They See Us* (2019), which she created, co-wrote, and directed. The series is based on events of the 1989 Central Park jogger case and explores the lives of the families and the five young Black male suspects who were prosecuted in 1990 on charges related to the rape and assault of a woman in Central Park, New York City, the year before.

When They See Us humanizes the five suspects who were prosecuted on charges related to the sexual assault of a female victim, by presenting them as individuals, as members of their families and communities, and as victims of intense racism. DuVernay thus dramatizes that the five young Black male protagonists of the series, who include Kevin Richardson (Asante Blackk), Antron McCray (Caleel Harris), Yusef Salaam (Ethan Herisse), Korey Wise (Jharrel

Jerome), and Raymond Santana (Marquis Rodriguez) were individual human beings with families and loved ones that were unjustly prosecuted. The young men were divided by the prosecutor into two groups for trial, and all were convicted by juries of various charges related to the assault, with four convicted of rape. They were sentenced to maximum terms for juveniles and the one adult, Korey Wise, who was 16 at the time of the crime, was held in adult facilities and served his time in adult prison.

After the true assailant was identified in 2002 by confession, DNA evidence, and other evidence in an investigation by the DA's office, the DA requested that the court vacate the convictions of the five men (a legal position in which the parties are treated as though no trial has taken place). By that time, all the men had served their sentences, and the state withdrew all charges against them from the 1989 case and removed them from the sex offender registry.

The by now young men and their families filed a suit against the city in 2003 for wrongful conviction and were awarded a settlement in 2014. They also filed a suit against the state, and received a settlement in 2016, although the latter settlement was not covered in the DuVernay's miniseries. *When They See Us* demonstrated that Black lives matter, and that racial injustice is an intolerable feature of U.S. society and culture. The mini-series shows Donald Trump exploiting the tragedy to call for the death penalty for the young victims in early stages of the trial, and that the media in general were prejudiced against the young Black men who could not have a fair trial with all the adverse publicity against them.

While Spike Lee's *BlacKkKlansman* and Ava DuVerny's *Selma, 13th*, and *When They See Us* use dramatic historical episodes and a variety of aesthetic strategies to present aspects of the recent history of racism in the U.S., George Tillman Jr.'s *The Hate U Give* (2018) draws on the 2017 novel of the same name by Angie Thomas to provide an exploration of police violence on the African American community with a focus on a typical Black family. The story centers on Starr Carter (Amandla Stenberg), a 16-year-old American Black girl who lives in the fictional, Black neighborhood of Garden Heights, but attends a white private school, Williamson Prep. The film opens with an introduction to Starr's family, and she recounts how her father, Maverick, who runs a local grocery store, gave her and her brothers "The Talk," telling them how to comport themselves when confronted by the police. Starr also learns of Tupac's "Thug Life" saying, "The hate U give little infants fucks everybody."

At a party Starr is attending, she meets her childhood best friend, Khalil. After gun shots ring out, Starr and Khalil flee, and Khalil offers to drive her home. They are stopped by a white police officer who orders Khalil to exit the car; while outside the car, Khalil reaches through the driver-side window to check on Starr and he picks up a hairbrush. The white officer sees Khalil has an object in his hand and fires three shots at him. Starr runs to Khalil and the officer tells Starr to sit then discovers that Khalil had a hairbrush, not a gun. The episode replicates the appalling shooting of young African Americans by the police and thus transcodes an issue of immense contemporary relevance into a cinematic narrative.

Although Khalil's death becomes a national news story, Starr's identity as the witness is initially kept secret from those outside Starr's family. Focus shifts to Starr's relationships with her white Williamson high school friends, Hailey and Maya, and Starr's white boyfriend, Chris. Starr suffers with the knowledge that she alone knows the story of Khail's death and her relations become strained with her white friends.

After pressure from Black activists, Starr agrees to be interviewed on television and to testify in front of a grand jury, demonstrating how Black activists use the media to promote a progressive agenda and dramatize compelling political issues. During the TV interview, in which her identity is hidden, Starr names the King Lords, the gang that controls her neighborhood and that her father was once involved in. The gang retaliates by threatening Starr and her family, forcing them to move in with her Uncle Carlos, who is a police detective. We learn that Carlos was a father figure to Starr when her father, Maverick, spent three years in prison for his gang activity with the King Lords. Following his release, Maverick left the gang and became the owner of the Garden Heights grocery store where Starr and her half-brother, Seven, work. Maverick was only allowed to leave the King Lords because his false confession to a crime kept gang leader King from being locked up. King, widely feared in the neighborhood, now lives with Starr's young brother Seven's mother and Seven's half-sister, Kenya, who is friends with Starr.

After a grand jury fails to indict the white officer, Garden Heights erupts into both peaceful protests and riots, replicating events that have occurred frequently in the last decades in an epidemic of police violence.[26] The failure of the criminal justice system to hold the officer accountable pushes Starr to take an increasingly public role, including speaking out during the protests, which are met by police in riot gear. Her increasing identification with the people of Garden Heights causes tension with Starr's school friends and especially with her boyfriend, Chris, and her girlfriend Hailey, who fails to recognize racist comments that she makes.

Near the end of the film, Starr and Seven get trapped in Maverick's grocery store, which is fire-bombed by King and his gang. The two escape with the help of Maverick and some other Garden Heights business owners. When the police arrive, Starr's younger brother Sekani points a gun at King, illustrating Tupac's Thug Life saying, "The hate U give little infants fucks everybody." Starr defuses the situation, and the community stands up against King, who goes to jail. At the end, Starr promises to keep Khalil's memory alive and to continue her advocacy against injustice, providing a positive, uplifting message for the audience.

The Hate U Give thus takes a strong stand against both police violence and gang violence, and warns how hate can be transmitted from generation to generation in a never-ending circle of violence. It portrays Starr coming of age, able to navigate multiple worlds, and to stand up for what is right. It shows how film can both be an important pedagogical tool and a force against racism and police violence, engaging important issues of the contemporary era.

Latino, immigration, and the American dream

While many noteworthy films appeared about African Americans during the past decades, other significant communities of color have been relatively ignored in the mainstream cinema,[27] although a large number of mostly independent films have undertaken exploring the lives and experiences of Latinos, Asian Americans, and other ethnic groups. In the mainstream Hollywood cinema, Latinos have tended over the last decades to be featured in dramas like *Traffic* (1990) or the TV series *Narcos* (2018–present) that deal with drug trafficking, or biographies of famous Latina women like *Frida* (2002) or *Selena* (1997).[28]

Luis Valdez, regarded as the father of Chicano theater in the United States for his creation of El Teatro Campesino, can also be seen as one of the founders of the contemporary Latino cinema.[29] Valdez's film of his successful play *Zoot Suit* (1984) was followed by his popular film *La Bamba* (1987) about rock and roll legend Ritchie Valens. *Zoot Suit* weaves a story involving the real-life events of the Sleepy Lagoon murder trial and the Zoot Suit riots of the 1940s, set against the background of fraught relations between Mexican Americans and the police and the events of World War II. The film focuses on Henry Reyna (Daniel Valdez), a pachuco gangster, and his gang, who were unjustly jailed for a murder they did not commit. Heavy with Latino cultural references, Reyna is doubled by an imaginary character El Pachuco, memorably performed by Edward James Olmos, who both advances and comments on the narrative.

Zoot Suit stands as a sharp indictment of the racism against Latinos and a cultural expression of Mexican American identity and cultural expression with its mixture of English and Spanish expression, Chicano style, and experimental rupture with the smooth narrative form and characters of Hollywood cinema. *Zoot Suit* careens from depictions of Henry's family life, his desire to serve in World War II, his arrest, incarceration, and trial – punctuated by the commentary and powerful presence of his alter ego El Pachuco who taunts his faith in the system and warns him against succumbing to the oppressive forces around him. The doubling itself expresses the hybrid identities of Mexican Americans and their occupation of a contested space within U.S. culture and society, although it also serves narratively as performing Henry's alter ego, his other self.

La Bamba also engages Mexican American identity and culture, depicting a young teenager Richard Steven Valenzuela (played by Lou Diamond Phillips) becoming a rock "n" roll superstar under the stage name Ritchie Valens. Ritchie meets and falls in love with high school classmate Donna Ludwig, an upper middle class Anglo whose father forbids them to date and tries to keep them apart. Ritchie writes a song for her, "Donna," an expression of forlorn love and loving that becomes a major hit and eventually wins her heart.

However, Ritchie's most important experience that constructs his cultural identity results from his brother Bob, who, sensing that Ritchie "needs to get laid," take him to a Tijuana brothel. In the brothel, Ritchie is initially mesmerized by the Mexican folkloric song "La Bamba," although eventually is initiated into the mysteries of sex as he awakens in a hut outside the city with an older Mexican shaman who skins a snake, which Ritchie eats, hallucinates, and returns home, ready to record "La Bamba" and become a rock superstar. While El Pachucho served as Hank Reynes' double, Ritchie's brother Bob serves as his double and other, the troubled and destructive sibling and alter ego who in some ways is his guide, but in others is the "bad dude" that Ritchie avoids. Portrayed as a drunk who steals Ritchie's girlfriend, impregnates, beats and abandons her, Bob is the "bad" destructive Other to Ritchie's sweet, sincere, loving and creative self who achieves great cultural success and brings happiness to his mother and relatives, while Bob's failures and destructive behavior are a source of shame.

Ritchie's rise to success is punctuated with a recurring dream of a midair collision between two planes over his school, which he tells Donna killed his best friend. Ritchie initially tries to avoid flying to his concerts and appearances, but must conquer his fear when invited to perform "Donna" on the popular show *American Bandstand*. Ritchie's record producer and manager, Bob Keane, helps him by giving him a little vodka to calm his nerves during the flight to Philadelphia.

The film, and Ritchie's life, concludes when he and fellow young rock superstars Buddy Holly and "The Big Bopper" take off in an airplane during a snowstorm for their fateful flight on February 3, 1959. Ritchie is shown to be extremely nervous, yet before the flight, he calls his brother Bob, to try to reconcile and even begs Bob to fly out to Chicago to join the tour, claiming that he needs "family" with him. However, Ritchie's dream of the exploding plane becomes a macabre reality, and the next day Bob and his fans of the period like myself, are shocked to hear a news bulletin on the radio that Ritchie Valens, Buddy Holley, and the Big Bopper were all killed on a plane crash without any survivors during "the night the lights went out."

Valdez is sometimes criticized for his male-focused narratives, though there have also been distinguished biopics of Latina female cultural icons like the artist Frida Kahlo and singer Selana.[30] *Frida* presents a sympathetic portrait of Mexican artist Frida Kahlo, centering on her relationships with her husband Diego Riviera, also a renowned Mexican painter. Directed by Julie Traymor, who has roots in theatrical, musical, and opera production, *Frida* combines a modernist fractured narrative of a 30-year span of Frida Kahlo's life with moments of surrealism and magical realism that illuminate her life and artistic production. The titular character is played by Salma Hayek who plays an important creative role in the film, shaping Kahlo as a strong but vulnerable woman who overcomes tragedy (this is made clear in interviews on the DVD of the film and in Molina-Guzman).

Frida begins with cuts of a mature Frida Kahlo being put on stretcher into an ambulance with colorful images of exotic plants, flowers, and a garden that would represent the colorfulness of Mexican life, a motif used throughout the film. Action quickly moves, however, to an earlier period of her life in which Kahlo suffered a traumatic accident at the age of 18. Traymore uses harsh expressionist images and music to portray the wooden bus Frida was riding colliding with a streetcar, sustaining injuries that would plague her for the rest of her life. The hospital scene cuts to harsh white lighting in which color is erased and Frida is plunged into a void.

Awakening three weeks later, her loving and supportive father brings her a canvas upon which to start painting and we see Kahlo beginning to paint fractured and sometimes grotesque images of her body. Some early scenes starts as paintings, then slowly dissolve into a live action scene with actors portraying Frida's struggles as a student with her boyfriend, mother, and others around her. *Frida* centers, however, on her tumultuous relationship with the great Mexican painter and muralist Diego Rivera (Alfred Molina). We see a young schoolgirl spying on Rivera, approaching him and demanding that he judge and critique her paintings, with her eventually seducing him and becoming his wife, political comrade in leftwing politics, and fellow and mutually supportive artists.

When Rivera proposes to Kahlo, she tells him that she expects from him loyalty if not fidelity and, from early on in the marriage, Diego has affairs with a wide array of women, while the bisexual Kahlo takes on male and female lovers, including in one case having an affair with the same woman as Rivera. Frida's gender doubling as male/female hybrid is a major visual and thematic motif of the film, emerging from her dressing in colorful Mexican folkloric attire and then men's suits, while also taking on male and female lovers, providing a spectacle of gender fluidity and ambiguity.

During a key juncture of their life, Diego and Frida travel to New York City so that Rivera may paint a mural *Man at the Crossroads* at the Rockefeller Center, a historical panorama of the achievements of science, industry, and technology in the twentieth century. While Rivera painted a man holding the globe at the center of the painting with the forces of science, technology, and industry radiating outwards, side panels depicted the masses, and prominent portraits of Marx, Lenin, and Trotsky, leading to demands that these figures be removed. Rivera refuses to compromise his communist vision of the work to the needs of the patron, Nelson Rockefeller (Edward Norton), and as a result, the mural is painted over and in effect erased.

The next section of *Frida* is marked by intense melodrama as Kahlo suffers a miscarriage, her mother dies in Mexico, and Kahlo and Rivera return to Mexico in despair. Back in Mexico, Kahlo's sister Cristina moves in with the pair and begins work as Rivera's assistant, although Kahlo soon discovers that her husband is having an affair with her sister. In great anger, Frida leaves him, and subsequently falls into alcoholism and despair. With the arrival of Leon Trotsky (Geoffrey Rush) in Mexico, who has been granted political asylum in

Mexico, Frida and Diego reunite, showing Trotsky the wonders of ancient Mexican civilization. However, Frida and Trotsky begin an affair, which forces the married Trotsky to leave the safety of his Coyoacán home, and Diego is scandalized.

The Trotsky section of *Frida* provides an illustration of Kahlo's leftwing politics and shows Rivera at first sympathetic to Trotskyism but moving closer to Stalinism and orthodox Soviet Communism while Kahlo supports Trotsky's leftwing revolutionism, calling for world revolution by the workers themselves, outside of the strictures of party and state. Stalin sends his agents to Mexico City to assassinate Trotsky, a serious rival for leadership in the world revolutionary movement, Rivera is temporarily a suspect, while Kahlo is incarcerated in his place when he is not found. Rivera helps get her released, and the two begin a difficult reconciliation.

Frida's condition worsens and she must have her toes removed when they become gangrenous forcing her to move about in a wheelchair. Diego asks her to remarry him, and she agrees, although her health continues to worsen, including the amputation of a leg, and she ultimately dies after finally having a solo exhibition of her paintings in Mexico, depicting her final triumph after a life struggling to become a serious artist.

Frida provides an epic panorama of the life and times of a major female artist of the twentieth century, focusing on Kahlo, while the also female centric biopic *Selena* (1997), written and directed by Gregory Nava, deals with the life and career of Tejano music star Selena Quintanilla-Pérez, a popular Mexican American singer and recording artist well known in the Latino communities in the United States and Mexico before she was murdered by her business manager at the age of 23.

Selena presents a strong family unit with Edward James Olmos playing her father and manager, while Constance Marie plays Selena's mother, managing to take care of all the kids in the family who made up Selena's band. The film opens in 1961 with her encountering a white restaurant where they are rejected for an audition due to the club's "Whites Only" policy, illustrating the racial segregation faced by Latinos at this time. When they perform at a Mexican nightclub, a riot ensues when they sing "We Belong Together," rather than music associated with the Spanish culture, and the band is forced to flee.

The narrative cuts to the 1980s with the father, Abraham, creating a band Selena y Los Dinos, with Selena as the lead singer, and her other siblings – with some reluctance – on bass and drums. Abraham opens a restaurant called "Papa Gayo's" and tells Selena to learn Spanish so she does not have trouble singing in front of Mexicans like he did. Unfortunately, due to the economic policy of Reaganomics being bad for small business, the Quintanilla family goes bankrupt and loses the restaurant. They move to Corpus Christi, Texas, to live with Abraham's brother. There, Selena performs at a carnival and is poorly received, but one day, while the family is on the beach hears a song on the radio "The Washing Machine," which helps her and her band become more popular.

In 1990, Selena meets a guitarist named Chris Perez, who after joining the band, develops a friendship with Selena. Abraham disapproves of Chris after his former rock band members trash a hotel suite even though he greatly helped in making music for the band. Chris and Selena's friendships grows into love and when Abraham catches them hugging before a concert, he fires Chris and threatens a heartbroken Selena that if she follows him, he will disband the Dinos.

Selena and Chris continue seeing each other behind Abraham's back, but soon Selena becomes tired and tells Chris that she wants to marry him right away. In 1992, Selena and Chris elope secretly, but their marriage soon makes headlines on the radio. Selena goes to see Abraham, who tells her he is glad she did what she did, only wanting what was best for her. Chris is accepted into the Quintanilla family and returns to being the guitarist for Los Dinos.

During one of Selena's live performances, Jose Behar (the head of EMI Latin) and his music associates tell Abraham that they want to make an English language album for Selena. By 1994, Selena opens her first boutique called: Selena Etc., which her fan-club president Yolanda Saldivar manages, and her album *Selena Live!* wins a Grammy Award for Best Mexican American album. As 1995 begins, she starts recording her Crossover Album and Saldivar gives her a friendship ring, lying that it was only from her.

Later, Selena finds out from Abraham that Yolanda has been stealing money from the fan club and a lot of business records have gone missing. At Q-Productions, Abraham, Selena, and Suzette confront Yolanda, but she denies the claim. Selena continues to achieve fame and her concert at the Houston Astrodome on February 26 attracts a record-breaking crowd. However, just one month later, on March 31, after an argument over the missing financial documents, Selena is shot to death by Yolanda at a Corpus Christi motel. Yolanda is arrested after a standoff with the police. As Selena's family, friends, and fans mourn her death, a montage of the real Selena plays during a candlelight vigil.

In the 2000s, Latinos have also been featured in comedies like *Real Women Have Curves, Maid in Manhattan*, or TV comedy series like *Ugly Betty* (2004–2010) and *Jane the Virgin* (2015–2019). There have been some cinematic dramas like *The Cell* (2000) and *Angel Eyes* (2001), often starring Jennifer Lopez, or featuring Lopez in in films like *The Wedding Planner* (2001) and *Gigli* (2003), or bio-pics in films like *Selena* (1997) and *El Cantante* (2007), discussed below. Yet in the contemporary era films dealing with immigration are assuming increased importance in an era marked by intense struggles over immigrants and borders. I will according first engage some dramas dealing with Latinos and everyday life in America, and then turn to some films about immigration of various ethnic minorities in multicultural America.

The past decades have been marked by expanding globalization that in turn has heightened gender, race, class, and state forms of oppression and domination on both a local and a global scale, as well as wide-spread resistance and struggle (see Kellner 2002 and 2007 and Kahn-Kellner 2007). The intersectionality of forces of oppression and domination is put on display in Alejandro Gonzalez Inarritu's *Babel* (2006), which weaves together a set of stories from around the world that puts on display unequal relations of class, gender, race, sexual, and state power.

Babel is the third in a series of collaborations by Inarritu and Guillermo Arriaga. Beginning with *Amores Perros* (2000) and continuing with *21 Grams* (2003), the trilogy is marked by complexity and fragmentation of plot, fast-editing, interconnections between disparate characters, and the possibility of explosive violence occurring at any moment.[31] The title "Babel" refers to the story in the Old Testament of the dispersion of peoples into different languages and cultures and the resulting confusion and chaos.[32] The film depicts massive differences across borders of space and class, gender, and racial divides, and shows how globalization complexifies the issue of borders and reproduces hierarchies of domination and subordination among peoples.

The mise-en-scène interrelates fragments of different stories, altering time sequence for dramatic effect, and eventually pulling the narrative threads together. The story unfolds with the sale of a gun to a Moroccan family that needs it to protect its goatherds from predatory jackals. The scene then cuts to a group of white tourists on a sight-seeing bus in Morocco, focusing on Richard (Brad Pitt) and Susan (Cate Blanchett) who have taken a vacation to mend their strained relationship after the death of a child. Susan is having stomach trouble and throws away some water her husband is about to drink, believing that it is contaminated, and signaling the alienation and problems of communication that the couple is having – issues that will run through the film.

A phone call to an older Mexican woman, Amelia (Adriana Barraza), in an up-scale brightly-lit kitchen filled with high-end appliances and expensive cabinetry, reveals that the woman is the domestic maid and nanny. The male voice on the phone tells her that they will be delayed in Morocco and she must take close care of their children. The woman protests that she must go to Mexico for her son's wedding, but the male voice insists that she stay with the children, establishing relations of class, gender, and race hegemony.

The fate of the tourists and Moroccans intersect as one of the boys playing with the newly purchased rifle tests its distance range and accidentally shoots Susan through the bus window, a symbol of the violence that can intrude into everyday globalized life at any moment. The shooting unleashes a narrative line where both the U.S. and Moroccan government interpret the incident as a terrorist attack, while Richard desperately seeks medical assistance for his wife. Due to miscommunication between the U.S. and Moroccan governments, adequate medical care does not arrive and Susan is dependent on a local Moroccan veterinarian and healer, and then a local country doctor. Richard desperately tries to get her adequate medical care, demands that the tourist bus remain with them and if necessary take her to where she can get better treatment, and commands local Moroccans and police and U.S. diplomatic authorities as if he were a White God. Played by Brad Pitt, his character, whiteness, Americanness, and gender dominates the narrative and other characters. Yet Richard and his wife are also dependent on chance and contingency, with the film suggesting that minor events in different parts of the world can have major unintended consequences elsewhere.

Meanwhile, Amelia, the Mexican nanny, cannot find anyone to take care of the children and gets her nephew Santiago (Gael García Bernal) to drive them to the wedding across the U.S./Mexico border. While the U.S. and Japanese scenes depict affluent houses, architecture, and modern cityscapes, the Mexican and Moroccan scenes highlight poverty, dusty desert landscapes, and overcrowded homes. The cutting is faster, the camera is jerkier, denoting instability and chaos in the developing countries. Gender divisions are strict, especially in the Moroccan scenes with men working and women staying in the house. In the Mexican scenes, men are strongly dominant and subject to excessive alcohol consumption and irrational behavior.

Another storyline, seemingly unrelated, opens in Tokyo where a young deaf Japanese girl Chieko (Rinko Kikuchi) desperately seeks attention from her stoic and distant father after her mother's death. She is also desperate for sexual attention from Japanese boys and men and is extremely provocative in dress and actions. Dressed in a school girl uniform, with her skirt shortened to expose her upper thighs, she epitomizes the infantilized look favored by sexist men and the highly sexualized representations of Asian and Asian American women (Hamamoto 2000).

Both the Japanese and Mexican scenes demonstrate overwhelming patriarchal power where the women are forced to submit to male domination and decisions. In the case of Amelia, she must submit to her nephew's decision to drive across the border after the wedding, although he is seriously intoxicated and has a dubious police record, a decision that leads to chaos after Santiago races away from the border guards who are questioning him and are about to detain him, dumping Amelia with the children alone in the desert. Implausibly, Amelia and the children are separated and the narrative reveals that Amelia is undocumented, portraying an irrational desire to endanger her job status and livelihood in the U.S. to attend the family wedding.

Once again the subordinate position of women is demonstrated. Although a dignified older male widower approaches Amelia at the wedding her sexuality is not allowed to be expressed and she is forced by her nephew to undergo a dangerous border-crossing. The border-crossing episode depicts how easy it is to cross from the U.S. into Mexico and how difficult it is to enter the U.S. *Babel* also illustrates in its representations of the border guard how people of color collaborate with police against other people of color thus serving the interests of the dominant class and race. Mexicans are stereotypically represented as friendly and festive in the wedding celebration, but who also irresponsibly drink and drive, putting at risk the children they are to care for, and risking arrest at the border.

Indeed, the well-being of the white couple and children is privileged throughout the film. Key emphasis is getting Richard and his wife safely out of the desert and then getting his children home safely when they are abandoned in the desert. The film thus shows how white Westerners have access to more advanced technology and political and social advances and throughout shows inequities in power between Western and non-Western, white and non-white, men and women, and the global effects of Western and patriarchal power, although, as I suggest below, the film also puts on display their limitations showing in an interconnected and globalized world control is not always possible (as the Bush–Cheney administration found out with disastrous consequences).

Meanwhile, in Japan, Chieko is becoming increasingly desperate for male attention, trying clumsily to seduce her dentist, and then taking her underpants off in a café as a group of young men ogle her and her girlfriends. The boys provide whiskey and pills to the young women and take them to a discothèque, but one disturbing scene shows Chieko wandering alone in the club with the loud soundtrack suddenly cutting off and replaced with silence, demonstrating her isolation in deafness, and signaling how all the characters are ultimately trapped in their own subjectivity. Indeed, as Oiyan Poon puts it (2007): "Chieko is presented as a metaphorical figure for the world itself and its inability to communicate" and "symbolizes the alienation and borderlines between individuals that the film thematizes."[33]

Continuing her desperate and destructive behavior, Chieko tries to seduce a policeman who wants to question her father concerning the gun that was used to shoot Susan in the Moroccan desert that, via global media, has escalated into an international incident. Earlier, one of the Moroccan boys was voyeuristically watching his sister undress through a window, with her complicity, and then masturbating, as if non-Western peoples have immature and primitive sexualities. While the Moroccan boys assume the patriarchal power of possessors of the gun (and penis), both get them in trouble and bring down social and family authority on them. Likewise, the Japanese boys are allowed to party as they please, although the drug and alcohol consumption with the young girls leaves Chieko alone and disoriented at the disco.

While the film puts on display unequal class, gender, and racial relations of power and dominance, indicating how they intersect, it also shows how the dominant groups are in turn subject to contingencies and limitations in a global world. *Babel* suggests a crisis of patriarchy and difficulties fathers are having in controlling and taking care of their families, motifs suggested in the American, Japanese, and Moroccan families. While the film shows the primacy of Whiteness with its focus on Brad Pitt's character, Richard, he is obviously unable to communicate significantly with his wife over a child's death, which motivated the trip, has no close friends to take care of his children when he is away and must rely on domestics, and is really not able to cut through bureaucratic red tape to bring medical help to his wife in the desert. The Japanese patriarchal father is obviously unable to nurture his deeply disturbed daughter and no doubt had serious problems with his wife that led to her suicide. The Mexican scenes show an absence of responsible males, forcing women to work and producing chaos through their problematic masculinist behavior (the Mexican bride at the wedding is pregnant, the nephew gets drunk and abandons his charges in the desert, and so on).

In the globalized world of *Babel*, a profusion of cultures, borders, unequal relations of power and subordination, and difficulties in communication and understanding create conflicts and disasters. In a globalized world, peoples and events are interconnected, and the contingency and chance of a moment can produce catastrophe in one part of the world that has impact elsewhere. Yet *Babel* does not really depict who is responsible for the globalized alienation, inequalities, and conflicts depicted in the film and lets the U.S. government and other powerful nations, multinational corporations, and global corporate culture off the hook. The concluding images contain a highly oblique critical vision of globalization, however, by showing the consequences of the globalized narrative on different groups. The Mexican housekeeper has lost her job and access to U.S. labor markets, but a news report suggests that the wife, Susan, is recovering from her gunshot and will be all right. In an extremely ambiguous set of con-cluding images, the Japanese girl Chieko connects with her father in an embrace that could be a sign of hope that communication can heal wounds and they can reconnect, but since the girl is naked and the narrative suggests that the mother may have committed suicide in the same luxury apartment, a happy ending here is far from certain.[34]

Other important Latino filmmakers include Leon Ichaso, a producer/director of chronicles of Latino life that have crossed over into the mainstream. Ichaso has fashioned compelling biopics of Panamanian singer Ruben Blades in *Cross-over Dreams* (1985) and Puerto Rican playwright Miguel Pinero in *Pinero* (2002), as well as directing his debut film *El Super* (1979) about the travails of Cuban/American life and his highly controversial anti-Castro film about contemporary Cuba *Bitter Sugar* (1996). Crossing over between film and television, Ichaso also directed episodes of Michael Mann's classic TV-series *Miami Vice* and *Crime Story* in the 1980s, and has directed many TV- series and episodes from the 1990s to the present, including the 2005 Showtime series *Sleeper Cell* that dealt with domestic terrorist threats in the United States.

Ichaso's films of the early 2000s include *Pinero* (2002) and *El Cantante* (2007), which provide critical interrogations of Latino culture. Pinero chronicles the life and early death of Nuyorican playwright Miguel Pinero (Benjamin Bratt) who burst onto the national scene in the 1970s with his prison drama *Short Eyes*, based on time spent in Sing Sing. The film is a strongly demythologizing biopic, presenting sharply critical visions of Pinero as drug addict, petty thief, and thor-oughly destructive individual who squandered his literary talent and an early reputation.

Set in grimy New York Latino and bohemian communities, the film is highly fragmented, telling Pinero's life in flashbacks. The frenzied style, cutting from Black and white to color, past to present, with a nervous, jiggling camera and jarring cuts captures the turbulent and hyperactive nature of Pinero's life. Interspersing his jazzy poetry, a cross between beatnik and rap style, with key events of his life, the narrative shows his rise to theatrical success with *Short Eyes* and founding of a lower Eastside poetry scene, the Noyorican Poets Café. A key scene shows his ambiguous relation to his native Puerto Rico. Abandoned by his father in New York as a youngster, Pinero returns to Puerto Rico where a group of intellectuals assembled in a lecture hall asks what rights does he have to speak for his country, and Pinero makes it clear he is only speaking for himself and his exile community. Tragedies, such as the death of his mother and a close friend from AIDS, happen fast, and it is clear that Pinero is on a swift path to destruction. Ravished by hard-living, Pinero seeks a new kidney in vain, and his hard life takes him down at the age of 41, leaving behind only his poetry and plays, and Ichaso's biopic.

Intersecting the dramas and sounds of gender and ethnicity, Ichaso's *El Cantante* (2007) tells the story of the meteoric rise to success of salsa superstar Hector Lavoe (Marc Anthony), focusing on his tumultuous relation with his wife Puchi (Jennifer Lopez). Narrated in Black and white segments around a 2002 interview with Puchi, about a decade after Lavoe had died of AIDS and shortly before her own death, the film captures the vibrancy of the New York Puerto Rican music scene of the 1960s and 1970s, and uses quick cuts and dazzling images, elaborate musical numbers, and fast-paced tableaux to portray the High Life of celebrity, partying, and drugs.

Like Ray Charles and Johnny Cash, Hector Lavoe met his nemesis in hard drug addiction, and much of *El Cantante* presents his inevitable devastation by the dual curses of drugs and AIDS. In these musical male biopics, it is as if drugs are a necessary accompaniment of male ambition and drive in the music business and part of the road to success, albeit one that if not overcome, or kept under control, can lead to death and destruction. Much of *El Cantante* dwells on Lavoe's growing addiction and downfall from drugs, as the film switches from the fast-paced frenzy of his early success to slow, painful dissections of his eventual demise.

El Cantante got mixed reviews with many of those involved in the New York/Puerto Rican music salsa scene criticizing the film for overemphasizing Lavoe's drug use and downfall, while others criticized Jennifer Lopez's performance and Pucci's narrative recollections framing the story. The film also did not do well at the box office, although it has an afterlife with a DVD that commemorates Lavoe's life and work.[35]

Gregory Nava had emerged as one of the finest Latino filmmakers in the world, from *El Norte* (1983) to *Bordertown* (2006) capturing political dynamics of relations between Latin America and the U.S., and documenting forms of oppression that Latinos undergo. Nava has documented multiple aspects of

Latino/a life, including some successful Hollywood cross-over films like *My Family/Mi Familia* (1995), which tells the story of three generations of Los Angeles Mexican Americans, as well as epic bio-pics like *Selena* (1997) and *Frida* (2002), about Mexican painting icon Frida Kahlo and her relation with Diego Rivera, on which he was screenwriter.

El Norte, which Nava co-wrote and directed with producing partner Anna Thomas, takes place in three countries, with the first part unfolding in a small rural Guatemalan village San Pedro where the Xuncax family, a group of indigenous Mayans, struggle for survival. The story opens with Arturo, a coffee picker, working in the fields, telling his son Enrique that, "to the rich, the peasant is just a pair of strong arms," and the theme of strong arms as the fate of the male worker will resonate in later episodes. Arturo calls a meeting to form a labor union among the workers and an informer tells the army chief where they are meeting. The army ambushes the workers, killing Arturo and others, and hanging Arturo's severed head on a tree.

The film combines a relentless naturalism capturing the textures, colors, and culture of the countries and peoples portrayed, with Latin American "magic realism," which brings in moments of fantasy and dream episodes. The narrative switches to Enrique's point of view as he desperately attempts to climb the tree to retrieve his father's head, and a soldier attacks him. After a violent fight, Enrique kills the attacker, then escapes with his sister, Rosa, and hides in a safe house until morning. Enrique and Rosa learn that many of their fellow villagers have been rounded up by soldiers, including their mother who "disappears," abducted by soldiers, reproducing the sort of political repression going on in Guatemala in the 1980s with a military government operating in the interests of the rich and landowners, and violently controlling workers and peasants.

Rosa and Enrique have heard stories about the wonders of "El Norte" from their godmother (toilets that flush! Electric lights!) who has apparently been receiving copies of *Good Housekeeping* from a friend. Hence, using money given to them by their godmother, Enrique and Rosa decide to flee Guatemala, the land of their birth, and head north to the promised land.

During the second part of the film the two teenagers flee Guatemala and travel through Mexico, meeting a Mexican coyote who tries to rob them, but is appalled when he sees how little money they possess. The teenagers eventually make it to a border town where a former coyote directs them to an abandoned sewer that crosses into the U.S. In a famously horrific scene, they crawl through the sewer pipe, attacked by rats, but manage to get across the border and into El Norte.

Part three deals with their challenges as undocumented immigrants in the U.S. Enrique finds a job in a restaurant where he appears to be succeeding, but a jealous co-worker calls immigration when Enrique gets a promotion the co-worker wanted, and Enrique is forced to flee and then work as a day laborer. Meanwhile, Rosa finds work in a factory, but also is the subject of an immigration raid and must find a new job. Working as a domestic, she is confused when her Anglo employer shows her a highly complex washing machine, and in a comic episode washes the clothes by hand and dries them in the backyard. Enrique becomes a busboy in an upscale restaurant and takes English classes begin to improve his command of the language.

Enrique had earlier been approached by a businesswoman who has a better-paying job for him in Chicago as a foreman, which he initially declines, but after losing his restaurant job, he seeks out the Chicago businesswoman who again offers the ambitious and charming young man a job and ticket to Chicago. Yet as Enrique's fortunes rise, Rosa becomes gravely ill with typhus contracted from the rat bites she received during their border crossing. Told of his sister's plight, Enrique is momentarily torn, but rushes to the hospital to be by her side. He discovers her near death, and just before dying, Rosa laments:

> In our own land, we have no home. They want to kill us … In Mexico, there is only poverty. We can't make a home there either. And here in the north, we aren't accepted. When will we find a home, Enrique? Maybe when we die, we'll find a home.

The film concludes with Enrique shown once again waiting with the other day-labor hopefuls in a parking lot, offering his services to a man looking for "strong arms," and we realize that his father's words about the poor being nothing but arms for the rich holds true even in El Norte. The film ends with a reprise of the severed head image that might connote Enrique's possible end or suicide, but certainly it represents a harsh fate for many immigrants.

Despite the grim narrative and extremely heavy scenes and suffering, *El Norte* was a major critical and audience success and opened the doors for Nava and Thomas to make a series of illuminating Latino/a themed films, including *Bordertown* (2006). Drawing on real historical events, the film deals with the rapes, murders, and disappearances of hundreds, perhaps thousands, of Mexican women factory workers in the multinational maquiladores factories that line the border between Mexico and the United States. Jennifer Lopez plays Lauren Adrian, a Chicago investigative reporter who is dispatched to Juarez by her editor, George Morgan (Martin Sheen), to cover the deaths and disappearances of the women there.

Bordertown opens with graphic titles describing the rise of the maquiladores factories along the U.S./Mexico border after NAFTA and the epidemic of murdered and disappeared young women in the factories. Interspersed among opening titles we see a local Juarez newspaper headlining a missing and murdered 16-year-old women, and see stacks of the papers confiscated by authorities, signaling the cover-up that will take place throughout the film. Illustrating the situation of the working women, *Bordertown* takes us into the assembly lines of the factories where for minimal wages women toil all day on machines to produce computers, televisions, and other gadgets, for mostly U.S. consumption. The work-day ends, the women workers file out on a bus, and clap with joy that they are free of their industrial prison.

Bordertown uses filtered lights, dark night scenes, and a fast-moving jittery camera to capture the Juarez environs and a yellow-desert like tint, gritty brown images, and hand-held long shots to capture Mexico as "other" to the U.S. scenes on the northern side of the border. Lauren is presented in flashbacks to her Latina youth in bright images, and quick cutting and eccentric camera angles cutting to her investigation create menace throughout the film as it is clear that there are forces who do not want the truth exposed and who threaten those on both sides looking into the murders.

The latter half of *Bordertown* becomes more of a detective and action movie as the reporters search for a bus driver and a man with a scar suspected in some of the murders. Lauren goes underground, working in maquiladores factories and takes the bus route upon which Eva, another factory worker, was raped and left for dead. At the end of the line the driver attacks her, and she barely fends him off, escaping through a junkyard where she discover mutilated bodies. Lauren and a news reporter friend, Diaz, are pursued by thugs and barely escape, while Lauren seduces a wealthy industrialist to try to get information about the scarred man who is a suspect who she saw at a party for the super-wealthy.

Politicians and the corporate elite of both sides of the border want to extend NAFTA trade rules to Central America and Lauren's boss at the newspaper says that they want no bad publicity now and should kill the story, offering her the international correspondent position she so coveted. Deeply involved in the story she explodes at her boss, telling him that there is no more real news any-more and that corporate America runs the show now and is destroying genuine journalism.

On her own now, Lauren has a flashback to the murder of her farm-worker father by corporate anti-union thugs, making the tenacity of her persistence clear. She continues to be menaced by forces who do not want the story published and in a melodramatic conclusion Diaz is shot, Eva flees with terror across the border and almost dies, but closing voice-overs indicate that Lauren will take over Diaz's struggle and edit his newspaper to continue to try to find out who was behind the murders and disappearance of the missing women.

While *Bordertown* was criticized for its melodramatic conspiracy theory, placing a bus driver and a perverted industrialist at the heart of the murders, early in the film Diaz suggested a variety of reasons for the murders including snuff films, extreme sex, bosses preying on workers, and other causes, and Lauren makes clear as well that the murders have multiple origins. The fact that these murders have neither been solved nor stopped is a major disgrace for Mexico and the United States and a badge of honor for those who made *Bordertown* to publicize the scandal.

Many films of the 2000s era dealt with immigration and difficult immigrant challenges in surviving in America from a variety of different perspectives, a topic that I will discuss in the following section.

Immigration to the promised land

Immigration is a cultural experience binding many Americans together and a variety of films of the 2000s dealt with contemporary problems of immigration. Many Latino films focused on this topic, that was so important for its community. Christopher Zalla's *Sangre de mi Sangre* (2007), a Grand Jury prize winner in Sundance, provides a powerful vision of the broken dreams and hard lives of two young Mexican immigrants boys who sneak into the country. A naïve young boy Pedro (Jorge Adrian Espindola) meets a hardened teenager Juan (Armando Hernandez), fleeing from a gang fight and hopping on a truck bound from the Texas border to New York City. The innocent Pedro tells Juan that he is carrying a letter from his mother, and hopes to find his father in New York, who supposedly owns a French restaurant and has been sending the family money for years, although the boy has never met his father. Seeing a possible U.S. meal ticket, Juan steals the letter and Pedro's meager belongings in his backpack, and finds the apartment of Pedro's father Diego (Jesus Ochoa) in Brooklyn, who has never seen his son and has no interest in him.

The real Pedro arrives in New York, remembering the address on the envelope, but soon discovering that there are numbered streets throughout the boroughs of New York. Pedro meets Magda, a tough, streetwise Mexican girl, who does drugs and supports her habit through prostitution and who helps the naïve Pedro out of pity and a vague hope of making some money out of the project. Meanwhile, pretending to be his son, Juan charms the old and bitter father Diego, who, although he works as a dishwasher rather than restaurant owner, has stowed away a stash of cash, which Juan hopes to find and steal. The narrative flows between Juan bonding with Diego, who secretly searches the apartment for money, and Pedro learning about survival in the street with Magda. The narrative machine inevitably brings them together at the end of the film, but none of the characters problems are really resolved and life goes on for the immigrants, hopeful, but uncertain.

The challenges of border-crossing are portrayed in Patricia Riggen's *Under the Same Moon* (2007). The film opens with a young Mexican boy Carlitos (Adrian Alonso), who talks on the phone to his mother, Rosario (Kate del Castillo), every Sunday at precisely 10:00 a.m. The mother has left Mexico four years previously and works in Los Angeles as a cleaning lady, dreaming of bringing over her son. Living with his grandmother in Mexico, Carlitos vows to cross the border to come to California to be with mother after his grandmother dies, and manipulates his employer to let him stow away in a minivan driven by two Mexican American students (Jesse Garcia and the popular TV series' *Ugly Betty* actress, America Ferrera). While Carlitos crosses the border safely, the students' van is compounded and the young but determined boy is on his own. Meeting a cynical Chicano with a big heart, Enrique, Carlitos learns to get around and after several adventures, eventually makes it to California.

Meanwhile, his mother, Rosario, considers marrying a Chicano named Paco (Gabriel Porras) for green-card privileges, and puts up with mistreatment by her rich, white employer (Jacqueline Voltaire), leading Paco to say of Americans: "First they screwed the Indians, then they screwed the slaves, and now they're screwing us Mexicans!" In a fairy-tale ending, Carlitos finds his mother as he tracks down the telephone from which she calls him every Sunday morning. Yet the aesthetic contrast in the film between the colorful and lively Mexican life, compared to the more drab and sterile U.S. life. raises questions whether the happy ending will really bring happiness.

Border-crossing and the travails of undocumented Latinos in the U.S. are also explored in the films of Pablo Veliz, who looks at immigration from the Mexican side and the standpoint of the dangers of border crossing and uncertain reception in the U.S. *La Tragedia de Macario* (2005) portrays a desperate but hopeless quest to cross the border and find salvation in the U.S., while *Clemente* (2008) explores the difficult life undocumented immigrants will have in surviving in the U.S. Opening with a beautiful young woman in the desert commemorating where a man died on a failed border crossing, we learn by the end of the film that it was the woman's father who died. The narrative cuts to a young man fighting in a fake wrestling arena and then struggling to provide sustenance to his family. Married to a permanent resident without citizenship, Clemente (Jorge A. Jimenez) is having trouble with his green-card application and one day is sent back to Mexico when the Migra enters the automotive factory where he works and sends him back to Mexico.

Clemente presents a sharply critical view of Mexican American permanent residents for whom the undocumented immigrants are second-class citizens. Clemente's wife (Mariana Watcher) is treated with contempt by the high-priced Mexican American immigration lawyer who seems to be doing nothing to advance her husband's case, and her documented mother is suspicious of whether her daughter should be involved with an undocumented individual. When Clemente goes missing, his boss at the automotive factory proclaims he will help the family – at the price of the attractive wife becoming his lover. Yet the most harrowing parts of Veliz's film involve Clemente's desperate attempts to return to the U.S. The director uses magic realism and hallucinatory fantasies of deliverance as Clemente dies of thirst and starvation in the relentless desert.

Hollywood films like *Crossing Over* (2007) provide more U.S.-centric views of immigration. Combining the multicultural vision of Southern California in *Crash* (2004) with the interconnected global world of *Babel*, Wayne Kramer's *Crossing Over* (2009) deals with the immigration challenges of a variety of immigrants intercrossed with the lives of U.S. immigration officers.

The film relentlessly marshals Hollywood and ethnic cinematic clichés and stereotypes in its story of how some immigrants and would be citizens are fortunate and become citizens, while others are victims of a bureaucratic, arbitrary, and sometimes corrupt, immigration system. U.S. immigration officials are depicted as either corrupt and bureaucratic, or helping and caring. Likewise, there are "good" representatives of various immigrant groups contrasted to "bad" ones.

Crossing Over opens with the bust of a sweat shop where a Mexican woman (Alice Braga) about to be deported desperately gives a U.S. Immigration and Customs agent (Harrison Ford) money and a phone number to take care of her daughter and pleads with him to find the child. The Ford character at first rebuffs her, but for the rest of the film pursues the child, who he finds and returns to his grandparents in Mexico, and keeps up a futile search for the mother who has allegedly fled Mexico and returned to the U.S.

In another plot-line, an Australian actress (Alice Eve) trying to make it in Hollywood crashes into the car of an INS arbitration officer (Ray Liotta) and he offers her an exceptional working permit as pay-off for frequent trysts in seedy hotels. It turns out his wife (Ashley Judd) is an INS lawyer who tries to get her husband to agree to adopt an African child lost in the system, and, in one of the film's main stories, tries to keep together an Arab family after the daughter has written a paper and defended in class the al Qaeda terrorists in the 9/11 attack, and is the subject of a Patriot Act interrogation and investigation that discovers half of the family is illegal.

The daughter of an Iranian family, which includes the Ford character's INS partner, is murdered when she is caught by her other brother having sex in a motel with a Latino with whom she works in a copy-machine office (that manufactures, among other things, fake I.D. cards). A British Jewish atheist is allowed citizenship as he fakes being an orthodox Jew and part of a religious congregation, while a Korean youth who has joined a gang is given mercy by Ford's partner who busts up a gang robbery gone bad. The final scene intercuts the U.S. citizenship ceremony for the Lucky Ones with the arrest of the Iranian IRS's brother who killed his sister allegedly to preserve family honor, and airport scenes showing the Australian actress and half of the Muslim family deported, laced with a report that the Mexican woman whom Ford had been seeking died in the border crossing.

Crossing Over is thus ultimately a celebration of U.S. citizenship and "good Americans" as the world's greatest country and citizenship as the ticket to a good life. Cary Fukunaga's *Sin Nombre* (2008) presents a look at the social conditions which drive Latin Americans to immigrate to the North and the perilous journey to enter the States. The film weaves together the stories of a young woman from Honduras Sayra (Paulina Gaitan), who has no prospects in her home country and joins her father and uncle in an odyssey through Central America and Mexico intended to take them to relatives in New Jersey who meets a young Mexican en route. In hard-hitting sequences Willy, nicknamed Casper (Edgar Flores), is a member of a vicious gang in southern Mexico, which has connections throughout the country and a Los Angeles franchise. El Casper initiates a young boy into the gang and watches him kill a member of a rival gang, is helpless when the gang leader attempts to rape his beloved girl-friend and accidentally kills her, and then breaks with the gang as they attempt to rob Sayra and her family who are traveling illegally through Mexico on train car roofs. The film uses the budding romance between Sayra and Casper, and the relentless pursuit of Casper by his former gang members who want revenge for the death of their leader that Casper caused when he aborted the robbery, to dramatize the difficult process of entering the United States.

Hence, many Latino filmmakers have dealt with immigration and the Latino/a experience in the United States. Negative aspects of the immigrant experience involved incarceration, and during the Trump era, immigration and incarceration has become a hot-button issue with Trump politicizing the border and creating detention camps in which children are separated from families and put in cages. This horrendous situation is graphically illustrated in Daniel Sawka's debut *Icebox* (2018). The film portrays a 12-year-old Honduran named Oscar (Anthony Gonzalez), whom we meet as he's being held down, screaming, while local gangsters tattoo the number "XVII" across his chest. With the gang violence pervading his native Honduras, Oscar soon leaves for the U.S. with the goal of finding his uncle and seeking refuge. En route in the dangerous crossing, Oscar is caught by U.S Border Patrol agents. After they ask Oscar a series of questions and inform him of a pending trial, they lock him up in what's described as a processing center for migrant children. The film unfolds in a child detention center known to the inmates as "Icebox," which describes cages in detention facilities that are freezing cold, the exposure of which during the Trump era on nightly news has outraged the nation and the world.[36]

Films dealing with immigration to contemporary U.S. society thus involve such diverse issue as the challenges of illegal immigration to conflicts that new immigrants to the U.S. face in diverse ways, often showing how immigrants maintain aspects of their culture while constructing new identities. Immigrant films thus deal with the intersectionality of race, class, and gender and feature key challenges and dynamics of the American experience, both historically and contemporary.

Notes

1 There has been much debate concerning what terminology to use to describe Black people of African and American descent in the U.S. In this study, I use the term "Blacks" and "African Americans" interchangeably. I am aware that there are problems with a white male professional in a privileged race, class, and gender position, writing about Black culture and politics, but I would defend this procedure by arguing that it is important for people of different subject positions to cross over and explore the terrain of difference and to exhibit solidarity with those engaged in liberation politics, while also engaging their interpretations and views of the media culture in question.

2 Lee's *She's Gotta Have It* cost only $175,000 and pulled in over $8.5 million; *School Daze* was budgeted at $5.8 million and took in over $15 million; *Do the Right Thing* was budgeted at $6.5 million and grossed over $25 million (Patterson 1992: 55, 92, 121). Many of Lee's films have also been profitable in the video-cassette market. Evidently, the money made on these films persuaded the Hollywood money establishment that Lee and other young Black directors were marketable and funded a renaissance of Black film in the early 1990s; see Guerrero 1993: 157ff and Patterson 1992: 223f. Reid, however, notes that Lee's own films draw on earlier Black cinema: "Lee's film

journals never recognize his debt to other black filmmakers, yet he borrows from their cinematic portrayals of urban black life and their use of contemporary black music" (1993: 107).

3 Guerrero also claims that in times of a general slump, Hollywood invests in low-budget Black films to up the profit-margin, whereas it ignores African American films when profits are high and the industry has "no need to continue a specifically black-focused product line" (1993: 165).

4 I am grateful to many people for critical comments on various versions of my study of Spike Lee, which was first presented in a symposium on organized by Mark Reid at the Society for Cinema Studies, and was then presented in a workshop on contemporary film at the American Sociology Association.

5 I do not know whether Brecht specifically influenced Lee, or if Lee (re)invented something like a Brechtian cinema out of his own experiences and resources. When I published the first edition of *Media Culture* in 1995 I had found only one mention of a possible Brecht/Lee connection in the growing literature on the Black director. Paul Gilroy, in a critique of Lee in *The Washington Post* (November 17, 1991), but an August 31, 2019, Google search of "Spike Lee, Brecht" found multiple reference to the Brecht–Lee connection throughout Lee's work; see Google at www.google.com/search?source=hp&ei=46pqXemcL5jz-gSHnoCgBA&q=Spike+Lee+Brecht&oq=Spike+Lee+Brecht&gs_l=psy-ab.12.0i22i30.741.5228.7697.0.0.0.140.1560.9j7...0..1.gws-wiz...0i131j0j0i10j0i22i10i30.u3g9LkNFnjc&ved=0ahUKEwipmsjwza3kAhWYuZ4KHQcPAEQQ4dUDCAc#spf=1567271655864 (accessed August 31, 2019). For a fuller presentation of Brecht's aesthetics and politics, see Kellner 1981.

6 See Barthes (1975) on "the writerly" modernist text that requires an active reader.

7 Jameson (1990, 1991) stresses the role of individual vision and style in modernism, while Bürger, Peter (1984 [1974]) analyzes the "historical avant garde" that attempts to change art and life, as opposed to more formalistically oriented modernist art.

8 This reading was suggested in conversation by Zygmunt Bauman after a series on postmodern film at the summer 1992 10th anniversary conference of *Theory, Culture, & Society*. In addition, Lee's *DRT* is read as a "postmodern" film in a somewhat indeterminate sense in Denzin 1991: 125ff; likewise, Baker (1993a: 174–5) describes Lee as a "true postmodern" with an "astute, witty, brilliant critique of postmodern, urban hybridity" in *DRT*, but without giving the term "postmodern" any substance. I will argue below that Lee basically grounds his politics and aesthetic strategies in modernist positions and is not in any important sense "postmodernist."

9 Of course, there are many postmodern politics, ranging from the nihilism of the post-1980s Baudrillard to the pragmatic reformism of Lyotard and Rorty, to the multiculturalist identity politics of many minority groups who identify as postmodern; see the survey in Kellner 1991. As I write the second edition in 2019, it appears that the discourse of the postmodern is neither as widespread or contentious as it was in the 1980s and 1990s.

10 This is an homage to the Robert Mitchum character in *Night of the Hunter*, who was, however, quite evil, thus Lee's appropriation of this symbolism perhaps inadvertently coded Raheem as more negative than Lee intended.

11 Lee indicates that he is down on Black youth exhibiting gold chains and the like ("They don't understand how worthless that shit is in the long run"), but doesn't do anything in the film to criticize this form of consumerism and in fact reproduces it in his cinematic images and capitalist ventures (see Lee and Jones 1989: 59 and 110 for Lee's disclaimers).

12 Patterson (1992: 125ff) notes some criticisms of Lee's commercial activity.

13 bell hooks (1990, 179) complains that a stuttering and inarticulate Black youth is chosen to represent the profoundly intelligent and articulate views of Malcolm X and Martin Luther King.

14 As I write the second edition of this book in the Trump era, I might note that there
    is a resurgence of nationalism as a major force of identity in the U.S. and throughout
    the world, often taking xenophobic, racist, and repugnant forms, such as the resur-
    gence of white nationalism, Nazism, Klanism, and other extreme right and often vio-
    lent forms during the Trump era, some of which is encouraged by the White House;
    see Kellner 2018.

15 Put differently, Lee's portrayal of racism does not take into account logical types, that
    there is a hierarchy of racial virulence, usually dictated by color (Blacks being subject
    to the most extreme racism, followed by Hispanics, Asians, and ethnics like Italians).
    Other hierarchies are those of gender (with women below men), sexual preference
    (with gays subject to prejudice from straights), and so on, such that Black, lesbian
    women would suffer significantly more oppression than, say, Hispanic men. The
    scene under question, however, portrays all forms of racism in terms of linguistic
    equivalence of cultural difference and racial hatred (I am grateful to Rhonda
    Hammer for this insight). I would argue in 2019, however, that the entire oeuvre of
    Lee's work constitutes one of the most impressive critiques of institutional racism and
    racist tendencies in the U.S. of any filmmaker.

16 In interviews after the release of the film, Lee said that he was constantly amazed at
    people indignant over the destruction of property, but few of these people seemed to
    focus on the Black youth's death. Lee was initially concerned to interrogate the condi-
    tions that could lead to wanton killings of Black youth, spurred on by the Howard
    Beach killings in Queens, New York, in 1986 in which white youth gratuitously
    assaulted Black youth, leading to one of their deaths. Thus, Lee seems to believe that
    violent protest is a legitimate response to the senseless killing of Blacks, as would, pre-
    sumably Malcolm X himself, and those who later formed the group Black Lives
    Matter.

    In a book on the making of *DRT* (Lee 1989), Lee remarks: "The character I play in
    Do the Right Thing is from the Malcolm X school of thought: 'An eye for an eye.' Fuck
    the turn-the-other-cheek shit. If we keep up that madness we'll be dead. YO, IT'S AN
    EYE FOR AN EYE" (34; Lee's capitals).

17 This reading was suggested by Kelly Oliver in a comment on an earlier draft of
    a paper on *DTR*. Indeed, as indicated in a note above, Lee was angry that many
    viewers and reviewers seemed to be very upset by the destruction of property, but
    were overlooking that a Black youth was killed by the police.

18 In a throw-away line, Mookie's sister Jade mentions that she'd like to see something
    positive happen for the community, but it isn't clear what she has in mind and in the
    absence of a more complete development of her political views, one can only guess.
    In his later work, of course, Lee interrogates many versions of Black oppositional
    politics and his work as a whole can be seen as an exemplary intervention in anti-
    racist politics.

19 It is precisely this nihilism that Cornell West warns Blacks against (1992b).

20 It was generally overlooked in the reviews of the film that a good part of *Jungle Fever*
    was spent attacking the crack scene, portraying it as a dead end and in extremely
    negative terms as a major force of destruction in the Black community. Lee avoided
    the issue of drugs, however, in his earlier films, for which he was criticized.

21 Brecht too was sympathetic to criminals and often presented them positively, as
    in the *Three-Penny Opera*. At times, they were figures of oppressed proletarians
    for Brecht, though he also used the gangster figure to present capitalists and
    fascists.

22 Although the narrative suggests that Malcolm was attracted to the white woman,
    Sophia, as a means of exerting sexual power and gaining racial revenge, there are
    both positive and negative images of the relationship, which is more favorably pre-
    sented than the image of interracial relationships in *Jungle Fever*, despite the fact

that Malcolm X himself came to sharply condemn Black men pursuing white women.

23 The Nation of Islam, for instance, preached Black superiority, presented the white man as a "devil," and in general engaged in racially dubious teachings, advocating Black separatism rather than structural social transformation. For some years, Malcolm X shared this perspective, but eventually distanced himself from such teachings and developed more revolutionary and internationalist perspectives. See such collections of Malcolm X's later writings as X 1992.

24 Obviously, the question of historical accuracy is important in evaluating a film that has the pretense of telling the truth about Malcolm X's life. Lee's book on the film (Lee and Wiley 1992) indicates that he was attempting to uncover the truth of Malcolm X's life through research and interviews, so one could validly examine the film for its historical accuracy; such a project, however, goes beyond the scope of this study. For some reflections on historical correctness and distortions of *X*, see the symposium in *Cineaste*, Vol. XIX, No. 4 (1993): 5–18 and the review by hooks 1993.

25 On the movement to abolish prisons, see Davis 2005 and my review "On Angela Davis and *Abolition Democracy*," *Radical Philosophy Review*, Vol. 10. Nr. 2 (2007): 149–156.

26 A police shooting database indicates that there have been 602 people shot and killed by the police already in 2019 by the end of August. See www.washingtonpost.com/graphics/2019/national/police-shootings-2019/ (accessed August 31, 2019).

27 A recent study by the Annenberg School of the University of Southern California revealed that Latinos are severely underrepresented in Hollywood in terms of films dealing with Latino characters and issues, directors, and producers, and utilize negative stereotypes. The survey indicated that "among 1,200 popular films released between 2007 and 2018 (a sample of the top 100 movies per year), just 4.5% of more than 47,000 speaking or named roles went to Latinx actors. Only 3% were leads or co-leads." Sonaiya Kelley, "Latinos Missing on Big, Small Screens. Representations is abysmal, with roles rare and stereotypical, a USC study finds," *Los Angeles Times,* August 27, 2019: E1, E3.

28 For an excellent study of Chicana and Chicano Film Culture, see Fregoso 1993 who presents a comprehensive and illuminating analysis of Chicano films, especially of the 1980s. On Latinos and Hollywood film, see Berg 2002 and Berumen 2016 and the excellent study of Latinas in film by Molina-Guzman 2010.

29 Rosa Linda Fregoso (1993: 1–9) has a detailed analysis of Valdez's early documentary film *I am Joaquin* (1969), and then an excellent chapter on Valdez's *Zoot Suit* and *La Bamba* (21–48), while Chon Noriega (2000: 1ff) provides an illuminating historical context for Valdez's cinematic and theatrical work which he discusses throughout his study of the rise of Chicano cinema.

30 Isabel Molina-Guzman (2010) has an outstanding study of *Dangerous Curves. Latina Bodies in the Media* which has an illuminating chapter on *Frida* (87–118) and provides an excellent analysis of Latina images and forms of cultural identity.

31 On *Babel*'s aesthetic, see Marina Hassapopoulou, "*Babel*: Pushing and reaffirming mainstream cinema's boundaries," *Jump Cut*, No. 50 (Spring 2008) at www.ejump cut.org/currentissue/Babel/index.html (accessed December 22, 2008). I am, however, providing a more political reading of the film that highlights the critique of the politics of representation and the effects of globalization.

32 As the Bible tells the story of the Tower of Babel: "In the beginning, all the Lord's people from all parts of the world spoke one language. Nothing they proposed was impossible for them. But fearing what the spirit of man could accomplish, the Lord said, 'let us go down and confuse their language so they may not understand one another's speech.'" *Genesis* 11: 1–9.

33 I am appreciative of Oiyan Poon sharing her paper on *Babel* written for my 2007 cultural studies seminar.

34 A conservative reading, which I would not assert, might hold that since the father represents Japanese capitalism and patriarchy the reconciliation suggests that capital and patriarchy, cemented with love, can resolve crises and overcome separation and alienation. However, this ending is undercut by the possibility that the scene is initiating an incestuous relation, or may not result in any significant changes. In fact, throughout, the sexuality of non-Westerners and especially the Japanese is presented as chaotic, aberrant, and disordered – from a Western perspective –, thus sexual and racial representation in *Babel* is quite problematical.

35 The total domestic gross of *El Cantante* was only $7,556,712; see www.boxoffice mojo.com/search/?q=EL%20CANTANTE (accessed September 2, 2019).

36 See the Human Rights Watch report, "In the Freezer Abusive Conditions for Women and Children in U.S. Immigration Holding Cells," February 28, 2018 at www.hrw.org/report/2018/02/28/freezer/abusive-conditions-women-and-children-us-immigration-holding-cells (accessed September 9, 2019).

5

GENDER AND SEXUALITY WARS

Media culture has always featured lavish displays of sexuality, and depictions of relations between men and women while gender representations have been among the most explored and debated in contemporary U.S. culture. Yet, interestingly, the conservative Bush–Cheney era and the Trump era witnessed an extensive panorama of portrayals of gays, lesbians, transsexuals, rebellious women, crises in masculinities, and gender struggles, as well as the expected cycle of post-feminist films and action/adventure films celebrating a hard masculinity – all trends that continued through the Obama and Trump era into the present. Thus, whereas there has been a backlash against Hollywood liberal gender and sexual politics evident in the 2000, 2004, and 2016 U.S. presidential elections, where gay marriage and other hot-button items mobilized Republican voters (see Kellner 2005, 2017), in U.S. media culture more diverse and positive representations of gays and lesbians and negotiations of masculinity and femininity continues apace in the contemporary moment.

In this chapter, I explore the culture wars over sexuality and gender and renegotiations of masculinity, femininity, and sexuality in the media culture of the 2000s. A cycle of women's films and TV series, and media culture focusing on men and their relationships, reveal that there was a renegotiation of femininity and masculinity in the contemporary era, although major films and TV series dealing with women in the genres of melodrama and comedy, as well as the emergent popular genre of "chick films," showed quite conventional women and traditional femininities. While hard, conservative hypermasculinities still dominated action-adventure films and TV series, a renegotiation and softening of masculinities was evident in the "dude flicks" that I examine in this chapter. Further, male biopics, that usually celebrate successful strong masculinities evidenced crises of masculinity and patriarchy, as I document below. And, perhaps for the first time in the 2000s, Hollywood seriously opened its doors to explore multiple sexualities and featured many important films on gays, lesbians, bisexuals, and transsexuals, with non-conventional sexualities becoming part of many mainstream films.

Women's films, female resistance, and empowerment

While women characters found some compelling roles in major Hollywood films and TV series of the epoch, representations of strong and independent women did not fare so well. The dominant genres of the period were male-dominated, and recent studies of the predominance of male producers, directors, writers, and industry workers over women across a variety of fields have shown that the entertainment industry is male-centric, and that women are subordinate throughout the spectrum of positions, jobs, and roles in the entertainment industry (Hunt et al. 2018). Yet, in the recent past, there has been an explosion of allegations of sexual abuse that the #MeToo movement has publicized and is fighting, sexual abuse from verbal harassment to rape across a variety of arenas. There have been strong media exposés of abhorrent sexual abuse by major film producers like Harvey Weinstein, directors like Brett Ratner, actors like Kevin Spacey, and a wide range of individuals in other sectors of the film and entertainment industry.

However, as long as most of the people creating the messages are male, patriarchy is likely to continue. Nonetheless, we have seen shifts in the media landscapes with more women becoming producers, writers, directors, and actors. Many of these women struggle to create more empowering roles for women and resist traditional stereotyped representations of women that limit narratives and images to presenting women as mothers, daughters, lover, or individuals who are subordinate to men.

There were, of course, many films and TV series in the 2000s that centered on women, and many major and minor media texts had strong roles for women. As we shall see in this section, although there were many women-centric films and strong portrayals of women in traditional "women's films," melodramas, romantic comedies, and the emergent genre of "chick flicks" (i.e. films made largely for women audiences like *Sex and the City*), the representations of women were quite conventional, centering women in heterosexual romance, and as wife and mother, or career women. Traditionally, Hollywood privileged representations of women as mothers, romantic objects, or fallen "bad" women. "Good women" submitted to traditional roles and accepted subordination to men whereas "bad women" defined themselves outside the boundaries of traditional women's roles and morality. Hollywood film, radio broadcasting, and the early years of network television also enforced heteronormativity with entire genres and mainstream films and TV series celebrating romantic relations between men and women, the family, and the norms of bourgeois morality, with those stepping outside of the norms often punished for "immorality." Furthermore, characters subtly coded as LGBTQ+ were often presented as outsiders, punished, or made fun of.

I should acknowledge, however, the shifting roles of men and women in media representations and the ways that representations of women have changed since the women's movements and sexual liberation movements of the 1960s. Previously, in Hollywood film, radio broadcasting, and early television in the 1950s, the dominant female genres such as melodrama and the women's film, women were represented as mothers or daughters in the family, romantic objects, or "bad women" who disrupted the bourgeois order. Women also were represented in comedic roles in Hollywood comedies and television series like *I Love Lucy* and *Our Miss Brooks* where they were often the butt of jokes in ways that reproduced sexism. Today, however, film and television feature women in a variety of roles in government, industry, and positions of power, as well as a variety and diversity of personalities and sexualities.

In the last decade, the superhero genre in comics and movies has been challenging its previous stereotypes for race, gender, and sexuality by adding more diverse characters, such as a Black Captain America, a Muslim Pakistani American hero in Ms. Marvel, a transgender character as Batgirl #1, and a gay marriage between Kyle and Northstar. Curtis and Cardo (2018) attribute these changes to more women drawing and writing the comics and "partly due to the centrality of intersectionality and pluralism to third-wave feminism" (p. 282). In the past ten years, Marvel and DC comics each have added about a dozen new female characters (Curtis and Cardo, 2018).

Yet traditionally, and continuing in the contemporary moment, Hollywood films associate women with fashion, femininity, and romance, and a series of films of the 2000s have continued that tradition. One of the most successful women's films, *The Devil Wears Prada* (2006), take place in the milieu of the contemporary fashion industry.[1] Based on the best-selling 2003 novel by Lauren Weisberger, which contains a savage indictment of the industry based on her experiences as assistant with a legendary editor of *Vogue*, the film is directed by David Frankel, who helmed multiple episodes of *Sex and the City* and arguably celebrates the industry with the images of fashion and various characters embracing the industry.[2]

In the fairy-tale narrative, just-graduated journalism student Andrea Sachs (Anne Hathaway) gets a job as second assistant to the powerful and ruthless Miranda Priestly (Meryl Streep), top executive of *Runway* fashion magazine. Mocked by Priestly's first assistant Emily (Emily Blunt) for her nativity and poor fashion sense, the art director and second banana Nigel (Stanley Tucci), takes Andrea under his wing and in a montage of celebratory spectacle, she is made over by the wonders of fashion and cosmetics, emerging as a beauty able to compete in the cut-throat world of image and fashion spectacle. Nigel also impresses upon her all of the creativity that goes into making fashion and the hopes and dreams it gives to women for a better life. Miranda's imperious and excessive demands keep Andrea racing to do menial and increasingly unimportant tasks day and night, straining her relation with her boyfriend Nate (Adrian Grenier), her family, and friends. But Andrea becomes increasingly competent and ruthless, managing to get copies of the unpublished *Harry Potter* manuscript for Miranda's twins and agreeing to replace Emily as first assistant in a coveted trip to Paris for the fashion show of the season, which breaks Emily's heart. Andrea's boyfriend, Nate, has become fed-up with how his sweet girl-friend has changed, while a girlfriend berates her for selling out and becoming like the fashion sharks that she initially was appalled by.

Yet Andrea appears completely taken by the glamour and wonder of Paris, and glitz of the yearly fashion spectacle, and, estranged from her boyfriend, submits to the charms of a *New Yorker* writer who she idolizes and met earl-ier, but warded off. He tells her the morning after that a new corporate owner has bought *Runway* and will replace Miranda with her major female industry rival. Nigel is meanwhile ecstatic to learn that a quickly rising fash-ion designer star is starting a new global line and wants him as his partner. Rushing to warn Miranda that her job is in jeopardy, Andrea quickly learns that Miranda has manipulated her rival to become partner with the fashion star of the day, crushing Nigel's dreams, and making sure that she will stay on as top editor. Although the audience is positioned to momentarily sympa-thize with Miranda as a fellow suffering human being who is losing her cov-eted job and having her marriage break up at the same time (a detail not in Weisberger's novel), ultimately her triumph validates her as a corporate genius and role model for aspiring young women. Brilliantly played by Meryl Streep, the audience is positioned to admire and ultimately affirm Miranda, despite her often monstrous behavior.

In a fake fairy tale ending, Andrea quits her job, gets her boyfriend back, and even receives a writing job at the *New Yorker*, thus ultimately fulfilling her dreams. The anti-feminist message is that that if you sell your soul to the Devil, completely compromise your values, ignore family and friends in favor of work, cheat on your boyfriend, and do exactly what you are told, you too will realize your dreams, especially if you look great and get a good letter of recommenda-tion from the Devil.

If one can believe chick flicks, marriage is the dream fantasy of all proper young women, and *27 Dresses* (2008) provides a thorough assemblage of all the clichés of romantic comedy leading inexorably to a wedding and happy ending. Directed by Anne Fletcher and written by Aline Brosh McKenna, who previ-ously was scriptwriter for the adaptation of *The Devil Wears Prada*, *27 Dresses* features Katherine Heigl as Jane, an amateur wedding planner and dedicated wedding junky who has collected 27 bridesmaids' dresses, the title of the film. Racing from one wedding in New York to another in Brooklyn one night, Jane meets a cynical journalist who writes on weddings and introduces himself as Kevin (James Marsden), although later he will be unveiled as a wedding col-umnist whose work Jane adores and even keeps his articles in a scrapbook.

Jane's day job is to serve as an assistant to an executive, George (Edward Burns), who runs an outdoor equipment company and with whom she is secretly in love. Her wise-cracking co-worker and girlfriend (Judy Greer) tells her to go for it and express her feeling for him. She is about to do so, but her beautiful sister, Tess (Malin Akerman), appears, flirts with George, who instantly falls for her insincere and deceitful patter, and sweeps him off his feet. The two are soon engaged and naturally select Jane as wedding planner. Meanwhile, Kevin becomes intrigued by Jane's always-a-bride's-maid-and-never-a-bride history, and plots to write a piece about her under the guise of doing an article on Tess and George's wedding. While Kevin and Jane, in typical screwball romantic comedy fashion, argue and bait each other, Jane puts on a home fashion show, donning the 27 dresses for Kevin and it is clear that they are falling in love.

Eventually, their Big Romantic Moment comes when they are stranded in the rain when Jane crashes her car and they proceed soaking wet to a local bar when they get stinking drunk and belt out heartfelt lyrics to Elton John's "Benny and the Jets." The morning after they must deal with their hangovers and embarrassment, and Jane must deal with her sister's upcoming wedding. Kevin's article about Jane is published by his editor without his permission and Jane is humiliated and her sister, Tess, is outraged because for once it was all about Jane, who herself was presented as a shallow and typical promoter of a $70 billion wedding business that forced prospective brides to spend big bucks on silly luxuries.

Tess forgives Jane, who was not in any case guilty, and proceeds with the wedding. In a totally out of character, and unbelievable performance, Jane reads the text that Tess had written for her at the wedding ceremony to the accompaniment of slides that demonstrate Tess is a lying hypocrite. Kevin is totally impressed with this cheeky act of subversion and dedicates himself to winning Jane, while George breaks off his wedding and tentatively expresses his feelings for Jane, but a failed attempt at a kiss shows that there is nothing there, and so Jane can get it on with Kevin and they can be married one year later, with George and Tess re-eyeing each other in a more mature fashion at the wedding ceremony, suggesting multiple happy endings …

While 27 Dresses takes a stab at a critique of the wedding industry, it ends up fully re-establishing big weddings as the key to What Women Should Want. The film version of the popular TV show Sex and the City (2008), directed and written by Michael Patrick King, continues to be an anthem of "fucking and shopping" feminism in which the four intrepid independent New York women are depicted five years into the future facing being 40-something.[3] We open with Samantha (Kim Cattrall) continuing to be driven by sex in a hot relation with a boy-toy TV star Smith in a Malibu beach-front California dream; Charlotte (Kristen Davis) is happily married to her divorce lawyer with whom she has adopted a Chinese child and during the course of the narrative their frequent sex produces pregnancy and a their own child; Miranda (Cynthia Nixon), however, learns from Steve that he had a brief affair and she immediately kicks him out of the house and it will take almost two filmic hours for them to reconcile. The narrative focus, of course, is on the narrator Carrie (Sarah Jessica Parker) who recounts her excitement concerning her forthcoming marriage to Mr. Big (Chris Noh), that she promotes in a *Vogue* article as a major event of the season, as well as her life.

When Big learns that there will be over 200 guests and that he will have to jump through a series of nuptial hoops, he gets cold feet and leaves the distraught 40-year old would-be-bride stranded at the altar. In the face of extreme crisis, the girls know that spending money is always good medicine and so the fabulous four go to a resort in Mexico where Carrie and Big were to honeymoon. Carrie is morose and sulky, however, and Charlotte is afraid to eat anything because of dreaded turista, but she allows a few drips from the shower to pollute her pure body and, sure enough, a couple of minutes later she gets Carrie and the girls laughing uproariously when a gurgling stomach and out of control bowels produce an event that everyone wants to avoid.

Back in NY, the girls try to cheer up Carrie with fashion shows, cosmopolitans, and fancy restaurants, but not even shopping until she drops, and providing product placement for several fashion companies, will quell her loneliness, and the rest of the movie is dedicated to the cornerstone of pop philosophy: ALL YOU NEED is LOVE. And so we learn that fashion and love are what young women desperately need for happiness, although a few, like Charlotte, need the supplement of marriage and children. So far, none of them have tried lesbianism, or joined a woman's group or social movement.

Diane English's update of *The Women* (2008) has a minor lesbian character, but it operates in the same upper class world and with the same post-feminist values as *Sex and the City*. Based on Clare Booth Luce's 1936 play, which carried out a biting assault on New York upper crust society women and George Cukor's witty 1939 women's picture classic, English's 2008 update lacks the bite, satire, and classy sophistication of the original versions. Opening appropriately with a paean to consumerism, much of the action takes place in Saks Fifth Avenue department store and revolves around perfume, manicures, face-lifts, and affairs. Women are either mothers or working women in the fashion industry (one edits a woman's fashion magazine and the other presents a designer fashion show after she learns her husband is having an affair and decides she needs a career). The film is resolutely classist, sympathizing with the trials and tribulations of its rich characters played by superstar actresses while presenting shallow caricatures of the working class women in Saks. Of course, there is a noble housekeeper and nanny in the house of the woman whose husband is having an affair with the Saks perfume spritzer who, surprise! surprise!, is Latina (Eva Mendez), presenting the worst stereotypes of the lower class seductress and social climber.[4]

Other women's films of the 2000s deal with how housewives contribute to economic survival in tough times, the challenges of working women, and dilemmas of unwanted or unplanned pregnancy. Steve McQueen's *Widows* (2018) uses the heist genre to explore female oppression and attempts at empowerment, while *A Star is Born* (2018) uses the oft-told story of a rising music star, who surpasses her male love/mentor in success leading to his tragic demise, to portray a narrative of female success. However, critics who have applied the Bechdel test to film, which asks whether a work features at least two women who talk to each other about something other than a man, indicates that only half of all films meet these criteria, according to user-edited databases and the media industry press.[5]

Yet the popular TV series *Orange Iis the New Black* provides perhaps the most diverse array of characters, ethnicities, and female bodies and women's lives of any popular text of media culture and engages the intersectionality of women's lives in the dimension of gender, race, sexuality, and class in a challenging and original fashion.

Epic of intersectionality: *Orange Is the New Black*

Orange Is the New Black is truly an epic of intersectionality with its many female characters of highly diverse ethnicities, social classes, backgrounds, and body types. The concept of *intersectionality* articulated by Kimberly Crenshaw (1991) calls for the importance of mapping the intersections of oppression and domination across the lines of race, gender, sexuality, class, and other forms of oppression, and *Orange Is the New Black* depicts how intersections of gender, race, class, sexuality, and religion construct hierarchies of oppression and domination but also lines of resistance and solidarity.

The TV series *Orange Is the New Black* was created by Jenji Kohan for Netflix, and is based on Piper Kerman's memoir, *Orange Is the New Black: My Year in a Women's Prison* (2010), about her experiences at FCI Danbury, a minimum-security federal prison. The series was one of the first Netflix-produced break-out series, premiering July 11, 2013, while in 2018 it was announced that its seventh season would be its last. The series has won Emmy awards as both a comedy and drama and it combines realist exposes of life in a women's prison with melodrama surrounding the prisoners, guards, and prison officials, punctu-ated with moments of love stories, horror, sometimes surreal comedy, and highly critical representations of the prison system in the U.S.A. today.

The series opens revolving around the shock of prison incarceration for Piper Chapman (Taylor Schilling), a white, educated woman in her thirties living in New York City, upon whose memoirs the series is based. Piper is sentenced to 15 months in Litchfield Penitentiary in a minimum-security women's federal prison in upstate New York. She was convicted of transporting a suitcase full of drug money for her girlfriend, Alex Vause (Laura Prepon), who was participat-ing in an international drug smuggling ring. Alex will also be arrested, sent to Litchfield, and serve as a major figure through much of the series.

The title *Orange Is the New Black* signifies that prisoners, who are forced to wear orange jumpsuits in Lichtfield, are the new oppressed class. The series features many Black, Latino/a, and a few Asian and other ethnic characters, and often shows how race continues to be a mark of oppression in varied social settings such as prison. Episodes often feature flashbacks of significant events from various inmates' and prison guards' pasts, and these flashbacks often reveal how an inmate and guard came to be in prison while developing a character's backstory. Hence, the series provides a diverse set of vignettes of people of color, and poor white people, struggling to survive in a racist and classist society, being driven into crime, and then finding themselves incarcerated in prisons.[6]

Early seasons focus on personal relations and the intersectional focus on race, class, sexuality, and gender dynamics in relations between the inmates, guards, and those in their past life. The series presents one of the more in-depth explorations of how the inmates' positionalities intersect and form multiple modes of oppression, as well as friendship and resistance. Relationships of domination and subordination are a major focus of the series, both in the cases of relations between prison officials and the inmates, and among the prisoners themselves. From the start, there was a vast panorama of characters of highly diverse ethnicities, sexualities, social classes, character types, and highly individual and idiosyncratic people.

For a diagnostic critique, *Orange Is the New Black* displays how prisons are inherently alienating and do little to rehabilitate prisoners. It highlights authoritarian power structures among both the guards and the prisoners, and shows guards and prisoners committing highly sadistic actions against other inmates. The fifth season features the prisoners revolting against the guards, wardens, and the system after a private prison corporation MCC, which took over running Lichtfield, attempted to cover up the handling of an inmate's death at the hands of a guard in the fourth season. The guard's crushing and choking to death of a popular inmate, Poussey, was reminiscent of the Eric Garner case, as was the prison system's covering up the killing and not bringing the guard to justice. The inmate death had followed a peaceful protest and subsequent instigation of an inmate fight by another guard. Fueled by oppressive conditions the inmates are forced to tolerate, as well as grudges against the prison guards, a three-day riot ensues. During the riot, some inmates attempt to negotiate better living conditions and seek justice for the death of the inmate Poussey, while others pursue their own interests and entertainment, and a few seek no involvement.

At the emergence of the riot, the guard who incited the fight in the prior season is critically wounded by an inmate who took the gun a guard illegally brought into the prison. A Latina inmate, Ruiz, picks up the gun and the ensuing scenes present it as an instrument of power. A brief "carnival" follows in which prisoners incarcerate guards, act out fantasies of power, and reverse social hierarchies. During these scenes there are rare moments of unity and solidarity as the prisoners overcome their racial, class, sexual, and ideological divisions to resist the prison system and to try to overturn and reform it.

At the end of season five, SWAT raids the prison to end the riot and remove all inmates from the facility. During this raid, a correctional officer is fatally wounded by a corrupt "strike team," which then conspires to blame the guard's death on inmates who hid in an underground bunker and had taken the guard hostage. The inmates are transported to other prisons and the last two seasons featured streamlined focus on the main characters with some new characters and themes.

The consequences of the riot are shown in the sixth season. A number of the inmates, including Chapman and Vause, as well as many other of the series' many characters, are transported to Litchfield Maximum Security. Most of these inmates are interrogated, and several of them charged and sentenced for their involvement in the riot. In "Max," new inmates are introduced, alliances are made, and a gang-like war emerges between two prison blocks, spearheaded by a longstanding feud between two sisters and a grudge harbored by them toward a former maximum-security inmate who returned. D-block is led by a hardened older inmate and drug addict Barb (Mackenzie Phillips), opposed to C-block, dominated by Barb's sister Carol (Henny Russell), a stone-faced killer in over-sized eyeglasses. Barb and Carol have long simmering rivalries and both seek control over Litchfield's drug-smuggling operation while demanding absolute loyalty and submission from their crew.

For a diagnostic critique, the war between C- and D-blocks replicates the country's political divide during the Trump years, with C-block resident Blanca derisively referring to her rivals as "D-plorables"), and it features new hardcore characters like Carol's nasty lieutenant Madison (nicknamed "Badison"), and Daddy, Barb's Latina enforcer. Season six also contains many scenes that show life outside of Lichtfield for former prisoners like Aleida (Elizabeth Rodriguez), who, unable to get a job because of her prison record, reluctantly begins selling herbal supplements while her resentful children languish in foster care. Aleida gets in an altercation with one of her daughter's boyfriends, trashes what she believes is his car, and is returned to prison to rejoin the characters in Licthfield. Her story is a grim but necessary reminder that freedom, for many of these women, will simply be a new phase of a lifelong sentence.

Season six portrays further corruption in the private prison system run by a for-profit corporation MCC whose officials are shown concerned primarily with the bottom line and not the well-being of the prisoners and guards. Throughout the series, it is shown how various forms of corruption, funding cuts, privatization of prisons, overcrowding, guard brutality and racial discrimination (among other issues), affect the prisoners' safety, health and well-being, as well as the well-being of the correctional officers, and the prison's basic ability to fulfill its fundamental responsibilities and ethical obligations as a corrections institution. One of the show's key conflicts involves one-time prison warden Joe Caputo, who undergoes a metamorphosis from hard-nosed prison administrator to warden who increasingly cares about the prisoners. This turn leads to constant conflict with the corporate interests of MCC and authoritarian guards, which acquired Licthfield when it was about to be shut down, and Caputo is constantly pushing for reform that will help the prisoners.

Episode five of season four "We'll Always Have Baltimore" presents Caputo going to a prison conference "Correction Con" with gung-ho MCC corporate honcho Linda. In satirical vignettes, Caputo and Linda pass by demonstrations of the newest laser guns, Tasers, and other high tech weapons used to control prisoners, hear about "faith based rehabilitation" programs, and encounter the keynote speaker, Kip Carrigan, who presents the corporate take on prisons as new sources of capital and speaks of immigrant detention camps emerging as "new profit centers." The speaker is interrupted by a young man who is working in prisons and argues that all of the corporate measures to increase profit harm the inmates, articulating a strong critique of prisons as corporate profit centers. These discourses transcode the for-profit corporate private prison line opposed to those who see this configuration as harmful to prisoners, guards, and administrators and society at large. On the whole, the series thus produces public pedagogies concerning the problems and limitations of private corporate prisons.

The final seasons, six and seven, focus significantly on Piper, her release, and challenges during reentry into a "normal" life. There is also intense focus on Taystee (Danielle Brooks), an African American woman blamed for orchestrating the prison riot that leads to the death of a guard, who is shown going though stages of anger and alienation, and then empowerment. Knowing that she is now in Max for life for a crime that she did not commit, Taystee adapts to her new situation, becomes a trusted assistant to a new young African American warden, and gains a measure of redemption.

Taystee is aided in her rehabilitation by prison official Caputo who increasingly reveals himself to be humane and sympathetic to the prisoners. He testifies to Taystee's innocence in regard to the guard's death in the riot and her good character and leadership. Yet he too falls in trouble when a former inmate accuses him of sexual harassment and he loses his job in a gesture toward the #MeToo movement. Caputo admits to his misdeed and tries to rehabilitate himself as a teacher in the prison, but his past comes out and he loses this job.

Filmed during the Trump era, the final seasons focus on a panorama of Latina characters and an ICE detention center is brought into the prison with highly authoritarian and abusive guards. Latina characters are shown being brought back into prison because of questions about their immigration status, and others are brought in, or not let out, because of their absence of a green card. One sequence focuses on Blanca Flores (Laura Gómez), shown as a particularly strong character who survives years in prison. When she becomes part of a group of convicts slated for early release, along with Piper and others, Piper notes that as they're being led off to be processed out, the line is divided in two. In one line are the Black and white women, while in the other line the brown ones, including Blanca, march out.

As the two groups emerge from the prison, the Blacks and whites run out to a gathered crowd of family waiting to meet them, while the Latina women are met by ICE officers and they are put into a bus that takes them to an ICE detention center. Cuffs are placed on Blanca's wrists, and she starts to weep. Her husband Diablo is left standing at the wire fence that stands between the prison and freedom forlornly holding a bouquet of flowers.

Interspersed within this sequence are scenes from a ritzy gathering hosted by PolyCon Corrections, the parent company of Litchfield's owners MCC. There, senior vice president Linda Ferguson (Beth Dover) unveils the company's expansion into the new and growing market of Immigration and Customs Detention centers, which indeed grew profitable during the Trump era, although they were plagued by scandals as families were separated, children were put in cages, and many immigrants died trying to cross the border or in detention centers.

Orange Is the New Black signals this situation with a title of episode 1 from season seven "And Brown Is the New Orange." In season seven, which was broadcast during Trump's war on immigrants, the show depicts the horror of immigrant detention as some previous characters, like Blanca, are re-arrested because they lack proper documentation and new characters are added to dramatize the horrors of arrest and incarceration in ICE and other immigrant detention centers. A popular character Maritza is shown free and partying at a club, and then arrested by ICE for having expired papers. The following sequences show her sequestered in the ICE detention center, sent back to Central America and injured on a dangerous trek in the mountains on a forced return to her country.

From the beginning, the series has presented a strong interrogation of white privilege, and depicted multiple forms of racial oppression against characters of color. An epic of intersectionality, it shows how middle and upper class white people are privileged in the court and prison system and have strong support networks waiting for them on the outside. People of color and the poor, by contrast, suffer deprivation and oppression that often forces them into prison, where they find a new hierarchical system of oppression that targets them in particular. Then, when they get out, they face new challenges that often are overwhelming and drive them back into the prison system, while privileged whites like Piper are able to re-enter their comfortable middle class existence, and have some possibility of happiness and even success.

Throughout its seven seasons, *Orange Is the New Black* grapples with narrative tension between intense drama and illustrating the many horrors of the prison system contrasted to its satire, comedy, and focus on interpersonal relationships and individual personalities and backstories. Major characters go through narrative arcs that allow them to develop as individuals and some are able to undergo positive growth and transformation, while others are victims of the prison system and its inherent oppression, especially for underclass inmates and prisoners of color. In some characters, such as Suzanne ("Crazy Eyes"), comedic scenes illuminate problems of mental illness, while the narrative also shows her developing serious relationships and undergoing positive growth, presenting an unusual tableaux of an individual struggling with mental health issues in the most difficult circumstances.

A Muslim character, hijab-wearing Abdullah (Amanda Stephen), is at first regarded with suspicion by other inmates, and then comedic episodes humanize her and normalize her relations with other inmates, providing a rare positive representation of Muslim characters. The transgender person Sophia Burset (Laverne Cox), however, whose depictions in the earlier seasons were hailed as ground-breaking and illuminating,[7] undergoes such intense suffering in later episodes that it perhaps sends a message that such transformation can only bring suffering and tragedy.

Despite the positive representations of gender, sexuality, religion, class, race, and other identity markers, the transformative developments of some of the characters, and the critical humanism that finds moments of empathy, unity, and humanity under the most difficult circumstances has led to debates over whether *Orange Is the New Black* sugarcoats the most monstrous activities in everyday prison life, or whether it accurately represents prisons in the U.S. during the contemporary era.[8] Does it undercut more radical positions on prisons such as Angela Davis' *Abolition Democracy* (2011), which documents the obsolescence of prisons, their role as a force of racial oppression, and the need for their abolition? Or does it advance the need for progressive and humane reform of the U.S. prison system which it presents in a critical light?

Ava DuVernay's documentary *13* (2016) also presents critical visions of the history of racial inequality in the United States, focusing on the fact that the nation's prisons are disproportionately filled with African Americans. DuVernay's film argues that slavery has been perpetuated since the end of the American Civil War through criminalizing African American behavior and enabling police to arrest poor freed Blacks and to force them to work for the state under convict leasing, which DuVernay presents as another form of slave labor. *13* also dramatically presents suppression of African Americans by disenfranchisement; periodic orgies of lynchings and restrictive Jim Crow laws; politicians declaring a war on drugs that weigh more heavily on minority communities; and, by the late twentieth century, mass incarceration of people of color in the United States. DuVerney's *13* thus present highly critical perspectives on the prison-industrial complex and the emerging immigrant detention-industrial complex, discussing how much money is being made by corporations from such incarcerations and the suffering it imposes on its victims.

In the next section, I shift focus from representations of women and their intersectional relationships to class, race, sexuality, and hierarchical oppression, to representations of men and masculinities. Gender analysis involves unpacking the social construction of masculinity and femininity and relations between men and women, and accordingly the next section will deal with "Men's films and crises of masculinity and patriarchy."

Men's films and crises of masculinity and patriarchy

The 2000s have seen myriad examples in cinematic culture and everyday life of multiple crises of masculinity. In *Guys and Guns Amok* (Kellner 2008), I analyze how crises of masculinity and their resolution through acts of violence that create media spectacle have proliferated from school shootings to domestic terrorism and frequent explosions of violence in everyday life. In Hollywood films of the epoch, there are also multiple examples of men in crisis, although few resort to violence and media spectacle to resolve their issues.

There are many forms of "crises in masculinities" rooted in fundamental transformations of the economy and society. In his classic *Manhood in America* (1996) and other texts, Michael Kimmel argues that throughout history men have been impelled to prove their masculinity through socially approved means and social roles, and he discusses a crisis of masculinity in the modern era when with the decline of industrial labor, many men lost their jobs and status as home providers, and then in the 1960s felt themselves under attack by feminism and other movements.

Susan Faludi argued in *Stiffed* (1999) that the crisis in masculinities was largely a product of the changing socio-economic conditions since World War II, in which the culture presented false ideals for men to live up to. In a highly sympathetic analysis of men's plight in the post-war economy, Faludi sagely notes in her Introduction that masculine ideals mutated in the post-war era from a prewar American ideal of the Westerner surviving in and controlling the wilderness, often through the gun and aggression. This was appropriate to the era of the frontier, but in the era during World War II, a new ideal emerged of the foot-soldier memorialized by Ernie Pyle who fought bravely and valiantly for his country, was part of a unit that worked together, and then returned to be husbands and fathers to the next generation – an ideal put on display in Ken Burns's populist epic *War* (PBS 2007), which focused on ordinary people and their bonding war experience.

Faludi pointed out that after the war, men were given a new "mission to manhood" with a "new frontier" (space exploration), a new enemy to fight (Soviet Communism), a new brotherhood (corporations and government agencies), and "the promise of a family to provide to and protect" (1999: 26). Men were let down in all of these promises: Space exploration was not a unifying ideal and the Russians got into outer space first with Sputnik, dealing a blow to American manhood; the Cold War with Communism got the U.S. stuck in unpopular wars like Korea and Vietnam with no clear-cut victory and foe, and produced devastation and personal defeat for many soldiers; corporations and government allowed "downsizing, restructuring, union-breaking, contracting-out, and outsourcing" (1999: 30), and thus the loss of job and economic security, as Faludi documents throughout her book. Many men would therefore not be able to provide for their families as they lost their jobs and suffered downward mobility, while women challenged them in the family, in part after the second wave of feminism.

I might note that I strongly agree with Faludi that it is certainly not feminism and women that are the origins of the crisis in masculinity, but changing socio-economic conditions that threw men into crisis and generated problematic images of masculinity that emerged. Feminists have importantly called attention to gender construction, highlighted themes of gender relations, and have helped generate and illuminate many of the issues explored in this book.[9]

Film biographies on the whole in the 2000s tended to feature men. *The Aviator* is one of the more critical of the series of successful male biopics of the 2000s while many focus on famous male singers and include *Ray* (Charles), Bobby Darin (*Beyond the Sea*, 2004), Cole Porter (*De-Lovely*, 2004), Johnny Cash (*I Walk the Line*, 2005), Hector LaVoe (*El Cantante*, 2007),[10] Bob Dylan (*I'm Not There*, 2007), and N.W.A. (*Straight Outta Compton*, 2015). They all in different ways deal with crises in masculinity and show the male protagonists struggling for success and identity.

Hence, many major male biopics can be read as a diagnostic critique of hegemonic masculinity and patriarchy. Martin Scorsese's biopic of Howard Hughes, *The Aviator* (2004), puts on display the crisis of patriarchy and masculinity in the post-World War II epoch. Howard Hughes embodies the hegemonic hypermasculinitiy of the day (to be sure in highly neurotic and idiosyncratic forms). Hughes is a Man's Man driven to success with business, women, and attaining celebrity. In Leonardo DiCaprio's interpretation, Hughes is portrayed as a control freak who must conquer every horizon in his chosen fields of aviation, filmmaking, and womanizing. He must break aviation speed records, significantly beat Lindbergh's record for flying around the world in record time, build the biggest airplanes and airline, and dominate all fields of aviation, hence the title of Scorsese's film *The Aviator*. Hughes also becomes a successful film producer and ultimately the richest man in the world when he eventually sells off his holdings in Transworld Airlines (TWA).

The Aviator presents Hughes as a compulsive womanizer, bedding cigarette-girls in fancy restaurants and scores of Hollywood starlets, as well as falling for Hollywood's most successful and attractive actresses. The women that Hughes gets most involved with are a patriarch's nightmare, an uncontrollable and ultimately unfaithful Katharine Hepburn (Cate Blanchett), and an ultimately unobtainable and unpossessable Ava Gardner (Kate Beckinsale). Hughes wins Hepburn's affections with his unconventional behavior, flying her over Los Angeles in his private jet and letting her take control at one point, a process coded as sexual turn-on and gratification, which highlights Hughes' power and manliness. Yet Hepburn obviously does not want to ultimately play second-fiddle and no doubt perceives Hughes' instability and dangerousness, eventually dropping him for Spencer Tracy.

Revealingly, and symptomatically, the film blames Hughes's obsessive compulsive disorders (OCD), which propelled him into madness, on his mother.

Echoing *Citizen Kane*'s "Rosebud," in which a closing scene provides a clue to Kane's personality and the movie, the opening sequence shows Hughes' mother bathing her eight-year-old son and warning him about germs and diseases, while teaching him to spell "quarantine." The images suggest incest and may explain Hughes' later obsession with milk and breasts, two figures that recurrently appear throughout his romantic interludes as well as his filmmaking and aviation feats. The plot highlights his search for clouds like breasts as a filmmaker, in which his epic film *Hell's Angels* (1930) was postponed for months until the proper cloud formation appears. There are also shots throughout of Hughes drinking milk from the bottle and focusing on the breasts of movie stars and starlets, leading to a battle with the censorship board over the cleavage revealed in *The Outlaw* (1943) that Hughes produced. It is as if all of Hughes' ultimately destructive obsessions are related to a mother-fixation, a coding highlighted at the end of the film as the camera flashes back, à la Kane's Rosebud, to his early scenes with his mother.

Hughes' interventions in the film business seem to be motivated in part to bed Hollywood stars and starlets, after the success of *Hell's Angels*, which documented his aviation obsession. Scorsese's film suggests that Hughes' major contribution to Hollywood was marketing film as a super-spectacle. *The Aviator* lavishes attention on the premiere of *Hell's Angels*, which reportedly caused the biggest traffic jam in Hollywood history as more than half a million people crowded Hollywood to get a look at the stars. While D.W. Griffith and Cecil B. DeMille helped create the aesthetics of the Hollywood spectacle, surely Hughes helped in marketing and promoting spectacle and made himself a spectacle celebrity, with an avid public focused on every detail of his private life, as images of tabloids of the era demonstrated in the film, even when he became more and more reclusive and eccentric.

In general, *The Aviator* is one of the more critical of the series of biopics of the 2000s. Hughes' madness and destructiveness, as well as his achievements and genius are shown in balanced measures. To be sure, the first half of the film tends to follow the form of the celebratory biopic as we see Hughes succeed in the film business, aviation, and with women. The editing and continuity shots flow into the typical arc of the rise of a powerful man who comes to dominate and control his environment, but as he unravels, so too does the film style mutate into fragmented, quick cutting, nervous jerky camera movements focusing on Hughes' phobias, using dark and shadowy backgrounds, and fast editing that creates a sense of events spinning out of control.

To some extent, Hughes landed on his feet, however, defeating corporate rivals like Juan Trippe (Alec Baldwin) who tries to force through a corrupt Congress an aviation bill that would give his Pan Am company a monopoly on overseas travel and would exclude Hughes' TWA from certain key markets. Hughes recovers from paranoia and his obsessive disorders to defeat the Maine Senator (Alan Alda) who sponsors Trippe's legislation and who calls a Senate hearing to destroy Hughes on charges of war-profiteering. Hughes brilliantly turns the tables on the Senator, exposing him as the corrupt pawn of Juan Trippe, and emerges stronger than ever from the hearings. These sequences put on display the corruption in the defense industry and their congressional tools, problems still going on and perhaps intensified in the contemporary configuration of the military-industrial complex.

Yet the liberal film soft-pedals Hughes' extreme rightwing politics and his more unsavory actions with business and womanizing. By focusing on "The Aviator," Scorsese's film shows Hughes at his best, truly a visionary in the field of aviation who mastered detail in design and business, and was himself a legendary flyer. Yet the film also puts on display a crisis of patriarchy and masculinity in which even the richest and most powerful person in the world cannot control business, politics, women, and his own demons, falling prey to his obsessional disorders and the limitations of his mind and body and life history to eventually fall apart, the last of the great corporate and industrial titans ending up alone in madness in a Las Vegas hotel room.

Another biopic that engages male crisis and obsession with success, *The Hoax* (2007), addresses the story of Clifford Irving who wrote a fake bio of Howard Hughes himself. Directed by Swedish filmmaker Lars Halestrom and staring Richard Gere in a bravura performance as writer turned conman Clifford Irving, the film puts on display the driven masculinity that will succeed at all costs. After his novel was rejected by New York publisher McGraw-Hill, Irving, desperate for a popular success, concocted the scam of writing a biography of the elusive Hughes. Faking intimate connections with Hughes and his closed circle, Irving gets the mega-bucks contract, pulls off fake-interview episodes, and gets enough information to produce a credible insider tale of Hughes' life, only to be exposed by Hughes himself in one of his few public appearances who reveals the hoax and kills the book. The film puts on display the compulsion to success and celebrity of ambitious men in the portrait of the driven writer Irving, obsessed with having a literary success at all costs, and the mysterious Hughes who stands as a figure who obsessively controls his environment and image.

Portraits of driven men who struggle for the pinnacle of success are also evident in the series of music biopics of the epoch. *Ray* (2004) portrays the obsessive genius of Ray Charles who overcomes blindness to achieve stunning musical success in a wide range of musical genres, and is able to seduce and carry out passionate affairs with a number of women. Brilliantly brought to life by Jamie Foxx, the film provides an intense dual focus on both Charles' musical success and his complex relations with women. The film ultimately suggests that while woman's role is to serve her man and accept all his limitations, men have a wider scope of ambition and achievement, thus projecting a largely patriarchal vision that it is man's world.

Beyond the Sea (2004) centers on the ambition, successes, and failures of Bobby Darin, frenetically played and directed by Kevin Spacey. The film, like

The Aviator, suggests that Darin's mother, who unconditionally loved and supported him, was the key to his ambition and triumphs – and later insecurities. The film opens with a musical number presumably documenting Darin at the height of his success, but suddenly the singer interrupts the number, criticizes the musicians, and the camera pulls back and reveals it is a film set with Darin playing himself in his own biopic. Later, the plot will reveal that male identity itself, like film, is an artifice and construct and something that can be transformed and reconstructed.

Much of the plot focuses on Darin's relations to women and his entourage, which includes Brenda Blethyn as Darin's mother, Caroline Aaron as his overbearing sister, Bob Hoskins as the sister's husband and part of Darin's entourage, and John Goodman as his manager. Flashbacks show a young child (William Ullrich), who will accompany the older Darin throughout the film, being initiated into music by his vaudeville mother and learning that he has a rheumatic heart condition and could die young. We also see the boy's mother encouraging his ambition to be a superstar, another Sinatra, and to overcome all obstacles. In the fast-moving musical story-line, Darin effortlessly gains his early successes from pop music stardom with "Splish Splash," buffo nightclub performances, and movie roles that pair him with America's sweetheart Sandra Dee (Kate Bosworth). After a whirlwind courtship he marries Dee, realizes his dream in playing New York's Copacabana nightclub, and gets an Academy Award nomination for best supporting actor.

Seemingly at the pinnacle of early success, the dream quickly crashes as Darin and Dee viciously fight the night when Darin doesn't win the Oscar and his male rage explodes. The smashup is presented in comedic form where after busting up his house and Cadillac, Darin reconciles with Dee, and accepts his role as husband and father. The retreat into domesticity leads the 1960s to pass Darin by. Out of touch with the counterculture and political and musical currents of the day, he retreats to Big Sur in a camper for a year, campaigns for Bobby Kennedy, tries to reconfigure himself as a folk singer, and is booed off the stage when he tries his new act and songs in a nightclub.

As Darin struggles to come back, his sister reveals that she is really his mother and that her mother faked having the child to avoid the embarrassment of a 17-year-old unmarried young mother with an illegitimate child. Seeing that his whole life was based on lies, the mid-30s Darin, near the end of his life, throws off his phoniness, discarding his hairpieces and returning to his former self as Walden Robert Cassotto. By the end of the film, in the face of impending death, he accepts himself as Walden/Bobby Darin, husband, father, son, nightclub performer, and celebrity, and in a final comeback concert knocks out the crowd, introduces his mother for the first time, and then collapses after the performance, soon to die. The film does not allow an explicit presentation of his collapse and demise, as the small boy, now integrated with the man, leads Darin into triumphant musical numbers that highlight his achievement and his ability to forge a healthy and integrated masculinity with all its limitations and flaws.

Beyond the Sea thus negotiates crises of masculinity by showing Walden/ Bobby overcoming challenges, renouncing hyper-masculinity, and achieving both male identity and success. The film projects a triumphant vision of the integrated personality that is able to reconcile and accept all parts of his self and life, thus achieving what Carl Jung championed as an integrated self. The film also follows Joseph Campbell's "hero myth" with the character setting out on adventures, meeting obstacles that he overcomes, leaving the world for deep meditation, suffering great humiliations, but returning intact to deliver his gifts of music and entertainment to the people.

James Mangold's Johnny Cash biopic *I Walk the Line* (2005) features Joaquin Phoenix as the famed country singer, a paragon of tough, heterosexual masculinity, struggling for male identity and provides a sharply critical vision of patriarchy. During a Thanksgiving dinner when Cash's parents meet June Carter's fabled music legend parents for the first time, Johnny Cash reveals the hurt his father inflicted when he blamed his brother's youthful death on him. Cash's father had been portrayed throughout the film as a harsh, judgmental, and unloving patriarch, and the story implies that this upbringing and the trauma of his brother's death caused Cash's severe emotional problems and dependence on drugs. Yet at the end of the film, Cash is united with his father after he finally marries June Carter, and the final shot contains a deep focus framing of Cash in the middle with his father closest to the camera and Carter's father at the end of the scene, an image that implies that Cash too has finally successfully inserted himself within the patriarchal system, which has been threatened by his waywardness and non-conformity.[11]

Todd Haynes' Bob Dylan anti-biopic *I'm Not There* (2007) carries through perhaps the most radical deconstruction of the biopic genre. In an interview with *Cineaste*, Haynes notes that "the biopic, as it's evolved, is a deceitful genre. And we know it. We know that these films blend fact and fiction in every scene, in every bit of dialog."[12]

Taking a postmodern fragmentation and splintering of identity as far as one can imagine, Haynes has at least six actors play part of the Bob Dylan persona or myth, and none is named Bob or even Robert Zimmerman. In a joke on origins, a young Black performer, Marcus Carl Franklin, plays Woody, an 11-year-old troubadour who hitches rides on trains and lives on the open road – while Dylan in his autobiography *Chronicles* (2004) admits that the story he hitched rides on trains à la Woody is a myth and that: "What I did was come across the country from the Midwest in a four-door sedan, '57 Impala – straight out of Chicago" (2004: 8).

Another "Dylan" character (Ben Whishaw) plays Rimbaud, obviously the poetic and aphoristic side of the Artist as a Young Man. Christian Bale plays Jack, the earnest young folksinger and man of the people, shown in recreations of known footage of Dylan singing the "Ballad of Hattie Carroll," about poor Black folks in the south. Later in the film, Bale plays an evangelical Christian preacher, alluding to Dylan's brief conversion to Christianity. Heath Ledger performs Robbie, who plays Jack Rollins, a Hollywood actor in a biopic whose chaotic celebrity life wreaks havoc on a marriage with a woman artist and his two children, recreating Dylan's marriage dramas. But the only real Dylan impersonation, and it is a stunning one, is carried off by Cate Blanchett's figure Jude Quinn, an innocent abroad in a tour of England, where Jude/Dylan puts everyone on and English media and society get their comeuppance. Finally, Richard Gere plays Billy, an outlaw on the run and in hiding, reprising Dylan's "Pat Garrett and Billy the Kid" stage, in a highly Sam Peckanpahesque plot about a greedy land developer who will displace a valley full of long-time inhabitants so that a six-lane freeway can be built.

Dylan's music holds together the fragmented plotlines and while much is revealed at the end of the film we may realize we don't really know much about Bob Dylan and perhaps we were foolish to think that a biopic was going to tell us the truth about a complex person's life. Or maybe Haynes' postmodern play with Dylan's life and music, film and pop culture references, media critique, and wild story-telling tells us about as much about Dylan as we could expect to find out. For while D.A. Pennebacker's documentary of Dylan's London tour *Don't Look Back* (1967), featuring a 1960s Dylan so brilliantly recreated by Cate Blanchett in *I'm Not There*, gives us a good look at one side of Dylan at one moment in time, there is much more to be seen. Even Martin Scorsese's multi-part TV documentary *No Direction Home: Bob Dylan* (2005) provides footage and a storyline largely familiar to hardcore Dylan fans, among whom the author must be counted. Yet *I'm Not There* suggests that there's a lot more there, that may be impossible to capture. Hence, biopics, documentaries, and other modes of representation may never fully probe the mysteries about the relationships between Bob Dylan's music, his life, and times, and provide at best partial perspectives.

Thus, if *Beyond the Sea* suggests it is possible to create an integrated self and a rich complex masculine identity, *I'm Not There* provides a postmodern vision of identity as multiple, fragmented, and disconnected, and a human life as a mystery, difficult to grasp and depict, and perpetually open to change and transformation.

Finally, some docudrama/biopics have dealt with rap singers/groups, their rabid rise to fame, and the personal dramas of their lives. Several documentaries deal with the lives of Biggie Thomas and Tupace Shakur, such as Nick Broomfield's *Biggie & Tupac* (2002), which depicts the rivalry and violence between East Coast and West Coast rap groups and fans.

Straight Outta Compton (2015) uses the form of docudrama to portray the rise and fall of the gangsta rap group N.W.A and lives of its members Eazy-E, Ice Cube, Dr. Dre, DJ Yella, and MC Ren. The members of the group were involved in the production, including Ice Cube and Dr. Dre as producers, along with Eazy-E's widow, Tomica Woods-Wright, while MC Ren and DJ Yella served as creative consultants. The film opens in Compton, California, in 1986, and introduces the characters in vignettes that delineate their characters and aspirations. We first see Eazy-E trying to do a drug deal, but his connections don't want to pay and are raided by the police, who use a demolition machine to wreck their house, signaling the theme of police hostility to young Blacks that will be a major motif of the film.

Dr. Dre (Corey Hawkins) is introduced as an aspiring disc jockey, while Ice Cube, played by his real-life son, O'Shea Jackson Jr., is portrayed as an aspiring rapper, shown writing lyrics in a bus that passes through the industrial area of his native Compton, California. We see the formation of the group with Dr. Dre convincing drug dealer Eazy-E (Jason Mitchell) to fund a startup record label, Ruthless Records, with Dr. Dre as record producer and using Ice Cube's "reality raps" on the crime, gang violence, and police harassment that they and other African Americans encounter daily.

After their song "Boyz-n-the-Hood" is rejected by a New York rap entrepreneur, Dre convinces Eazy-E to perform it instead. It becomes a local hit, and Eazy-E, Ice Cube, Dr. Dre, DJ Yella, and MC Ren form the group N.W.A ("Niggaz Wit Attitudes"). At this point a Jewish record promoter Jerry Heller (Paul Giamatti) enters the story and Eazy-E accepts his offer to manage N.W.A and co-run Ruthless Records. At around the same time, Priority Records offers N.W.A a record deal. While recording their debut album, *Straight Outta Compton* (1988), the group are harassed by police due to their race and appearance, prompting Ice Cube to pen the song "Fuck tha Police."

The group assumes the image of aggressive masculinity and their album becomes a controversial hit due to its profanity, violent lyrics, and expressions of rage caused by ghetto life. The group's style is dubbed gangsta rap by the press and rap music becomes a major phenomenon of the epoch.[13] N.W. A. repeatedly clashed with the police with the F.B.I. demanding during a 1989 concert tour that the group should stop performing "Fuck tha Police" because it was allegedly encouraging violence against law enforcement.

Police in Detroit forbid them from performing the song, and a riot breaks out when they perform it anyway. Their manager, Jerry, delays producing the individual members' contracts with Ruthless, and when he insists that Ice Cube sign without legal representation, Ice Cube quits the group. His debut solo album, *AmeriKKKa's Most Wanted* (1990), becomes a hit, but when Priority Records is unable to pay him his advance on his next album, he trashes the label's head office. When N.W.A heavily insult Ice Cube on their next record, *100 Miles and Runnin'* (1990), he responds with the diss track "No Vaseline," criticizing Jerry and his former bandmates and prompting accusations of antisemitism. This, combined with Cube's outspoken criticism of the Los Angeles Police Department in the wake of the beating of Rodney King, and starring role in the 1991 film *Boyz n the Hood*, make him even more famous and controversial.

Dr. Dre hires Suge Knight as his manager, through whom he learns that Jerry has been underpaying him. Dre leaves N.W.A to form Death Row Records with Suge, who has his men threaten Jerry and beat Eazy-E to pressure them to release Dr. Dre from his contract with Ruthless. Dr. Dre enjoys his newfound freedom and begins working with other rappers including Snoop Dogg. Snoop's debut solo album, *The Chronic* (1992), sells over five million copies, even as he becomes disturbed by Suge's violent behavior and the community is rocked by the 1992 Los Angeles riots.

Eazy-E, whose fortunes and health have declined, is devastated by the comparative success of his former bandmates. Learning that Jerry has been embezzling money from Ruthless from the beginning, he fires him and rekindles his friendships with Ice Cube and Dr. Dre, who agree to an N.W.A reunion. However, before recording can begin, Eazy-E collapses and is diagnosed with HIV/AIDS. Amid emotional visits from his bandmates, he dies on March 26, 1995 and is mourned by fans.

A year later, Dr. Dre splits from Suge Knight and Death Row to form his own label, Aftermath Entertainment. Clips shown during the film's credits highlight Ice Cube's subsequent roles as a film actor and Dr. Dre's career as a producer and entrepreneur. Several famous rappers credit Dr. Dre with helping to launch their careers, and Beats Electronics, which he co-founded, is bought by Apple Inc. in 2014 for $3 billion.

Crises of masculinity and patriarchy, however, do not always find creative resolutions, and male violence is a pervasive feature of U.S. society and some Hollywood films like Stanley Kubrick's *The Shining* (1980), which uses the occult to show an inspiring writer, husband, and father driven by his crises of masculinities into extreme terror and violence, presenting an allegory of the disintegration of the family in contemporary U.S. society.[14]

While Hollywood film traditionally established hegemonic hard-masculinity as the ideal for men, or at least a smooth corporate identity, able to effectively wield societal and male power, Hollywood film on the 2000s has many portraits of males in crisis. Many of the dude flicks that I discuss in the next section show men renegotiating masculinity through male bonding or creating more liberal and flexible male identities.

Dude flicks and the renegotiation of masculinity

In the 2000s, female-centric "chick flicks" have been supplemented by "dude flicks," which often use comedy to present sex and relationships from a male point of view. Judd Apatow, Seth Rogen, and a group of young male collaborators have contributed mightily to the expanding subgenre of "dude flicks," although in this section, I'll show how the development is more complex and complicated than it may appear at first glance, as in its best efforts there have been interesting renegotiations of masculinity.

Romantic comedies are and have long been a highly popular stable of Hollywood film comedies. Previously, "chick flicks" presented romantic comedy from a women's point-of-view, while "dude flicks" use comedy to present sex, relationships, and life from a male point of view. While there are strong sexist and homophobic moments in some dude flicks, the genre as a whole can be read as a renegotiation of masculinity, undercutting the hard-bodied macho masculinity dominant in 1980s and many 1990s films.[15] In a broad sense, dude flicks range from the juvenile humor evident in popular teen comedies like the *American Pie* (1999, 2002, 2007) series, or Farrelly brother comedies, to films that seriously renegotiate masculinity and present alternative masculinities. Some dude flicks present men as victims who renounce romance and women in favor of male bonding and companionship, contrasted to dude flicks that work out more complex negotiations and egalitarian relations between men and women. Yet there are also dude flicks that use comedy to support a form of hegemony that re-inscribes male domination and superiority over women in fantasies in which often homely or untraditional romantic male heroes obtain beautiful women.

Judd Apatow and his collaborators have been the most prolific creators of dude flicks in the past decades that mostly present relationships from a male point of view. While there is some renegotiation of masculinity in the films produced by Apatow and his crew, for the most part they conservatively re-affirm the old hegemonic male-dominated relationships and heteronormativity. Apatow's *The 40 Year Old Virgin* (2005) features Steve Carrell as Andy Stitzer, a nerdy dude who has just never had sex. When the guys at work find out that he is a virgin, they tease him endlessly and scheme to get him laid. The film deals with male bonding at work featuring four guys who work and socialize together, eventually integrating Andy into the pack. At first, their female boss is presented as a castrating female, but as the film proceeds she softens and good-naturedly becomes obsessed with taking Andy's virginity herself.

Just as the dudes in the film bonded in the gym and sports, they also bond at work and bars. Each of them has issues with women, and their homosocial relations suggest this dude flick is something of a bromance film (i.e. brotherly romance), in which the men really love each other more than women, although the possibility of homosexuality will be exorcised by the end of the film.

After failed attempts to connect Andy with hot babes in bar pick-ups, he decides he really wants to date a nice woman who works across the street, Trish (Catherine Keener) who sells people's unwanted possessions on eBay. The film takes the format of a traditional romantic comedy with the couple falling in love, fighting, and overcoming obstacles to their relationship, and finally cementing their relation with superhot sex. Apatow's film, however, not only ends up with heteronormativity and conventional male-female romance, but puts on display anxieties about homosexuality. One improvisational sequence, expanded in the DVD, has the dudes teasing each other about their behavior with the retort "I know you are gay because … " repeated over and over.

Although the narrative suggests some of the characters, including Andy, may be gay, they are all paired heterosexually by the end of the film, establishing an ideal of heteronormativity for all.

Another subtheme of dude flicks shows men having trouble forming relations with women that can take the form of rejection of women in favor of male bonding, although, as in Apatow's films, they usually end up in a romantic relationship with an attractive woman. Some of these films present men as victims of women's scheming and misunderstanding. A major theme, though, seems to be men overcoming their problems with forming relationships with women and renegotiating their masculinity so they become more sensitive and capable of love.

While many dude flicks satirize the hegemonic hard masculinity and redefine masculinity, the recent dude flicks of Judd Apatow and his collaborators, by contrast, present fantasies of conventional, uncool, unsuccessful and not always good looking guys getting beautiful blonde trophy girls like the Seth Rogen character in *Knocked Up*, or in *Zack and Miri Make a Porno* (2008). These films also sometimes re-establish male-dominated romance and relationships, as in *Forgetting Sarah Marshall* (2008). Directed by Nicholas Stoller and produced by Apatow, the film features an ordinary guy protagonist Peter Bretter (Jason Segel, who wrote the script), in love with blonde beauty and TV star Sarah Marshall. Peter discovers Sarah is having an affair with a British pop star and when he travels to Hawaii to mend himself and get over Sarah, he discovers Sarah and the pretentious Brit dude are at the same resort. Sarah eventually is fed-up with the Brit, who is about to take off anyway on a two-year tour, and seems to be ready to go back to Peter, who, however, dumps her in favor of a new beauty waiting in the wings and ready to marry him.

Throughout the film, homely men are seen with beautiful women, and representations of women are generally quite negative. Indeed, often in Apatow-stable dude flicks, women who realize men's fantasies and subordinate themselves to the guys are represented positively, while women who do not submit and/or reject the dudes are presented negatively, portrayed as "bitches." These are obviously male fantasy films and tend to look at relationships from men's point of view. They also generally feature puerile male humor and are often politically incorrect, enjoying playing with taboos and hot buttons concerning the representation of gender, sexuality, race, or ethnicity. Finally, dude flicks, on the whole, show guys overcoming crises of masculinity by coupling with women in romantic relationships or by bonding with men, or both, which usually re-establish a threatened male-dominated heteronormative order.

The LGBTQ+ movement and Hollywood's exploration of gays, lesbians, transsexuals, and multiple forms of queer identity

Despite the Bush/Cheney administration and following attacks assault on gay marriage and the continual conservative attack on gays and lesbians, contemporary Hollywood has revealed growing acceptance of alternative sexualities. *Brokeback Mountain* swept major awards for 2005 and crossed over to mainstream audiences. Philip Seymour Hoffman won the Academy Award for his portrayal of *Capote* in 2005 bringing to the screen the conflicts that the gay writer and personality Truman Capote faced in writing *In Cold Blood*, and in 2006 another film devoted to Capote's life *Infamous* appeared. Felicity Huffman in turn won an Academy Award nomination and acclaim for her 2005 performance as a transsexual man in *Transamerica*, a boundary breaking film that presented a teenage son dealing with his father's sex change operation. And in 2008 Gus van Sant won an Academy Award for *Milk*, based on the life of murdered gay activist Harvey Milk, while Dustin Lance Black won an Oscar for his screenplay.

These works were influenced by the rise of New Queer Cinema that emerged in the 1990s,[16] including the 1991 documentary *Paris is Burning*, directed by Jennie Livingston, which portrayed New York's drag balls and houses, focusing on the people of color who occupied these spaces. Other influential works of New Queer Cinema included Todd Haynes's *Poison* (1991), Isaac Julien's *Young Soul Rebels* (1991), Tom Kalin's *Swoon* (1992), and Gregg Araki's *The Living End* (1992), where two gay and HIV positive guys go on a road trip after one kills a homophobic police officer.

It is appropriate that two films about Truman Capote would create breakthroughs in bringing gay figures and life into mainstream Hollywood cinema since it was Capote himself in the 1950s and 1960s who helped introduce to mainstream U.S. culture what we now call a gay sexual orientation, sensibility, and life-style to mainstream U.S. culture through his writings and literary success, frequent TV appearances, and status as a major figure in the New York celebrity and social scene, in which he became increasingly famous and written about.

Both Bennett Miller's highly successful 2005 film *Capote* and Douglas McGarth's 2006 release *Infamous* focus on Capote's life in the period during which he read a November 15, 1959 *New York Times* article about the brutal murder of a Kansas farm family through the completion of his non-fiction novel about the incidents *In Cold Blood* in the mid-1960s. Both films stress how this experience led to Capote's downfall as a major writer and collapse as a human being, and both are highly critical of the writer who manipulates those around him to attain his literary success and celebrity.

Both films strongly emphasize Capote's gayness, presenting him as a flamboyant and out homosexual, at a time when most gay men were closeted. Both films stress his serious and committed relationship with writer Jack Dunphy and his close homoerotic bond with Kansas murderer Perry Smith, although *Infamous* presents the latter relation more explicitly as a homosexual love affair. Both stress Capote's close friendship with his childhood friend Nelle Harper Lee, who came into great literary success herself with the publication in 1960 of *To Kill a Mockingbird*, and who is Truman's moral and practical center and grounding in the two Capote films. Both Capote films stress the traumatic effects of his investigations of the Kansas murders on him and the devastating impact of the eventual execution of the murderers, and how this led to Capote's downfall as a writer and human being. The two films also put on display the tremendous cultural divide between Capote's social scene in New York and mid-Western life in Kansas, and show how he used the same manipulative techniques and mendacity to maneuver people around him into getting what he wanted out of them.

The success of gay-themed films has important predecessors that have brought a gay sensibility into U.S. culture. During the 1960s, Andy Warhol and his factory, an ironic term for the site where Warhol and his colleagues produced an astonishing amount of paintings and films, publicized gay life-styles and helped create a gay cinema and subculture, contributions put on display in a series of documentaries in the 2000s about the Warhol scene.[17]

A gay and camp sensibility is highly evident in the work of John Waters who has crossed-over from the indie movement into the mainstream with the adaptations of films like *Hairspray* (1988) into a Broadway hit and cinematic 2007 remake directed by Adam Shankman. Waters established himself as a staple of gay camp cinema in the 1970s with his so-called "trash trilogy" of *Pink Flamingos*, *Female Trouble*, and *Desperate Living*. In the 1980s and 1990s, Waters produced a more mainstreamed camp cinema with films like *Polyester*, *Hairspray*, *Cry-Baby*, and *Serial Mom*.

Waters, a one-man gay camp impresario, also helped to generate spin-offs of his films into popular Broadway plays like *Hairspray* and *Cry-Baby*, and frequently appears on television and in documentaries. His stand-up comedy routine in *John Waters: This Filthy World* (2006) provides an engaging overview of his cinematic work and quirky personality. Waters' films of the 2000s return to the hyper-campy bad taste of his earlier films. His *Cecile B. Demented* (2000) provides a very extravagant satire on Hollywood and independent films in its story of how an indie director (Stephen Dorff) kidnaps a fading movie star (Melanie Griffith) and gets her to play in his crazed and demented movie (hence the title). Based on the Patricia Hearst kidnapping, and featuring Hearst in a small role, the actress totally gets into the role when she hears her kidnapping has raised her celebrity stock and she gleefully romps with porn stars, drag queens, and the usual Waters cast of misfits and sexual rebels.

A Dirty Shame (2004) can be seen as Water's sexual and cinematic manifesto as he concocts a highly absurdist and campy story about repressed individuals becoming sex maniacs after having been knocked in the head. The narrative, such as it is, features battles between Waters' beloved sexual "freaks" and anti-sex "neuters," sympathizing, not surprisingly, with the former. The film opens with a doughty middle-aged woman Sylvia Stickles (Tracey Ullman) refusing to have sex with her husband, Vaughn, and ashamed of her nympho daughter, Caprice (the diminutive Selma Blair), who has giant, inflated breasts and is a night-club go-go dancer.

Sylvia and her mother, Big Ethel, are appalled by the sexual promiscuity in their neighborhood, including a house-full of promiscuous bears (i.e. burly, hairy gay men), and create a group that self-identifies itself as "neuters" and promotes conservative sexual morality. But Sylvia accidentally bumps her head and her sexual yearnings explode, especially when she meets sexual guru Ray Ray Perkins, who introduces her to his group of libertines, who practice every conceivable fetish and "perversion." Waters mixes campy satire with trashy humor to ridicule prudery and to champion sexual expression, but outside of his fans who welcomed his return to raunch after forays into less transgressive fare, critics were generally harsh to the film, which won few new fans for Waters.

Duncan Hunter's *Transamerica* (2005) introduces mainstream America to transsexuals and the world of gender-bending. The film boldly puts on display the socially constructed nature of sexuality and the performative nature of gender. The film opens with Felicity Huffman's character Bree (born Stanley) mimicking a tape teaching her a proper male accent and speech mannerisms. An interview with a hostile male psychiatrist describes Bree's desire to be a woman as "gender dysphoria."[18] The shrink is unfriendly to the idea of a sex-change operation, but Bree describes the operation that will remove her male genitals as a "sexual reassignment," and in discussions with her sympathetic therapist Margaret (Elizabeth Pena) insists she will go through with the operation.

A call from a junior detention center in New York distracts her from her mission, but she gamely goes to bail out her son, who has never met his father, who is in jail for prostitution and minor theft. The therapist tells Bree that she cannot undergo her operation until she deals with the responsibility of finding care for her son Toby (Kevin Zegers), and the two undertake a cross-country road trip where they will get to know each other, for better and worse, and ultimately come to accept and love each other.

One of the first stops is to the town where Toby was raised where Bree learns that the stepfather had sexually abused the boy and his mother had committed suicide, obviously ruling this place out as a refuge for the boy. Another highlight involves a stop in Arkansas to a transgendered group meeting and party where Toby and the audience learn of the variety of gender-bending goings on in the country. Toby begins to understand and respect people wanting to be themselves and to accept differences. After a peyote-addled hustler steals their car and Bree and Tony brave a night in the woods together, hitching the next day, they are picked up in Texas by a Native American (Graham Greene) in a cowboy hat who seems to take to Bree as a female, delighting her immensely.

Rebecca Scherr argues that *Transamerica* analogizes racial with sexual discrimination and points out that throughout the film people of color are much more comfortable with Bree, and she with them, than white folks.[19] *Transamerica* builds to a melodramatic psychodrama where Bree and Toby turn up in Arizona at Bree's upper-middle-class home. At first her ultra-Christian and conservative mother (Fionnula Flanagan) and her easy-going Jewish father (Burt Young) react to Stanley/Bree's transformation with horror, but are soon and surprisingly accepting. The mother dotes on her handsome grandson and insists that he stay with the family, leading to a confrontation where Bree must admit that she is his father, a revelation he receives with horror that drives her son, Toby, to run away to California and Bree to return for her operation.

Bree borrows money from her family and soldiers on to California and has her operation, returning to her jobs as a waitress in a Mexican restaurant and telemarketer. Toby appears as a bleached blonde actor in porn movies, realizing part of his California dream, but seeks out his father and at the end it appears that they have reunited and will continue to try to understand and love each other. The film promotes tolerance, acceptance of otherness and difference, and is an important milestone in gay, lesbian, and transgendered cinema.

Gays and lesbians have long been active in musicals and the sensational Broadway run of *Rent* guaranteed a film version of Jonathan Larson's musical based on Puccini's *La Bohème*. Directed by Chris Columbus (2005), *Rent* opens in 1989, when the AIDS epidemic had already decimated segments of New York city gay culture and the country was learning to cope with the epidemic and feel empathy with people with AIDS. The Broadway musical success of *Rent* helped create understanding for people suffering with AIDS and the play brought sympathetic representations of gays and lesbians to a mainstream audience. The film follows the play in associating gays and lesbians with "la vie Bohème" and creativity in its stories of how marginalized but talented young people struggle for survival and recognition in the mean streets of New York.

The play/film is also highly multicultural in its story of a young Black philosophy professor Tom Collins (Jesse L. Martin), a gay man who is HIV-positive, falling in love with a transvestite fashion model Angel (Wilson Jermaine Heredia). The characters include Mimi, a Latina exotic dancer and heroin user (Rosario Dawson), who contracted HIV through drug use and her Anglo songwriter love-interest Roger (Adam Pascal), a former drug user who also contracted HIV, as well as performance artist Maureen (Idina Menzel) who is presented as the partner of an African American lesbian lawyer Joanne (Tracie Thomas). Their lives and loves are taped by aspiring documentary filmmaker Mark (Anthony Rapp) and in the background hover their ex-roommate Benny (Taye Diggs), an ambitious African American who has married a rich white woman and who conspires to turn their run-down loft into a cyberstudio with the latest technology to produce a variety of new media and art projects.

A subtheme involves the conflict between selling out and maintaining artistic integrity and independence, a dilemma the filmmaker Mark tries to resolve when he gets a well-paying TV job to make his indie docs about life in New York. One of his projects is taping an AIDS support group, which serves to educate the audience about coping with AIDS. In another scene, prescient concerning the hot-button issue of gay marriage, Mark tapes a gay wedding announcement party put on by the African American lawyer's upscale parents who liberally accept their daughter's sexual choice, as do the parents of the performance artist Maureen. In real life, the topic would be and still is a source of political conflict. *Rent* ends with Tom Collins dying of AIDS and his friends celebrating his life but unlike Puccini's *La Bohème*, Mimi survives her near death AIDS crisis, bonding with Roger in a feel-good Happy Ending.

Not surprisingly, there have been fewer major Hollywood films featuring lesbians than gays, and many of the outstanding lesbian-centric films of the past decades have come from the independent film movement, including *Desert Hearts* (1985), *Fried Green Tomatoes* (1991), *Bound* (1996), *But I'm a Cheerleader* (1999), *Imagine Me & You* (2005), *Loving Annabelle*, (2006), *Can't Think Straight* (2008), and *The Duke of Burgundy* (2014). Prestige lesbian-themed films like *The Hours* (2002) center on three women of different generations and sexualities whose lives are interconnected by the novel *Mrs Dalloway* by Virginia Woolf, while Todd Haynes' *Carol* (2015) takes on a 1952 semi-autobiographical novel by Virginia Highsmith *The Price of Salt* and uses it to present a love story between a would-be young theater set designer taking a part-time job in a department store during the Christmas vacation who meets a wealthy older woman Carol with whom she has a passionate affair.

Stephen Daldry's *The Hours* focuses on the emotional and sexual dissatisfaction of three women in different historical epochs with different sexual orientations with each woman passionately kissing another at a crucial narrative moment, suggesting to many viewers that a straightforward lesbian relation would be the most appropriate and satisfying for the protagonists in question. [20] The theme of "the hours" is first posed by a young man dying of AIDS who tells his woman caregiver that he is facing the momentary end of his life and desperately wants more hours to live. The film ends with a voice-over in which the Virginia Woolf character thanks her husband, Leonard, for loving her in a suicide note, concluding: "Always the years between us. Always the years. Always the love. Always the hours."

One implication of this thematic is that one should use the hours allotted to gain maximum satisfaction and meaning from life and that society traps women in conventions and institutions which imprison them and restrict their possibilities for happiness and self-realization. Todd Haynes' *Carol*, by contrast, shows two women in unfulfilling heterosexual relationships who meet by accident in a New York department store and go on to have a passionate relationship. Yet the narrative shows the obstacles that women in the 1950s in particular faced in pursuing same-sex relations and the dangers that such forbidden relationships subjected them to.

Gay life and activism, once largely consigned to documentaries, also made it into the mainstream and even won Academy Awards, such as Gus van Sant's *Milk* (2008, a powerful film about the assassination of Harvey Milk, the first gay San Francisco city supervisor and the country's first elected totally out gay politician). The film reminded the country of vicious and pathological hatred for gays and lesbians among some sectors of U.S. society, recalling oppression of gays and struggle for their basic rights at the very time when even California voters supported a proposition to ban gay marriage after it was legally approved. While the California state Attorney General, former Governor Jerry Brown, called upon the California Supreme Court to invalidate the measure, it shows that struggles for gay and lesbian rights were passionate and hot-button items.

Opening with somber Black and white archival images of gays being arrested in police bar busts and beaten up in protests, the film cuts to Sean Penn playing Harvey Milk in 1978, audio-taping his story with the expectation that he would be assassinated and should get his story down in his own words. Next, *Milk* cuts to New York in 1970 where approaching his 40th birthday, Milk is shown as a closeted gay who works on Wall Street. He meets a charming young hippie on the subway who he picks up to help celebrate his birthday, telling him that so far he has done nothing that he is proud of and needs to radically change his life.

In a tender montage sequence, the two men make love and the film exuberantly cuts to San Francisco where Milk and his new partner Scott (James Franco) set up a camera shop in the Castro and immediately become deeply involved in gay politics, evoking the Castro area as a Mecca for gays and lesbians and winning Milk renown as "The King of Castro Street." Much of the film concerns Milk's own political education as he learns to make alliances, speak to crowds, organize campaigns, find and articulate issues, and eventually win elections. Defeated three times in runs for a seat on the San Francisco Board of Supervisors, their equivalent of a powerful city council, Milk eventually wins in 1977 and uses his position as a platform to push gay issues.

As backdrop to Milk's political ascendancy, van Sant intersperses documentary footage of Anita Bryant campaigning nationally against gays and lesbians, events central to Rob Epstein's 1984 Oscar-winning documentary *The Times of Harvey Milk* that van Sant heavily draws upon. A major challenge to gay rights emerges in a 1978 ballot initiative Proposition 6, sponsored by a California assemblyman John Briggs, influenced by Anita Bryant, that would fire gay and lesbian schoolteachers. Polls indicate a 2 to 1 lead for the conservatives in polling on the proposition going into the election, but Milk debates its defenders, organizes against the proposition, and in a surprise upset it is defeated handily on election night.[21]

A subtext of *Milk* that brought an anticipated and tragic ending to the activist's life involves his relation with conservative Supervisor Dan White (Josh Brolin), who represented a highly Catholic ethnic neighborhood in the city. Initially antagonistic, Milk tries to charm White, who invites him to his child's christening, and they attempt to forge alliances on issues important to them. White is portrayed as deeply disturbed, a heavy drinker, and possibly a closeted gay who snaps when at the last minute Milk does not back him on a measure important to his district. White resigns in anger and when he tries to negate his resignation the Mayor George Moscone, portrayed as a strong ally of Milk, refuses to take White back and in premeditated anger White coldly assassinates Moscone and then walks to Milk's office to assassinate Milk.

Closing titles indicate that Dan White was arrested, tried and found guilty, but sentenced to a minimum charge of manslaughter, was released after five years, and then committed suicide. In a wonderful closing montage, titles described the activities of those associated with Milk, juxtaposing the actors' faces with photographs of the real characters, all of whom had highly productive and successful lives, devoted to progressive political causes.

In addition to genre cycles dealing with gender, race, and sexuality, with many films developing their intersectionalities, there has also been a wealth of films and TV series dealing with youth, which I engage in the next chapter.

Notes

1 *The Devil Wears Prada* grossed over $300 million globally and finished in the top 20 films of 2006 ratings both domestically and internationally; see the detailed production and reception information on the film at http://en.wikipedia.org/wiki/The_Devil_Wears_Prada_(film) (accessed December 24, 2008).

2 In the DVD commentary, the creators of *The Devil Wears Prada* not only make it clear that they were not attacking the fashion industry but that they were clearly celebrating it.

3 On "shopping and fucking" feminism, see Michelle Goldberg, "Feminism for Sale" at AlterNet.org, January, 8, 2001, discussed in Hammer 2002: 33–34.

4 *The Women* got bad reviews with A.O. Scott of the *New York Times* calling it "a witless, straining mess" of a film; September 12, 2008 at http://movies.nytimes.com/2008/09/12/movies/12wome.html?ref=arts&em. Richard Schickel of *Time* described it as "one of the worst movies I've ever seen"; September 11, 2008 at www.time.com/time/arts/article/0,8599,1840522,00.html (accessed December 24, 2008).

5 "Bechdel Test," Wikipedia at https://en.wikipedia.org/wiki/Bechdel_test (accessed October 28, 2019).

6 My analysis below focuses on seasons six and seven of *Orange is the New Black*, and after engaging these seasons it is highly interesting to re-view the first seasons that do an excellent job of introducing the characters and their backgrounds.

7 Harron Walker, "Laverne Cox Looks Back on Historic Role in *Orange is the New Black*," *Out*, August, 05 2019, at www.out.com/television/2019/8/05/laverne-cox-looks-back-historic-role-orange-new-black (accessed August 17, 2019).

8 Jeff Smith, "A Former Prisoner On What 'Orange Is The New Black' Gets Right – And What It Doesn't. The Netflix drama depicts life in prison with some degree of accuracy. But with far too much skin, for one." *Buzzfeed*, August 22, 2013, at www.buzzfeed.com/jeffsmithmo/a-former-prisoner-on-what-orange-is-the-new-black-gets-right (accessed August 17, 2019)

9 Faludi (1999) documents ways that feminism was scapegoated for men's crises, is highly sympathetic to men, and critically engages the socio-economic and cultural forces that have helped produce a crisis in masculinity in the contemporary moment. In Faludi's analysis, the media and consumer society created new false ideals for men in terms of images, performance, style, celebrity, wealth, and looks (37ff). In a "culture of ornament," she writes, "manhood is defined by appearance, by youth and attractiveness, by money and aggression, by posture and swagger," and by competitive success. While Faludi is strongly critical of a problematic ideal of masculinity, she fails, however, to note the emergence of a more virulent notion of violent masculinity that is apparent in the film and television superheroes, computer and video

games, sports extravaganzas, and the rise of a gun and military culture. To be sure, she notes how violent masculinity has mutated into media images of superheroes, or star athletes like Mike Tyson, but claims that by and large men are relegated to spectatorship or cosmetic masculinity.

10 I discussed *El Cantante* in the previous chapter in my discussion of Latino films.

11 A review in *World Socialist Website* argues that Mangold's film cuts out all the progressive politics from Cash's life and work in favor of presenting a more subjective portrait of the singer, showing the inability of some in Hollywood to engage progressive politics. See Joanne Laurier and David Walsh, "Two recent films: *Brokeback Mountain* and *Walk the Line*," *World Socialist Website,* January 5 2006 at www.wsws. org/articles/2006/jan2006/film-j05.shtml (accessed February 15, 2010).

12 Richard Porton, "The Many Faces of Bob Dylan: An Interview with Todd Haynes," *Cineaste,* Winter 2007: 20.

13 In the first edition of *Media Culture* (Kellner 1995: 174–187), I sketched an overview of the genesis of rap from the 1980s up to publication date in 1995, but have not kept up with the later developments of rap and hip hop which has remained globally popular up to this day, still generating excitement and controversy, but would require a large book to adequately cover.

14 The same template is found in the remake of Stephen King's *Pet Cemetery* (2019) which focuses on the crisis of patriarchy but shows the whole family in crisis and dissolving in a highly dark and pessimistic scenario.

15 On the hard-bodied hyper masculinity dominant in 1980s cinema, see Jeffords 1994 and the studies of cinema and masculinity collected in Cohan and Hark 1993.

16 The term "New Queer Cinema" was introduced by B. Ruby Rich who continued to explore the genre (see Rich 1992, 2000, 2013). See also Benshoff and Griffin's 2006 history of gay and lesbian film in America.

17 Two documentaries in the 2000s go back and capture the Warhol scene, including Chris Rodley's *Andy Warhol: The Complete Picture* (2002) that focuses on Warhol himself. By contrast, the three-part TV series Catherine O'Sullivan Scharr's *Andy Warhol's Factory People* (2004) provides the most extensive documentation yet concerning the extent of Warhol's gay coworkers and associates, the contributions they made to his paintings, film, and celebrity image, and the ways that collectively they brought a gay sensibility into art, film, and more generally 1960s culture. Featuring new interviews with Warhol's associates, and interview footage from those who died, the series provides a comprehensive look at Warhol's work, its relation to gay culture, and the way he and his crowd provided new breakthroughs in inserting gay themes, culture, and figures into the mainstream. Another archaeological documentary into the origins of gay culture, Lisa Ades and Lesli Klainberg's *Fabulous! The Story of Queer Cinema* (2006) provides new historical insight into films "by, for, and about" gays and lesbians in the United States and highlights the ways that Hollywood film culture has promoted gay and lesbian themes, figures, and sensibilities, as well as also promoting negative and biased stereotypes.

18 Rebecca Scherr points out that "gender identity disorder" was labeled a mental illness in the *Diagnostic and Statistical Manual of Mental Disorders* just at a time when homosexuality was taken out of the closet. See "(Not) queering 'white vision' in *Far from Heaven* and TransAmerica," *Jump Cut,* No. 50 (Spring 2008) at https://www.ejump cut.org/archive/jc50.2008/Scherr/text.html (accessed December 22, 2008).

19 See Scherr, op. cit. Scherr also argues that *Transamerica* analogizes transsexuality and being non-white racially, but does not really engage the people of color in the film who recognize and affirm Bree, and that the film thus implicitly privileges whiteness. For me, it also provides another example of the intersectionality of gender, sexuality, race, and class, and how they interact in complex ways in life and cinematic representations.

20 Michael Giltz, "The Golden Hours: With Meryl Streep as a Lesbian, Nicole Kidman as Virginia Woolf, and Julianne Moore Kissing Toni Colette, the Hours Would Seem to Be the Gayest Movie Ever Nominated for Nine Oscars. but the Actresses and Filmmakers Argue That Transcending Such Labels Is Exactly What Has Made the Film So Successful." *Questia* at www.questia.com/magazine/1G1-99850228/the-golden-hours-with-meryl-streep-as-a-lesbian (accessed November 19, 2019).

21 Reviewers of *Milk* noted that uncanny resonance of the infamous Proposition 6 initiative to the Proposition 8 initiative on the 2008 California ballot that would ban gay marriage, previously approved by the courts, and that would thus take away hard-won gay and lesbian rights. This time, despite fierce opposition, strong financial support for the initiative by the Mormon church and evangelical Christians pushed the ballot through, producing protests, that I observed shortly after the election in both San Francisco and Los Angeles, which had strong echoes of the earlier gay rights struggles that Harvey Milk was involved in. The power and success of the film *Milk* provides hope that gay marriage rights will be restored and nasty and bigoted homophobes will be forced back into the closet.

6

YOUTH, IDENTITIES, AND FASHION

As the social historian Philippe Aries reminds us (1962), "childhood" and "youth" are socially constructed conceptions of age and not biological givens. Indeed, the idea that a transitional period of youth occurs between childhood and adulthood is a relatively recent invention, beginning with Rousseau's *Emile* in mid-twentieth-century Europe, which celebrated childhood and delineated stages of youth. Generational terms referring to the "lost generation" of the 1920s, or the "silent generation" post-World War II (1950s), began emerging in the twentieth century. During the post-World War II period, "youth culture" was widely used to describe the growing music and rock culture and consumer and fashion styles of the era that mutated into the counterculture of the 1960s.

British cultural studies were focused on youth and youth culture from the beginning of their work in the Birmingham center for Contemporary Cultural Studies in the 1960s, and cultural studies has maintained a focus on youth since much media culture is informed by youth culture and aimed at young audiences. Further, a major goal of a critical media/cultural studies and pedagogy is teaching critical media literacy (Kellner-Share 2019). Consequently, critically engaging youth, youth culture, identity and fashion is important since youth can create a new and better world and are a crucial fulcrum of hopes for the future.

In fact, since the 1960s, there has been multiple oppositional youth cultures, and theorists in the Centre for Contemporary Cultural Studies emphasized youth culture's counter-hegemonic and "generational" qualities and examined the ways in which working-class youth sub-cultures resisted subordination through the production of their own culturally subversive styles (Hall and Jefferson 1976). From this perspective, youth of the 1950s celebrated beatniks and rebels in the U.S., teddy boys in the U.K., and the styles associated with American rhythm and blues music throughout the world. A decade later, when these became appropriated by the mainstream, 1960s youth turned to the mods and rockers in the U.K., and hippy and countercultural styles of sex, drugs, and rock and roll in the U.S. After the commercialization and appropriation of the 1960s counterculture in the 1970s, youth turned to new movements like punk and, with the rise in global popularity of hip-hop culture from the 1980s onward, youth have turned increasingly to more urban and underclass "gangsta" styles of hip-hop sub-cultures (Kellner 1995), as well as a diverse range of styles and identities generated by new technologies, forms of culture, and youth and political movements.

Contemporary youth embrace a wide array of young people and its youth culture is equally heterogeneous. Post-boomers include those who helped create the Internet and the culture of video-gaming; the latchkey kids who are home alone and the mallrats quaffing fast food in the palaces of consumption; the young activists who helped generate the anti-globalization and peace and antiwar movements of the 1990s; the cafe slackers, klub kidz, computer nerds, and sales clerks; a generation committed to health, exercise, sustainability, ethical dietary practices, and animal rights, as well as anorexics and bulimics in thrall to the ideals of the beauty and fashion industries. Today's youth also include creators of exciting 'zines and diverse multimedia such as can be found on sites like Facebook, Instagram, YouTube, and other forms of social media; the bike ponies, valley girls, and skinheads, skaters, gangstas, low-riders, riot grrrls, and hip-hoppers – all accompanied by a diverse and heterogeneous grouping of multicultural, racial, and hybridized individuals seeking a viable identity in oppositional groups like the Occupy Movement, Black Lives Matter, #Metoo, and as of yet unnamed movements emerging as I write and you read.

Youth subcultures can comprise an entire way of life, involving clothes, styles, attitudes, practices, and identities. Youth sub-cultures contain potential spaces of resistance, though these can take various forms ranging from narcissistic and apolitical to anarchist and environmental and social justice activist cultures promoting alternative life-styles to right-wing skinheads and Trumpsters, Islamic jihadists, and those promoting startlingly reactionary ideas and values. Thus, although there might be elements of opposition and resistance to mainstream culture in youth subcultures, such counterculture might not be progressive and must be interrogated in specific cases concerning their forms of cultural expression, politics and effects.

Today, youth culture is increasingly global with the Internet, new media, and social networking transmitting transnational forms of culture through proliferating channels and media of communication. Yet one should distinguish between a youth culture produced by youth themselves that articulates their own visions, passions, and anxieties, and media culture produced by adults to be consumed by youth. One also needs to distinguish between youth cultures that are lived and involve immediate, participatory experience as opposed to mediated cultural experience and consumption, and to be aware that youth cultures involve both poles. Moreover, one should resist both reducing youth culture merely to a culture of consumption, or glorifying it as a force of resistance. It is best instead to ferret out the contradictions and both the way in which youth cultures are constructed by media and consumer culture and the way in which youth in turn construct their own communities.

I begin by discussing youth culture films from the 1950s that influenced my generation and Richard Linklater's film *Slacker* (1995) and subsequent youth culture films, followed by a study of "Social Anxiety and Class: Mike Judge From *Beavis and Butt-Head* to *Idiocracy*." I then turn to analysis of *"Buffy the Vampire Slayer* as Spectacular Allegory: A Diagnostic Critique," which I read as a critical analysis of young women dealing with the challenges of family, high school, and then college, Next, I engage "Fashion and Identity" with studies of "Pop Icons From Madonna to Lady Gaga and Beyoncé." In this section, I engage the role of popular music, stars and fashion in contemporary media and youth culture. I argue that Madonna's shifts in image and identity articulate transformations in values and politics of the epoch, as well as reflecting stages of her life and career, while Lady Gaga, Beyoncé, and subsequent superstar performers represent further changes in style, fashion, identity, and gender politics.

Youth films from Alan Freed to *Slacker*

One of the types of youth films emerged in the 1950s as corporate products that exploited popular youth musical cultures in films produced by New York DJ Alan Freed, and drawing on his concerts and featuring top rock and roll artists of the day. Freed's 1956 films *Rock, Rock, Rock* and *Rock Around the Clock* featured Bill Haley & His Comets, The Platters, Chuck Berry, Frankie Lymon and the Teenagers, Johnny Burnette, LaVern Baker, The Flamingos, and other popular singers, many who came from Black R&B cultures. Freed continued these films featuring insipid teen romances and exciting concert fare in *Mister Rock and Roll* (1957), *Don't Knock the Rock* (1957), and *Go, Johnny Go!* (1959). Alan Freed briefly broke into television with a primetime show *The Big Beat*, which was scheduled for a summer run, with the understanding that if there were enough viewers, it would continue into the 1957–1958 television season. While the ratings for the show were strong, it was suddenly terminated after four weeks, as during the second episode, Black singer Frankie Lymon had been shown dancing with a white girl from the studio audience. In a still heavily segregated country, the incident caused an uproar among ABC's local affiliates in the South and "would allegedly lead to the show's cancellation" (Jackson 1991: 186).

My brother and I went to Freed's rock and roll concerts at the Times Square Paramount and Brooklyn Paramount in New York in the mid-1950s, and were electrified by the music. The first time our mother chaperoned us, as there were rumors of riots and immorality in the audience, but when she saw it was just an enjoyable music experience with teens jumping up and down to the rhythms and cheering their favorites, we were allowed to go unchaperoned. We also compiled an extensive collections of 45-rpm record format of the most popular songs and 33-rpm record format albums of the top stars that became a major feature of teen culture in the 1950s.

Freed continued to organize his concerts and promote rock and roll culture on television into the late 1950s when he was caught up in a payola scandal in 1960, whereby he and other disk jockeys were paid by music companies to play songs on the radio. Meanwhile, a more conservative and white-bread Dick Clark hosted *American Bandstand* from 1957 to 1988, which featured clean-cut teens dancing in Philadelphia to the most popular hits of the day, with guest appearances by Fats Domino and other representatives of the early pantheon of rock and roll. Clark also introduced new rock and roll artists, including Iggy Pop, Ike & Tina Turner, Smokey Robinson and the Miracles, Stevie Wonder, Prince, Talking Heads, Simon & Garfunkel and Madonna. Dick Clark continued to host Blacks and whites performing on the same stage, and also featured racially diverse live studio audience and dancers. Although pop singer Paul Anka claimed that *American Bandstand* was responsible for creating a "youth culture," in fact, Freed and other DJs, as well as Hollywood directors who featured James Dean, Marlon Brando, Natalie Wood, and other teen idols in films like *The Wild One*, *East of Eden*, *Rebel Without a Cause*, and many others were part of the culture industry that promoted youth culture which helped shape my generation which came of age in the 1950s.

While rock and roll helped promote racial integration and made Black culture a strong pillar of the emerging youth culture and even mainstream culture, there was also an exploitation and cultural appropriation of Black artists in which white singers like Pat Boone, Frankie Avalon, Patti Page, and others covered Black hits and ended up dominating the pop record charts. Elvis Presley was another appropriator of Black culture and became one of the major music/pop culture sensations of all time, although I would defend Elvis as an original talent and synthesizer of country, R&B, gospel, rock, and pop musical forms of the day (see Kellner 2007). After releasing a popular album on the country-oriented Sun label, Presley's RCA single, "Heartbreak Hotel," was released in January 1956 and became a number-one hit in the United States. Elvis' TV appearances became cultural moments as he rocked, gyrated, and drove studio audiences wild, worrying executives about censorship and losing sponsors. Yet Elvis' over-the-top ratings led cultural conservative Ed Sullivan and others to feature him on their TV shows, helping make Elvis the "King of Rock and Roll."

With a series of successful network television appearances and chart-topping records, Elvis became a leading figure of the rock and roll revolution and a major pop idol on the scale of Frank Sinatra for a previous generation. Elvis's flamboyant interpretations of blues, pop, country, and other musical genres, and sexually provocative performance style, combined with a singularly potent mix of influences across class and color lines during a transformative era in race relations and an explosion of youth culture, made him enormously popular – and controversial.

In November 1956, Presley made his film debut in *Love Me Tender*, and I recall seeing the film with teenage girls in the audience screaming with ecstasy every time Elvis came on screen. Drafted into military service in 1958, Presley relaunched his recording career two years later with some of his most commercially successful work. Elvis held few concerts however, and guided by his conservative manager Colonel Tom Parker, proceeded to devote much of the 1960s to making Hollywood films and soundtrack albums, most of them critically derided.[1] In 1968, following a seven-year break from live performances, Elvis returned to the stage in the acclaimed television comeback special *Elvis*, which led to an extended Las Vegas concert residency and a string of highly profitable tours. In 1973, Presley gave the first concert by a solo artist to be broadcast around the world, *Aloha from Hawaii*. Years of prescription drug abuse severely compromised his health, and he died suddenly in 1977 at his Graceland estate at the age of 42.

I was a major Elvis fan until he was drafted into the army in 1958, returning two years later to make formulaic records and insipid movies. A turn in the 1960s toward more oppositional youth culture had its roots in R&B and rock and roll, but was given a political inflection by folk music in which Bob Dylan, Joan Baez, Pete Seeger, Peter, Paul, and Mary and other folk singers of the era became the heroes of youth, including myself, who continue to love to this day 1960s and earlier and later folk music. The popular folk singers/songwriters just mentioned became part of the civil rights movement and 1960s countercultural movement. Dylan's "The Times They Are a Changin," "Blowing in the Wind," and "A Hard Rain's Gonna Fall," became anthems of the time and the generation, as did songs by Baez, Seeger, Joni Mitchell, and others. Films like *Easy Rider, Bonnie and Clyde, The Graduate*, and many other youth films of the 1960s also became major components of youth culture (see Kellner and Ryan 1988). Indeed, popular music and film continue to be vital components of youth culture and major forms of media culture. In the following sections, I will examine some significant artifacts of film and television of the past decades that became noteworthy forms of youth culture, and then will examine some popular recording artists of the post-1980s and their impact on fashion and identity.

Richard Linklater: auteur of youth

For insight into the plight of youth in contemporary U.S. culture, one can look to Richard Linklater's *Slacker* (1990) and *Dazed and Confused* (1993) and to a selection of Linklater's subsequent films. An Austin, Texas, based independent filmmaker, Linklater followed his early success by making a trilogy of films dealing with romantic encounters every ten years or so between a young woman (Julie Delphy) and man (Ethan Hawke) comprising *Before Sunrise* (1995), *Before Sunset* (2004), and *Before Midnight* (2013). Linklater also experimented with a technique in which live actors are shot on film and then animated in *Waking Life* (2001) and *A Scanner Darkly* (2006). Linklater made some Hollywood films including *School of Rock* (2003), a remake of *Bad News Bears* (2005), *Fast Food Nation* (2006), *Me and Orson Welles* (2008), *Bernie* (2011) and his most successful film, *Boyhood* (2014).

I was teaching philosophy at the University of Texas in Austin during the period when Rick first came to town and we immediately connected over our mutual love of film. Before becoming a filmmaker, Rick founded the Austin Film Society in 1985, which brought in many young filmmakers who later became major directors such as Quentin Tarantino, and provided a showcase for independent films, obscure cult films, and eclectic film festivals. Rick's film *Slacker* featured a number of Austin young people, including some of my philosophy students, and eventually became a national sensation, bringing youth to Austin who wanted to become slackers and gaining a cult following. When I was lecturing on what became the first edition of *Media Culture* (1995) I would invariably be asked about Austin, Linklater, and *Slacker*, which were becoming increasing well-known and loved by youth.

The Slacker *effect*

Slacker is probably the quintessential cinematic dissection of the plight of the post-1960s generation of disaffected youth, bombarded with media culture and alienated from the conservative hegemony of "straight" middle class society. The youth of *Slacker* all live on the margins of society and pursue offbeat lifestyles, refusing to play the game of academic achievement, career, marriage, and family espoused by the dominant ideology of success and disseminated in the mainstream films.

The film pursues a day in the life of Austin, Texas, youth during the late 1980s. The narrative opens with director Rick Linklater playing a character arriving in Austin on a bus. He embarks at the bus station and gets into a taxi where he proceeds to recount the "weird" dream he has just had and philosophizes concerning the possibility of alternative universes and lives, consisting of choices not made, which he had just read in a book. The film then pursues an aleatory itinerary in which one character accidentally encounters another and the narrative proceeds to trek from each new character to another, leaving the previous ones behind. The result is a vision of youth leading aimless, disconnected lives, wandering from one scene and situation to another without specific goals, or purpose.

Yet the young slackers are in a totally media-saturated society in which the products of media culture provide the warp and woof of their conversations, fantasies, and lives. A political conspiracy buff tells of government conspiracies and cover-ups from the space program, referencing *World Weekly News*; another speculates that Elvis still lives; an agitated young woman tries to sell Madonna's pap smear, complete with Black pubic hair; another slacker recounts statistics indicating the lack of genuine mandate for Bush in the 1988 presidential election, which it turns out, come from the *Dallas Morning News*; a young Black sells Free Mandela T-shirts and pamphlets, while doing a political rap derived from media clichés; a video artist/activist has a room full of TV sets and video-tapes, trying to capture everything on tape; the local music scene is a major sources of interest and entertainment, as are movies and television; two slackers philosophize about the cartoon characters Scooby-Doo and the Smurfs in a cafe; and many of the slackers spout fragments of pop philosophy derived from media culture.[2]

The slackers, however, appropriate media culture for their own ends, turning artifacts from conservative media sources into material for radical social and political critique, while using media technology for their own purposes (as does obviously director Linklater and his team). The slackers are not passive products of media effects, but active participants in a media culture who use media to produce meaning, pleasure, and identity in their lives. The ubiquitous T-shirts often have logos or images derived from media culture, and TV and music are constant backgrounds for the cinematic events of the film.

Thus, the media form the very warp and woof of the slacker's lives and allow diagnostic critique to discern that for many segments of youth today media culture *is* their culture. Previous studies of media effects were too restricted in their (pseudo)scientific research methods and thus failed to see how media culture circulate images, artifacts, information, and identities which are appropriated by audiences who use media culture to create their pleasures and identities. Researchers concluded too quickly that media culture had no discernible and measurable effects because their experimental situations were too artificial and their methods inappropriate to tap into the texture of everyday life to see how people actually use the media to produce meanings and identities.

Slacker thus allows a diagnostic critique of how media culture saturates contemporary youth culture and provides the materials from which young people produce meanings, identities, and their own youth culture. In a sense the film presents a "postmodern" vision of the plight of contemporary youth.[3] The youth are lost in the moment and seemingly live completely fragmented and disconnected lives, going from one activity to another through largely accidental mediations. No one seems to have any long-term plans or projects, and all seem to only live for the moment, drifting through life as if in a dream with no dreamer.

Yet as the characters in the film wander from one scene to another, and as some characters leave the frame, while others enter, one gets a sense of something of a Slacker community in which the Slackers are connected to each other, even if temporarily or minimally. However, the community consists of nomadic wanderings, accidental connections, unstructured comings and goings, and a vision of life as consisting of disconnected moments of euphoric intensity, punctuated with periods of banality and meaningless.

The style of *Slacker* thus utilizes the postmodern strategy of fragmenting and disconnecting narrative unity, presenting a series of slices of barely connected lives, meandering through the surface of things, without any depth or deeper meaning. A young man picks up a young woman outside of a music club, takes her home, and we see her get out of bed and leave the next morning, while the roommate watches TV in the same room, without any dialogue shown passing between the characters.

The film thus explores the surfaces of everyday life, and while there are moments of great humor and intense conversation, there is no character development, plot development and resolution, or the production of deep meanings that link sequences, or tie the narrative strands together. Moreover, Linklater pastiches modernist movies, as where he draws on Luis Buñuel's film *The Milky Way* (1969) as the principle of narrative (dis)organization of the film. Buñuel's film presented the voyage of religious pilgrims on their way to Spain in a timeless space and placeless time, in which the main characters encounter one eccentric figure after another, who soon disappear as another strange person enters the narrative sequence. *Slacker* also presents a world of accidental connections and absurdist juxtapositions, though while Bunuel's film had some main characters who remained in the narrative, and utilized allegorical probing of Christian myths, *Slacker* has no main characters, with each Slacker disappearing after her/his few moments of narrative focus, and the film eschews allegory or symbolic meaning.

Slacker's concluding sequence plays with Godard's *One Plus One*, substituting for Godard's Black revolutionaries proclaiming revolution a "Postmodern Paul Revere" (as described in the titles) riding in a car with loud-speakers, describing a government weapons program. And while the end of Godard's film shows his camera apparatus on the beach, scooping up his then wife Anne Wiazemsky and raising her to the sky in a fade-out, in a delirious romantic image of transcendence through love and cinema, *Slacker* shows a group of all-night party animals driving up to Mount Bonnell, the highest point of Austin, with a movie camera that they throw off the cliff. The camera pans to the cover of Paul Goodman's book *Growing up Absurd* before spiraling images of the camera swirling down the cliff cut to black in a nihilistic conclusion that nothing really matters in a totally absurd world, neither love, nor cinema, nor creativity, nor transcendence of any sort.

Yet in another sense, *Slacker* represents a modernist auteur with a distinctive vision and style, which adds up to a sharp, insightful view of the plight of contemporary youth, alienated from the American dream and traditional American values, floating on the media surfaces of contemporary life with their attention focused and shaped by media culture. The film was financed on a very low budget and shares the innovative ethos of the independent film movement. In an early scene in an Austin coffee house, a student picks up a copy of Hal Foster's collection of essays on postmodern culture, *The Anti-Aesthetic* (1983), and a copy of Marshall Berman's book on modernity and modernist culture, *All That is Solid Melts Into the Air* (1982), is visible on a table and I would argue that Linklater combines modernist and post-modernist aesthetic strategies and that the film is thus between the modern and the postmodern.[4]

Moreover, *Slacker*'s vision of multiple possibilities of life, with a wide range of individuals producing their own meanings, might have emancipatory effects. The characters are not conforming or submitting to an over-arching structure of domination, and while they all get opinions and images from the media, they process them in their own individual and idiosyncratic ways. Such a vision especially appealed to young audiences and indeed *Slacker* was felt deeply, producing distinctive "Slacker effects" (see my earlier study of the Rambo effect). The film became a cult favorite throughout the country and indeed world. During the years following the release of the film when I would lecture on *Media Culture*, someone in the audience, upon learning that I had lived in Austin, mentioned *Slacker* and how much they love the film. Moreover, in 1993, city officials in Austin were worried about the large number of homeless youth on the streets and margins of the city, many of whom had seen *Slacker* and came to Austin in search of like-minded cohorts and to pursue the "Slacker" life-style, now identified with Austin.

Slacker articulated experiences of disaffection of youth from contemporary U.S. society and produced a new concept to describe contemporary youth, mythologizing the life-styles of slackers in Austin, Texas. It obviously tapped into deep feelings of contemporary youth, striking a highly responsive chord in its audiences who used the film to articulate their own experiences and feelings. The success of the film also won Linklater a $6 million Hollywood contract to make another youth film, *Dazed and Confused* (1993), which traced a day in the life of Austin high school students on graduation day of 1976. Linklater's "Hollywood" film presents graduating seniors who also lack any guiding purposes or goals and who are alienated from their parent's "straight" middle class world.

Hence, Linklater's early films present a diagnosis of the situation of youth in an absurd society in which traditional norms and values no longer have any hold on many of the young. They present the opportunity for a diagnosis of the situation of contemporary youth and suggest that large numbers of young people are disconnected and alienated from the mainstream culture celebrated by network television and conservative Hollywood film. Another wildly popular TV series of the 1990s *Beavis and Butt-Head*, also produced in Austin, Texas, by Mike Judge, articulates the situation and anxieties of youth in the contemporary era.

Social anxiety and class: Mike Judge from Beavis and Butt-Head *to* Silicon Valley

Many of Richard Linklater's films focus on middle-class youth while much of Mike Judge's work focuses on alienation and the plight, first, of working class youth, and then the challenges of work and the work place in high tech America. Judge's first media culture phenomenon was his animated MTV television series *Beavis and Butt-Head* (1993–1997; 2011). Judge morphed the series into a feature-length film, *Beavis and Butt-Head Do America* (1996), and after his early success, co-created another popular TV series, *King of the Hill* (1997–2009), which dealt with life in a small suburban town in Texas, followed by movies and TV- series that dealt, among other topics, with working in a corporate environment in *Office Space* (1999), *Extract* (2009) and the popular TV-series *Silicon Valley* (2014–). In the following discussion I shall first engage Judge's MTV series *Beavis and Butt-Head* and then his satires of working life in corporate America, focusing on his TV series *Silicon Valley*.

Animated cartoon characters Beavis and Butt-Head sit in a shabby house much of the day, watching television, especially music videos, which they criticize in terms of whether the videos are "cool" or "suck." When they leave the house to go to school, to work in a fast-food joint, or to seek adventure, they often engage in destructive and even criminal behavior. Developed for MTV by animated cartoonist Mike Judge, the series spoofs precisely the sort of music videos played by the music television channel.[5] *Beavis and Butt-Head* quickly became a cult favorite, loved by youth, yet elicited spirited controversy when some young fans of the show imitated typical Beavis and Butt-Head activity, burning down houses, and torturing and killing animals.[6]

The series provides a critical vision of the current generation of youth raised primarily on media culture. This generation was possibly conceived in the sights and sounds of media culture, weaned on it, and socialized by the glass teat of television used as pacifier, baby sitter, and educator by a generation of parents for whom media culture, especially television, was a natural background and constitutive part of everyday life. The show depicts the dissolution of a rational subject and perhaps the end of the Enlightenment in today's media culture. Beavis and Butt-Head react viscerally to the music videos that they watch hour after hour, snickering at the images, finding representations of violence and sex "cool," while anything complex which requires interpretation "sucks." Bereft of any cultivated taste, judgment, or rationality, and without ethical or political values, the characters literally react in a mindless fashion and appear to lack almost all cognitive and communicative skills.

The intense alienation of Beavis and Butt-Head, their love for heavy metal culture and media images of sex and violence, and their violent cartoon activity soon elicited heated controversy, producing a "Beavis and Butt-Head" effect that elicited literally thousands of articles and heated debates, even leading to U.S. Senate condemnations of the show for promoting mindless violence and destructive behavior.[7] From the beginning, there was intense media focus on the show and strongly opposed opinions of it. In a cover story on the show, *Rolling Stone* declared them "The Voice of a New Generation" (August 19, 1993) and *Newsweek* also put them on its cover, both praising them and damning them by concluding: "The downward spiral of the living white male surely ends here: in a little pimple named Butt-head whose idea of an idea is, 'Hey, Beavis, let's go over to Stuart's house and light one in his cat's butt'" (October 11, 1993). "Stupid, lazy, cruel; without ambitions, without values, without futures" are other terms used in the media to describe the characters and the series (*The Dallas Morning News*, August 29, 1993) and there were countless calls to ban the show.

Indeed, a lottery prize winner in California began a crusade against the series, after hearing about a cat that was killed when kids put a firecracker in its mouth, imitating Beavis and Butt-Head's violence against animals, and a suggestion in one episode that they stick a firecracker in a neighbor boy's cat (*The Hollywood Reporter*, July 16, 1993). Librarians in Westchester, New York ranked *Beavis and Butt-Head* high "on a list of movies and television shows that they think negatively influence youngsters' reading habits," because of their attacks on books and frequent remarks that books, or even words, "suck" (*The New York Times*, July 11, 1993). Prison officials in Oklahoma banned the show, schools in South Dakota banned clothing and other items bearing their likeness (*Times Newspapers Limited*, October 11, 1993), and a group of Missouri fourth graders started a petition drive to get the program off the air (*Radio TV Reports*, October 25, 1993).

Yet the series continued to be highly popular into 1994, and spawned a best-selling album of heavy metal rock, a popular book, countless consumer items, and a movie contract that resulted in a film in 1996. *Time* magazine critic, Kurt Anderson, praised the series as "the bravest show ever run on national television" (*The New York Times*, July 11, 1993), and there is no question but that it has pushed the boundaries of the permissible on mainstream television to new extremes (some critics would say to new lows).

Beavis and Butt-Head is interesting for a diagnostic critique because the main characters get all of their ideas and images concerning life from the media and their entire view of history and the world is entirely derived from media culture. When they see a costumed rapper wearing an eighteenth-century style white wig on a music-video, Butt-Head remarks: "He's dressed up like that dude on the dollar." The 1960s is the time of hippies, Woodstock and rock "n" roll for them; Vietnam is ancient history, collapsed into other American wars. Even the 1950s is nothing but a series of mangled media clichés: referring to the twin sons of 1950s teen idol Ricky Nelson, Gunnar Eric Nelson and Matthew Gray Nelson who formed the band Nelson, Butt-Head remarks that: "These chicks look like guys." Beavis responds: "I heard that these chicks' grandpa was Ozzy Osbourne." And Butt-head rejoins: "No way. They're Elvis' kids."

The figures of history are collapsed for Beavis and Butt-Head into media culture and provide material for salacious jokes, which require detailed knowledge of media culture:

> Butt-Head: What happened when Napoleon went to Mount Olive?
> Beavis: I don't know. What?
> Butt-Head: Pop-Eye got pissed.

In a certain sense, *Beavis and Butt-Head* is "postmodern" in that it is purely a product of media culture, with its characters, style, and content almost solely derivative from previous TV shows. The two characters Beavis and Butt-Head are a spinoff of Wayne and Garth in *Wayne's World*, a popular *Saturday Night Live* feature, spun-off into popular movies. They also resemble the SCTV characters Bob and Doug McKenzie, who sit around on a couch and make lewd and crude remarks while they watch TV and drink beer. Beavis and Butt-Head also take the asocial behavior of cartoon character Bart Simpson to a more intense extreme. Their comments on the music videos replicate the popular Comedy Central Channel's series *Mystery Science Theater 3000*, which features two cartoon stick figures making irreverent comments on god-awful old Hollywood movies and network television shows. And, of course, the music videos are a direct replication of MTV's basic fare.

Moreover, Beavis and Butt-Head seem to have no family, living alone in a shabby house, getting enculturated solely by television and media culture. There are some references to their mothers and in one episode there is a suggestion that Butt-Head is not even certain who his father is, thus the series presents a world without fathers.[8] School is totally alienating for the two, as is work in a fast-food restaurant. Adult figures who they encounter are largely white conservative males, or liberal yuppies, with whom they come into often violent conflict and whose property or goods they often destroy.

There is a fantasy wish-fulfillment aspect to *Beavis and Butt-Head* that perhaps helps account for its popularity: kids often wish that they had no parents and that they could just sit and watch music videos and go out and do whatever they wanted to. Kids are also naturally disrespectful of authority and love to see defiance of social forces that they find oppressive. Indeed, Beavis and Butt-Head's much maligned, discussed, and imitated laughter ("Heh, heh, heh" and "Huh, huh") may signify that in their space THEY RULE, that Beavis and Butt-Head are sovereign, that they control the television and can do any damn thing that they want. Notably, they get in trouble in school and other sites of authority with their laugh, but at home they can laugh and snicker to the max.

And so the series has a utopian dimension: the utopia of no parental authority and unlimited freedom to do whatever they want when they want to. "Dude, we're there" is a favorite phrase they use when they decide to see or do something – and they never have to ask their (absent) parents' permission. On the other hand, they represent the consequences of totally unsocialized adolescent behavior driven by aggressive instincts.[9] Indeed, their "utopia" is highly solipsistic and narcissistic with no community, no consensual norms or morality to bind them, and no concern for other people. The vision of the teenagers alone in their house watching TV and then wreaking havoc on their neighborhood presents a vision of a society of broken families, disintegrating communities, and anomic individuals, without values or goals.

After the successful run of *Beavis and Butt-Head* on MTV, Mike Judge co-created the show *King of the Hill* with former *The Simpsons* writer Greg Daniels based on his experiences growing up in a small town in Texas and satirizing Texas and male culture (1997–2001). Judge followed with the film *Office Space*

(1999), which satirizes the everyday work life of a typical mid-to-late-1990s software company, focusing on a handful of individuals fed up with their jobs, a theme taken up again in his film *Extract* (2009), which deals with work in a flavor extract factory, and his recent TV-series *Silicon Valley* (2014–2019), which satirizes high-tech start-up and work culture.

Silicon Valley presents a satirical vision of how the computer youth culture mutated into corporate high-tech culture. The series focuses on five young men who founded a startup company in Silicon Valley led by Richard Hendricks who creates an app known as Pied Piper, which contains a revolutionary data compression algorithm. A venture capitalist Peter Gregory acquires a stake in Pied Piper, and Richard hires a group of high-tech misfits, illustrating how youth was taking over Silicon Valley culture.

The plot of season one involves a rival corporation Hooli who attempt to reverse engineer Pied Piper's algorithm and develop a copycat product called Nucleus, satirically presenting the cut-throat competition among Silicon Valley companies. Both Pied Piper and Hooli are scheduled to present their product at a convention TechCrunch Disrupt, which satirically depicts Silicon Valley's quirky claims to disruption and innovation. It appears that Hooli is outperforming Pied Piper as its "compression technology," cobbled from Pied Piper, is integrated with all of Hooli's services and has compression performance equal to Pied Piper. However, Richard has a new idea and spends the entire night coding. The next morning, Richard makes Pied Piper's final presentation and demonstrates a product that strongly outperforms Nucleus and he is mobbed by eager investors.

Succeeding seasons show multiple venture capital firms offering to finance Pied Piper's new projects, lawsuits between different companies, and the drama of working with different venture capitalists, which cumulatively provides a satirical take on Silicon Valley and the challenges of youth prospering in a volatile high-tech environment. The series deploys the mode of satirical comedy, but it shows the serious drama of high-tech youth trying to make it and survive in the high-tech economy surrounded by corporate sharks, young idealists, techie nerds, and a multicultural rainbow of different individuals struggling in a Brave New High Tech world. The different episodes feature revolutionary innovations of the Internet and the cloud, the challenges of artificial intelligence (AI), the seductions of cryptocurrency, the adventures of global capital as Chinese capitalists enter the fray, the drama of video game culture, and the ever present threats of Amazon and other high tech corporations taking over their product with the future up for grabs and great success or wretched failure facing the youth and other denizens of Silicon Valley.

Although there are female characters in *Silicon Valley* the culture itself is notoriously male-dominated as is reflected in the series. The popular fantasy TV series *Buffy the Vampire Slayer*, by contrast, centers on major female characters and shows contemporary youth dealing with the challenges and nightmares of growing up and living in a bizarre and confusing world in the mode of the fantasy horror genre.

Buffy the Vampire Slayer as spectacular allegory: a diagnostic critique

Since the appearance of the 1992 film *Buffy the Vampire Slayer* (hereafter *BtVS*) and the popular 1997–2003 TV series based on it, Buffy has become a cult figure of global media culture with a panorama of websites, copious media and scholarly dissection, academic conferences, and a fandom that continues to devour reruns and DVDs of the 144 episodes. The series caught its moment and its audience, popularizing Buffyspeak, the Buffyverse (the textual universe of the show), and Buffypeople, who dedicated themselves to promoting and explicating the phenomenon and exemplified the British cultural studies ideal of the active audience, able to both quote and interpret, while citing episode and season. A globally popular TV series, by the time the series reached its apocalyptic conclusion in summer 2003, it was widely recognized as one of the most striking cult TV shows of the epoch.[10]

In this chapter, I argue that *BtVS* functions as an allegorical spectacle about contemporary life and provides a diagnostic critique concerning some of what the series tells us about life in the U.S.A. today and the situation of contemporary youth. Popular television articulates in allegorical forms fears, fantasies, and dreams of a given society at a particular point in time. Reading popular fantasy TV like *The X-Files* and *BtVS* provides access to social problems and issues and hopes and anxieties that are often not articulated in more "realist" cultural forms.[11] The richness of symbolic allegorical structure and content in these shows allows the production of meanings and identities beyond that of more conventional TV and provides a wealth of different readings and appropriations.

BtVS features the adventures of Buffy Summers (played by Sarah Michelle Gellar), a 16-year-old high school student who had just transferred to the small town of Sunnydale from Los Angeles, where she got into trouble with school authorities for her erratic behavior (which we learn later was fighting vampires). Buffy's parents were divorced and so she and her mother attempt to begin life anew, a theme of renewal and change that will become central in the unfolding episodes.

In the series mythology, Sunnydale high school is located on the Hellmouth, a portal to nether regions where demonic forces enter to threaten everyday life and wreak havoc, portending apocalypse. The opening episode introduces a hideous Master who plans to open the Hellmouth to legions of monsters who will unleash their demonic fury. Buffy learns that she is the Chosen One with the powers to fight evil monsters and bonds with the bookish Willow (Alyson Hannigan) and awkward but loyal Xander (Nicholas Brendon) who are all tutored by the English librarian Giles (Anthony Stewart Head), who possesses a vast collection of books that identify the various monsters who emerge in

Sunnydale. Giles serves as Buffy's "Watcher," providing guidance and mentor-ship to help her deal with her occult powers and provides a rare TV image of a nurturing mentor able to relate to and work with youth.

Buffy's "Scooby gang," named after the *Scooby-Doo* cartoon series featuring young detectives, fight various vampires and demons each week, as well as grap-pling with their own personal and interpersonal problems. Encompassing realist, mythological, and allegorical levels, *BtVS* provides a polysemic and complex hermeneutical challenge to contemporary criticism to depict how the series works and how it presents a startling diversity and intensity of themes. The series combines genres of horror and fantasy, gothic romance, teen dramas, soap operas, and epic adventure tales. It pastiches the perennial figures of the vampire, werewolf, witch, and a panorama of traditional monsters, while adding some new ones. Mixing comedy and drama, *BtVS* offers social satire and insight embodied in a wide array of compelling characters, engaging narratives, and clever commentary on contemporary culture.

On the realist level, the show presents down-to-earth and revealing relations between teenagers, and between young people and parents, teachers and men-tors, and a diverse range of authority figures. *BtVS* engagingly deals with social relationships, love, rejection, loss, and all the complexities of family, school, work, constructing identity and finding oneself, growing and evolving, or failing and regressing as a human being.

BtVS is particularly realistic and boundary-breaking in its depiction of sexual relations with a considerable amount of gay and lesbian sexuality, and quite frank and explicit depictions of an extensive variety of sexualities. The series abounds with steamy sex and mutating relations where hate turns to love and violence to erotic entanglement. Playing with S&M and taboo-breaking eroti-cism to a degree hitherto unseen on U.S. television, *BtVS* sizzles and titillates with throbbing music, yearning looks, passionate kisses, and more.

BTVS depicts typical relationships and problems, such as teen and young adult angst, needs for love, acceptance, identity, community and a panorama of teen desires and fears. It engages painful problems like rejection and loneliness; drugs and addiction; violence, gangs, rape, destructive behavior, death and a range of other issues that concern young people and adults, although it often does this, as I argue below, in the mode of allegory, rather than movie-of-the-week style realism. It deals with the hell of high school with its group conform-ity, hierarchies and ostracisms, anti-intellectualism and oppressive authority fig-ures and meaningless rules and regulations. Moreover, *BtVS* deals with existential crises like coping with parents' divorce, creating a relationship and life with one's single mother, and dealing with a parent's or loved one's death.

Families are presented as essentially dysfunctional in Buffy's world and the mothers depicted are largely ineffectual or perhaps destructive, while fathers are mostly absent and divorce appears to be a norm. Depicting ways to cope with the problems of contemporary life, the series shows how teenagers and young people often have to forge alternative families and in effect create friendships and communities as traditional families disintegrate. Clearly, Buffy's group the "Scooby gang" offer its members a substitute family that it can count on in times of trouble, as well as a cadre of friends and lovers with whom one can experience the agonies and ecstasies of growing up and becoming initiated into life's pleasures and disappointments.

One of the series' most distinctive themes concerns how individuals with exceptional powers and abilities can develop these capacities and find and culti-vate love, friendship, affirmation of difference, and identity. Its grappling with difference, otherness, and marginality is a major theme of the show and puts on display its affinity with postmodern theory.[12] On the one hand, it affirms certain types of difference and otherness, as it shows the main positive characters as out-siders who refuse to conform to the dominant teen subculture and cultivate their individual powers and abilities, while relating to others in respectful ways. However, the series also shows how certain types of otherness, embodied in the program's monsters, threaten school, community, and everyday life and must be stood up to and dealt with. The dialectic of otherness is complicated further, as I will note, by showing slippages between "good" and "bad" otherness, as, for example, when the vampires Angel and Spike exhibit abilities to do both signifi-cant good and evil, and are forced to make important moral choices.

In addition, *Buffy* can be read, on the more traditional and realist narrative level, as a female *Bildungsroman*, that is a coming-to-age and growing up story, focused on a young women. It provides a fantasy of an empowered women able to control her environment and to hold off and defeat forces of evil. While the *Bildungsroman* is associated with Goethe, Thomas Mann and novels about young men coming-to-age,[13] *Buffy* is different and ground-breaking in having a female protagonist. Indeed, the series exhibits perhaps the most fully developed female *Bildungsroman* narrative in history of popular television and earned a cult follow-ing and dedicated audience.

The theme of how to cultivate exceptional abilities and deal with monstrosity obviously takes us to the level of the series' mythology as Buffy is a vampire slayer and her antagonists are often demons and monsters of a certain pop cult genre type. I'm using "mythology" as Chris Carter did in relation to *The X-Files* and Joss Whedon does with Buffy as the particular mythical universe and narra-tive of the series, rather than in the traditional sense of mythology, which I'll argue takes us more to the allegorical level that I'll come to shortly. The series' mythology comprises the particular supernatural powers that the characters pos-sess, the demons they fight, and the conflicts they are involved in within par-ticular story arcs and narrative sequences.

The specific *BtVS* mythology was introduced by series creator Joss Whedon in the 1992 film *Buffy the Vampire Slayer* on which Whedon is cred-ited as writer and Fran Rubel Kuzui is credited as director (she would serve as long-time producer on the TV series). The film opens with the portentous narrative frame:

> Since the dawn of man the vampires have walked among us, killing, feeding. The only one with the strength or skill to stop the heinous evil is the Slayer … Trained by the Watcher, one Slayer dies and another is chosen.

A caption appears "Europe: The Dark Ages" showing the vampire slayer emerging and then after the titles, the picture cuts to a title "Southern California: the Lite Ages." Buffy and her friends are introduced as Valley Girls who are into cheerleading, shopping, boys, and the prom. However, the Chosen One, Buffy (Kristy Swanson), has dreams of dark events in the past involving vampires, and her Watcher Merrick (Donald Sutherland) tells her of her "birthright" and initiates her into the art of vampire slaying. First resisting her calling, as the vampires invade the student prom, Buffy displays her mythical powers and slays the Evil Ones.

The film sets up the Buffy mythology and displays its blend of humor, horror, and social satire, but the TV series that appeared on the fledging Warner Brothers WB channel in 1997 went much further into developing a complex mythology, set of characters, and plot lines that generated a genuine pop culture sensation. The WB channel was looking for programming that would appeal to a youth market and was willing to gamble on more offbeat and idiosyncratic programming that would give the fledging network buzz, publicity, and ratings in the competitive world of network television.[14] Although *BtVS* was never a major ratings hit, as was *The X-Files* for some years, it picked up enough viewers so that a new smaller network like the WB would be inclined to promote and renew it.

Joss Whedon called his company Mutant Enemy and the corporate logo that appeared at the end of *BtVS* featured a squiggly animated character tearing across the screen and screeching Grrrr … Arrgh![15] The logo codes the series as subversive and offbeat and the show at its best has dissident and oppositional features, although it also reproduces some dominant female gender ideology motifs and has its problematic aspects.

On the series mythology level, *BtVS* creates stories about vampires and the vampire slayer, monsters, various forms of evil and their defeat; the mythology follows story arcs, as does the realist narrative level of the series. From our retrospective position at the end of the series, we can see that the first three seasons dealt with high school and introduced the mythology; season four dealt with college life; and succeeding seasons five through seven dealt with work and college and post-college life and initiation into adulthood.

The two-part 1997 opening episodes "Welcome to the Hellmouth" and "The Harvest" introduce viewers Buffy and her friends who are positioned as outsiders and non-conformists who bond together in a close community. The episodes unfold the mythology of the Hellmouth over Sunnydale High where demonic forces enter the world and introduce an aging vampire demon, the Master, who threatens apocalyptic destruction of the community, opening the Hellmouth to an invasion of demons.

Season one put on display a series of salient fears of contemporary youth and won a devoted audience by providing characters, situations, and narratives that embodied contemporary worries and anxieties.[16] It is remarkable that the series resists the assaults on youth and negatively stigmatizing the young that is a major theme of many films, media representations, academic studies, and political discourse.[17] Instead *BtVS* presents images of youth who are intelligent, resourceful, virtuous, and able to choose between good and evil and positively transform themselves, and who are also capable of dealing with their anxieties and grappling with the problems of everyday life.

I'll return to some of the specific mythologies of the series, but want to argue that *BtVS* also has an allegorical level that makes it more interesting than just a self-contained vampire-slayer narrative and Slayer mythology or conventional story of growing up teen in the contemporary U.S. The allegorical level builds on the previous levels I've mentioned and has its own complexities.

In general, a complex and multidimensional allegory like *BtVS* has a theological and religious dimension that copes with life and death; sin, guilt, and redemption; the choice between good and evil; and how to understand and deal with life and an afterlife.[18] There are also moral and philosophical allegories that present ethical lessons ranging from children's stories to philosophical treatises like Kant, Hegel, and Marx, which convey specific ethical, or social and political ideals or lessons, as when the Brothers Grimm terrify their young audiences into accepting conservative German values or the Disney factory indoctrinates its audiences into proper white middle-class American small town morality. More sublime philosophical allegories would include Kant's presenting Enlightenment as a mode of salvation, or Marx positing the proletariat and socialism as solutions to the damnation and evils of capitalism and modernity. As critics ranging from Georg Lukacs to Fredric Jameson tell us, literature can also be read as allegory about life in specific milieux, in particular historical periods that convey concrete socio-historical truths. And, finally, popular culture can be allegorical in a moral and socio-political mode, telling stories about contemporary life in a symbolic and narrative structure, providing specific life lessons, as well as commentary and critique of contemporary life and specific events, institutions, values, and types of persons.

Although media culture allegory can provide a vehicle for ideology, reproducing the values and prejudices of the dominant class, race, and gender, it can also resist and subvert the dominant ideology, valorizing outsiders, resistance to hegemonic norms, and can present alternative ways of relating, living, and being, as I'll argue in the succeeding analysis. Thus reading complex texts like *BtVS* involves both critique of its ideologies and politics of representation, as well as presentation of its critical and subversive moments.

Applying this model of allegory, I argued in Chapter 3 that the *Poltergeist* films, *The Amityville Horror* and other horror/fantasy films of the era, as well as season one of *American Horror Story*, depicted fears of losing your home, economic downwards mobility, the family falling apart and other fears of the era. These truly horrifying problems were too distressing and traumatizing for a realist aesthetic depiction, so horror and fantasy could represent these themes in ways that audiences could deal with the fears and dangers of class downward mobility, the breakup of the family, or losing your house. Horror and fantasy films could also allegorize themes such as the corruption of capitalism or opposition to patriarchy more accessibly and less threateningly than more realist films.

BtVS can be read the same way as an allegory about contemporary life with its monsters as metaphors for societal difference and threats, and Buffy and her friends' special powers can be read as metaphors for how knowledge, skill, and courage which can help solve problems and dispatch evil. Classically, monsters like vampires symbolize predatory sexuality; werewolves connote bodily energies and forces exploding out of control; witches signify traditional female powers, including sexuality, which threaten the rational patriarchal order; while a wide range of demons signify various sorts of deviance and threats to contemporary order and security. In the current situation, for instance, many of the demons on *BtVS* point to dangers of drug addiction and the gangs of monsters signify dangers of gang violence. Obviously, many of the monsters are figures for alienated teens who strike out at their classmates with violence and often murder.

The vampire as addict was clearly depicted in the figures of Spike (James Marsters) and Drusilla (Juliet Landau) in the second season. In the episodes introducing her, Drusilla appeared zoned out on hard drugs like heroin and the show's creators contend that the duo was modeled on *Sid and Nancy* (1986), a popular film of the era based on Sid Vicious, the heroin-addicted punk rocker with the Sex Pistols and his girlfriend, Nancy. Spike and Drusilla's need for blood is a clear metaphor for drug addiction and their sexual nihilism and ambiguous ménage à trois with the vampire Angel suggests sexual degradation associated with addiction and amorality.

As Gregory Erikson suggests (2002), vampires have a historical specificity as well as more universal connotations. Early vampires in European folklore were peasants who emerged from the grave to avenge grievances while by the time of Bram Stoker's *Dracula* novel, it was aristocrats who embodied vampiric evil and required elaborate rituals to destroy. In the representation of vampires in German expressionist horror films of the 1920s like *Nosferatu*, the vampire was disturbingly similar to representations of Jews, such as one seen in the anti-Semitic *Jude Suss*. In contemporary U.S. culture, vampires have been largely represented as anarchic individuals, who can emerge from any class, age, or social grouping.

The allegory of *BtVS* is that all of these teen monstrosities create a conflictual and dangerous situation for youth today that must be dealt with skillfully and successfully to defeat the evils of the contemporary era. Buffy's method of dispatching vampires is literally "dusting" the creatures with a stake or sharp weapon, turning them into dust and avoiding the blood squirting associated with more traditional vampire-slaying. The series provides positive characters and models who embody a creative otherness and difference, and who are able to overcome and destroy the more monstrous threats to community and security.

A critical media/cultural studies interrogates the politics of representation, as well as the allegorical meanings and cultural resonances and effects of a media culture spectacle. Most of the ideological focus on *BtVS* has been on its representations of gender and sexuality, in which its powerful images of strong women and alternative sexualities have been positively valorized. Indeed, the series provides a systematic critique of patriarchy showing how its structures permeate schooling, politics, the military, and other social institutions. Curiously, though, patriarchy in the family on the series is glossed over, as fathers are usually extremely weak or in most cases absent, although the opening mythology of the Master and his minions arguably contains a satirical critique of patriarchy. The minor demons treat the Master with obsequious obedience and a young child, the Anointed One, arguably constitutes a parody of patriarchal succession, an ideological trope subverted on the series by having a female slayer.

Further, patriarchal conservativism is shown as ascendant and negatively portrayed in schooling in the representations of high school Principles Flutie and Snyder (the latter in particular is presented as an authoritarian conservative, not really concerned with students or learning, while the former is merely ineffectual and quickly dispatched with). The swim team coach who exposes his swimmers to steroids is an example of the destructive nature of patriarchy in school sports, and Buffy and Giles both rebel against the patriarchal structure of the Watcher Council. In season three, the presentation of the mayor and his political associates as monsters constitute a tongue-in-cheek attack on patriarchy in the sociopolitical system, as does season four's assault on the patriarchal military that I engaged above.

Yet, although *BtVS*'s gender politics are progressive in many ways, the ideal women are almost invariably thin and beautiful. The images of high school and college women depicted in the series are largely white, middle classed, and conventional. More punkish or countercultural types of women are usually associated with monsters in the series and working class women are shown as largely unattractive. As noted, mothers are usually ineffectual, absent, or malicious. Hence, while the images of Buffy, Willow, and some of the other women are unusually strong and women's relations and solidarities are at the heart of *BtVS*, the series is at best Feminism Lite, soft-pedaling feminist ideas in images and narratives rather than discourses or more progressive representations and narratives.

Hence, traditionally feminine ideals of beauty and desirably are upheld although patriarchy is under assault. Likewise, *BtVS*'s representations of class and race are problematic. The main characters are identifiably white and middle class, and many monsters appear to be rough, threatening working-class types and people of color. Faith is the most identifiably working class character of the major figures in the series and she is introduced and often presented as an unruly, undisciplined, amoral, and potentially destructive person, although eventually she is more or less integrated into the community, a figure of working-class mobility and assimilation. At the start of season three, Buffy is presented as a waitress while in season four, she is shown working in a burger joint and Xander is presented in a series of menial working-class jobs, all portrayed as dead end jobs, to be overcome and transcended by proper(ly middle-class) individuals.

The series is also extremely limited and seriously problematical with its representation of race. In the first seasons, there were few Black characters and those presented were often either killed or were vampires. There was little interaction among Buffy's Scooby gang with people of color and while the final season displayed a variety of young women from varied ethnicities as potential slayers, few exhibited any individuality and the attempt at multiculturalism was largely cosmetic and visual, putting on display a diversity of rainbow-colored bodies, rather than racially interactive groups and social relations.

Whiteness and middle-class ideals are thus privileged throughout the series as Buffy is the model balanced Slayer while the Afro Jamaican Kendra is shown as compulsive and fanatical, and working-class Faith is often erratic and unbalanced. Moreover, throughout the series, threats to the middle-class community come from outside, not only from Hell, but from non-Western cultures. "Inca Mummy Girl" (season four, #4) features a vampirish Inca princess from an ancient Peruvian culture who comes to life and causes Xander much pain as he falls in love with her and then discovers her monstrosity. The subtext of the story is a foreign exchange program and the episode implies that members of other cultures can be seductive and dangerous. "Half-breeds" and "non-humans" also come from Egypt, Pakistan, the Middle East, or other countries once labeled Third World, so the cultural ethos is rather parochially southern California white and middle-class.

While *BtVS* is sometimes presented as critical of religion, there is a privileging of Christianity in iconographies of the cross, holy water, and other images as well as themes such as salvation and redemption. Willow is "kinda Jewish," but Jewish or themes of other world religions do not centrally appear in the series' episodes, thus there is a theological privileging of Western Christianity, although, admittedly, the demonology undermines strict Christian theology and there are some episodes which depict monstrous demonic rites taking place before Christian iconography (as in the episode "Innocence" [season four, #4]), thus presenting contradictory relations to Christianity and provoking fundamentalist Christian attacks upon the series.[19]

On the level of the politics of representation, then, *BtVS*, like most television, reproduces some dominant gender ideology, although it is in many ways highly subversive. A popular medium that must attract mass audiences and that does not want to catch flak from conservatives or traditionalists of various sorts must be careful to be subtle and sly in its subversion. The "Mutant Enemy" production team of *BtVS* has in many ways, as I've argued in this chapter, provided significant satire and subversion of many dominant societal and social codes, as well as rather consistently attacked patriarchy. Moreover, it has engaged the situation of contemporary youth with engaged critical awareness, often brilliant social satire and commentary, and narrative arcs that together constitutes one of the classics of contemporary television and an important artifact of youth culture that deserves serious critical attention.

Fashion and identity

Reflections on Madonna, Brittany Spears, Lady Gaga, Beyoncé, and other pop culture icons of the contemporary era reveal how their work, popularity, celebrity, and influence demonstrate important features of the nature and function of fashion and identity in the contemporary world. Media culture icons become role models and help young women and men construct identities. Elvis Presley and male icons of the early rock and roll era provide images of rebellion, individuality, and fashion that influenced a generation of youth while later rock stars of the 1960s, alternative rock icons of the 1970s and 1980s, and hip-hop stars and music videos of the 1990s influenced the fashion choices, life styles, and generations of youth. In this section, I will discuss how certain female pop music idols have influenced fashion and identity.

Indeed, fashion offers models and material for constructing identity. Traditional societies had relatively fixed social roles and sumptuary codes, so that clothes and one's appearance instantly denoted one's social class, profession, and status.[20] Identity in traditional societies was usually fixed by birth, marriage, and accomplishment, and the available repertoire of roles was tightly constricted. Gender roles were especially rigid, while work and status were tightly circumscribed by established social codes and an obdurate system of status ascription.

During the medieval period, identities in Western Europe were especially circumscribed and rules even dictated what members of different classes could or could not wear. Modern societies eliminated rigid codes of dress and fashion, and beginning around 1700 changing fashions of apparel and appearance began proliferating (Wilson 1985). Although a capitalist market dictated that only certain classes could afford the most expensive attire, which signified social privilege and power, in the aftermath of the French Revolution, fashion was democratized in countries that carried through a democratic revolution, so that anyone who could afford certain clothes and make-up could wear and display what they wished (whereas previously, sumptuary laws forbid members of certain classes from dressing and appearing like the ruling elites; Ewen and Ewen 1982; Ewen 1988).

Modernity also offered new possibilities for constructing personal identities. Modern societies made it possible for individuals to produce – within certain limits – their own identities and to experience identity crises. Already in the eighteenth century, the philosopher David Hume formulated the problem of personal identity, of what constituted one's true selfhood, even suggesting that there was no substantial or transcendental self. The issue became an obsession with Rousseau, Kierkegaard, and many other Europeans who experienced rapid change, the breakdown of traditional societies, and the emergence of modernity (see Antonio and Kellner 1994).

In modernity, fashion is an important constituent of one's identity, helping to determine how one is perceived and accepted (see Wilson 1985; Ewen 1988). Fashion offers choices of clothes, style, and image through which one could produce an individual identity. In a sense, fashion is a constituent feature of modernity, interpreted as an era of history marked by perpetual innovation, by the destruction of the old and the creation of the new (Berman 1982). Fashion itself is predicated on producing ever new tastes, styles, dress, and practices. Fashion perpetuates a restless, modern personality, always seeking what is new and admired, while avoiding what is old and passé. Fashion and modernity go hand in hand to produce modern personalities who seek their identities in constantly new and trendy clothes, looks, attitudes, and style, and who are fearful of being out-of-date or unfashionable.

Of course, fashion in modern societies was limited by gender codes, economic realities, and the force of social conformity, which continued to dictate what one could or could not wear, and what one could or could not be. Fashion in modernity itself underwent complex stages of historical development, though by the beginning of the twentieth century, modern fashion rationalized clothing and cosmetics and mass markets began to make changes in fashion open to mass consumption (Ewen and Ewen 1982; Ewen 1988). Yet fashion codes continued to be relatively fixed for some classes and regions. Documentary footage from the U.S. in the 1950s, shown in the 1982 ABC documentary *Heroes of Rock* and other sources, depicted parents, teachers, and other arbiters of good taste attempting to dictate proper and improper fashion, thus policing the codes of fashion and identity. Crossing gender codes in fashion was for centuries a good way to mark oneself as a social outcast or even to land in jail or a mental institution.

The 1960s exhibited a massive attempt to overthrow the cultural codes of the past and fashion became an important element of the construction of new identities, along with sex, drugs, and rock and roll, phenomena also involved in the changing fashions of the day. In the 1960s, anti-fashion in clothes and attire became fashionable and the subversion and overthrowing of cultural codes became a norm. So-called fashion-subversion continued in vogue during the following decades, and the fashion industry allowed new flexibility and marketed an ever-changing array of new styles and looks. By means of such fashion moves, individuals could quickly produce their own identities through resisting dominant fashion codes and producing their own fashion statements, or using dominant styles in their own ways. One of Stuart Ewen's students provides interesting testimony concerning how it was possible to produce one's own style against dominant fashion codes:

> I went to Catholic school for twelve years. In grammar school, I wore a uniform for eight years. I used to try to rebel against this in little ways, such as not wearing the tie I was supposed to, or by wearing the wrong type of collar … It was a way of finding myself a little freedom, a way of fighting the system in a small way.
>
> *(cited in Ewen 1988: 5)*

Indeed, Madonna herself tells in an early interview how she expressed adolescent rebellion through fashion from the time she was a young girl, indicating she and her girlfriend dressed extravagantly:

> Only because we knew that our parents didn't like it. We thought it was fun. We got dressed to the nines. We got bras and stuffed them so our breasts were over-large and wore really tight sweaters – we were sweater-girl floozies. We wore tons of lipstick and really badly applied makeup and huge beauty marks and did our hair up like Tammy Wynette.
>
> *(Madonna, cited in Lewis 1993: 142)*

During this period, media culture became a particularly potent source of cultural fashions, providing models for appearance, behavior, and style. The long-haired and unconventionally dressed rock stars of the 1960s and the 1970s influenced changes in styles of hair, dress, and behavior, while their sometimes rebellious attitudes sanctioned social revolt, as when Bob Dylan proclaimed that "The Times They are a-Changin'," or that change was "Blowing in the Wind." Groups like the Beatles, the Rolling Stones, the Jefferson Airplane, and performers like Janis Joplin or Jimi Hendrix sanctioned countercultural revolt and the appropriation of new styles of dress, behavior, and attitudes. The association of rock culture with long hair, social rebellion, and non-conformity in fashion continued through succeeding decades with successive waves of heavy metal rock, punk, and new wave attaining popularity.

More conservative television programming, films, and pop music by contrast provided mainstream models for youth. During the past several decades, cultural conservatives have been reacting strongly against 1960s radicalism and fashion, and youth culture and fashion have become battlefields between traditionalist conservatives and cultural radicals, attempting to overturn traditional gender roles, fashion codes, and values and behavior. Thus, fashion and social identities are themselves part of a process of social struggle and conflict between opposing models and ideologies. Conservatives have their fashion models and style, as do subcultural rebels. Political struggles thus are partly played out in fashion wars as well as elections and political debate.

High school in particular is a period in which young people construct their identities, attempting to "become someone" (Wexler 1992).[21] High school has been a terrain of contradiction and struggle for the past decades. While some parents and teachers attempt to instill traditional values and ideas, youth culture is often in opposition to conservative culture. Although the 1980s was a predominantly conservative period with the election of Ronald Reagan and a "right turn" in U.S. culture (see Ferguson and Rogers 1986; Kellner and Ryan 1988; Kellner 1990a), the images from popular music figures sometimes cut across the conservative grain. Michael Jackson, Prince, Boy George, and other rock groups undermined traditional gender divisions and promoted polymorphic sexuality. Cyndi Lauper reveled in offbeat kookiness, while Pee-wee Herman engaged in silly and infantile behavior to the delight of his young (and older) audiences. Throwing off decades of cool sophistication, maturity, respectability, and taste, Pee-wee made it OK to be silly and weird, or at least different.

Pop culture icons from Madonna to Beyoncé and Lady Gaga

From the origins of post-World War II U.S. youth and media culture, pop cultural icons have thus become fashion models and role models for youth, creating fusions between youth culture and media culture. For the past decades, Madonna Louise Ciccone has been a highly influential pop culture icon and the center of a storm of controversy. For decades, she has been one of the best-selling and most discussed female singers in popular music, one of the most prominent stars of music video, a movie actress, writer, producer, and, most of all, a superstar of media culture.

Madonna has become a site of contestation and controversy, adored and abhorred by audiences, critics, and academics alike since her emergence in the 1980s. Most of the polemics, however, are contentious, of an either/or and pro or con nature, and they fail to grasp the many sides of the Madonna phenomenon. While some celebrated her early work as a subversive cultural revolutionary, others attacked her as anti-feminist, or as irredeemably trashy and vulgar, although her image changed significantly over the decades. Against one-sided attacks or celebrations, however, I argue that "Madonna" is a site of genuine contradiction that must be articulated and appraised to adequately interpret her images, works, and their effects.

My argument is that Madonna's image and reception highlights the social constructedness of identity, fashion, and sexuality in today's youth culture and media culture. By exploding boundaries established by dominant gender, sexual, and fashion codes, she encouraged experimentation, change, and production of one's individual identity. Yet by privileging the creation of image, looks, fashion, and style in the production of identity, Madonna reinforces the norms of the consumer society, which offers the possibilities of a new commodity "self" through consumption and the products of the fashion industry. I argue that grasping this contradiction is the key to Madonna's effects and to interrogating the conditions under which the multiplicity of discourses on Madonna, and contradictory readings and evaluations, are produced. In her work, Madonna pushes the most sensitive buttons of sexuality, gender, race, and class, offering challenging and provocative images and cultural artifacts, as well as ones that reinforce dominant conventions. The Madonna construct *is* a set of contradictions and in the following analysis I'll explore some of the images, codes, and effects that constitute the Madonna phenomenon.

It was during the 1980s, in which youth identities were being renegotiated in a conservative era, that Madonna first came to prominence. Her early music videos and concert performances transgressed traditional fashion boundaries and she engaged in overt sexual behavior and titillation, subverting the boundaries of "proper" female behavior. Thus, from the beginning Madonna was one of the most outrageous female icons among the repertoire of circulating images sanctioned by the culture industries. Although there were no doubt many more far out and subversive figures than Madonna, their images and messages did not circulate through mainstream culture and thus did not have the efficacy of the popular. The early Madonna sanctioned rebellion, non-conformity, individuality, and experimentation with fashion and life-styles. Madonna's constant change of image and identity promoted experimentation and the creation of one's own fashion and style. Her sometimes dramatic shifts in image and style suggested that identity was a construct, that it was something that one produced, and that it could be modified at will. The way that Madonna deployed fashion in the construction of her identity made it clear that one's appearance and image helps produce what one is, or least how individuals are perceived and related to.

Thus, Madonna problematized identity and revealed its constructedness and alterability. Madonna was successively a dancer, musician, model, singer, music video star, movie and stage actress, "America's most successful businesswoman," and a pop superstar who excelled in marketing her image and selling her goods. Consciously crafting her own image, she moved from being a boy toy, material girl, and ambitious blonde, to artiste of music videos, films, and concerts.[22] Her music shifted from disco and bubblegum rock, to personal statements and melodic torch singing, to (with the aid of her music videos) pop modernism. Madonna's hair changed from dirty blonde to platinum blonde, to black, brunette, redhead, and multifarious variations thereof. Her body changed from soft and sensuous to glamorous and svelte to hard and muscular sex machine to futuristic technobody. Her clothes and fashion changed from flashy trash, to haute couture, to far-out technocouture, to lesbian S&M fashion, to postmodern pastiche of all and every fashion style. New images and a new identity for all occasions and epochs. As it turns out, Madonna's fashion moves generally caught shifts in cultural style and taste, and thus achieved the status of the popular, providing fashion models and material for appropriation by her vast and varied audiences.

While there is sufficient material both to celebrate and to criticize her, one should grasp the many-sidedness of the Madonna phenomenon and her multiple and contradictory effects. Indeed, Madonna is a provocative challenge to cultural studies. Unpacking the wealth of her artistic strategies, meanings, and effects requires deployment of a full array of textual criticism, audience research, and analysis of the political economy and production of pop culture in our contemporary media society. Her work has become increasingly complex and it is precisely this complexity that has made Madonna a highly controversial object of academic analysis for decades. Madonna allows many, even contradictory, readings, which are grounded in her polysemic and modernist texts and her contradictory cultural effects. At dull gatherings, mention Madonna and you can be sure that there will be violent arguments, with some people passionately attacking and others defending her.

Other young popular singers quickly followed Madonna in becoming pop icons, models of fashion, and super-celebrity heroes of youth. Britney Spears' first two studio albums … *Baby One More Time* (1999) and *Oops! … I Did It Again* (2000), were global successes and made her the best-selling teenage artist of all-time, helping to revive a genre of teen pop during the late 1990s. Her early 2000s albums *Britney* (2001) and *In the Zone* (2003) adopted a more mature persona and themes and she made her feature film debut in a starring role in *Crossroads* (2002).

Like Madonna, Britney Spears excelled in singing, dancing, performance, and image production, winning her a global fan base. She had difficulties, however, managing her personal life and has had difficult marriages, has been the subject of tabloid scandals, and undergone health issues, which have periodically side-lined her career. In recent years, for example, there has been controversy about Britney being put under a conservatorship controlled by her father since 2008, but she has continued to perform and produce popular albums.[23]

Other pop icons succeeded in becoming global superstars like Beyoncé Giselle Knowles-Carter who emerged as a rising superstar and pop icon, coming to fame in the late 1990s as lead singer of the R&B girl-group Destiny's Child, and appearing in films like *Austin Powers in Goldmember* (2002). The release of her first solo album, *Dangerously in Love* (2003) established Beyoncé as a superstar artist worldwide, debuting at number one on the U.S. Billboard 200 chart and earning her five Grammy Awards.

Following the break-up of Destiny's Child in 2006, Beyoncé released her second solo album, *B'Day*, and continued her acting career with starring roles in *The Pink Panther* (2006), *Dreamgirls* (2006), and *Obsessed* (2009). Throughout her career, Beyoncé has sold over 100 million records worldwide as a solo artist and a further 60 million records with Destiny's Child, making her one of the best-selling music artists of all time. She is acclaimed for her vocals, music videos, and live concert shows. The documentary film *Homecoming*, sub-titled: "A Film by Beyoncé" (2019) provides illuminating insight into the Beyoncé phenomenon and displays her spectacular performance and style, as well as fervent adulation by her audience. Depicting her headlining role in the 2018 Coachella Valley Music and Arts Festival, the concert and documentary film was presented as a Netflix special on April 17, 2019. Written, directed, and executive produced by Beyoncé herself, *Homecoming* thus provides her self-presentation of her life, music, and versatility as a performer.

The concert show is an over-the-top spectacle with Beyoncé backed with male and female dancers, chorus, and orchestra, with Beyoncé dominating every scene. Yet it is also a spectacle of Blackness with the performers of color putting on display spectacular moves, lyrics, and spectacle of Black culture. The documentary intersperses between each scene words from top African American writers like Toni Morrison, Maya Angelou, Alice Walker, and poet/songress Nina Simone who states: "To me, we are the most beautiful creatures in the whole world, Black people." The Black is beautiful motif runs through the concert and documentary, and in a voiceover, Beyoncé states: "When I decided to do Coachella, instead of me pulling out my flower crown, it was more important that I brought our culture to Coachella."

Another video clip edited into the montage has Malcolm X proclaiming "The most disrespected person in America is the Black woman. The most unprotected woman in America is the Black woman. The most neglected woman in America is the black woman." The documentary also features W.E. B. DuBois stating: "Education must not simply teach work – it must teach life." *Homecoming* stresses the importance of Black education and Historically Black Colleges and Universities (HBCUs) with footage from an actual homecoming celebration at Black colleges. Voice-over narration notes where the various Black luminaries quoted studied, while Nina Simone speaks about the importance of Black culture and of her ambition to teach others, with the theme of education highlighted throughout *Homecoming*.

Beyoncé opened her two-hour set dressed as an Egyptian queen – with a royal headdress and long black cape, also paying homage to Egyptian goddess Nefertiti, whose name and insignia was emblazoned on the back of her cape. Her dancers were dressed in ethnic cat suits, which included an image of the ancient Greek symbol, the Sphinx, before they all changed to perform, "Crazy in Love." Beyoncé's lyrics in the concert/film range from aggressive and self-affirming as she belts out lyrics from "Freedom" telling of her struggle to "break chains all by myself" and be truly free. In "Formation," she talks of her background and proclaims that she's a star "Cause I slay …" On "Diva," Beyoncé states "I'm a diva" and watching the wildly cheering and ecstatic fans in the audience, there is no question but she is! Other songs present her as more vulnerable when in "I Care" she notes hurt and rejection in a relationship and the pain of love. And, importantly, *Homecoming* affirms the power of women when Beyoncé proclaims in "RUN THE WORLD" that "GIRLS" should "run this motha, yeah"!

Homecoming was described as providing an "intimate, in-depth look" of Beyoncé's concert, revealing "the emotional road from creative concept to a cultural movement".[24] *Wikipedia* documents that *Homecoming* received widespread acclaim from critics with the review aggregator website *Rotten Tomatoes* reporting an 98% approval rating while *Metacritic* "assigned the film a weighted average score of 92 … indicating universal acclaim," which makes "*Homecoming* the most acclaimed television special of all time."[25] Further, *Wikipedia* notes:

Several publications named *Homecoming* as one of the greatest concert films of all time, including *RogerEbert.com*, *The Washington Post*, *The Hollywood Reporter*, *Deadline*, *Refinery29*, *Chatelaine*, *The Guardian*, and *Chicago Sun-Times*. Spencer Kornhaber of *The Atlantic* called *Homecoming* "one of Beyoncé's masterpieces", adding that the film's "combo of well-edited stage spectacle and behind-the-scenes segments – intimate, hard-fought, occasionally tense, politically explicit, personally specific segments – make it a career-defining document." David Ehrlich of *IndieWire* wrote that "Beyoncé managed to fit the whole spectacle into a euphoric, triumphant, and exhaustingly fierce documentary that should help see Beychella enshrined as one of the definitive pop culture events of the century."[26]

Other female pop idols have also risen to the heights of superstardom in the 2000s. Stefani Joanne Angelina Germanotta a.k.a. Lady Gaga burst on the scene with her debut album, the electropop record *The Fame* (2008) and its chart-topping singles "Just Dance" and "Poker Face." Gaga is a sensational performer and astute media personality who quickly assembled a rapturous band of followers who emulated her rebellious fashion style, her unconventional behavior, and assertive personality.

Lady Gaga's second major album, *Born This Way* (2011), explored electronic rock and techno-pop, and became one of the fastest and best-selling albums of all time. Gaga experimented with Electronic Dance Music (EDM) on her next album, *Artpop* (2013), which reached number one in the U.S. and included the single "Applause." Her collaborative jazz album with Tony Bennett, *Cheek to Cheek* (2014), her soft rock-influenced fifth studio album, *Joanne* (2016), and her songs from *A Star is Born* (2018), in which she also acted to great acclaim, became best sellers as well.

Fans got a revealing look into Lady Gaga's performing life in the documentary *Gaga: Five Foot Two* (2017), which presents the events around the production and release of Gaga's fifth studio album, *Joanne*, and her halftime performance at Super Bowl LI. The film, directed by visual artist and documentarian Chris Moukarbel, deploys a cinéma vérité style to give viewers "unfiltered, behind-the-scenes access" to a year in the life of Gaga, during which she produced and released her fifth studio album, *Joanne*.[27] Many events are covered in *Gaga*, including her experiences with her entourage, her encounters with fans, and her struggle with chronic pain caused by the onset of fibromyalgia. The film also offers an extensive look at the creation and execution of her critically lauded Super Bowl LI halftime performance, in addition to a variety of other topics and events, including her home life, the filming of her guest role as the character Scáthach on *American Horror Story: Roanoke*, and a discussion about her feud with Madonna, among other things.

And so the major female icons of pop music have become masters of media spectacle, merging performance, videos, albums, and movies to publicize their work creating an implosion between popular music, video, performance, and spectacle in the contemporary moment. In the next chapter, we shall see how politics has also been dominated by media spectacle in the 2000s, which reflects changes in presidential politics in the past decades and the emergence of the Obama and Trump spectacles.

Notes

1 Elvis fans and scholars, including myself (Kellner 2007), see Parker's management as extremely harmful to Elvis's career as the Colonel pushed him into making an endless series of mediocre films and then releasing albums of the songs in the films, rather than producing original work (see Guralnick 1995, 2000).

2 On the other hand, unlike *Beavis and Butt-Head*, which I discuss below, the slackers also read books, referencing Tolstoy, Dostoyevsky, Sade, and various other writers and poets, though the differences between books, TV, and movies seem to be levelled, with the various characters reducing everything to sound bites and clichés.

3 The conception of "postmodernism" that I am using here is that of Jameson (1991) who focuses on flat, one-dimensional experiences or images, disconnected and fragmented, but punctuated by moments of euphoric intensity. This concept describes both the form of the film *Slacker* and the texture of its characters' experiences and life-style. For my take on postmodern theory see Best and Kellner 1991, 1997, 2001.

4 Coincidentally, I was teaching a course on modernity/postmodernity at the University of Texas the semester of *Slacker*'s shooting, was using the two books shown in the coffee house in my course in a scene with two slackers talking, and several of my students were in the film, including Tommy Palotta who confirmed the two books in the coffee house filmed were texts in my modernity/postmodernity course (discussion in Los Angeles, November 2019). Thus, aesthetic debates concerning modernism and postmodernism were in the air in Austin during the 1990s, and Linklater, who I have known for years, obviously picked up on these ideas, blending them in an innovative fashion in his film. So perhaps it is not just an accident that I choose to discuss these films.

5 *Beavis and Butt-Head* was based on an animated short by Mike Judge, in which the two characters play "frog baseball," shown at the Sick and Twisted Animation festival, and was taken up by MTV's animated series Liquid Television. The series itself premiered in March 1993, but because there were only four episodes, the show went on hiatus, returning on May 17 after Judge and his team of creative assistants put together 32 new episodes (see *The San Francisco Chronicle*, June 29, 1993). The series tripled MTV's ratings and MTV ordered 130 more episodes for 1994 (*The New York Times*, October 17, 1993).

6 An October 9, 1993, story in the *Dayton Daily News* reported that a five-year-old boy in Dayton, Ohio, ignited his bed clothes with a cigarette lighter after watching the pyromaniac antics of Beavis and Butt-Head, according to his mother. The boy's younger sister, two, died in the ensuing blaze. The mother said her five-year-old son had become "obsessed" with Beavis and Butt-Head and imitated their destructive behavior. I provide more examples of the "Beavis and Butt-Head" effect throughout this section.

7 An October 23, 1993, Senate Hearings on TV violence focused media attention on the show, though U.S. Sen. Ernest Hollings (D-SC) botched references to it, saying: "We've got this – what is it – Buffcoat and Beaver or Beaver and something else. ... I haven't seen it; I don't watch it; it was at 7 o'clock – Buffcoat – and they put it on now at 10:30, I think" (*The Hartford Courant*, October 26, 1993). Such ignorance of media culture is often found in some of its harshest critics.

8 Beavis and Butt-Head's family genealogy in a book on the series puts a question mark in the place of both of their fathers (Johnson and Marcil 1993). Their mothers

were never shown in the series, though there are some references to them. It is also unclear exactly whose house they live in, or are shown watching TV in, and whether they do or do not live together. One episode suggests that they are in Butt-Head's house and that his mother is always out with her boyfriend, but other episodes show two beds together in what appears to be their highly messy bedroom and as of early 1994, their parents have never been shown.

9 Psychoanalysts could identity Beavis and Butt-Head with the Freudian Id, with uncontrolled aggression and sexual impulses that they cannot understand or control (they were often shown masturbating, or talking about it, and Beavis uncontrollably "moons" attractive female singers while watching music videos). There is also a barely repressed homoerotic element to their relationship, expressed in the endless "butt" jokes and references, their constant use of "sucks," and other verbal and visual behavior ("Hey Beavis, pull my finger!").

10 For an introduction and overview of the Buffy phenomenon see the book edited by David Lavery and Rhonda Wilcox, *Fighting the Forces: What's at Stake in Buffy the Vampire Slayer* (2002); the website www.slayage.tv; *Bite Me* by Sue Turnball and Vyvyan Stranieri (2003); and the study by Carolyn Cocca in *Superwomen* (2016), pp. 157–182.

11 My study of *The X-Files* can be seen in Kellner 2012.

12 Parenthetically, I'd argue, although this would require a separate discussion, Joss Whedon and his gang have produced on the one hand a modernist text with a very specific vision and systemic structure while on the other hand engaging in postmodern pastiche, irony, metacommentary and hipness. On different notions of modern and postmodern culture, see Kellner 1991; 1997, 2001.

13 On the *Bildungsroman*, see Herbert Marcuse's study of the German artist novel (1978 [1922]) and the commentary in Kellner 1984.

14 At a 1998 seminar at the Museum of Broadcasting in Los Angeles, Whedon and other cast members and producers stressed the importance of working with the then new WB Network in terms of producing for a younger and hungrier network that needed to take chances to gain hits and was prepared to work more closely in largely supportive and unoppressive ways in comparison to traditional networks who are often heavy-handed in their treatment of programs and do not allow more experimental and offbeat material. The marriage with the WB did not last, however, as the network refused in 2001 to meet Mutant Enemy's financial demands and so the series went over to the rival UPN network with Joss Whedon commenting: "I've been dumped by my fat old ex and Prince Charming has come and swept me off my feet. I'm mostly very excited because I now have a network that cares about my show as opposed to one that insults it." In "'Buffy' picks up stakes, leaves WB for UPN," *CNN.Com*, April 23, 2001 at http://edition.cnn.com/2001/SHOWBIZ/TV/04/23/buffy/ (accessed September 19, 2019).

15 Whedon is a third-generation TV creator. As David Lavery points out (2002: 47ff): "[After working in radio,] Whedon's grandfather went on to contribute to *Donna Reed, Mayberry RFD, Dick Van Dyke Show, Room 222*. His father wrote for *Captain Kangaroo, The Dick Cavett Show, The Electric Company, Alice, Benson, Golden Girls*, and *It's a Living*."

16 The series is available on DVD with extras and commentary, making *Buffy* accessible for in-depth study. In referring to specific episodes, following recent *BtVS* scholarship, I will cite season and episode number with the year and episode as, for instance, 1007, for season one, episode seven. I might also signal the growing connection between critical television research and DVDs and the Internet. When I began doing television research in the 1970s, you had to go to archives to find much classical TV material. But with, first, video-recorders and VHS tapes of popular series, and DVDs, and now the Internet and streaming video, it is possible to do serious in-depth research on television programming. There are also incredibly rich resources on-line:

in addition to the www.slayage.tv and a profusion of Buffyverse websites, there are many other articles and resources online, including archives of scripts, laboriously typed out by fans. Kaaza has archives of *BtVS* episodes, there are chatrooms, media commentary, and much material on the series production and reception of a degree not available earlier.

17 On the war against youth in contemporary U.S. culture, see Giroux 2009; Males 1996; Best and Kellner, 2001.

18 In presenting interpretation of Buffy as allegory at a couple of *Buffy* conferences, I received skepticism from some prominent *Buffy* scholars who seemed to equate allegory as a theological type of Christian structure, or rigid type of literary structure. While it is true that allegory developed in biblical traditions and had a full-blown development with *The Pilgrim's Progress*, Dante and Milton's poetic epics, and other Christian allegorical texts, as Walter Benjamin already in the early modern period noted (1977), another, more secular allegorical tradition emerged and it is on this model that I read *Buffy* as an allegory about contemporary teenage and college student life.

19 For a discussion of how various Christian groups perceived *BtVS* see Todd Hertz, "Don't Let Your Kids Watch *Buffy the Vampire Slayer*," at www.christianitytoday. com/ct/2002/136/31.0.html (accessed July 17, 2004). The article is generally positive toward the series, although it has links to evangelical Christian groups who demonized *BtVS*. Series creator Joss Whedon consistently insisted that he is an atheist and not privileging any religious tradition, although he admits that Christianity and Judaism are the ones he is most familiar with; see the interview with Laura Miller, "The man behind the Slayer," Salon (May 20, 2003) at www.salon.com/2003/05/20/whedon/ (accessed August 22, 2019).

20 The ideal type constructing a distinction between traditional and modern societies is in some ways an over-simplification, but I am using the distinction to attempt to highlight key features linking fashion, image, and identity in modern societies. For more on the discourses of modernity, their contributions and limitations, see Antonio and Kellner 1992; 1994.

21 As I am editing this chapter for the second edition, a *Los Angeles Times* columnist writes that middle school should receive more attention from media culture and the society at large as increasingly youth identities are being formed in middle school grades as well as high school; see Mary McNamara, "Taking Tweens More Serious. Middle School Should be a Place for Pop Culture," *Los Angeles Times*, August 22, 2019: E1.

22 In the first edition of *Media Culture* I go into detail describing the stages of Madonna's work into the mid-1990s, but since then her development has continued to be complex and many sided and I do not have space to engage it here as I want to discuss female music icons who followed Madonna in this edition.

23 Laura Newberry. "Rich, Productive, but not Fully in Control of her Life. #FreeBritney Calls Abound after Decade-plus Conservatorship," *Los Angeles Times*, September 18, 2019: A1, A8.

24 Cos Staff, "Intimate, in-depth look" of Beyoncé's concert, revealing "the emotional road from creative concept to a cultural movement". April 17, 2019 at https://consequenceof sound.net/2019/04/beyonce-homecoming-netflix/ (accessed November 27, 2019).

25 "Homecoming," Wikipedia at https://en.wikipedia.org/wiki/Homecoming (accessed November 7, 2019).

26 Ibid.

27 Hilary Hughes, "They're Really Conjuring that wWorld." *MTV News*, September 26, 2017) at www.mtv.com/news/3037852/gaga-five-foot-two-american-horror-story/ (accessed November 27, 2019).

7

NEWS, ENTERTAINMENT, AND DOCUMENTARY AS POLITICAL SPECTACLE

This chapter focuses on the role of media culture in U.S. politics and society over the past decades. I first examine the politics and ideology of presidential politics in media culture from the Reagan to Bush II administrations, and demonstrate how the media culture of the era produces narratives concerning successful and failed presidencies and argue that presidential reputations depend importantly on representations in media culture that are always subject to contestation and revision. This analysis of "Presidential politics: the movie" discusses the often contested narratives of competing political regimes of the past decades using as examples the presidencies of Reagan, Bush I, Clinton, and Bush II.

Next, I engage the shift from Obama's liberal presidency to Trump's rightwing "shitstorm in a dumpster fire" – to cite the colorful phrase of George Conway, the husband of Trump advisor Kelly Anne Conway who popularized the equally revealing term "alternative facts."[1] I show how laudatory and derogatory documentaries preceded Barack Obama's election and then examine how his presidency was presented in documentary and fictional films. In a separate section on Trump, I take on his emergence as a national figure of media culture celebrity in his hit TV series *The Apprentice* and his initial role as a political commentator on *Fox and Friends* to his 2016 election campaign and his reality TV show media presidency, focusing on Trump and his exploitation of media culture.

Throughout the chapter, I focus on news and infotainment as a contested terrain in which political and cultural battles are waged in media culture from TV news and entertainment to films and newspapers and digital media. Finally, I engage the documentaries of Michael Moore who has critically dissected major events in contemporary U.S. society for decades, and will discuss some of his recent films taking on corporate America and capitalism, the conservative political establishment, and the presidency of Donald Trump.

Presidential politics: the movie

In an age of spectacle politics, presidencies are staged and presented to the public in cinematic terms, using media spectacle to sell the policies, person, and image of the president to vast and diverse publics. The media are complicit in the generation of spectacle politics, reducing politics to image, display, and story in the forms of entertainment and drama. Daily news is increasingly structured by the forms of entertainment and sound-bite, as are documentaries and TV magazine-style features on politics, while fictional films or TV mini-series narrativize especially dramatic events or entire presidential dynasties. Consequently, publics come to see presidencies and politics of the day as narrative and spectacle in an era when entertainment and information inexorably merge. In the media entertainment society, politics and everyday life are modeled on media forms, with entertainment becoming a dominant mode of media culture and a potent and seductive factor in shaping politics and everyday life.

Consequently, one can depict the relationship between media and politics from the Reagan administration to the Trump debacle in terms of the narrative and cinematic spectacle that framed the respective presidency. From this perspective, successful presidencies presented good movies that succeeded in being effective and entertaining in selling a presidency to the public. Failed presidencies, by contrast, can be characterized as bad movies that fashioned a negative public image that bombed with the public and left behind disparaging or indifferent images and reviews of the presidency in question. And, of course, there can be contradictory and conflicted narratives of more ambiguous and contested presidencies.

In the contemporary era, politics is thus becoming a mode of spectacle where the codes of media culture determine the form, style, and look of presidential politics, and thus party politics in turn becomes more cinematic and spectacular, in the sense of Guy Debord's concept of spectacle. Consequently, American presidential politics of the past several decades can be perceived as media spectacles, in which media politics becomes a major constituent of presidential elections, governance, and political success or failure.

Hence, I will examine how presidential politics, the movie, produced a set of the collective images, spectacles, and narratives of the Reagan through the Trump administrations. These presidencies in turn generated series of presidential narratives, some good, some bad, and some conflicted. Certain presidencies themselves engendered epic Hollywood political films, which help construct public images of the presidency and of recent history. The ongoing circulation and revision of representations and narratives of media-focused presidents and their specific histories help continue to nurture cinematic politics and media spectacle as a basic component of political strategy and governance.

Ronald Reagan, the acting president

With the election in 1980 of Ronald Reagan, the U.S. had its first acting president and professional actor qua president. The election of former movie star and

California governor Ronald Reagan represents the first time that a Hollywood actor and TV personality ascended to the presidency and the Reagan presidency was scripted as if it were a movie (Cannon 1992). Not surprisingly, in an era of media saturation, Reagan was a popular and effective president, despite lacking in political experience. Reflection on the Reagan presidency suggests that Hollywood is the New Aristocracy, both in terms of cash and life-style, but also a network of connections and glamorous public image, so it is not accidental that Hollywood would produce a president. The Reagan presidency also combined the aura of celebrity and political leader, making the attainment of celebrity status part of future successful presidencies.

The Reagan administration (1980–1988) was one of the most successful media presidencies and set of political spectacles in recent U.S. political history. Michael Rogin has written a book *Ronald Reagan the Movie* (1982) that documents the intersection of Reagan's film and political career. Reagan, contrary to some popular misrepresentations, was a top-line A and not B movie actor. His presidency was scripted to act out and play his presidential role. Reagan rehearsed his lines every day and generally gave a good performance. Every move was scripted and his media handlers had camera on hand to provide the image, photo opportunity, and political line of the day that they wanted to convey to the media.

Reagan was also a celebrity, a superstar of media culture, an American icon and perhaps the first intersection of celebrity and politics in an era in which celebrities were increasingly not just role models but political forces who ran for office, or were active politically. Like Reagan, entertainers George Murphy, Sonny Bono, Shirley Temple, Jesse Ventura, and other celebrities attained political office during the Reagan–Bush era. A wide array of media celebrities campaigned for causes and candidates on both sides, including Jane Fonda, Robert Redford, Warren Beatty, Barbra Streisand, Rob Reiner and others on the left, contrasted to Bruce Willis, Arnold Schwarzenegger, and a few B or C-list Republicans celebrities on the right.

For two administrations, the Reagan team carried out a politics of media spectacle with coordinated daily political events and extravagant media spectaculars: rallies, special events, and speeches with flags, crowds, and a photogenic background. After a slow start, the new Reagan administration was given a big boost by the spectacle of the attempted assassination of Ronald Reagan in 1981 by a disturbed young man who was trying dementedly to win the affections of actress Jodie Foster who attracted his attention as a teen prostitute in Martin Scorsese's *Taxi Driver* (1976).[2] The event created intense drama, but also sympathy for a man who reacted to his tragedy with humor and fortitude, and Reagan was on a positive media roll that would continue for years.

The Reagan administration also had a good plot line and narrative for his presidency: deregulation and the triumph of market capitalism and defeat of communism in the Cold War. Ultimately, the Reaganites claimed victory on both of these themes, and Reagan continues to this day to score high in presidential ratings and to get positive media coverage. Of course, there were significant and sometimes unperceived costs to his presidency: in his two terms, Reagan doubled the national debt, and redistributed wealth upward from poor to rich, greatly increasingly the divide between haves and have not. His military build-up was costly and wasteful, his deregulation politics created the Savings and Loan scandal, that cost taxpayers over a trillion dollars to cover bad loans, and, in retrospect, the Clinton years were far more prosperous than the Reagan years, which, in fact, were an economic disaster for many.[3]

The Reagan presidency was partly done in by the consequences of the October Surprise, the Iran-Contra Affair, and his overly aggressive foreign policy and military policy, which are narratively linked. Iran-Contra was itself a great political spectacle, which could have made great movies, but was perhaps too complex and has never been presented in blockbuster popular narrative form. Yet some films have dealt with the scandal including the documentary *Coverup: Behind the Iran Contra Affair* (1989), and fictionalized films *Kill the Messenger* (2014) and *American Made* (2017), both of which dealt with the Contra-connected CIA drug ring.[4]

One of Reagan's failed policies involved a "Star Wars" missile defense program that would send nuclear weapons to outer space to be launched by satellite in the event of a nuclear war with Russia. The Star Wars program was broadly ridiculed, denounced by scientists and eventually scrapped by the Clinton administration, although it was resurrected in part by Bush II and especially Donald Rumsfeld, the U.S. Secretary of Defense, a retread of the failed Ford administration. Rumsfeld was popularly referred to as "Dr. Strangelove" before September 11 because of his strange faith in a missile defense shield and unconventional ideas on the military, although he became a respected media star in the Terror War of 2001–2002.[5]

Finally, the Reagan image has benefited in retrospect from sympathy from his suffering Alzheimer's disease. While images of Reagan falling asleep when visiting the Pope, nodding off at a major arms negotiations meeting, or failing to distinguish between reality and some of his movie roles, created a culture of Reagan ridicule and accusations of senility, the tragedy of his disease rendered it mean and unsympathetic to attack his mental failings when it was revealed that he was suffering from Alzheimer's.[6]

Hence, although one could indeed argue that the Reagan administration was in many ways a failure, it was not presented in this way by the media or any films or television programs and was thus not perceived negatively on the whole by broad sectors of the public, either then or now. In fact, generally speaking, certain political or economic scandals and failures do not make for good movies or coherent narratives, as these events, like the S&L scandal, Iran-Contra, or election theft of 2000, are too complex to capture in an easily consumable film. There are, arguably, great films to be made of Reagan era scandals. Yet since Reagan has been deified by the Republican establishment and never really investigated or scandalized by the mainstream media (see Hertsgaard 1988), it is highly unlikely that there will be a cultural and political reconstruction and rethinking of the Reagan era in the near future. Thus Reagan's acting presidency emerges as one of the most successful presidential narratives of recent history.

Bush I, mixed spectacle, problematic presidency

In 1988, George H.W. Bush ran one of the great media campaigns of all time, as I described in my 1990 book *Television and the Crisis of Democracy*. Trailing Democratic Party candidate Michael Dukakis by 10–15 points after the late summer Democratic convention in 1988, Bush ended up handily winning, after an excellent TV campaign. The Bush I team presented positive images of the candidate in their daily photo ops and pictures, that showed Bush surrounded by flags, on stage with the police or military, and in scenes of presidential power, as he drew on his vice president image, and projected the spectacle of an experienced, energetic, and hard-working public servant. In his TV ads, there were copious pictures of his family, with Bush ladling out soup in one ad, a giving father ready to serve and provide.

Of course, Bush I also ran a highly effective negative campaign and his Willie Horton TV ads are now icons of dubious negative advertising.[7] The Horton ads, which portrayed images of prisoners of color revolving out of open prison doors, evoked the story of a Black convict Willie Horton whom Bush's Democratic Party contender Michael Dukakis had released in a prison furlough program when Governor of Massachusetts, and who then had brutally beaten a Maryland couple and raped the woman. The ad insinuated that Dukakis was a liberal, soft on crime, and it played on racial fears, as Trump would later do. The ad was totally unfair as many states, such as Texas, had similar furlough programs, and Dukakis's Republican predecessor in Massachusetts had initiated the program. Another completely mendacious Bush team negative ad portrayed a polluted Boston Harbor, as if Governor Dukakis was weak on the environment. In fact, it was the failure of the Reagan–Bush administration to release mandated funds to clean up Boston Harbor and other environmental sites that was responsible for the continued pollution in the harbor.

Bush's campaign was run by Lee Atwater and George W. Bush, both fierce attack dogs running a down and dirty campaign that was one of the most negative in recent history. Roger Ailes was another top campaign official, who became president of *Fox TV* news, where he continued his ideological service for the right-wing of the Republican Party until accused of multiple sexual harassment in May 2018, after which he resigned and then died.

Bush's 1988 opponent, Massachusetts governor Michael Dukakis, was highly qualified, but just could not produce strong enough positive images and sell his candidacy to the public. At times, Dukakis appeared as a doofus, as when he was photographed driving a tank, an image that Republicans used in attack ads.

Using a McCarthyite tactic, Bush 1 denounced Dukakis as a "card-carrying lib-eral in the ACLU," but Dukakis himself wouldn't admit he was a liberal until the end of the campaign. He also seemed too cold and detached in debates when he was bushwhacked with a question concerning how he'd respond to his wife's rape, an incredible question that showed the tabloid nature of the media Mafia who performed in presidential debates.

And, crucially, although Bush played hardball politics against Dukakis, the Democratic Party candidate just didn't go after Bush. Dukakis had any number of great scandals he could play against Bush, but the Democrats wimped out, refusing to go after Bush and the October Surprise, or his roles in the Iran-Contra affair, the S&L crisis, or other scandals of the Reagan era.[8] The Demo-crats played softball in a hardball era, engaging in an earlier form of civil and gentlemanly politics in a smashmouth era when Republicans excelled in dirty tracks, slime and slander, and doing everything possible to present their oppon-ents in a negative light.

And so Dukakis lost and George H.W. Bush won after a highly effective media campaign. Moreover, Bush got off to a strong start as president with a great dramatic TV movie opener, the Panama Invasion and arrest of Panama dictator Manuel Noriega that created a wave of patriotism, macho assertiveness, and high ratings for the CIA-president.[9] But by 1990, the economy was tanking, taxes were going up, and Bush's popularity was heading south. Bush had pledged "Read my lips, no new taxes" and had then raised taxes, so he was losing his conservative base and looking bad in the media. Footage of his pledge not to raise taxes was repeated over and over in the media, while economic bad news was relentless, creating an image of Bush as failed economic manager and hypocritical politician (both true).

Consequently, another great movie was needed to boost Bush I's popularity and save his presidency: the Persian Gulf TV war, a cinematic spectacle of the highest order. I am not suggesting that Bush's war movie of 1991 was merely an effort to sell the Bush presidency, as there were also geopolitical interests involved, oil interests that have defined Bush family politics for decades, and a desire of the military to fight and win a war to redeem their defeat in Vietnam and to increase their military budget. Major political events are always overde-termined and require multicausal analysis. Yet, as I recount in my 1992 book *The Persian Gulf TV War*, Bush I's Iraq adventure was one of the great media spectacles and propaganda events in recent U.S. history. By the return of U.S. troops from the Gulf after kicking Saddam Hussein out of Kuwait, Bush's popularity was soaring at 90% and it looked like he'd be a shoo-in for a second term.

Bush failed to follow-up on the defeat of Iraq's military and overthrow Saddam Hussein, established by Bush's propagandists as another Hitler, thus he could not claim complete triumph in the Gulf war. Moreover, images of sup-pressed uprisings in southern and northern Iraq, with heartbreaking images of Kurdish refugees, contrasted with Bush playing golf on vacation, made Bush look disengaged and heartless. These scenes, and the survival of Saddam Hussein, created a bad aftermath regarding the Gulf war, and with the economy faltering again during the latter part of Bush's presidency, he was vulnerable to a challenge.[10]

Bush's opponent in 1992 was a brash young Arkansas Governor named Bill Clinton who was relatively unknown on the national scene. Yet Clinton ran an excellent media campaign, like Bush's 1988 effort, and is considered one of the best politicians in modern U.S. political history, celebrated in the documentary *The War Room* on Clinton's 1992 campaign, a biopic *Primary Colors* (1992) with John Travolta as a good-old-boy Bill Clinton overcoming obstacles to win the 1992 election, and countless fawning books by Clintonistas and savage attacks by the Clinton haters that continue to the present.

Clinton was self-consciously a John F. Kennedy-type figure, a younger generation politico, who cultivated the JFK look, called attention to the lineage endlessly, playing repeatedly the campaign video of a young Bill Clinton shaking hands with Jack Kennedy in the White House. Clinton was also entertaining as a campaigner, using every major TV genre to cultivate votes, many for the first time. Clinton played his sax on the late night Arsenio Hall show; did teary and soulful melodrama and soap opera with Hillary on *60 Minutes*, as he admitted he'd had affairs, that their marriage had suffered problems, but that they'd worked hard to solve the problems and strengthen the marriage, a narrative-line many in the audience could buy and identify with. Clinton bantered about underpants and boxers on MTV; he had a serious conversation about marriage with talk show superstar Phil Donahue, and was the first presidential candidate to appear on these popular talk show venues – now a campaign necessity after Clinton's successful manipulation of popular TV genres.

Clinton also did well in debates, and had a good spectacle moment in one of his debates with George H.W. Bush when an African American woman in the audience asked if any of the well-off candidates understood the distress of those in the underclasses. Bush was clichéd and perfunctory in his answer, but Clinton strode down the stage to eyeball the woman (and the TV audience) saying that he felt their pain, he cared, and he'd work hard to improve the economy for everyone. During the same debate Bush looked bored and detached, glancing at his watch at several points, as if he just couldn't wait until this ordeal was over.

On the whole, Bush I ran a surprisingly bad campaign in 1992. He appeared detached from everyday reality when he went into a supermarket and looked amazed at a scanner in the checkout area, obviously a chore that Bush had never performed. He seemed unhappy with having to sell himself to a fickle public, and his campaign never caught fire. His political manager, Lee Atwater, had died of cancer, his son George W. was preoccupied with personal affairs and not yet ready for prime-time, there was friction between the Bushes and long-time friend James Baker who was running the campaign, and Bush never really connected with the public.

Of course, Clinton also had political issues on his side, with his team endlessly telling the public, "It's the economy stupid!," and indeed the economy was in a slump during the latter part of Bush's one-term reign. Bush doubled the national deficit while raising taxes, seemed to have no economic plan or policy other than giving big corporations whatever favors they wanted, and lost favor with the public. There was also the irritant of Third Party candidate Ross Perot, with his nerdy charts demonstrating the economic woes under Bush and stealing votes from the center and right alike from Bush with his twangy-Texas pseudo populism.[11]

However, in a media-saturated era, it was also clear that Bush just didn't have the image or political skills to work the media, was a poor president, and ran a losing campaign. While U.S. politics are not all spectacle and image, it certainly helps and Bill and Hillary Clinton projected more youthful, attractive, and energetic images than the Bushes. *Saturday Night Live!* made jokes about Barbara Bush as George's grandmother, and the Bushes had poor body language, always looking awkward with each other and disconnected. The more youthful and attractive Clintons made a far more appealing couple, and then provided the thrills of weekly tabloid soap opera entertainment and family melodrama, continuing to the present.

The Clinton spectacle

The two Clinton terms (1992–2000) were probably the most contested and melodramatic spectacle of any presidency in modern U.S. history, with endless conflict, scandal, crisis, and their miraculous overcoming by the "comeback kid" Bill Clinton. It's almost as if Clinton needed scandal and crisis to function, requiring challenges to perform and connect with a public that ignored everyday politics but loved political battles, scandal, and spectacle. Consequently, as president, like Reagan, and unlike Bush I, Clinton gave good spectacle: sex scandals, soap opera, melodrama, impeachment, cultural war with the right, and ultimately the spectacle of survival under constant adversity.

The Clinton years were highly entertaining and unfolded during a period of unparalleled expansion of media culture and a high-tech revolution that produced the Internet, cyberculture, and a new culture of celebrity. In this situation, the president had the potential to become First Celebrity, top dog in the Instant Recognition hall of fame sweepstakes. John F. Kennedy had achieved positive celebrity status, as had Reagan, whereas more mundane politicians like Johnson, Ford, Carter, and Bush I ultimately failed in the celebrity popularity race and were not able to get re-elected.

There was, however, a price to be paid for attaining a celebrity presidency in an Age of Spectacle Politics. Never before had the media delved into the personal lives of a presidential couple to the extent of the media trials and tribulations of Bill and Hillary Clinton – which continue to this day. The Whitewater scandal unfolded during the first year of the Clinton presidency and there was unending media focus on every detail of the Clinton's economic, political, and ultimately sex and family life. No longer was the president free from the taint of scandal and tabloid journalism. The blending of information and entertainment in media culture during the Clinton years, the fierce competition for audiences, the rise of the Internet and cyberculture, and perhaps especially the rise of three competing U.S. cable news channels all made for a volatile media mix and feeding-frenzy that exploited the topic or scandal of the day for maximizing audiences and profits.

Indeed, Fox News, owned by conservative media baron Rupert Murdoch and run by former right-wing Republican operative Roger Ailes, vilified the Clintons from the beginning, as did certain Talk Radio hosts like Rush Limbaugh, and right-wing Internet sites like *The Drudge Report*. Never before in the modern era, had a president been so viciously and continuously attacked by different forms of media, and henceforth the media spectrum would become more and more differentiated between hardright, conservative, liberal, and left-progressive television, radio, newspapers, Internet and new media sites, including the TV networks that had previously been centrist and attempted to be non-ideological. Since the Clinton years television news and documentary has been highly ideological and partisan with, currently in the 2020s, Fox News on the hardright, MSNBC on the liberal left, and CNN and the major TV networks ABC, CBS, and NBC shooting for the mainstream but frequently taking partisan stances.

In the 1996 election, Bill Clinton faced off against aging Republican Bob Dole. The election itself was purely contrived with staged town hall meetings, scripted and managed conventions, sound-bite "messages" tested by polling and focus groups, and constant attempts to sell the candidates as if they were commodities. Clinton won easily, in part because the economy was relatively strong, partly because Dole was a poor candidate, and to a degree because Clinton was a good politician, in tune with many sectors of the electorate.

Clinton was seemingly able to empathize with audiences. He had highly developed social and political skills, and was, more than the longtime actor Reagan, a great person-to-person communicator – at least to those who were open to his communication. Precisely because of Clinton's easy-going personality, morality, and pragmatic politics, conservatives deeply loathed him, and were furious when he won two presidencies and overcame scandal after scandal. The Internet burned with anti-Clinton screeds and there was a cottage industry of books that demonized the Clintons and cumulatively sold millions.

Indeed, the Monica Lewinsky sex scandal was broken on the Internet when Matt Drudge published an outline of a story that the *Washington Post* and *Newsweek* seemed reluctant to push, concerning rumors of a sexual relationship between Clinton and a young White House intern (Toobin 2000). Eventually, the story broke and Bill and Monica were the hot item of the season. There were endless replays of the footage of the perky intern with a beret hugging Clinton at a White House reception, or greeting him at another event in revealing cleavage. When Clinton insisted that he "never had sex with that woman," this image came back to haunt him and encouraged conservatives that they could destroy Clinton. His opponents attempted to use a videotape in which Clinton denied the sexual relation to charge him with lying under oath and then undertook impeachment proceedings that came close to succeeding.

Conservatives were outraged, however, that every time a new scandal broke in the Lewinsky affair, Clinton's popularity went up. When Clinton's prosecutors, led by the puritanical and ultraconservative Ken Starr, released the video of Clinton lying under oath, they figured his popularity would collapse, but, no, it went up. Likewise, when Clinton's prosecutors released the Starr report that detailed his sexual adventures with Lewinsky and others, once again Clinton's approval rating climbed in public polls. In the Congressional impeachment proceedings and Senate trial, yet again Clinton's ratings improved as his conservative attackers attempted to discredit and destroy him.

Clinton was fortunate that he had such unpleasant and hypocritical right-wing foes and benefited from political sympathy from liberals and Democrats that did not want to see an election victory overturned and to allow the Republicans to get their way. Moreover, broad sectors of the centrist and apolitical public sympathized with Clinton, to some extent because of the obnoxiousness of his prosecutors, and in part because of empathy and identification with the spectacle of the president under attack. It seems that many in the audience had experienced similar predicaments and could empathize with Clinton and his pain.

Despite the scandals, Clinton became a celebrity and cultural icon, however tarnished, and his popularity soared in part because his years were an entertaining spectacle and in part because of the unprecedented growth of the U.S. and global economy. It appeared by the end of the Clinton years that in an age of media spectacle possessing good looks and a pleasing personality had become important markers of a successful presidency, especially plentiful hair, a nice smile, and a good body image. The most popular presidents of the post-JFK years had abundant hair and a pleasing smile and engaging personality (i.e. JFK, Reagan, and Clinton). LBJ and Ladybird Johnson came off as Texan Gothic types; Richard Nixon seemed untrustworthy and shifty, someone you'd hesitate to buy a used car from; Gerald Ford looked to be bumbling, unappealing, and incompetent; Jimmy Carter was presented by the media as too moralistic and ineffective, as he tried to micromanage every issue and situation; Robert Dole was perceived as unpleasant and mean; and George H.W. Bush came across as too patrician and disengaged, not really caring about ordinary people.

The presidential culture of personality and swing toward media politics reflects in some ways shifts in the economy and culture from the post-World War II to the contemporary era, sometimes theorized as a shift to postmodern culture and society (see Kellner 1991, 1997; Best and Kellner 2001). Sociologists have argued that U.S. culture in the twentieth century moved from a culture of individualism with inner-directed people searching for authentic meaning and shaping their own life, to an other-directed culture of conformity in which people are guided by the media and external social authorities and influencers. Further, as the economy and society moves from emphasis on production to consumption, media culture is defined by image, look, and spectacle, requiring presidents to have a pleasing personality and to sell themselves to voters. Hence, the importance of public relations, media handlers, polls, focus groups, and media spectacle to promote candidates and policies.

To connect with audiences, politicians also have to look like just plain folks, one of the people, as well as to appear nice and attractive. Note also how some recent politicians have been committed to working out and gym culture (i.e. Clinton, Gore, Bush II, and Obama), while earlier golfing was (and still is) de rigeur for presidents, a role happily assumed by Trump who has already spent more time on the golf course than any president in history. All of these trends typify a media president who strives to make a good impression and manage his image to promote his presidency and his policies, and this syndrome of media politics is evident in the ascension to power of George W. Bush – and later Barack Obama and Donald Trump.

Bush II, *Grand Theft 2000,* and Terror War

During Campaign 2000, the Republicans had a mediocre presidential candidate, the least qualified of my lifetime until Donald Trump appeared on the scene. Yet the Bushies constructed a first-rate script: Bush II was a different kind of Republican, a compassionate conservative, a uniter, not a divider, who could get Democrats and Republicans together to "get things done." Arguably, none of these claims were true (see Kellner 2001), but they created a positive image and the media generally went along with them. The mainstream media for the most part overlooked that Bush's Texas record as governor was not compassionate conservatism, but hardright pandering to corporate interests who funded his campaign, and tax breaks for the wealthy that bankrupted the state of Texas, which had enjoyed a surplus under Democratic governors. Bush had bullied or cajoled select Democrats in Texas to go along with his right-wing corporate agenda, and was not really a consensus-builder or bipartisan.

Moreover, by and large, the mainstream media neglected a lifetime of scandal, which marked George W. Bush's life and was well documented in the Internet and a series of books, but largely stayed off the mainstream media radar during Election 2000. It was, in fact, astonishing that after eight years of scandal-mongering and mudslinging during the Clinton years, none of the rich history of Bush family scandal or George W. Bush's personal failings were focused on. Nor did the softball Democrats under Al Gore go after Bush's record, or personal and family history, a courtesy for which they were repaid with hardball "smashmouth" politics during the Battle for the White House after the dead-locked 2000 election.[12]

The war for the White House was indeed one of the greatest political dramas and media spectacles in U.S. history, as I recount in my book *Grand Theft 2000* (Kellner 2001). While the purloining of the presidency is arguably one of the major scandals of U.S. political history, the story has rarely been told by the mainstream media, although you can find big chunks of the story on the Internet and in a series of books, including my own.

Bush's first months in office were marked by hardright conservatism with bold payoffs to the key corporations who had supported his campaign in the form of deregulation, changing governmental rules, and tax giveaways. After the Democrats seized control of the domestic agenda in late May 2001, with the defection of Republican Senator Jim Jeffords, Bush's hard-right and corporate agenda seemed sidetracked. But the September 11 terrorist attacks strengthened his hand and enabled his cronies to carry through even more radical hardright assaults on civil liberties and the free and open society, as well as to attempt more federal theft through the mechanism of an economic "stimulus" package. Such stimulus, as proposed by the Bush administration, would constitute even greater corporate giveaways and tax breaks to the rich and his biggest contributors.[13]

The September 11 terror attacks, succeeding anthrax hysteria, and war fever following the Bush administration military intervention in Afghanistan created a situation of unparalleled media and popular support for the Bush presidency and elevated Bush into a top-tier celebrity, almost immune from criticism. In early 2002, a *USA Today* poll rated Bush as the most admired person in the United States and he enjoyed the highest approval ratings in modern times during the post-9/11 period, although his rating would later collapse.[14]

On the whole, the media have been kind to the Bush family who are elite establishment to the core, a fact evident in the elaborate celebrations of George H.W. Bush's life during the week of December 3, 2018 following his death at 94. Yet the media can destroy what they build up, and future historians could reverse the symbolic fortunes of the Bush dynasty with a series of crime dramas, political corruption and conspiracy narratives, and family melodramas that would rival any comparative saga in American literature or history. I would indeed recommend to a future Theodore Dreiser or Oliver Stone a trilogy of books or films starting with *Prescott*, that detail the stunning story of Bush family patriarch Prescott Bush who was, in effect, Adolph Hitler's financial agent. Prescott helped manage through the Union National Bank several key Nazi businesses that ran in the U.S. and globally, including Hapag-Lloyd Shipping Lines and Thyssen United Steel Works. The Union Banking Corporation was seized by the U.S. government in 1942 under the Trading with the Enemy Act, and Prescott Bush was listed as a top board of director. The Bushs held onto the bank through the war and sold out in the 1950s, attaining their family fortune through an institution that had help finance National Socialism. But somehow the scandal never came out during Prescott's senate campaigns and he died a respected family patriarch.[15]

This epic history of ruling class scoundrels would also present the story of *George Herbert Walker*, Prescott Bush's close business associate and father of his wife, Dorothy Walker. George H.W. Bush aka 41 and George W. Bush aka 43 were named after George Herbert Walker, the man who helped run businesses for Stalin's Russia, Mussolini's Italy, and Hitler's Germany. The secretive wheeler dealer is perhaps best known for his golf spectacle the Walker Cup and the construction of Madison Square Garden, while his son Herbert Walker junior ("Uncle Herbie") was one of the owners of the New York Mets, a sports spectacle that helped get George W. Bush interested in baseball. The Walker–Bush alliance is one of the shadiest and most scandalous in U.S. economic and political history and uncovering this story will be one of the great spectacles of the new millennium if it ever happens.[16]

The second part of the trilogy would tell the remarkable saga of *George* (Herbert Walker Bush), detailing an astonishing life of intrigue in economic and political scandals, including a stint as CIA director that involved interesting but largely unknown relations with scoundrels like Saddam Hussein and Manuel Noriega. *George* would also have engaging spy thrillers like the October Surprise, the Iran/contra scandal, and support of Islamic fundamentalist groups in Afghanistan era that later helped form the al Qaeda network and Taliban. This monumental epic would include Reagan-era scandals like the S&L crisis and the tremendous increase in the global drug business when George was given drug-czar responsibilities during the Reagan years. It would include some curious business relations with the bin Laden family and the Saudis (see Unger 2004), strange relations with Rev. Moon and some other sinister figures on the right, and could delve into the affairs of the Carlyle Fund. The latter constitutes one of the biggest holders of military stocks at a time when the bin Laden family and Bush–Baker cliques were chief investors and managers of the fund (Kellner 2003). At the same time, their sons George Junior and Osama bin Laden were protagonists in the Terror War (2001–present) that was one of the defining spectacle of the new millennium, and a source of great profit for the Bush–Baker and bin Laden cliques.

The Bush family saga could also present the remarkable business careers of George H. W. Bush's three sons, looking into the Silverado S&L scandal, and the involvement of Neil Bush; it could examine how Jeb Bush was involved in businesses with right-wing Cuban crooks who scammed HUD and Medicare for millions, and made a fortune for Jeb who became governor of Florida and one of the architects of theft of the White House in Election 2000. And it would require an entire separate study of how George W. Bush (a.k.a. W.) made his fortune and then succeeded in state and presidential politics. This story, found in a series of books and Internet sources, but generally left out of mainstream media, would tell the remarkable tale of how George W. Bush made his fortune, obtained the presidency through *Grand Theft 2000* (Kellner, 2001), and fronted the Terror War that saved his failing presidency and enriched his family, friends, and wealthiest supporters.

The *W.* story would recount how after years of frat boy ribaldry at Yale, Bush got his father to pull strings so he would not have to go to Vietnam and then got into the Texas National Guard Air Reserves. During his lost years in the 1970s, W. reportedly went AWOL for a year from military duty,[17] was a heavy alcohol and drug abuser, and a ne'er-do-well failure who finally decided to put together an oil company when he was already well into his 30s. Investors reportedly included the bin Laden family and other unsavory types. His initial company, went bust and was eventually taken over by Harken Energy Corporation, with family friends again jumping in to bail Junior out. Harken soon after received a lucrative Bahrain oil contract in part as a result of Bush family connections, and the Harken stock went up. But as a member of the Board of Directors, Junior knew that declining profits figures for the previous quarter, about to be released, would depress the value of the stock, so W. unloaded his stock, in what some see an in illegal insider trading dump. Moreover, young Bush failed to register his questionable sale with the SEC, although later a paper was produced indicating that he had eventually registered the sale, some eight months after he dumped his stock (it helped that his father was president when Junior should have been investigated for his questionable business dealings).[18]

With the money made from his Harken disinvesture, George Junior invested in the Texas Rangers baseball team and was made general manager when some other Texas good old boys put up the money. Using a public bond issue that he pushed upon voters to finance construction of a new Rangers stadium, the stock value of the baseball team went up. Once again, Bush Jr. sold out for a hefty profit and then ran as Governor of Texas, despite no political experience and a shaky business history. His two terms in office wrecked the state economy as it went from surplus to deficit thanks to a tax bill that gave favors to the wealthiest and sweetheart deals and deregulation bonanzas to his biggest campaign contributors. Governor Bush helped make Texas the site of the most toxic environmental pollution and outrageous corporate skullduggery in the country. Bush provided questionable favors to a nursing home corporation that faced state investigation and strong support for the wheelin' and dealin' Enron Company, one of the biggest financial contributors to Bush's campaigns and a corporation that underwent the biggest collapse of any U.S. company in history, under highly questionable circumstances.

To be sure, Oliver Stone made a film, *W* (2008), about George W. Bush, yet reviewers deemed it "surprisingly sympathetic" and it was not a critical or financial success.[19] Stone envisaged a behind the scenes approach that would focus on Bush as a rowdy and undisciplined young man who eventually overcame his alcoholism and went into politics, become governor and then president. The third act of the drama presents Bush's disastrous foray into the Iraq war (2003) and the sinister machinations of his vice president, Dick Cheney.

Cheney has been sharply criticized in many biographies and a film *Vice* (2018) presents an engaging docudrama about George W.'s villainous Vice President

Dick Cheney directed by Adam McKay. The film provides an entertaining and insightful portrait of Cheney's vices and misdeeds, and opens with Dick Cheney and other White House officials and staff responding to the September 11, 2001, terror attacks. McKay provides a fractured narrative flashing back to Wyoming in 1963, where Cheney finds work as a lineman after his alcoholism led him to drop out of Yale University, and showing how his longtime sweetheart and future wife, Lynne, forced him to stop his drinking and carousing, and to get his life together or she would not marry him.

Vice depicts Cheney's service as a White House intern during the Nixon administration, his lifelong alliance with Donald Rumsfeld, and his rise as a political insider and operative for the Republican Party. After Nixon is forced to resign the presidency and Gerald Ford loses his bid for election in 1976, *Vice* shows Cheney returning to Wyoming, overcoming a heart attack and with his wife Lynne's help winning a seat in Congress and returning to Washington to work for the Reagan administration in the 1980s. Here Cheney once again pushes a hardright agenda, pushing pro-business policies favoring the fossil fuel industries, and supporting the abolishment of the FCC fairness doctrine, which led to the rise of Fox News, Conservative talk radio, and the rising level of party polarization in the United States.

Climbing the ladder of Republican politics, Cheney becomes Secretary of Defense under President George H. W. Bush during the Gulf war and a media celebrity. Outside of politics, Cheney and Lynne come to terms with their younger daughter, Mary, coming out as a lesbian. Though Cheney develops ambitions to run for president, he decides to retire from public life to spare Mary from media scrutiny.

During the presidency of Bill Clinton, Cheney becomes the CEO of Halliburton while his wife raises golden retrievers and writes books. McKay fools the viewer with an epilogue in the middle of the film, claiming that Cheney lived the rest of his life healthy and happy as a successful business executive, and credits begin rolling, only for them to abruptly end as the film continues. *Vice* picks up showing how Cheney was named to help George W. Bush choose a running mate during the 2000 United States presidential election, and then chose himself as vice president, demanding that young Bush delegate "mundane" executive responsibilities, such as energy and foreign policy, to him.

Vice depicts Cheney working with Secretary of Defense Rumsfeld and a cabal of right-wing White House personnel to push through a hardright and pro-business agenda, highlighted by the U.S. invasions of Afghanistan and Iraq, resulting in the killing of hundreds of thousands of civilians and the torture of prisoners. While the film points to the disasters of the Iraq war, Cheney's endorsement of the unitary executive theory, which assigns to the president unchecked power, various other scandals of the Bush–Cheney years, and record-low approval ratings by the end of the administration, it does not arguably depict what I consider Cheney's major political scandal and crime.

In *Vice*'s version of the Cheney saga, Dick becomes CEO of Halliburton during his years in the private sector between his stints at public service, but the film does not depict the episode in which Cheney makes a deal with the Texas-based Brown and Root construction company. It turns out that Brown and Root, which among other scandals produced cages for U.S. "enemies" in the Vietnam war, was also subject to major lawsuits for using asbestos in its domestic construction projects. The lawsuits threatened to bankrupt Halliburton, which would cost Cheney millions in pension funds, and once he became Vice President Cheney desperately fought to get Halliburton government contracts to avoid bankruptcy. In particular, Cheney pushed hard, against other members of the Bush administration like Colin Powell, to get the U.S. to invade Iraq and overthrow Saddam Hussein.[20]

As is well-documented, Cheney got his war, gave Halliburton its contracts, and saved his pension, although most historians and political experts see the Iraq war as a major catastrophe in U.S. history that cost the U.S. about $1 trillion and destabilized the Middle East, leading to the rise of ISIS and other terrorist groups. Moreover, it turned out that Halliburton provided shoddy services in Iraq, and has been sued.[21]

The Bush family spectacle is therefore not yet over and it will be highly instructive to see how the family history continues to be constructed and perceived in the media and by the general public. It will also be interesting to see if the Internet spectacle replaces television and Hollywood spectacle as the foremost conveyer of news, information, entertainment, and politics as the millennium proceeds, providing multiple sources of information and entertainment that will be impossible for the Bush clique to control. Or will the travails and scandals of Donald J. Trump provide a spectacle that will enable the Bush administration to evade closer scrutiny (see below)?

The American presidency, from John F. Kennedy to Barack Obama,[22] has thus produced a series of political narratives, some of which were successful and other unsuccessful. In the Age of Media Spectacle, politics is mediated more and more by the forms of spectacle culture and in particular look, image, style, and presentation, but also narrative. What sort of stories a presidential administration generates determines success from failure, and a positive from an ambiguous or negative legacy. The centrality of media spectacle and political narrative to contemporary politics means that making sense of the current era requires the tools of a critical social theory and cultural studies in order to analyze the images, discourses, events, and narratives of presidential politics. Of course, politics is more than merely narrative, there are real events with material interests and consequences, and often behind the scenes maneuvering that are not part of the public record. Yet publics see presidencies and administrations in terms of narrative and spectacle, so that theorizing the cinematic and narrative nature of contemporary politics can help us understand, critique, and transform our political system, as well as to help understand the key role of media culture and spectacle in U.S. and global politics today.

News and infotainment as contested terrain

In an analysis of "Presidential politics: the movie," I have just presented how media culture constructed for each U.S. president from Reagan to the Bush presidencies narratives that capture their presidency in news reports, documentaries, and films, and thus demonstrate how media culture helps construct our understanding of recent history through media narratives. To be sure there are conflicting narratives of each presidency found in books, magazine stories, documentaries, and feature films, and so media culture is a contested terrain out of which each individual constructs their own culture, identity, and modes of thought and behavior.

Perhaps the contested terrain of media spectacle in presidential politics has some roots in Colorado Senator (Dem.) Gary Hart's run for presidency in the 1980s depicted in Ivan Reitman's 2018 film *The Front Runner*. The film opens in the turbulent 1984 Democratic Party primaries, as Hart loses the nomination to Vice President Walter Mondale. With a roving camera, multiple dialogues, and quick editing, Reitman throws the audience into the confusion and chaos of a political campaign, a technique he will use throughout the film in his depiction of the interactions between the press and the candidates. The film depicts insightfully the chaotic process through which elections are fought, and the media construct their daily stories and commentaries, which in turn become part of the election.

Reitman's ambition is to illuminate the moment in which the media become a form of infotainment and the line between tabloid and conventional political journalism blurs, beginning the media circus that has continued to the present. After losing in 1984, Hart decides to run again in 1988 for the presidency, and quickly becomes the "frontrunner" with highs polls and the most fervent following of any political candidate. The Democrats were desperate to win after eight years of the conservative rule of Ronald Reagan, and the film shows Hart assembling a strong campaign team of veterans and enthusiastic youth.

Throughout the film, Reitman shows show how the media were transforming politics into a form of media spectacle and that presidential politics, as Hart notes in the film, was becoming a "sport," a strenuous competition in which anything goes, thus planting the seeds of the terrain that Barack Obama and Donald Trump would harvest in very different ways in the 2000s. Likewise, the media were become more frenzied, competitive and prepared to transgress traditional boundaries as they hounded candidates, dug into their private lives, and even followed their every movement while hanging on their every word.

The Front Runner captures the frenzied state of both political campaigns in the 1980s and the media fighting to cover them and get scoops. Based on Matt Bai's book *All the Truth Is Out: The Week Politics Went Tabloid* (2014), the film depicts the shifting relationship between the media and politics by focusing on three weeks in the 1988 Democratic Party primaries in which Hart emerges as the "front runner" with "new ideas," good lucks, passion, charisma, an attractive family, a scrappy campaign team, and the momentum that could drive him to the presidency. Hugh Jackman convincingly depicts Hart's complex personality, from his eloquence as a speaker, to the introspective private person who sometimes appears off-putting and arrogant when the press tries to delve into his private life.

Throughout the film, the viewer is forced to question whether the press is doing its democratic function of probing the character and life of presidential candidates or wallowing in muck and sensationalism. Using overlapping conversations, multilayered sound effects and fast pacing to capture the frenzy of the campaign, Reitman takes the viewer from overheated campaign stops to backroom strategizing by the political operatives and the hustle to get a story by the media. Suddenly, there is a shift in the narrative when a couple of ambitious reporters from the *Miami Herald*, acting on an anonymous tip that Senator Hart was having an affair, decide to pursue the story, stalking Hart, parking in their car to surveil comings and goings in Hart's Washington townhouse, and even hiding in the bushes outside his house to photograph the lighted windows in his bedroom. The reporters then confront Hart in an alley behind his house asking about a young blonde woman who was seen going into his house, not coming out, and asking if Hart was having an affair with her.

The reporters publish the story alleging an affair, create a media spectacle, and generate a media frenzy the next weeks of the short-lived campaign. Hart reveals in a press briefing that the overzealous reporters missed that he had a back door in his townhouse and claimed that various people from his campaign would come in the front door and out the back, temporarily embarrassing the *Herald* reporters and creating the possibility that Hart would survive the scandal.

The scandal concerns Donna Rice, who Hart met on the campaign trail and who told him that she was "very interested in getting into fund raising," and wanted to join his campaign. The film makes Rice a somewhat shadowy figure who we see Hart talking to in a boat full of campaign donors and young women, calling her on the telephone, and meeting her at his apartment in Washington, although the film never shows us the details of the relation. Both Hart and Rice denied having an affair, yet the rumors threatened Hart's marriage, and the media frenzy forced Hart to abandon his campaign.

Yet there have been recurrent rumors that Donna Rice was a Republican operative set up to trap Gary Hart,[23] and on his deathbed Republican Party super operative and dirty trickster Lee Atwater confessed that he had a rented a boat the *Monkey Business* on which Hart went sailing with Rice and various donors and others, yielding a famous picture of Rice sitting smiling on Hart's lap.[24]

The Front Runner thus depicts a moment in which media spectacle becomes a major determinant in U.S. and global politics in which different politicians would use media spectacle to promote their candidacies and presidencies while also using media spectacle to destroy their opponents. In this context, media culture became a contested terrain over which political battles are fought, won, and lost. Gary Hart was an early victim of media spectacle producing a candidacy that was appearing to master the media and use it to promote his campaign, but he fell victim to a tabloidization of journalism in which previous boundaries were crossed and the media delved into his private life making him a sacrificial victim of the new turn toward media sensationalism.

Hart himself, of course, bears some responsibilities for the reckless actions that caused his downfall, and it is a primary virtue of *The Front Runner* that it centers on the issue of media, political, and personal responsibility and accountability. The film shows the horrific impact of the Hart scandal on his family, campaign, and followers, and the story of politicians rising and falling via media spectacle has become a major feature of the culture and politics of our time.

The intensity of media spectacle became even more feverish with the rise of 24-hour-a-day cable news channels, the Internet, and explosion of new media and social networking that is going on to this day. In the 1990s, the rise of cable news channels like *Fox News* on the right and *MSNBC*, which has veered to the left, has created a partisan situation in which audiences have segregated into tribes who religiously follow their newsfeeds of choice, a situation intensified by the exploding development of the internet, new media, and social networking.

To follow two more stages in this evolution, let us next engage "The Barack Obama media spectacle," in which a young African American rises from little-known novice senator to president of the United States, followed by analysis of "The Donald Trump reality show," in which a faux billionaire and TV celebrity becomes president in one of the most controversial elections in history in 2016.

The Barack Obama media spectacle

In the contemporary era of media politics, image and media spectacle has played an increasingly important role in presidential politics and other domains of society.[25] As corporate journalism became increasingly tabloidized, the line between news and information and entertainment blurred, while politics became a form of entertainment and spectacle. In this context, presidential candidates become celebrities and they are packaged and sold like the products of the culture industry. Candidates enlist celebrities in their election campaigns and are increasingly covered in the same way as celebrities, with tabloidized news media and social networking obsessing about their private lives.

Celebrities are mass idols, venerated and celebrated by the media. It is indeed the media that produce celebrities, and so naturally the most popular figures in media industries become celebrities. Entertainment industry figures and sports stars have been at the center of celebrity culture, employing public relations and image specialists to put out positive buzz and stories concerning their clients, but business tycoons and politicians have also become celebrities in recent years. Chris Rojek distinguishes between "ascribed celebrity," which concerns lineage, such as belonging to the Royal Family in the UK, or the Bush or Kennedy families in the U.S.; "achieved celebrity" is won by outstanding success in fields like entertainment, sports, or talent in a particular field; and "attributed celebrity" who achieve fame through media representations or spectacle, as in scandals or tabloid features (2004: 17ff), with Paris Hilton, the Kardashian family, and the latest YouTube or Instagram "influencers" as obvious examples of this category in U.S. culture.[26]

Celebrity is dependent on both constant media proliferation, and the implosion between entertainment, news, and information in which celebrity culture infuses every sphere of life. The proliferation of new media and social networking has created an ever more intense and diffuse celebrity culture with specialized publications, Internet sites, and social networking fanning the flames of celebrity culture, and with mainstream media further circulating and legitimating it. Celebrities have thus become the most popular figures in their field, and publics seem to have insatiable appetites for inside information and gossip about their idols, fueling a media in search of profit in a competitive market to provide increasing amounts of celebrity news, images and spectacle.

Indeed, celebrity culture is such that there is a class of faux celebrities – think Paris Hilton or social media influencers – who are largely famous for being famous and being in the media. Celebrity culture is bolstered by a tabloid media that is becoming more prevalent in the era of the Internet, new media, and social networking sites that circulate gossip and celebrity trivia, enabling anyone caught in the media circus to become famous for 15 minutes, as Andy Warhol once predicted could be the aspiration of anyone. In this context, it is not surprising that politicians, especially political leaders who are frequently in the media spotlight, have become celebrities, as publics seek news, information, and gossip about their private and public lives, turning some politicians into media superstars and relegating politicians caught in scandal to tabloid hell and damnation.

In addition, politics in the United States and elsewhere in global culture have become propelled in recent years by media spectacle. The mainstream corporate media today in the United States increasingly process events, news, and information in the form of media spectacle. In an arena of intense competition with 24/7 cable TV networks, talk radio, Internet sites and blogs, and ever proliferating social media sites like Facebook, Instagram, Twitter, and YouTube, competition for attention is ever more intense, leading the corporate media to go to sensationalistic tabloidized stories, which they construct in the forms of media spectacle that attempt to attract maximum audiences for as much time as possible, until the next spectacle emerges.

In the following pages, I will engage some of the ways that the logic of the spectacle promoted the candidacy of Barack Obama and informed his presidency, and will indicate how he became a master of the spectacle and global celebrity of the highest order. I first discuss how Obama became a supercelebrity in the presidential primaries and general election of 2008 and utilized media spectacle to help win the presidency. Next, I discuss how Obama deployed his status as global supercelebrity in his presidency, which has also revealed the limits of celebrity politics and spectacle.

While documentaries were appearing in the last days of the Bush–Cheney era attacking their regime (Kellner 2010), documentaries about Barack Obama began to appear before he was even elected. Already in 2007, Bob Heracles released *Senator Obama Goes to Africa* which portrayed the Senator from Illinois searching for his roots in Africa, a focus in Obama's book *Dreams From my Father* (1995). Once Obama declared himself candidate for president, a series of documentaries on Obama appeared. The compilation film *Barack Obama: The Power of Change* (2008) provides some of Obama's most memorable campaign speeches, but reveals little of the man and his history.

Maria Arita-Howard's *President Barack Obama: The Man and His Journey* (2008), by contrast, charts key moments of Obama's life and career, and intersperses moments of his speeches with testimonies from a variety of people who knew him, ranging from his Harvard Law Professor Larry Tribe who cites Obama's brilliance and early promise to some grassroots supporters who tirelessly campaigned for him.[27] The documentary notes how Obama first came to public attention through his successful 2004 campaign for the Senate in Illinois and his spellbinding speech at the 2004 Democratic convention. The film cites Elder Berenice King, daughter of Martin Luther King, recounting that after hearing this speech, her mother, Coretta Scott King, stated: "I think we've got somebody," indicating that Obama was in the King tradition and represented someone who could help realize the promises of the civil rights movement in their struggle for equality and racial justice. Another commentator claimed that Obama was "the real deal," and throughout, the film attempted to put Obama's candidacy in the historical context of civil rights struggles.

Maria Arita-Howard's *Barack Obama – The Man and History Journey* (2009) highlights how Obama was the only major Democratic Party 2008 presidential candidate who had opposed the Iraq war from the beginning, and cites commentators and colleagues that praise his work as state legislator in Illinois. There is dramatic footage of Obama's February 10, 2007 announcement of his candidacy for the presidency on the steps of the Illinois State Capital where Abraham Lincoln himself declared he was standing for president. The rest of the film follows Obama's successful campaign for the presidency, accentuating his themes of hope, change, and new leadership. Commentators note that Obama ran a campaign for a twenty-first-century digital age, using music videos, email lists, websites, and social networking to organize his supporters and raise money, while other candidates of his party and the 2008 Republican Party candidates were running a twentieth-century analogue campaign. Commentators note how Obama's Democratic Party acceptance speech reflected Martin Luther King's "I Have a Dream" speech, and members of the King family and commentators note the historical continuity and spiritual resonance of the Obama candidacy with King and the Civil Rights movement.

By contrast, *Hype: The Obama Effect* (2008) presents a critique of Obama released during the election campaign with an A-list of conservative commentators attacking Obama and his record. Directed by Alan Petersen and co-produced by conservative activist David Bossie and Citizens United,[28] the film functions as a position paper against Obama, arguing exact opposite positions to those in Arita-Howard's pro-Obama film. While the latter produced positive comments on Obama's work in the Illinois state senate, on his record in the U.S. Senate, and positive presentations of his campaign, *Hype* presented negative commentaries from right-wing pundits on his political service in the Illinois State Senate and U.S. Senate, and his speeches on the campaign trail, dismissed as "Hype."

The film opens with a young-looking Obama dancing on TV with Ellen DeGeneres and then making speeches highlighting his slogans of Change, Unity, and Hope. Adoring crowds chant Obama's name and Oprah Winfrey introduces him as "The One." The opening montage attempts to present Obama as a celebrity attracting irrational devotion, but the rest of the polemical film attempts to present Obama as a left-wing radical and outside of the U.S. mainstream. Highlighting Obama's admiration for radical Saul Alinsky during his community organizer years, his association with the radical preacher Rev. Wright, and contacts with Bill Ayers, formerly of the Weather Underground, the film suggests that Obama's "Associates" prove he is an out of the mainstream radical. Various conservative pundits and activists also assault Obama's "Judgment" on Iraq and foreign policy, and raise questions whether he has the experience to defend America against terrorism (there is no comparison of Obama with George W. Bush, who was less prepared then Obama on every issue and no doubt the same conservative pundits have never noted that Donald Trump had no previous political experience whatsoever). The film negatively presents Obama's record on taxes, immigration, energy, health care, guns, abortion, and foreign policy, as embodying left-wing positions, thus attempting to dissuade moderate voters from supporting Obama.

The Big Lie of *Hype: The Obama Effect* was that Obama was coming in to raise taxes, a point made throughout the film, which was highlighted in a concluding sequence in which Arkansas Governor Mike Huckabee and a Republican presidential candidate, told viewers that: "if you want to pay higher taxes, Obama's your man." In fact, Obama's first days in office he lowered taxes for all but the top 2%, and throughout his presidency he attempted to keep lower tax rates in place for 98% of the population, raising taxes only for the top 2%.

Hype and the pro-Obama films were intended as political interventions in the 2008 election, which Obama won. After Obama's paradigm-shifting victory, several post-election documentaries quickly appeared to celebrate or demonize Obama. Amy Rice and Alicia Sam's *By the People: The Election of Barack Obama* (2009) covers Obama's campaign for U.S. senator and 2008 run in the presidential election, presenting him as a spectacular campaigner who evoked idolatrous support. The film also examines the grassroots movement that helped Obama secure the election. Largely filmed during the 2008 presidential election campaign, the documentary goes behind the scenes, showing Obama and his aides fighting for the presidency, evoking an inside-the-campaign look, as did the more acclaimed cinema verité documentary *The War Room* (1993), which portrayed Bill Clinton's aides and campaign, providing insight into how the Clinton team won the presidency in 1992.

Danny Schechter's *Barack Obama: People's President* (2009) provides a largely celebratory spectacle of Obama's winning the 2008 election. Putting himself on camera and into the action à la Michael Moore, we see Schechter interacting with members of Obama's grassroots campaign. Himself a prolific media critic, Schecter documents Obama's mastery of old and new media and interviews a number of media analysts, journalists, political insiders, and activists to illuminate Obama's victory, with emphasis on Obama's groundingbreaking use of the Internet and social networks to spread his message and organize his supporters.[29]

Not surprisingly, fierce critiques of Obama began appearing early in his presidency in documentary film, as well as Fox television, Talk Radio, and the rightwing Internet. Conspiracy theorist and popular radio host Alex Jones released two 2009 films, *The Obama Deception* and *Fall of the Republic*. Jones combines right-wing populism with anti-world government tirades that attack both parties and claim that the mainstream media and political culture manipulate the public in the interests of the banks and global capital. Indeed, Jones' films express his view that a cabal of international financiers guided by the Bilderberger groups, the Trilateral Commission, the Council for Foreign Relations, and other elite/insider groups control Washington and global politics – conspiracy theories that would continue to percolate on the extreme right during the 2016 U.S. presidency election and the Trump presidency.[30]

Jones' *Fall of the Republic* appears to be an extension and updating of his earlier anti-Obama film that continues fierce attacks on Obama and Al Gore's crusade against global warming, situating Jones and his cohort as climate-science deniers (they attribute rising temperatures to the tilting of the sun). While Jones et al. appear to present radical attacks of the control of the system by a global cartel of bankers and advocates of a World Government that will replace national sovereignty, the constitution, and our "freedoms," in fact, his critical attention is often aimed at Obama, Al Gore, and liberal Democrats, from what Jones variously describes as a "paleoconservative," or "libertarian" perspective.

While Jones does raise serious questions about Obama and his policies, especially his putting Wall Street foxes to run the economic hen house, and outdoes Michael Moore in attacking the banks for engineering the financial collapse of 2008, Jones also goes off the deep end with some issues, vehemently denying global warming and climate change, and claiming (via some of the people interviewed in the film) that Lenin, Stalin and the Bolsheviks, Hitler and the Nazis, Mao, and all recent American presidents (except Kennedy who apparently gets dispensation because he was assassinated) are tools of a cabal of British and American Capital. Jones is the ultimately Big Conspiracy theorist whose sometimes valid criticisms of the U.S. political system and economy are undermined by his advocacy of global banks as the primary source of contemporary evil (letting off oil and energy corporations, and many other major contributors to the manifold evils of our times).

Two sympathetic fictional films appeared on different phases of the early life of U.S. President Barack Obama at the end of his presidency. Richard Tanne's *Southside with You* (2016) chronicles the summer 1989 afternoon when the future President Barack Obama (Parker Sawyers) woos his future First Lady, Michelle Obama (Tika Sumpter), on a first date across Chicago's South Side. The story opens with Michelle talking about Barack to her parents ("Barack o-what-a?" says Dad), while Obama tells his grandmother about Michelle. At this point, Barack is a Harvard law student spending his summer working for a law firm in Chicago, where Michelle Robinson works, as his supervisor.

The plot revolves around plans the couple have to attend a community meeting in an impoverished neighborhood on what Robinson insists is not a "date." During the first portion of the film, Michelle repeatedly asks Barack about his plans for the future, and makes it clear that their outing cannot be a date because that would undermine her position in the law firm, where she already struggles as a Black woman. Obama reveals that he tricked Robinson into coming with him several hours early and has made plans for them to attend an art gallery and eat lunch together. Robinson hesitantly agrees, but only if he agrees to be strictly "professional." When interrogated about his future plans, Obama admits that "Something else is pulling at me," and he ponders whether "I can write books or hold a position of influence in civil rights." Michelle responds, "Politics?," while Barack shrugs, "Maybe."

Those who have followed Obama's career know that indeed he was to write books, become active politically in Chicago, and then state and national politics, while becoming president of the United States in 2008 and was re-elected in 2012. In *Southside with You*, we see Michelle and Barack wander through Chicago and get to know each other on what is indeed their first date, and we learn that Barack wants to go to Harvard Law School, while Michelle has actually done that and is now practicing law. Eventually, the two make it to the political meeting, and Michelle is embarrassed to be seen as Obama's "women," by his friends, but she overcomes her annoyance, after Obama demonstrates his oratorical skills, giving a rousing speech that helps the group overcome their discouragement following the city's rejection of their proposal to build a community center.

Michelle then agrees to accompany Obama to the movies, and they see Spike Lee's *Do the Right Thing*. While exiting the theater, the couple cross paths with one of the law firm's partners, who tells Robinson to "take good care of" Obama. While she is initially annoyed and tells Obama she really shouldn't ever go out with him again, he wins her over after he buys her favorite kind of ice cream and they seal the date with a kiss, before returning to their respective homes. As the credits begin to roll we see that both are smiling and know that this will not be their last date.

Another biopic about Obama, *Barry* (2016), directed by Vikram Gandhi, deals with Obama's life at Columbia University where he arrives to study as a transfer student in 1981. The 20-year-old Barack Obama, commonly known as Barry at the time, arrives in New York City, but is unable to contact his expected roommate, Will, and spends the night in the streets. Soon after, Barry meets Will and they both begin to live in their off-campus apartment on 109th Street, a block away from where I once lived when I was studying Philosophy at Columbia University in the 1960s.

Barry depicts young Obama as a typical new graduate student, searching for his way in the world, having a girlfriend, and playing basketball to "chill out." We see young Obama in Harlem discussing the contrast of Black life in New York City and the south, buying *The Souls of Black Folk* by W. E. B. Du Bois, and encountering everyday racism in the streets. Barry's white mother, Ann Dunham, comes to visit and he meets a white student, Charlotte, who questions Ann about Barry's father and childhood, as it appears that Barry keeps much of his private life to himself.

Barry learns that his father has died in a car accident and at Charlotte's sister's wedding Barry meets Grace Lee Boggs and James Boggs, a mixed race couple in their late 50s who were civil rights activists in the 1960s. Barry confides to the Boggs about his inner turmoil and conflicts between his white and Black identity, and the Boggs reassure him that he will find his way and should seek inspiration from those who came before him and carry the baton of hope as far as he can, allowing Barry to begin finding peace within himself.

Barry concludes with young Obama breaking up with Charlotte and working to write a book about his father in Africa, as the film ends it is clear that Barry is now comfortable with who he is and is ready to meet challenges of the future. *Barry* and *Southside With You* thus both present Obama as a young man moving into his future, using cinematic narratives to showing him mature and eventually bond with his future wife, Michelle, develop as a community organizer, and envisage possibilities in law and politics.

A documentary *The Final Year* (2017), directed by Greg Barker, provides a chronicle of the Obama administration's foreign policy team and the events of Obama's final year in office. While President Obama is featured at certain points, the documentary crew mainly follows the activities of Secretary of State

John Kerry, UN Ambassador Samantha Power, National Security Advisor Susan Rice, and Deputy National Security Advisor Ben Rhodes. Although the documentary does not present Donald Trump, the emphasis among the main players switches as the final year progresses from producing a foreign policy legacy to taking measures to protect that legacy from being dismantled by the incoming administration.

Enjoying rare access to Barack Obama and some of his top aides during the last year of his presidency, *The Final Year* captures the urgency of White House foreign policy experts as they hasten to cement Obama's global legacy. The film argues that the Obama administration's foreign policy approach was different from that of previous administrations in that it favored engagement without immediate resort to the threat or use of force. Barker's documentary shows various administration officials implementing that approach, and discussing their foreign policy decisions, thus providing an interesting look at the people who worked behind the scenes during the last year of Obama's presidency.

As the final year of Obama's presidency progresses, we see his team focusing on establishing his foreign policy legacy and taking measures to protect that legacy from being dismantled by the incoming administration. Indeed, the 2016 U.S. presidential election brought in Donald Trump who would attempt to undo Obama's legacy in every arena from domestic to foreign policy to the conducting of the presidency. Accordingly, the next section will attempt to explain the election and the presidency of Donald Trump.

The Donald Trump reality show presidency

Explaining the Donald Trump phenomenon is a challenge that will occupy critical theorists of U.S. politics for years to come. My first take on the Trump phenomenon is that Donald Trump won the Republican primary contest and then the U.S. presidential election because he is the *master of media spectacle*, a concept that I've been developing and applying to U.S. politics and media since the mid-1990s and explicated earlier in this chapter. In this section, I will first discuss Trump's use of media spectacle in his business career, in his effort to become a celebrity and reality TV superstar, and in his political campaign. Then I shall examine how Trump embodies Authoritarian Populism and has used racism, nationalism, xenophobia, and the disturbing underside of American politics to mobilize his supporters in his successful Republican primary campaign and in the hotly contested win in the 2016 general election. Finally, in line with the conception of the dialectics of digital culture, I will stress how Trump has used digital culture to win and advance his presidency, but argue that his use of digital culture and media spectacle may contribute to his undoing, suggesting that digital culture in the contemporary era can empower and destroy, has both an emancipatory and a regressive and destructive side, and thus creates a highly unstable and unpredictable social and political situation in the contemporary era, embodied and illustrated by the chaotic political career of Donald J. Trump.

Donald Trump and the politics of the spectacle

I first came up with the concept of media spectacle to describe the key phenomenon of U.S. media and politics in the mid-1990s. This was the era of the O.J. Simpson murder case and trial, the Clinton sex scandals, and the rise of cable news networks like Fox, CNN, and media MSNBC and the 24/7 news cycle that has dominated U.S. politics and media since then.[31] The 1990s was also the period when the Internet and New Media took off so that anyone could be a political commentator, player, and participant in the spectacle, a phenomenon that accelerated as new media morphed into social media, and teenagers, celebrities, politicians, and others wanting to become part of the networked virtual world joined in.

In the 2016 U.S. presidential election, Donald Trump emerged as a major avatar of media spectacle and has long been a celebrity and master of the spectacle with promotion of his buildings and casinos from the 1980s to the present, his reality TV shows, self-promoting events, and his presidential campaign and presidency. Hence, Trump was empowered and enabled to run for the presidency in part because media spectacle has become a major force in U.S. politics, helping to determine elections, government, and more broadly the ethos and nature of our culture and political sphere, and Trump is a successful creator and manipulator of the spectacle.

Trump's biographies reveal that he was driven by a need to compete and win,[32] and entering the highly competitive real estate business in New York in the 1980s, Trump saw the need to use the media and publicity to promote his celebrity and image. It was a time of tabloid culture and media-driven celebrity and Trump even adopted a pseudonym "John Baron" to give the media gossip items that touted Trump's successes in businesses, with women, and as a rising man about town.[33]

Trump derives his language and behavior from a highly competitive and ruthless New York business culture and an appreciation of the importance of media and celebrity to succeed in a media-centric hypercapitalism. Hence, to discover the nature of Trump's "temperament," personality, and use of language, we should recall his reality TV show *The Apprentice*, which popularized him into a supercelebrity and made the Donald a major public figure for a national audience. Indeed, Trump is the first reality TV candidate who ran his campaign (and then his presidency) like a reality TV series, boasting during the most chaotic episodes in his campaign that his rallies are the most entertaining, and sending outrageous tweets into the Twitter-sphere, which than dominate the news cycle on the ever-proliferating mainstream media and social networking sites. Hence, Trump is the first celebrity candidate whose use of the media and celebrity star power is his most potent weapon in his improbable and highly surreal campaign.[34]

The Apprentice, Twitter and the Summer of Trump

Since Trump's national celebrity derived in part from his role in the reality TV series *The Apprentice*,[35] we need to interrogate this popular TV phenomenon to help explain the Trump phenomenon. The opening theme music "For the Love of Money," a 1973 R&B song by The O'Jays, established the capitalist ethos of the competition for the winning contestant to get a job with the Trump organization, and obviously money is the key to Trump's business and celebrity success, although there is much controversy over how rich Trump is and so far he has not released his tax returns to quell rumors that he isn't as rich as he claims, that he does not contribute as much to charity as he has stated, and that many years he pays little or no taxes.

In the original format to *The Apprentice*, several contestants formed teams to carry out a task dictated by Trump, and each "contest" resulted with a winner and Trump barking "you're fired" to the loser. Curiously, some commentators believe in the 2012 presidential election that Barack Obama beat Mitt Romney handily because he early on characterized Romney as a billionaire who liked to fire people, which is ironic since this is Trump's signature personality trait in his business, reality TV, and now political career, which has seen him fire two campaign managers and more advisors by August 2016.

The Apprentice premiered in January 2004, and after six seasons, a new format was introduced: *The Celebrity Apprentice*. The celebrity apprentice series generally followed the same premise as the original, but with celebrities as contestants participating to win money for their chosen charities, rather than winning a job opportunity with the Trump organization. There have been seven seasons of *The Celebrity Apprentice* since 2008, although NBC announced on June 29, 2015 that it was severing all business ties with Trump due to the latter's comments about Mexican immigrants, but has said its relationship with Mark Burnett and the show will continue.

When NBC started negotiating with Trump concerning the reality TV series in 2002, according to NBC producer Jeff Gaspin, the network was not sure that the New York-centric real estate mogul would have a national resonance and the initial concept envisaged different billionaires each season hiring an apprentice. The show immediately got good ratings and Trump became a popular TV figure as he brought the contestants into his board room in Trump Tower, appraised their performances, insulted those who did not do well, and fired the loser.[36]

The Apprentice's TV producer Mark Burnett broke into national consciousness with his reality TV show *The Survivor*, a neo-Darwinian epic of alliances, backstabbing, and nastiness, which provides an allegory of how one succeeds in the dog-eat-dog business world in which Donald Trump has thrived, and spectacularly failed as many of the books about him document. Both Burnett and Trump share the neo-Darwinian (a)social ethos of nineteenth-century ultracompetitive capitalism with some of Donald Trump's famous witticisms proclaiming:

> When somebody challenges you unfairly, fight back – be brutal, be tough – don't take it. It is always important to WIN!
> I think everyone's a threat to me.

> Everyone that's hit me so far has gone down. They've gone down big league.
>
> I want my generals kicking ass.
>
> I would bomb the shit out of them.
>
> You bomb the hell out of the oil. Don't worry about the cities. The cities are terrible.[37]

In any case, *The Apprentice* made Trump a national celebrity who became well-known enough to plausibly run for president and throughout the campaign Trump used his celebrity to gain media time. Trump had also became a regular commentator on *Fox & Friends*, a discussion show on the right-wing Fox TV network that introduced him in a positive way to conservative viewers.[38] Trump began appearing as a guest and topic of discussion on *Fox & Friends* when he was expanding his national profile as a celebrity after the success of *The Apprentice*. Eventually he became so popular a guest that in March 6, 2011, *Fox & Friends* began a new segment "Mondays with Trump," and so Trump was able to bond with conservative *Fox* viewers and had *Fox* heavily promoting him years before his presidential run, as well as during the 2016 presidential campaign and his presidency.[39]

In addition to Trump's 2016 campaign's ability to manipulate broadcast media, Trump is also a heavy user of Twitter and tweets his messages throughout the day and night, thus becoming a master of digital culture as well as media culture. In this section, I want to suggest how media/digital culture has both empowered Trump and sown the seeds of his possible destruction, thus revealing a perverse dialectic of digital culture that can both empower and destroy individuals and groups – and I would argue even corporations in the #MeToo Era, but that is a topic for a different study.

Donald Trump may be the first major Twitter candidate, and certainly he is the one using it most aggressively and frequently with arguably contradictory results. Twitter was launched in 2006, but I don't recall it being used in a major way in the 2008 election, although Obama used Facebook and his campaign bragged that he had over a million "Friends" and used Facebook as part of his daily campaign apparatus (Kellner 2015). I don't recall, however, previous presidential candidates using Twitter in a big way like Donald Trump, although many politicos now have accounts.

Twitter is a perfect vehicle for Trump as you can use its 140 character framework, and in November 2014, 280 character platform, for attack, bragging, and getting out simple messages or posts that engage receivers who feel they are in the know and involved in TrumpWorld when they get pinged and receive his tweets. When asked at an August 26, 2015, Iowa event as to why he uses Twitter so much, he replied that it was easy, it only took a couple of seconds, and that he could attack his media critics when he "wasn't treated fairly." Trump has also used Instagram – an online mobile photo-sharing, video-sharing and social networking service that enables its users to take pictures and videos, and share them on a variety of digital social networking platforms, such as Facebook, Twitter, Tumblr, and Flickr.

Twitter and social media are perfect for General Trump who can blast out his opinions and order his followers what to think and in some cases what to do. It enables Businessman and Politician Trump to define his brand and mobilize those who wish to consume or support it. Trump Twitter gratifies the need of Narcissist Trump to be noticed and recognized as a Master of Communication who can bind his warriors into an online community. Twitter enables the Pundit-in-Chief to opine, rant, attack, distract, and proclaim on all and sundry subjects, and to subject TrumpWorld to the indoctrination of their Fearless Leader.

Hence, Trump is mastering new digital media as well as dominating television and old media through his orchestration of media events as spectacles and daily Twitter Feed. In Trump's presidential campaign kickoff speech on June 16, 2015, when he announced he was running for president, Trump and his wife Melania dramatically ascended down the stairway at Trump Towers, and then Donald strode up to a gaggle of microphones and dominated media attention for days with his drama. The opening speech of his campaign made a typically inflammatory remark that held in thrall news cycles for days when he stated:

> The U.S. has become a dumping ground for everybody else's problems. [Applause] Thank you. It's true, and these are the best and the finest. When Mexico sends its people, they're not sending their best. They're not sending you. They're not sending you. They're sending people that have lots of problems, and they're bringing those problems with us. They're bringing drugs. They're bringing crime. They're rapists. And some, I assume, are good people.

This comment ignited a firestorm of controversy and a preview of Things to Come concerning vile racism, xenophobia, Islamophobia, and the other hallmarks of Trump's Cacophony of Hate. Debate over Trump's assault on undocumented immigrants would come to dominate daily news cycles of the Republican primaries and would continue to play out in the general election in fall 2016 and throughout Trump's presidency. In the lead up to the first Republican primary debate in fall 2015, Donald Trump got the majority of media time, and his daily campaign appearances and the Republican primary debates became media spectacle dominated by Trump. Every day that Trump had a campaign event, the cable news networks would hype the event with crawlers on the bottom of the TV screen proclaiming "Waiting for Trump," with airtime on cable TV dominated by speculation on what he would talk about. Trump's speeches were usually broadcast live, often in their entirety, a boon of free TV time that no candidate of either party was awarded. After the Trump event, the rest of the day the pundits would dissect what he had said and his standing vis-à-vis the other Republican candidates. If Trump had no campaign event planned, he would fire off a round of Tweets against his opponents on his highly active Twitter account – which then would be featured on network cable news discussions as well as social media (Kellner 2016, 2017).

Hence, Trump's orchestration of media spectacle and a compliant mainstream media was a crucial factor in thrusting Trump ever further into the front runner status in the Republican primaries and winning for him the overwhelming amount of media attention and eventually the Republican nomination. The first major quantitative study released notes that from mid-June 2015 after Trump announced he was running through mid-July, Trump was in 46% of the news media coverage of the Republican field, based on Google news hits; he also got 60% of Google news searches, and I will bet that later academic studies will show how he dominated all media from newspapers to television to Twitter and new media to social networking during the Republican primaries and then during the general election.[40]

At a press conference on August 26, 2015, before his appearance at a rally in Dubuque Iowa, Trump bragged how all three U.S. cable news networks, as well as the other big three networks and even foreign news networks, were following him around all day, broadcasting all his live campaign appearances. The same day, Trump bragged about how one major media insider told him that it was the "Summer of Trump" and that it was amazing how he was completely dominating news coverage. Trump also explained, correctly I think, why he was getting all the media attention: "RATINGS," he explained, "it's ratings, the people love me, they want to see me, so they watch TV when I'm on." And I do think it is ratings that leads the profit-oriented television networks to almost exclusively follow Trump's events and give him live TV control of the audience. This wall-to-wall Trump coverage of all his campaign events, media stunts, and daily tweets continued throughout the presidential campaigns and into his presidency, giving Trump an unparalleled domination of digital and broadcast media.

Trump rose to prominence in New York during the Reaganite 1980s as an embodiment of wild, entrepreneurial cowboy capitalism in an era of deregulation, the celebration of wealth, and the "greed is good" ethos of Wall Street, enabled by the Reagan administration. Trump's success was tied to an unrestrained finance capital that loaned him immense sums of money, often with minimal and problematic collateral, to carry through his construction projects. Trump was an extravagant consumer with a three story penthouse at the top of Trump Towers, a 118 room mansion in Palm Beach, Florida Mar-A-Lago, that he immediately opened for TV interview segments, and an obscene array of properties. He flaunted a yacht bought from Saudi arms dealer Adnan Khashoggi, and a personal airplane to jet him around the world to luxury resorts. Trump was featured on TV shows like *Life Styles of the Rich and Famous,* and his life-style was the subject of multi-page spreads in fashion and other popular magazines, making Trump the poster-boy for excessive "conspicuous consumption," of a degree that I doubt Veblen could have imagined (1994 [1899]).

Trump's financial fortunes hit the economic slowdown that followed the Reagan orgy of unrestrained capitalism in the late 1980s,[41] and in the 1990s Trump almost became bankrupt. Fittingly, Trump had overinvested in the very epitome of consumer capitalism, buying a string of luxury gambling casinos in Atlantic City. The financial slump hit Trump's overextended casinos, driving him to put them on the market. The banks called in loans on his overextended real estate investments, and he was forced to sell off properties, his yacht, and other luxury items. Having temporarily lost his ability to borrow from finance capital to expand his real estate business, Trump was forced to go into partnerships in business ventures, and then sold the Trump name that was attached to an array of consumer items ranging from water to vodka, and men's clothes to fragrances.

Most significantly, Trump has been particularly assiduous in branding the Trump name and selling himself as a businessman, a celebrity, and then as a presidential candidate and eventually a president. Trump's presidential campaign represents s successful branding of a loudmouthed faux billionaire into a political candidate whose campaign and then presidency was run on bombast and hyperbole, dominating on a daily basis the mediascape, and gaining the attention of voters/consumers. Trump has adeptly orchestrated political theater like he orchestrated a business and media career, and his daily presidential theatrics are highly entertaining to some, and in any case set the media agenda and dominate the daily mediascape.

Trump thus represents another step in the merger between entertainment, celebrity and politics. While Ronald Reagan arguably played a key role as our first actor president, Trump is arguably the first major presidential candidate and then president to pursue politics as entertainment, and thus to collapse the distinction between entertainment, news, and politics. He is also the first authoritarian populist to have been a party nominee and then president in recent times.

Trump's presidency, populist authoritarianism, and the war on democracy

Throughout the first term of Trump's presidency, he has consistently governed as an authoritarian populist, and from the beginning of his presidency, Trump has relentlessly attacked the basic pillars of American democracy. As an autocrat, he constantly assaults the major institutions of the American system of checks and balances, especially the Fourth Estate of the media, the judiciary, and Congress – unless it enacts his will and flatters him (Kellner 2017). The Trump presidency is arguably the most authoritarian in recent history with the president engaging in all-out war against the media, judiciary, the U.S. intelligences services, and any other organ of government or individuals that criticize Trump, impede him in any way, or raise his ire.

Trump's ascendency as 45th president of the United States will likely be seen as the most disruptive opening of a presidential regime in modern U.S. history.

Trump and his administration began by waging battles against the media, the courts, the Congress, and the majority of the people of the U.S. who strongly opposed him and found Trump thrust upon them as president because of an outdated and thoroughly dysfunctional Electoral College system. Yet from the beginning there has been resistance to Trump's presidency beginning with the Woman's March on Washington, the largest demonstration in U.S. history the day after Trump's inauguration and continuing with an ever-growing Trump Resistance movement (Kellner 2017).

Trump's war on the media has been a defining feature of his presidency. Calling the media "the enemy of the people," terms used by Comrade Stalin and Chairman Mao, Trump derides every media report that criticizes him as "fake news" and personally attacks critical media reports on his daily Twitter feed, and attacks reporters for their fake news at his few press conferences and many rallies.

Trump also has had a contentious relation to the courts and law throughout his litigious career (see D'Antonio 2015), and as president he had continually attacked judges, the courts, and key institutions of the legal system, including the FBI, CIA, and U.S. intelligence agencies. On May 9, 2017, Trump fired FBI director James Comey creating the most stunning and perhaps consequential media spectacle of his presidency.

There is a dialectic of the spectacle whereby those who prosper and thrive through the spectacle may undergo their downfall and destruction through media spectacles of scandal and delegitimation. Miraculously, Bill Clinton survived the spectacle of the Monica Lewinsky sex scandal and impeachment perhaps because the spectacle of the noxious Grand Inquisitor Ken Starr and a blood-thirsty Republican Congress turned public opinion to support Clinton despite his failings (Kellner 2002). Michael Jackson, by contrast, during the same era, had his career destroyed by revelations that he invited young boys to his home and bed for sleepovers. Yet after his death, Jackson underwent a miraculous resurrection of the spectacle as millions around the world mourned his death and gave his career and work an afterlife.

Trump's firing of Comey, however, generated negative media spectacles highlighting his pathological mendacity as he claimed that he fired Comey because of the mishandling of Hillary Clinton's email problems during the 2016 presidential election. Few outside of Trump supporters believed this, however, especially after it was revealed that Comey had requested more resources to investigate the connections between the Trump organization and campaign and the Russians during the 2016 presidential election when there was strong evidence that the Russians had hacked the democrats and released embarrassing, or distracting, emails from the Clinton campaign to the press with the aid of WikiLeaks and Facebook (see Nance 2016, 2018; Kellner 2017; Isikoff-Corn 2018).

The Russian hacking, which reportedly continues into his presidency, and has evoked indictments by the Mueller investigation and Congressional and media inquiries, may affect the trajectory of U.S. elections in years to come, which in turn will impact the fate of the Trump presidency. Only after the 2016 election was it revealed that the Russians, perhaps in conspiracy with the Trump campaign, used Twitter, Facebook, and other forms of digital culture to attack Clinton and promote Trump, and continued Russian cyberwarfare is still being investigated into Trump's presidency.

Jack Bryan's *Active Measures* (2018) is the first major documentary to address the allegations of collusion between the Trump campaign and agents of the Russian state. The term "active measures" has long been used by Soviet and Russian security services to describe measures of political warfare intended to influence the course of world events. It also involves collecting intelligence and producing efficacious uses of it, since as was involved in the Russian hacking of the Clinton campaign and the use of hacked data to help Trump and hurt Clinton.

The documentary puts the Russian hacking in the context of a 30-year history of covert Russian political warfare in which Russian president Vladimir Putin, a former KGB agent, has been involved in. Trump had long called the Russian investigation a hoax and "fake news," but the very fact of firing Comey who was vigorously investigating the Trump/Russia connection as head of the FBI, and Trump's obsessive attacks on the media and the legal system suggest that he has been deeply worried about the various investigations by Congress, the media, the Mueller Commission, and other state and federal investigations.

Trump seems to have survived the Mueller Report as of summer 2019, but many scandals could eventually do him in. A 2019 Netflix documentary *The Great Hack* directed by Karim Amer and Jehane Noujaim's provides new insights into the 2016 presidential election and the role of Cambridge Analytica, Facebook, and the Trump organization using the Clinton campaign stolen emails to help Trump win. Focusing on a Cambridge Analytica employee Brittany Kaiser, the documentary explores how data producing voting profiles and providing a sense of "persuadable" voters, accompanied by relentless targeting of those voters, can sway an election whether it's in the 2016 Brexit vote, the U.S. presidential election, or Trinidad and Tobago where Cambridge Analytica was allegedly active.

Brittany Kaiser tells how she was recruited by Cambridge Analytica and worked with Facebook and the Trump organization. She describes the shock when it was revealed in early 2018 that Cambridge Analytica had harvested the personal data of millions of people's Facebook profiles without their consent and used it for political advertising purposes. The documentary also interviews Carole Cadwalladr, a reporter for *The Guardian* who broke stories about the Cambridge Analytica/Facebook/Trump/Brexit/Russia nexus. The documentary is especially harsh on Cambridge Analytica and Facebook, and depicts former Cambridge Analytica CEO Alexander Nix's anger when investigations lead to his firm's bankruptcy. It also records the shock when news reports revealed that Brittany Kaiser had met with WikiLeaks' Julian Assange, leading Kaiser to insist she had never worked with WikiLeaks, Assange, or Russia, raising questions as to what exact linkages were operative between these organizations.

The Great Hack concludes with arguments that data rights and privacy are now a human rights issue when it is now clear what nefarious political use can be made of data harvested from social media like Facebook and distributed through Facebook and other social media outlets. Near the end of the documentary, we also see data scientist David Carroll worrying that "by letting algorithms make all our choices for us, we are surrendering our free will."

No doubt, the many investigations into the Trump–Russia connections, Trump's financial dealings, and the always mushrooming scandals of his presidency have produced impeachment proceedings that are unfolding as I write in fall 2019,[42] and there is no doubt that the Trump presidency will continue to be a major media spectacle of the contemporary era and perhaps one of the most momentous political spectacles in U.S. history. Indeed, one of the most disgusting scandals of the Trump presidency and most appalling media spectacle, are the internments camps on the U.S./Mexico border and Trump's exploitation of immigration to appease the right-wing, anti-immigrant and racist segments of his base. The horrors of family separation, children dying in camps and border crossings, and multiple forms of suffering caused by Trump's failure to create a rational border and immigration policy is certainly one of the many major stains on Trump's presidency. U.S. politics are now totally bound up with the logic and dynamic of media spectacle, and the fate of the nation depends on how the U.S. public and political system responds to the ongoing Trump scandals after he survived a 2020 impeachment yet continues to be investigated by the courts, political parties, and media.

Political documentary: Michael Moore vs. Corporate America and the conservative political establishment

Michael Moore has emerged as one of the world's best known documentary filmmakers. His films *Bowling For Columbine* (2002) and *Fahrenheit 9/11* (2011) are the two highest grossing documentary films in history, and he has emerged as one of the most successful and controversial filmmakers of his day. *Bowling* won an Academy Award for best documentary and in 2002 was chosen by 2,000 members of the International Documentary Association (IDA) as the best documentary of all time. *Fahrenheit 9/11* was even more successful at the box office and garnered a perhaps unparalleled legion of passionate fans and bitter detractors alike.

In addition, Moore has a stack of best-selling books, and a popular website that promotes his products and receives millions of hits. He engages in lecture tours with packed houses and adoring fans, has produced TV series *TV Nation* (1994), *The Awful Truth* (1999), and *Michael Moore Live* (1999), still circulating in DVD and streaming video, and has been a frequent presence in the mainstream media. This success is surprising given that Moore is one of the most high-profile critics of corporate capitalism, U.S. military policy, several U.S. political administrations, and the manifold injustices of U.S. society.

What is the secret of Moore's success? He is a populist artist who privileges his own voice and point of view, inserting himself as film narrator and often the subject of action. Moore plays the crusading defender of the poor and oppressed, and stands up to and confronts the powers that be. He uses humor and compelling dramatic and narrative sequences to engage his audiences. He deals with issues of fundamental importance, and convinces his audience that the problems he presents are highly significant, involve everyone, and concern the health of U.S. democracy. Moreover, despite the severity of the problems he portrays, the films and filmmaker imply that the problems are subject to intervention, and that progressive social transformation is possible and necessary.

I have written previously on Moore's particular documentary strategies, aesthetics, and politics (Kellner 2010), and in this study will limit myself to his more recent films, and in particular his recent critiques of the U.S. political and economic system and documentaries on Donald Trump. From an aggressively left-wing perspective, Michael Moore's *Capitalism: A Love Story* (2009) takes on the capitalist system itself, excoriating a socio-economic system in which the top 1% owns 95% of the wealth and in which an unregulated economy is allowed to wreak havoc. Illustrating the flaws of laissez-faire capitalism, Moore focuses on the home mortgage and financial crises that exploded in public in fall 2009. Interviewing people who were victimized by easy home loans that soon morphed into increased monthly mortgages that they could not pay, as well as interviewing individuals involved in the scandal, who were obviously motivated by greed, Moore shows the human consequences of an unregulated economic system.[43]

After an opening montage sequence that compares the fall of the Roman Empire with images of the failing Bush–Cheney administration, Moore contrasts families being evicted from their homes with a brazen operative for a Florida real-estate company that buys up condos being foreclosed with the appropriate name of "Condo Vultures," who declares: "That's capitalism!"

Moore makes the argument that a system run by greed, competition, and profit-seeking above all will obviously ignore morality, social justice, and the negative impacts of an unregulated economy, and that stronger regulation, more progressive taxation (which Moore points out was the norm in the U.S. in the postwar period until the Reaganite era of the 1980s), and guaranteed rights to health care, education, and social welfare are minimal components of a just social system. To ground the latter argument in political history, Moore provides documentary footage of one of the last speeches of Franklin Roosevelt presenting an argument for a "second bill of rights" in his final State of the Union address, footage believed lost that Moore's researchers unearthed in an archive in South Carolina. In this forgotten speech, FDR urged legislation which would guarantee eight specific rights:

Employment, with a living wage
Food, clothing and leisure
Farmers' rights to a fair income
Freedom from unfair competition and monopolies
Housing
Medical care
Social security
Education.[44]

Other horrors of contemporary corporate capitalism documented in the film include the "Dead Peasants" insurance scheme whereby big corporations take out life insurance policies on workers and get to cash in the policy for themselves after the workers die, not sharing the benefits with the workers' family. Moore also exposes, in the mode of his former TV shows *TV Nation* and *The Outrageous Truth*, how a privately owned juvenile detention center owner bribed judges to get them to sentence juveniles to maximum sentences in his institution. For positive looks at alternatives to capitalism, Moore shows how a successful occupation of Republic Windows and Doors in Chicago after the firm went out of business in December 2008 gave back control of their workplace to the workers themselves – interestingly, anticipating the Occupy movements of 2011 that became a global political force (see Kellner 2012).

Once again Michael Moore inserts himself into the center of the film and part of his concluding argument contrasts the situation of his father and his own family as members of a working class community in which strong unions and reasonable salaries made it possible for working class families to achieve what was recognized as a stable middle class existence and to realize the "American dream." Although Moore captures the moment of capitalist crisis with the near-collapse of the mortgage and financial system, he does not follow Marx in citing the endemic crisis tendencies in an unregulated capitalist economy, the injustice and horrors of exploitative industrial labor, or the argument central to the Marxist tradition of how capitalism inevitably leads to imperialism and war (see Marx 1867 in Marx-Engels 1978).

In *Capitalism: A Love Story,* Moore does, however, indicate what policies and individuals were largely responsible for the deregulation of the economy and global economic crisis of 2007, and criticizes Obama for bringing into his administration advocates of neoliberalism, who were in part responsible for the economic failures of the era, including Treasury Secretary Timothy Geithner, who was part of the failed Wall Street regulatory apparatus and Larry Summers, a neoliberal who was brought in as a top economic advisor. In interviews, Moore gives Obama the benefit of the doubt, and offers subtle pressure (perhaps with tongue in cheek), to follow his best progressive instincts, telling audiences that he hoped Obama had brought the neoliberals into his administration in the same way that some banks hire robbers to help them prevent future theft:

"Maybe that's what Obama's doing – he hired the people who robbed all the money to help him get it back. That's the optimistic version."[45]

His first Trump film *Michael Moore in TrumpLand* (2016) focuses on the 2016 U.S. presidential election campaign. The film is based on a one-person show that Moore held at the Murphy Theatre in Wilmington, Ohio, with the movie based on a recording of that performance over two nights in October, just before the election. Moore immediately released the film on DVD and streaming video and obviously intended his one-man performance to mobilize anti-Trump voters in the Midwest where he was performing his anti-Trump skits.

Surprisingly Moore, a strong Bernie Sanders supporter, spends more energy extolling Hillary Clinton than attacking Donald Trump. Moore compares Clinton to Pope Francis, arguing that she will be as activist in assuming the office as has been the Pope, and like the Pope, Clinton will take surprisingly progressive positions. Moore fantasizes that if elected she will release the pent-up idealism she's been clinging to since college, resulting in a flurry of landmark legislation reminiscent of Franklin D. Roosevelt's famous first 100 days.[46]

Moore' *Fahrenheit 11/9* (2018) is a predictably stronger attack on Trump than his previously low-budget one-man show documentary *Michael Moore in TrumpLand*. Again, Moore focuses on the 2016 United States presidential election, and then the subsequent presidency of Donald Trump. Moore shows montage of himself and Trump joking around with Roseanne Barr when both were on her TV show in the 1980s and then cuts to a creepy montage of Trump with his daughter Ivanka as he gushes about how beautiful she is, what great breasts, how he would date her if he wasn't her father and the usual sexist blather from Trump. An ugly montage captures Trump's racism with his demanding of the death penalty for the Central Park Five, his real estate company's efforts not to rent to people of color, and the racist remarks about Mexicans that launched his 2016 presidential campaign

Moore than switches gears to the crisis in his hometown of Flint Michigan resulting in the election of Republican governor Rick Snyder, who Moore holds responsible for shifting Flint's water supply to the Flint river that resulted in thousands of people poisoned with lead and dying of polluted water-related diseases. In a surprising section Barack Obama appears in Flint and one might imagine he would be the savior of the town, but instead he makes light of the situation before a hopeful crowd as he raises a glass of Flint water to barely sip it, as if the water was now safe to drink as the Republican governor claimed. The Flint residents register their disgust and disappointment with Obama, which one presumes Moore shares.

From the horrors of Trump and Flint, Moore shifts to West Virginia activists struggling for change and devotes a segment to West Virginia teachers who go on strike and who won their demands even when their union advised conciliation, sparking a national teachers' movement. Moore especially bonds with the survivors of the Parkland, Florida school shooting who organized a youth march against gun violence and campaigned for gun reform. They offer genuine hope for the future as does a cadre of young progressive activists running for Congress such as Alexandria Ocasio-Cortez, who won the Democratic primary in the Bronx and Queens and then the election, and Rashida Tlaib who won in Michigan.

The most shocking segment near the end of *Fahrenheit 11/9*, builds as Moore returns to Trump and his movement, showing their thuggery in rallies and suggesting that the U.S. could be on the verge of a fascist takeover at the same time as there are signs it is on the cusp of a progressive revolution. Moore recutting footage of Hitler speaking at Nazi rallies while seeming to show Trump's voice issuing from Hitler's mouth raised controversy. Moore also interviews a 99-year-old Nuremberg prosecutor who makes the parallels between Trump's movement and Hitler's shockingly clear, a danger Trump himself highlights with footage of him bragging that he may seek a third term or become President for Life.

Moore concludes with an argument that Trump is not the only problem U.S. democracy faces, but, in fact, the whole system is the problem: the Electoral College doesn't work in the interests of representation of the American in highly populated urban areas; over 100 million citizens failed to vote in the last election; in places like West Virginia where the Democrats won more votes in every county, the Republicans ended up getting more electoral college votes; and many people Moore interviewed have simply given up on the system. Moore concludes with a call for action, fueled by a sense of urgency and anger – qualities he is especially well-equipped to inspire, leading one critic to proclaim: "Watching *Fahrenheit 11/9* often feels like getting socked in the gut, but it leaves you with your blood pumping hard and fast, ready to get up off the floor and throw the next punch."[47]

Throughout the film, Moore makes and documents the point that Donald Trump has always committed acts of corruption and outrages in plain sight. "It's not that we don't see them; it's that he has a gift for getting people not to mind them," Moore comments. Indeed, after the release of Moore's films, the *New York Times* published a blockbuster expose of the finances of Fred Trump and the Trump family, which revealed that Fred Trump did not pay income taxes for decades and used his children as fronts for phony tax shelters.[48] No doubt but that the Trump family and the Trump presidency will provide material for blockbuster films and shocking documentaries for years to come and that Michael Moore and other filmmakers will be up to the challenge.

Notes

1 Melissa Quinn, "George Conway: Trump Administration Like a 'S–t Show in a Dumpster Fire.'" Washington Examiner, November 16, 2018 at www.washingto nexaminer.com/news/george-conway-trump-administration-like-a-s-t-show-in-a-dumpster-fire (accessed November 18, 2018).
2 The Reagan assassination attempt was perhaps the first time that a Hollywood movie triggered a presidential assassination spectacle, as the shooter thought his action

would win the affection of actress Jodie Foster who he had a crush on; see Herts-gaard 1988.

3 For negative appraisals of the Reagan presidency, see Hertsgaard 1988 and Kinsley 2014.

4 In the Iran-Contra Affair, the CIA directed a Central American drug ring to siphon profits to the counterrevolutionary forces, the Contras, who fought a war against the left-wing Sandinista government in Nicaragua since the U.S. Congress would not fund the enterprise. For a full discussion of the Iran-Contra affair, see Malcolm Byrne, Iran-Contra: Reagan's Scandal and the Unchecked Abuse of Presidential Power. Lawrence, Kansas: University Press of Kansas; Reprint edition, 2017.

5 Donald Trump had a similar fantasy of a "space force" which he wanted to create but so far nothing has come out of his fantasy.

6 "How Ronald Reagan Dealt With His Alzheimer's Diagnosis," Newsweek, April 2, 2016 at www.newsweek.com/ronald-reagan-alzheimers-disease-442711 (accessed September 10, 2019).

7 K.H. Jamieson (1989) "Context and the Creation of Meaning in the Advertising of the 1988 Presidential Campaign," American Behavioral Scientist, 32(4), 415–424.

8 A Google search for "scandals of the Reagan era" opens with a long list of the scandals followed by links to literally millions of sites; see www.google.com/search?source=h p&ei=6AR4XcaSDvOT0PEPltqBoAQ&q=scandals+of+the+Reagan+era&oq=scandals +of+the+Reagan+era&gs_l=psy-ab.12..33i22i29i30l2.4023.4023..10761... 0.0..0.96.96.1......0....2j1..gws-wiz.uhpJ9RJA-zw&ved=0ahUKEwjGpoLHicfkAhXzCT QIHRZtAEQQ4dUDCAs#spf=1568146672863 (accessed September 10, 2019).

9 Bush, however, had a complex background with Panama dictator Manuel Noriega who served as a source of support for the Nicaraguan contras during the Reagan administration and who allegedly sold drugs while delivering arms to the contras; see Howard Kohn and Vicki Monks, "The Dirty Secrets of George Bush. The Vice President's Illegal Operations," Rolling Stone, November 3, 1988 at www.rolling stone.com/politics/politics-news/the-dirty-secrets-of-george-bush-71927/ (accessed December 4, 2018).

10 As I am working on this study of media narratives of recent U.S. presidents in Decem-ber 2018, a media spectacle erupted after the death of George H.W. Bush at the age of 94. Glowing reviews were cast upon the mediascape of Bush's heroism in World War II as a young fighter pilot of 18, his remarkable political career and the achievements of his presidency including managing the end of the Cold War, creating an atmosphere of bi-partisan consensus, and serving the U.S. with honor. Yet the negatives of his presi-dency were played down in the mainstream U.S. media summaries of his life and presi-dency, and at present he is being celebrated as one of the great U.S. presidents of the modern era. For a critique of the George H.W. Bush presidency that stresses the nega-tive side of his legacy, see Kellner (1990: 239ff) and Parry (2004).

11 I was in Texas teaching philosophy at UT Austin in the 1990s, and heard Perot recount how he didn't like it that George H.W. Bush's three sons Jeb, George Jr, and Neil were involved in shady business deals and indeed Neil almost went to jail from his involvement in the Silverado Colorado scandal, while Jeb escaped from eco-nomic scandals he was involved with in Florida, including possibly illegal support for the Nicaraguan contras, while George W. had failed in business and was believed to be taking solace in heavy drinking. Perot eventually got almost 20% of the vote, which many believed tipped the balance from Bush to Clinton. For instance, on July 9, 2019 following Perot's death, Chris Wallace reported on Fox News that George H.W. Bush told him he believed that Perot cost him the election, a common view among Bushies; see www.foxnews.com/politics/chris-wallace-bush-41-felt-ross-perot-cost-him-re-election-against-bill-clinton (accessed September 10, 2019). Others believe that this is a myth as argued in the film by John Watkin and Eamon Harrington for FiveThirtyEight and ESPN Films called "the Perot Myth."

See the announcement of the film on October 6, 2016, at "The Ross Perot Myth. Deep Voodoo, Chicken Feathers and the 1992 Election" at https://fivethirtyeight. com/features/the-ross-perot-myth/ (accessed September 10, 2019).

12 See Dana Milbank's *Smashmouth: Two Years in the Gutter with Al Gore and George W. Bush* (2002).

13 For the astonishing story of the Bush gang election theft, see Kellner 2001 which also cites documents grounding the thumbnail sketch of Bush's life presented above. All of these stories are well-documented in websites like www.bushwatch.com, as well as a series of books that I draw upon in Kellner 2001, but the mainstream media prefer to neglect the more unsavory aspects of the life and times of George W. Bush, in favor of puff pieces on the rascal.

14 This would change by the end of his presidency when after a failed Iraq war, a collapsing economy in 2007–2008 that aided the election of Barack Obama, and eight years of ridicule that created a (correct) image of Bush as a jerk and buffoon, Bush's final presidential ratings were among the lowest in U.S. history upon his termination of office in 2008, with a low 22% approval rating; see "Bush's Final Approval Rating: 22%," CBS News, January 16, 2009 at www.cbsnews.com/news/ bushs-final-approval-rating-22-percent/ (accessed December 3, 2018). George W.'s positive media presentations after his father's death in 2018, and after two years of the really horrific presidency of Donald Trump will perhaps boost Bush Jr.'s standing with the public in future years.

15 My favorite book on Prescott Bush and the Bush Dynasty is Robert Parry, *Secrecy & Privilege: Rise of the Bush Dynasty from Watergate to Iraq* (Washington, DC: The Media Consortium, 2004) which is consistent with the research I've done for my trilogy of books on the Bush–Cheney Gang (see Kellner 2001, 2003, 2005). A search on Amazon for popular books on the Bush dynasty include texts by right-wing anti-Bush critics that surprisingly overlap in substance with critique of the Bush dynasty from the left, including books by respectable conservative Kevin Phillips, best-selling popular author Kitty Kelley, and notorious Republican operative arrested in the Trump-Russia-WikiLeaks scandal Roger Stone (and co-author Saint John Hunt); see the Amazon page on "the Bush Dynasty" at www.amazon.com/s?k=the+bush+dynas ty&i=stripbooks&crid=2N41QB0OX9CRX&sprefix=The+Bush+dyn%2Cstripbooks %2C189&ref=nb_sb_ss_i_1_12 (accessed September 10, 2019).

16 I could find no biography of George Herbert Walker but information on his life is found in Parry 2004 and the other Bush dynasty books I list in note 15 and there are also Internet sources on George Herbert Walker (see the Wikipedia entry listed at https://en.wiki pedia.org/wiki/George_Herbert_Walker (accessed September 11, 2019).

17 *Truth* (2015), a fictionalized account on Bush's missing year directed by James Vanderbilt, shows Dan Rather attempting to document the scandal and then getting fired from CBS News, after an illustrious career, because he allegedly put out an erroneous story concerning Bush's missing year.

18 For the insider trading allegations, widely circulated in the Texas press during Bush's first run for governor against Ann Richards, see Hatfield 2000 and Ivins and Dubose 2000; for an update on the story by investigative reporter Knut Royce, released on the Center for Public Integrity website, see "Bush's Insider Connections Preceded Huge Profit on Stock Deal" at www.public-i.org/story_01_040400.htm (accessed January 22, 2018).

19 See the critics' consensus at the *Rotten Tomatoes* film review site at www.rottentoma toes.com/m/w_2008/ (accessed September 11, 2019).

20 "Halliburton's Iraq Role Expands," *BBC News*. May 7, 2003. Archived from the original on May 25, 2006. Retrieved April 28, 2006.

21 AFP, "Halliburton, KBR Sued for Unsafe Conditions at Iraq Base." *Business and Human Rights Resource Center*, December 5, 2008 at www.business-humanrights.org/ en/halliburton-kbr-sued-for-unsafe-conditions-at-iraq-base (accessed September 11, 2019).

22 I will discuss media spectacle and the Obama presidency below through the prisms of documentary films and books that appeared as he was running for president in 2007–2008 and into his presidency.

23 In a December 11, 2018 showing of *The Front Runner* at the Hammer Museum in Los Angeles, which I attended, Reitman recounted how he came personally to know Hart and his wife, Lee, as well as Donna Rice, and how he discussed the film and presented showings for them, gaining their approval.

24 See Bai 2014 and James Fallow, "Was Gary Hart Set Up?
     What Are We to Make of the Deathbed Confession of the Political Operative Lee Atwater, Newly Revealed, that He Staged the Events that Brought Down the Democratic Candidate in 1987?" The Atlantic, November 2018 at www.theatlantic.com/magazine/archive/2018/11/was-gary-hart-set-up/570802/ (accessed September 18, 2014). In the Hammer Museum Q&A which I reference in the note above, Reitman noted the Atwater confession, but seemed to indicate that he did not give much credence to the story. In any case, the shadowy role of Donna Rice in the film is in my opinion a defect and given Lee Atwater's history and the trajectory of "smashmouth" politics over the past decades there is good reason to believe that Hart was the victim of political dirty tricks.

25 On my concept of media spectacle, see Kellner 2001, 2003a, 2003b, 2005, 2008.

26 Sean Redmond (2014) astutely notes that these categories of celebrity might overlap.

27 The DVD of President *Barack Obama: The Man and His Journey* contains an interesting interview with Director Maria Arista-Howard and two producers that highlights the speed with which they produced and released the film, beginning in March 2008 and completing it in time for the election campaign.

28 The Citizens United Productions group had earlier in 2008 produced *Hillary: The Movie*, thinking Hillary Clinton was going to be the Democratic Party candidate, and then rushed into production an anti-Obama polemic when it appeared he could win the Democratic Party nomination. In 2012, Citizens United released an anti-Obama Film *The Hope and the Change* which they distributed to activists and paid to air on TV.

29 I have a similar analysis of how Obama mastered media spectacle and deployed old and new media to become the world's most famous celebrity and to mobilize support to win the presidency; see Douglas Kellner, "Barack Obama and Celebrity Spectacle." *International Journal of Communication*, Vol. 3 (2009): 1–20 at http://ijoc.org/ojs/index.php/ijoc/article/view/559/350 (accessed September 18, 2014).

30 Alex Jones continued to do a syndicated radio show, participates in public access television, makes films, and is an active Internet presence; see http://en.wikipedia.org/wiki/Alex_Jones_(radio_host) (accessed September 18, 2014). However, in 2019, Jones was banned from Roku, Facebook, Instangram, and other social media sites for disseminating hate speech. See Sarah Wells, "Here Are the Platforms that Have Banned Infowars so Far," August 8, 2018 at https://techcrunch.com/2018/08/08/all-the-platforms-that-have-banned-infowars/2018/08/08/all-the-platforms-that-have-banned-infowars/ (accessed October 29, 2019).

31 I provide accounts of the O.J. Simpson trial and the Clinton sex/impeachment scandal in the mid-1990s in Media Spectacle (Kellner 2003b); engage the stolen election of 2000 in the Bush/Gore presidential campaign in *Grand Theft 2000* (Kellner 2001); and describe the 9/11 terrorist attacks and their aftermath in From 9/11 to Terror War (Kellner 2003b).

32 See D'Antonio, 2015; Blair, 2000; Kranish and Fisher 2016. Blair's chapter on "Born to Compete," op. cit., pp. 223ff., documents Trump's competitiveness and drive for success at an early age.

33 Marc Fisher, Will Hobson, "Donald Trump 'pretends to be his own spokesman to boast about himself.' Some reporters found the calls disturbing or even creepy; others thought they were just examples of Trump being playful." *The Independent*, May 13,

2016 at http://www.independent.co.uk/news/world/americas/us-elections/donald-trump-pretends-to-be-his-own-spokesman-to-boast-about-himself-a7027991.html (accessed August 9, 2016).

34 For my take on celebrity politics and the implosion of entertainment and politics in U.S. society, see Kellner 2015: 114–134. On celebrity politics, see also Wheeler 2013. One of the best studies of Trump, the media, and his long cultivation and exploitation of celebrity is found in O'Brien 2005.

35 Trump's book *The Art of the Deal*, co-written with Tony Schwartz (2005 [1987]), helped introduce him to a national audience and is a key source of the Trump mythology; see Blair, op. cit., 380ff.

36 Gaspin was quoted in CNN, "All Business. The Essential Donald Trump." September 5, 2016.

37 *Quotations From Chairman Trump*, Pogash, Ed. (2016: 30, 152, 153).

38 For an excellent analysis of Trump's appearances on Fox and Friends, see Poniewozik (2019: 159ff).

39 Apparently Trump reciprocates his support from *Fox & Friends* every morning by calling into the program frequently. Trump also reportedly has the *Fox News* channel on all day long and spends hours viewing its coverage of him, leading commentators to note that not only does *Fox News* support Trump, but they also influence him; see James Poniewozik, "Watching '*Fox & Friends*,' Trump Sees a Two-Way Mirror,' *New York Times*, at https://www.nytimes.com/2017/07/19/arts/television/donald-trump-fox-friends.html (accessed on October 30, 2019).

40 Ravi Somaiya, "Trump's Wealth and Early Poll Numbers Complicate News Media's Coverage Decisions." The New York Times, July 24, 2015 at www.nytimes.com/2015/07/25/business/media/donald-trumps-wealth-and-poll-numbers-complicate-news-medias-coverage.html (accessed July 22, 2016). Later, there were reports that Trump received $3–5 billion of free media time during his 2016 presidential campaign, as documented in a Google search on this topic on August 3, 2018 at www.google.com/search?source=hp&ei=jp5kW8-JJa2V0PEPsu2t2Ao&q=Trump+received+over+%243+billion+of+free+media+time+during+his+2016+presidential+campaign&oq=Trump+received+over+%243+billion+of+free+media+time+during+his+2016+presi dential+campaign&gs_l=psyab.12...2942.2942.0.3758.3.2.0.0.0.0.79.79.1.2.0....0...1c..64.psy-ab..1.0.0.0...86.00ElM-S99jQ-.

41 For the story of Trump's financial downfall and near collapse in the 1980s and 1990s, see the detailed and well-documented narratives in Barrett, op. cit.; John O'Donnell and James Rutherford, *Trumped!: The Inside Story of the Real Donald Trump – His Cunning Rise and Spectacular Fall*. New York: Simon and Schuster, 1991; D'Antonio 2015; Kranish and Fisher, op. cit.

42 As it turns out, Trump was impeached by the House of Representatives but was not impeached by the Republican-controlled Senate and continues as President as I correct these page proofs in March 2020.

43 For my earlier comprehensive analysis of Moore's films, see *Cinema Wars* (Kellner 2010), Chapter 3.

44 Ken Burns 2014 documentary series *The Roosevelts* ends with this list of human rights that FDR believed needed to secure in the future.

45 Michael Moore, cited in Alec MacGillis, "For 'Capitalism,' Moore Sells Short Politicians of All Denominations," *Washington Post*, September 16, 2009 at www.washingtonpost.com/wp-dyn/content/article/2009/09/15/AR2009091503314.html (accessed December 15, 2009). In a generally sympathetic review in Cineaste (Summer 2010: 51), Gary Crowdus notes that a "standard criticism of Moore's latest film has been that, no matter how compelling a case it makes against capitalism, it offers 'no solutions.'"

46 Moore has a strong streak of pragmatism and just before the highly contested 2000 election in a showing of his films at the Director's Guild in Los Angeles, I witnessed

Moore making a plea for Nader supporters, like himself, to vote for Al Gore in the swing states of Florida and New Hampshire, even though he had been a strong supporter of Nader and the Green Party. Moore was right as Bush was awarded Florida and the presidency by his Daddy's Supreme Court and given the presidency in a controversial decision. Nader was seen as a spoiler and his political career tanked. On the stolen election of 2000, see Kellner 2001.

47 Sam Adams, "Michael Moore's New Movie Is a Much-Needed Punch to the Gut. *Fahrenheit 11/9* is a rousing piece of propaganda and a worthy successor to the highest-grossing documentary of all time." Truth Out, September 7, 2018 at https://slate.com/culture/2018/09/fahrenheit-11-9-review-michael-moores-trump-movie-is-rousing-propaganda.html (accessed October 30, 2019).

48 David Barstow, Suzanne Collins, and Russ Buettner, "Trump Engaged in Suspect Tax Schemes as He Reaped Riches From His Father. The President Has Long Sold Himself as a Self-Made Billionaire, but a Times Investigation Found that He Received at least $413 Million in Today's Dollars from His Father's Real Estate Empire, Much of It through Tax Dodges in the 1990s." *The New York Times*, October 2, 2018 at https://www.nytimes.com/interactive/2018/10/02/us/politics/donald-trump-tax-schemes-fred-trump.html (accessed November 30, 2019).

8

FANTASY, TECHNOCULTURE, AND DYSTOPIA

Since the 1970s, media culture has been feeding on a rich tradition of fantasy literature and stories, myths, and legends that resurrect heroes of a long-forgotten past for entertainment and moral guidance in a degraded and confused present world, as well as creating new narratives and forms of fantasy. Following the trauma of Vietnam, the *Star Wars* films nourished fantasies of adventure and redemption in a mythic world where the distinction between Good and Evil was clear, heroes were paragons of virtue and villains embodiments of malevolence. *Superman, Batman, Conan, The Hulk*, and other cycles of superhero films drawn from DC and Marvel comics have nourished fantasies that powerful figures would triumph over evil and maintain order and stability.

In this chapter, I discuss the popular genres of science fiction and fantasy to show how representations of the future in these genres can illuminate the present, as well as anticipate future trends. It is perhaps Peter Jackson and his colleagues' *Lord of the Rings* (hereafter *LOTR*) cycle that goes furthest in providing a fully developed alternative fantasy world that provides moral instruction, compelling mythical narratives, and epic transcendence of the challenges of the contemporary world, and so I begin this chapter with analysis of Jackson's film cycle of the beloved Tolkien epic. I follow with a discussion of "David Cronenberg, the technoculture, and the new flesh," which engage the horrors of out of control technologies that are creating new forms of human life and visions of a frightening future.

I then discuss how optimistic utopian visions of the future in a certain type of traditional science fiction have been largely supplanted by more negative dystopic visions of the future in the *Blade Runner* films. I argue that these visions of the future often involve contemporary debates over race, gender, class, the environment, and politics.

Fantasy entertainment as political allegory: reading *LOTR*

Certainly, the *LOTR* trilogy has been the most popular, acclaimed, and fetishized film cycle of the twenty-first century, which has intensified and expanded Tolkien readership for the novels that are the basis of the cinematic epic, while generating a devoted following for the films. In this study, I counter the reading that *LOTR* films are mere escapist fantasy and argue that they reproduce the dominant conservative and patriarchal militarist ideology manifest in the United States and elsewhere during the past years and should be read in the light of the epochal Terror War still raging to help grasp its power and effects, as well as to decode their ideological subtexts. Although Tolkien scorned allegorical readings of his *LOTR*, I assert that the novels and film cycle can be read as socio-political and moral-existential allegory that articulates conservative ideology of the present age.[1] Of course, the text is highly polysemic, subject to multiple readings, and has been widely read as religious allegory, a reading whose popularity I will take as symptomatic of its conservative ideological underpinnings.

As a moral-existential allegory, *LOTR* relates to the German *Bildungsroman* theme of maturity and development.[2] Like the figures in Joseph Campbell hero's myth,[3] the young heroes of *LOTR* have adventures, undergo challenges, and grow and mature into exemplary moral figures and their relationships and fellowship convey specific social values, a range of which I engage in this study. As a political allegory, both the novels and films are clearly conservative attacks on industrial and technological modernity, yearning for an idealized past of stable communities, social hierarchy, and romantic attachment to the soil and earth. The thematics, as I will highlight, have profound similarities to Nazi ideology and the films articulate at the time of their release (2001–2003) with the patriarchal conservativism and crusading militarism of the George W. Bush/ Cheney administration (2001–2008). Indeed, I will argue that despite their contradictions, complexities, and positive aspects, *LOTR* film cycle provides ideological sustenance for aggressive rightwing conservativism and militarism.[4]

Tolkien's *LOTR* fantasy novels were written during an epoch of world war and the rise of totalitarian systems that threatened democratic countries like England who were forced to enter into alliances to defend themselves against fascism. Although the film cycle was largely conceived and begun before the September 11, 2001, terror attacks on the United States, their release and reception followed the events and the context of its reception has been within a Terror War that has been raging since the September 11 spectacle of terror. In this context, the film cycle can be seen as projecting a crusading militarism that celebrates feudal values, social hierarchy, patriarchal masculinism, and a deeply conservative vision and critique of the modern world. By interrogating the narrative, discourses, cinematic spectacle, and specific film stories, sequences, and scenes of the film cycle, I will unfold the "political unconscious" of the cinematic epic and its allegorical articulations of highly conservative notions of gender, sexuality, race, class, and politics. Utilizing a multiperspectivist approach, I will also be interested in articulating the ambiguities and contradictions of the film, the tensions with Tolkien's novel, and its reception and critical and audience response. My main interest in the film cycle and its reception is to use the material to provide a diagnostic critique of the contemporary era, illuminating patriarchal, conservative, and militarist ideologies.

From this diagnostic perspective, popular films provide important insights into the psychological, socio-political, and ideological make-up of a society or culture at a given point in history. Reading films diagnostically allows one to gain insights into social problems and conflicts, and to appraise the dominant ideologies and emergent oppositional forces. Moreover, diagnostic critique enables one to perceive the limitations and pathologies of mainstream conservative and liberal political ideologies, as well as oppositional ones. This interpretive approach involves a dialectic of text and context, using texts to read social realities and context to help situate and interpret key films of the epoch.

LOTR films were illustrative of a global fantasy production machine with a creative team drawn from all over the English-speaking world. The novel cycle that inspired the films was penned by English writer J.R.R. Tolkien; the film was funded by American corporations like Miramax and Time Warner; the director, writers, and production crew were largely from New Zealand where the films were shot; and actors came from throughout the English-speaking world. The global popularity of *LOTR* films was related to a deep need for fantasy, escapism into alternative worlds, and distractions from the turbulent and distressing conflicts of the contemporary era, as well to the enticements of a technologically dazzling cinematic epic machine generating a fully-articulated fantasy universe. Yet, as I argue, the "escape" was precisely into the tentacles of conservative ideologies.

Shire, Gemeinschaft and *The Fellowship of the Ring*

The film trilogy in *LOTR* begins with *The Fellowship of the Ring* (2001), which opens with a Prologue announcing that "the world has changed" and the old ways have been lost forever, a conservative lament that pervades the cycle. A narrator tells the story of the Rings that were forged to give leaders of respective human, dwarf, and elf worlds the power and wisdom to govern successfully. This envisaged idyllic world, however, is threatened by a Master Ring, the One Ring, which was produced by the Dark Lord Sauron to give him power over all domains. His attempt to control the world led to an alliance of peoples and nations threatened, and to a war against him in which Sauron was defeated and the Ring passed into the hands of a human, Isildur, the ruler of Gondor.

The Prologue in both Tolkien's novel and the film takes place in a long past prehistory, evoking a mythic time that is being destroyed by the advent of modernity. Tolkien's project, in part, was to create a specifically English mythology to compete with German and other European mythologies, although, curiously, his Ring story, and how the Ring was produced and corrupted, was remarkably similar to Richard Wagner's reworking of the Nibelungen Saga in his highly Germanic operatic Ring cycle. Jackson and his crew are faithful to the mythic and epic scale of Tolkien's saga, as was Fritz Lang in his two-part cinematic rendition of the Nibelungen tales (1924), a high cinematic level to which Jackson and company aspire.

Isildur is corrupted and destroyed by the Ring and it is lost in a lake. Much later, the Ring is found by a hobbit, Gollum, who is obsessed and ultimately ruined by the Ring. After years of exile, Gollum loses the Ring in an isolated mountain where it is found by another hobbit, Bilbo Baggins (Ian Holm). Baggins, seemingly oblivious to its corruptive force, takes the Ring and returns to his home in the Shire, a land in Tolkien's imaginary Middle Earth, which most scholars and fans recognize as a fantasy vision of Middle Merry Olde England. The Shire is a Gemeinschaft, or organic community of the sort valorized by conservatives against the intrusion of *Gesellschaft*, the encroaching industrial society. I will argue that Jackson's *LOTR* films share this conservative *gemeinschaftlich* ideological vision and that the trilogy as a whole can be read as a critique of industrial and technological modernity – a somewhat ironic critical vision in view of the astonishingly complex cinematic technology that went into the film cycle's creation. Indeed, Tolkien's narrative and Jackson and company's adaptation provides a vision of a fall from harmony, community, peace, and stable values into an anarchic, violent, and hostile world – exactly the vision of modernity projected by conservatives since the 18th century or earlier.

The hobbits are introduced as small, good-natured folk who love hearth and home, a good smoke and a good brew. Baggins returns to pen *A Hobbit's Tale* and his nephew Frodo (Elijah Wood) is excited by the visit of the old wizard Gandalf (Ian McKellen) who arrives to celebrate Baggins' 111th birthday. Baggins seeks adventure and leaves the Shire, giving his house and the Ring to Frodo, after which an uneasy Gandalf travels to read the account of Isildur, which conveys the story of Sauron's Ring and its dangers. Gandalf intuits the return of Sauron and tells Frodo that the Ring is dangerous and that they must take it from the Shire and hide it until Gandalf receives further instruction concerning how to deal with the problem. Another hobbit, the gardener Sam (Sean Astin), overhears the story of the Ring, and Gandalf decrees that Sam and Frodo together leave the Shire to hide the Ring from Sauron.

On their way to an inn, The Prancing Pony, where they are to meet Gandalf, Sam and Frodo are pursued by nine faceless riders, the Ringwraithes or Nazgul, who represent the nine Kings who lost the power of their original Rings when Sauron gained the one Ring. They are now his slaves and are on a mission to retrieve the Ring for him. Running from the faceless men in black on black horses, Sam and Frodo encounter fellow young hobbits Merry (Dominic Monaghan) and Pippin (Billy Boyd) stealing food and they are chased together by the farmer and the Nazguls. In a frightening scene, the black-clad Riders suddenly attack the hobbits, riding on black horses, hissing, and chasing the terrorized hobbits through the woods. Seen through the eyes of the diminutive hobbits, the Black Riders appear as dangerous forces of evil.

In the inn, some of the hobbits fill up on excessive amounts of brew while a mysterious cloaked man called "Strider" (Viggo Mortensen) smokes and watches over the proceedings. He reveals himself to be a friend and when the Men in Black come for the hobbits, he tries to help them. A frightened Frodo puts on the Ring to become invisible and connects with Sauron who has psychic access to those who put on the Ring. Seeing Sauron's Eye, shaped like a flaming vagina, Frodo learns the fearful power of the Ring but also the danger that threatens them if Sauron is to get the Ring.

In a parallel story, Gandalf goes to his old friend the wizard Saruman the White to help get advice concerning what to do about the dangers of the Ring. Saruman, however, has gone over to Sauron's side and warns Gandalf that their only chance of survival and maintaining power is to merge with Sauron and get hold of the Ring. Resurrecting Cold War imagery, Saruman (Christopher Lee) looks like the evil Russian Rasputin with his tall, emaciated stick-beard, maniacal eyes, and over-all aura of Evil. Saruman and Gandalf fight and Gandalf barely escapes alive. We also see that Sauron is breeding a monstrous race of fighters by crossing orcs and goblins. They appear as the horrible and bestial Uruk-hai, with extremely bad teeth, dark swarthy skin with awful complexion, and violent and barbarian behavior. Both the orcs, whom Sauron created by torturing and mutilating humans, and the Uruk-hai whom Saruman has bred, represent fears of eugenics and genetic engineering, such as were visualized by the Nazis and are taking form in the cloning laboratories of the present. The beasts are extremely ugly and menacing killing machines and can serve to represent a threat from massified non-Western peoples of color, a fear that haunted the Nazis and a variety of conservatives and liberals.

Sensing the dangers of Sauron's hordes, Gandalf, the four hobbits, and Strider travel to the Elf Kingdom Rivendell where they meet up with the elf Legolas (Orlando Bloom), the dwarf Gimli (John Rhys-Davies), and the human Boromir (Sean Bean). The mysterious Strider, who is soon revealed as Aragorn, the relative of Isildur and rightful heir to Gondor, meets up with the elf-princess Arwen (Liv Tyler), who has chosen to sacrifice her immortality to be with the human she loves. While Arwen will appear occasionally throughout the epic, it is basically a male adventure with little space for women.

Aragorn must overcome his fear and hesitancy and assume the sword of his father and prove himself in war. In the Elf Kingdom, the groups congregates in the Council of the King Elrond where they debate what to do with the Ring. While the group bickers over who will take the Ring to destroy it in the fires of Mount Doom in Sauron's Kingdom of Mordor where it was forged, Frodo assumes responsibility and Elrond declares the rest of the crew "Nine Companions, the Fellowship of the Ring." Elrond gives Aragorn and the hobbits Merry and Pippin daggers and their ascendant to masculinity will involve using the dagger to successfully kill villains, hardly a healthy model of male socialization and maturation.

At first the Fellowship is divided into squabbling groups with elves and dwarves hostile toward each other and the hobbits suspicious of all. Tolkien is extremely racialist, creating races and different species that have specifically delineated features and that are often hostile to other groups, and these species worlds are replicated in Jackson's film. Dwarves are somewhat shorter and rougher than humans and the hobbits are diminutive and childlike, while the elves are tall, immortal beings. Humans and others contemptuously refer to hobbits as "Halflings," and groups like elves and dwarves exhibit intense distrust and hostility toward each other. The squabbling groups in the Fellowship must overcome their differences and bond together to fight Sauron and his monsters, whose armies are ruthless killers and devoid of any moral scruples.

The Fellowship and positive figures in Jackson's trilogy are largely white, often with blond hair and/or blue eyes, signifying distinctly Aryan configurations, while the villains are invariably dark in complexion or soul, setting up a deeply racist problematic that I will engage in detail. While Gandalf appeared at first to be the wise leader, he is often uncertain and as the Fellowship begins the long trek to Mordor to destroy the Ring, they get lost, almost die in snowy mountainous trails, become entangled in the Caves of Moria, and encounter numerous enemies. In the Caves of Moria, Gandalf is pursued by a fire-monster Balrog who appears to kill him in a fiery blast as he hurtles into the pits of a mountain, seemingly consumed by flames. Another human member of the Fellowship, Boromir, is shown to be overly attracted to the Ring, wanting to use it to defeat Sauron and protect his Kingdom. Indeed, Boromir is so attracted to its power that he is corrupted, trying to steal it from Frodo and use it for himself. Boromir is shot in battle and his death represents another cautionary warning how the Ring as a sign of absolute power corrupts and destroys those who want it for questionable purposes.

Through their travels and battles, the group is bonded together into a true Fellowship, where it is All for One, and One for All. Each member achieves heroic deeds and is recognized by others in the group as a valuable member. While the Council of Elrond appeared to be democratic and the Fellowship could debate and make choices, as they get bonded in battle, natural leaders come to the fore and in the succeeding episodes democracy disappears, as if it is a conflicted, ineffectual way of dealing with problems and making decisions. The novel and film cycle suggests that only a few individuals are moral enough to resist the temptations of power (i.e. the Ring) and that superior individuals will rise to leadership and eventually produce a King and stable social structure.

The politics are thus on the whole highly antidemocratic and conservative. A white-clad and ethereal elf-queen, Galadriel (Cate Blanchett), warns Frodo of the great dangers of the Ring and herself appears monstrous when she gets too close to it, dramatizing the self-transforming and corruptive power of the Ring.

Curiously, the two major female characters in the novel and film cycle are elves, presented as idealized embodiments of female virtue, although in the brief scene where she is attracted by the Ring, Galadriel presents the dangerous side of women, and later images will present extremely sexist spectacles of female castration in the spider Shelob. Thus, on the whole, the patriarchal cycle exhibits extremely problematical representations of women.

The narrative projects dangers of a total destruction of established societies and as the story proceeds it produces an aura of unease and fear, uncannily like the mood in the United States and other Western countries threatened by terrorism in the post-9/11 environment. Like George W. Bush, *LOTR* promotes a bifurcated metaphysical division between Good and Evil and advances a notion of Absolute Evil. Like the Bush/Cheney administration, *LOTR* films could help generate paranoia and anxiety about dire threats from the East and Evil Ones, as bin Laden, al Qaeda, and assorted terrorist groups proclaimed Jihad against the United States and the West. Jackson's film cycle, largely conceived and produced pre-9/11, thus uncannily resonated with the mood of the time, perhaps increasing fear and the need for authoritarian leadership, while embodying notions of a "clash of civilizations" and privileging military action as the most effective mode of fighting "evil."

As the Fellowship leaves the Elf Kingdom and undergoes more battles with Sauron's legions as they weave toward Mordor, the members are separated from each other, with Merry and Pippin captured by the Uruk-hai, and Frodo and Sam separated from the others, soldiering on alone. Yet the essential bonding has taken place through common suffering and military action and henceforth the Fellowship is a *Bruderbunden*, a Band of Brothers, tightly bound together to fight the forces of Evil and complete their mission.[5]

Mountains, Bruderbunden, and *The Two Towers*

The Two Towers (2002) opens in media res with gorgeous panoramic shots of mountains, and much of the action in the film will take place in high cliffs, valleys, elevated towers, hillside fortresses and caves. A popular genre of Nazi cinema unfolded in mountains, which filmmakers like Leni Riefenstahl presented as transcendent sites of glorious nature where Volkish Aryans could be free and united in a Gemeinschaft with like-minded people. Threatening forces would emerge to disturb the idyll, but good Aryan heroes would triumph and restore the community to peace, order, and fascist bliss. Riefenstahl's 1932 film *Das Blaue Licht (The Blue Light)*, for instance, shows a beautiful young woman, played by Riefenstahl herself, saving an idyllic mountain town from a mysterious blue light that led men to death, a film that so inspired Hitler he asked her to lead his film industry.

The Two Towers opens with the main characters of the Gemeinschaft and Fellowship already expelled from paradise and separated into three groups on their perilous quest to defeat the forces of evil. Eschewing narrative preamble, the opening montage quickly cuts to a replay of Gandalf's battle with the fire-breathing monster Balrog in the first film. The exploding flames that appear to consume Gandalf evoke the images of the fiery and hellish images of the industrial forges in the film cycle that produce iron and thus destroy preindustrial modernity and threaten the earth itself. This visual and thematic attack on industrial production and modernity stands at the center of *The Two Towers* and Jackson's entire trilogy, in a faithful reprise of Tolkien's vision.

Appearing to be consumed in fire in the first film of the trilogy, magically, Gandalf is resurrected as Gandalf the White, reborn as an even greater symbol of Good, a metamorphosis signaled by the religious glow of light and a white halo that bathes his transformed face, drawing on religious iconography to present the very white and patriarchal symbol of Good. Eschewing the visual racism that plagued *Star Wars* with its all-too-black Darth Vader, *The Two Towers* pits Gandalf against a very White Lord Saruman, although it is clear from the narrative and to much of the audience that Saruman is a Force of Evil and has gone over to the Dark Side, serving Sauron, the Lord of Darkness himself and the very embodiment of absolute evil.

Women have little part in the Fellowship/Bruderbund. Aragorn, who will emerge as a major figure in the trilogy, is separated in this episode from the hobbits and is portrayed as the romantic love interest of the Rohan King's daughter Eowyn (Miranda Otto). Flashbacks, however, establish that Aragorn's true love is the elf princess Arwen who has renounced elfish immortality to be with him. The hopeless love of Eowyn will enable her in the following film to become a warrior heroine, but the second installment sacrifices focus on romance for the more male pursuits of valor and military heroism.

In fact, neither Tolkien's novels nor Jackson's films have any complex heterosexual relationships, sexuality, or even erotic desire and conflict. While novelists like Jane Austin and Henry James eschew portraying sexual relations, their work teems with sexual desire, tensions, conflicts, and ambiguities – exactly like in life. In *LOTR*, however, there is no overt sexuality or heterosexual relationships besides chaste and extremely conventional roles and depictions (until, perhaps, the third film, which provides a powerful visual assault on female sexuality in the figure of the Spider monster Shelob).

Separated into three groups, Frodo and Sam journey towards Mordor to dispose of the Ring once and all. They are pursued by the mysterious Gollum (Andy Serkis), a computer-generated character who provides much of the narrative tension of the film. The story will reveal that Gollum was formerly a hobbit named Smeagol who got possession of the Ring and was corrupted by its power. He has become hideously deformed by the interaction, appearing like an emaciated and barely human survivor of the German concentration camps. Yet beneath the monster is a benign hobbit, wishing to do good, and the conflict between his good and bad side (a conceit also utilized in the *Star Wars* films) becomes a major focus of the narrative.

In general, Gollum provides a cautionary warning figure showing what obsession with the Ring and addiction to power can do to someone. Deprived of its power, he craves his "precious" talisman of power, although he knows its destructive force. Obviously, here we have a parable of addiction, and Gollum is a being torn apart by his need for the destructive substance. Captured by the two hobbits, Gollum agrees to lead them to Mordor if they will release him. During the course of *The Two Towers*, Frodo himself undergoes a Gollumesque conflict, torn between wanting to carry out his mission and destroy the Ring and yet seeking its power for himself. The conflicted and increasingly despondent Frodo is kept on mission by the steady and solid friendship of Sam, who shows that ordinary fellows can rise to the occasion and become heroes if they loyally serve their master and follow orders – a good conservative message to keep underlings in their place.

Meanwhile, freed from the orcs, Merry and Pippin wander through a mysterious forest where they are captured by the Ent Treebeard, who informs them that he is a forest herdsman, whose task is to protect the forest from destruction. Mixing traits of trees and humans, the Ents provide moments of comic relief as they stomp through the forest, protecting Merry and Pippin from danger, while enunciating solemn ecological pronouncements. The Ents kick in, like Birnam Wood in *Macbeth*, as they step forth to fight the army of Sauron whose minions they see as a threat to their dominion. Trees too are living, talking, and mobile beings, providing a vision of Nature as a living, breathing force, worthy of preservation, although also dangerous, as a tree catches the hobbits in its tentacles.

The vision of nature is on the whole complex and quite engaging in Tolkien's novels and Jackson's films and the ecological theme quite endeared audiences in the 1960s to Tolkien and in the contemporary period infuses Jackson's cinematic trilogy with a warm ecological glow. Yet the vision of ecology in the films is limited, showing the dangers to forests and the earth from industrialism and war, but yet celebrating the warfare that is a highly dangerous threat to the very survival of human beings and the earth.

While the action unfolds, Merry and Pippin find themselves in the forest with the Ents who warn them of dangers ahead and advise them to return to the Shire, expressing conservative traditionalism that affirms minding your own business and staying out of trouble. Pippin is taken by the advice and suggests they indeed return to the Shire, but Merry proclaims that they should join their comrades in battle and, of course, they chose the path of peril, danger, and eventually ascension to manhood through military valor.

In the DVD commentary and documentaries, Peter Jackson, his partner, Fran Walsh, and scriptwriter, Phillipa Boyens, go out of their way to proclaim that this passage has been misinterpreted as an embrace of militarism in Tolkien's novel and the film. Jackson and his colleagues insist in their commentary that Pippin and Merry's choice to soldier on to battle is not a pro-war message, but rather an injunction that there are some things worth fighting for, like the Good

War of World War II where the enemy was indeed a threat to life, liberty, and the pursuit of happiness, and that did threaten Europe, the United States, and much of the world with totalitarian domination. But the two hobbits' choice of war, and that of other more obviously militarist characters in the film, is not for a clear cause and good war against a determinate enemy, but rather a war against the Forces of Evil themselves. Indeterminate crusaders against Evil articulate in the contemporary moment in which the Jackson trilogy was globally released with the Bush/Cheney administration's war against terrorism, where you're either with us or against us fighting the Evil Ones and Evil itself – a vast panorama of enemies in which Saddam Hussein soon morphed into Osama bin Laden.

Yet the two coalitions fighting the key conflict at Helms Deep and in the final battle in *The Return of the King* are themselves both multicultural and disparate. While Saruman's army is presented as Evil, in the key scene where he recruits masses of ordinary townspeople and soldiers, the army is shown to consist of diverse groups of people coming together to join in the fight. The iconography of the scene, that Jackson and company highlight in their DVD commentary and interviews, is clearly that of Hitler at Nuremburg, casting a spell over the masses and leading a massified totalitarian horde to battle. And perhaps Tolkien had German fascism and Russian Communism in mind when he imagined the destruction of countries and peoples by evil political forces and evoked an alliance to fight and defeat them (although he vigorously proclaimed that he was not producing a political or religious allegory).

However, in *LOTR* film cycle there are no clear political referents in the battles, no specific political goals, and no politics except for fighting for land, achieving heroism, and, ultimately, restoring monarchy. There is little democracy in the film being fought for, and indeed the iconography is profoundly anti-democratic with wizards like Gandalf and heroes like Aragorn proclaiming higher truths and carrying out great deeds that lesser beings follow. The political structure throughout is that of feudal and premodern hierarchy with celebration of military valor as one of the highest forms of human achievement. The film trilogy is itself strongly militarist, spending tremendous amounts of time, energy, and money on creating the great battle scenes that were acclaimed by fans and uncritical critics. As I will argue in the next section, the trilogy on the whole is a celebration of military valor and heroism linked with valorizations of patriarchy, whiteness, and hierarchy, highly conservative themes that articulate the film with contemporary conservativism.

Indeed, there are few film cycles that have shown more bodies stabbed, shot with arrows, crushed by monsters, and killed off in a myriad of ways than *LOTR*. The trilogy is one of the bloodiest epics in contemporary cinema and celebrates military valor as the highest form of human virtue and necessary for survival in a world full of violence and evil. Yet to the film's credit, the cost of warfare is clearly shown and *The Twin Towers* has an extremely melancholy feeling to it. Faramir of Gondor notes after killing an enemy that his enemy's sense of duty was no less than his own, and asserts: "War has made corpses of us all."

Jackson's trilogy does not flinch from showing bloody killings, corpses strewn about on the battlefield, and the melancholy horrors of war. Few cinematic blockbusters have such a sense of the frailty of human life, where one stray arrow can mean death. Conflicts between courage and fear, and goodness and greed, lay at the heart of the narrative that has a strong sense of the mortality of human beings and the need for good character to survive in a violent and uncertain world to preserve fragile order and social stability.

Yet the evocation of finitude, contingency, and the frailty of human life is undercut somewhat in *The Return of the King* as Gandalf solemnly invokes belief in an afterlife, "another path" to higher states of being. Gandalf evokes the "White Shores" and beyond of the afterlife, bathed in a glow of white light, obvious invocations of a (white) Christian heaven and the possibilities of salvation. Indeed, the trilogy is teeming with Christian references to sin, redemption, and salvation, giving rise to a cottage industry of Tolkien Christian readings. But, as I will attempt to show in the next section, on the whole the trilogy has more to do with conservativism and militarism than faith and Christian redemption.

The Return of the King and triumph of conservatism

The Fellowship of the Ring (2001) appeared in the months following the September 11 terror attacks on the U.S. when battles against the forces of "evil" were being fought in Afghanistan and elsewhere in a world war in what the Bush/ Cheney administration proclaimed a global war against the Evil Ones and terrorism (see Kellner 2003). The marshalling of the Fellowship corresponded with the attempts at organization of a coalition to fight global terrorism by the Bush/ Cheney administration, and so the film resonated uncannily to key historical events of the era, which gave it extra relevance and force (although one could argue that the largely unilateralist and militarist Terror War waged by the Bush/ Cheney administration failed to learn the lessons of alliances and multilateralism from *LOTR*, leading to eventual identifications of Bush with Sauron.

The Two Towers (2002) appeared in the tense period between a seeming victory over bin Laden and al Qaeda in Afghanistan. Yet it was a period in which bin Laden and Taliban leaders remained at large, while the Bush/Cheney administration marshaled its energies for a big fight against Saddam Hussein and Iraq. The melancholy, unnamed apprehension, and anxious mourning of the second film thus also uncannily responded to its historical epoch. *The Return of the King* (2003) however, opened at the end of the year after Bush and Blair's largely unilateral militarist invasion and occupation of Iraq, about the time Saddam Hussein was captured, giving rise to momentary euphoria, that quickly died as the Iraqi insurgency greatly intensified its fight against the occupation.

At this moment, *The Return of the King*, arguably provides ideological ballast to Bush and Blair administration militarism, while ultimately legitimating military intervention in terms of its assault on dangerous and absolute Evil.

While *The Two Towers* takes place in a mountainous terrain and the dark night of the soul where superior beings can rise above the masses to become warrior heroes, or in the case of Frodo and Sam can fight temptation and lust for power to exemplify goodness, *The Return of the King* takes place on a vast canvas in which the epic quest of destroying the Ring of power is achieved, Sauron's minions are defeated, order and harmony are restored, the heroes mature and establish themselves and the narrative threads are pulled together.

Cinematically, *The Return of the King* is an epic paean to Whiteness and never before has White had such extravagant visual apotheosis, nor has it triumphed so completely in cinematic spectacle. The film unfolds a panorama of white clouds, snowcaps, towers and fortresses, tents, long flowing gowns worn by both men and women, and, of course, white faces bathed in a reverential halo of white light. Rarely has a film had so many blond-haired and/or blue-eyed characters, and even the darker-complexioned Caucasian characters often have their face suffused with a white glow to signify their goodness. There are even some white-faced/masked orcs in the film, although there are still many very black evil forces, including the darkest villain of all, Sauron, described as a Dark Lord, who lives in a Black Land and unleashes Black Riders, a faceless monster dressed in black, with a black flying dragon that looks like a pterodactyl.

In the film and the trilogy as a whole, Whiteness is affirmed as the sign of Good and Virtue while black is the color of evil and villainy in a passion play between the forces of Light and Darkness. There also seems to be an aesthetic in play in which the more virtuous characters are portrayed as beautiful, or at least attractive, or cute and homey like the hobbits, while the monsters are largely ugly and even hideous and repulsive. The idealized heroes and few women characters are portrayed in classical Western terms of beauty, while the evil ones are so extremely ugly that one can almost read the moral value of a character as to where they fit on a scale of Beauty to Ugly.

At first, it appears that the powerful army of Sauron will take the Gondorian stronghold of the very white fortress city Minas Tirith, which is assaulted by armies of orcs, bestial Trolls pulling back the springs for catapults to hurl boulders against its walls and towers, and a fire-breathing assault machine that pounds against its gates. Even Gandalf is pessimistic, believing that Frodo has been taken and that defeat is on its way, but Aragorn appears in a fleet of ships with an Army of the Dead which in the Battle of Pelennor Fields joins the Fellowship and their allies who together carry out an epic struggle against Sauron's Legion of Evil with its mechanized orc army, assorted Trolls and mutants, giant elephants, winged dragons, and other beasties.

Audaciously drawing on the imagery of Abel Gance's *J'Accuse* (1919) which showed legions of wraithlike spirits in a March of the Dead sequence bemoaning their senseless deaths on the battlefields of World War I, Peter Jackson's army of souls comes from a painful Purgatory and are mobilized by Aragorn, who promises to release them after the defeat of Sauron's legions. Transforming Gance's anti-war symbology into figures of military heroism gives away the militarist proclivities of the film trilogy, which invests its most energy and cinematic elan in the spectacular war scenes. The battle is also graced by Eagles, which are allies of the Coalition of the Willing, and eventually Gandalf will fly away with the Eagles, perhaps joining with another military force to provide a future hegemony of the Good against emergent evil forces in future wars.

As noted, the trilogy is an epic of militarist patriarchy as each hero solemnly takes up the sword in scenes bathed in white light and accompanied by operatic or soulful music. Militarism is the privileged route to Manhood and Virtue in *LOTR* and the manly character takes up the sword, displays valor and achieves honor, thus sending out the message that the sword and military is the best route for manhood and social validation.

In a parallel story, Sam and Frodo trek to Mount Doom to destroy the Ring. In one horrifying sequence, Frodo battles a horrible giant spider in a cave, evoking fear and loathing of female sexuality. The spider monster Shelob has what appears to be a threatening vagina detenta, classically signaling fear of castration. Curiously, the Eye of Sauron also appears as a flaming vagina, putting on display male fear of women and presenting images of the feminine as menacing and castrating, thus infusing the film cycle with infantile and harmful notions of female sexuality. Indeed, Jackson's *LOTR* cycle bifurcates its female characters into idealized female fantasy figures or symbolic images of castration, with the exception of Eowyn who becomes a Woman Warrior after she is spurned.

The spider entangles Frodo in its web and it looks like it might be curtains for the little hobbit who has been alienated from Sam by Gollum who convinces him that Sam wants the Ring for himself. But Sam turns out to be a loyal servant, stealthily taking the Ring away when Frodo is captured by Sauron's minions and then accompanying him through Sauron's territory and up Mount Doom. Just as Frodo fights temptation to throw the Ring into the fiery depths that will consume it, Gollum creeps up to snatch the Ring, and after a fight with Frodo, they both appear to fall off the top of the mountain into the fiery pit below, but Frodo emerges seconds later, intact and now a full-fledged hero and True Man, as he has carried out his task and defeated Evil.

Sam embraces him with joy and Frodo returns Sam's affection saying that "I'm glad to be with you Sam Gamgee, at the end of all this." After a series of manly embraces and visual homoerotic bonding, Sam fantasizes returning to the Shire and marrying Rosie Cotton, which he does to demonstrate that he and Frodo are not gay. The same cannot be so easily affirmed of Merry and Pippin who after the victory over Sauron's forces discover themselves still alive on the battlefield, upon which both have attained manhood, and fulsomely embrace and demonstrate their manly love.

Yet *LOTR* is on the narrative surface a heterosexual text and so Aragorn and Arwen marry in a triumph of Whiteness and Matrimony. When the couple reunite and then marry, the spectacle is bathed, as usual, with intense white light and their very white faces are brightly lit and gleaming. Aragorn declares that "Now comes the day of the King," establishing that all of the fighting was for the restoration of monarchy. The Royal Couple bow to the hobbits, Merry and Pippin, affirming their ascension to manhood and the audience is told that "the Fourth Age of Middle Earth, the Fellowship of the Ring, founded by friendship and love, has ended."

Before the audiences can return to Real Life, in a series of premature endings, Frodo and Sam return to the Shire, bathed in a warm glow of white light (although the crystal ball the Palintir revealed that there had been devastation and suffering while the boys were away becoming men, as is described in Tolkien's novel). Sam marries and has a family and Frodo writes *LOTR*, following Baggin's *Hobbit Tale*, and thus achieves his own patriarchal succession as the hobbit chronicler. The life of the writer is not so cheery, however, for Frodo appears despondent in the closing scenes and is shown at the end taking leave of Sam and his family and joining Gandalf on a ship for unknown adventures.

And so it is that the writer and the critic of *LOTR* do not live happily ever after but have further tales of the Battle between Good and Evil to recount and ideological extravaganzas to follow and critique. Novels and films are quite dissimilar, enable various readings, and have disparate effects in diverse social contexts. In an era of Terror War, *LOTR* enjoins patriarchal and crusading militarism that articulates with the Bush/Cheney administration's crusade against terrorism and post-2005 as yet not articulated Jeremiad tyranny.

In earlier historical periods, Tolkien's novels articulated politically with anti-German fascism in the 1930s and 1940s and with countercultural rebellions against the "system" in the 1960s and succeeding years. The story is rich and complex enough that it could also motivate alliances between forces of Good against Evil forces of the present, such as an alliance against the Bush/Cheney administration and its militarist agenda, or Trump as the Evil Lord Sauron.[6] The Ring could stand for capital and the ways that greed for money corrupt individuals. Yet the cinematic militarist and patriarchal spectacle of *LOTR* is so great that more progressive readings are undercut by the mis-en-scène and its presentation by Jackson and his crew. Moreover, the fetishistic attention to details is so loving, and the creation of an alternative universe is so involving that many viewers may miss the ideological subtexts and political unconscious of the film cycle altogether – that makes it an even more potentially powerful political force. It is thus a challenge for diagnostic critique to say the unsaid and articulate the often-mute meanings beneath the cinematic façade.

Canadian filmmaker David Cronenberg, a prophet and poet of the posthuman condition, has explored the dynamics of the emergent and ever-expanding technoculture, the implosion between technology and humans, and the challenges and paradoxes of living in a new high-tech world, and it is to his imaginative cinematic mappings of his nightmare visions of the future that we now turn.

David Cronenberg, the technoculture, and the new flesh

The battle for the mind will be fought in the video arena, the video-drome. The television screen is the retina of the mind's eye. Therefore, the television screen is part of the physical structure of the brain. There-fore, whatever appears on the television screen emerges as new experience for those that watch it. Therefore, television is reality, and reality is less than television.

(Professor Brian O'Blivion in Videodrome)

Words beget image and image is virus.

(William Burroughs, Naked Lunch)

The films of David Cronenberg contain terrifying visions of science and tech-nology creating new viruses, species, and implosions of technology and the human. While literature can evoke images of the novelties of a high-tech society and provide prescient warnings of the dangers of technoscience and culture, film and the visuals of media culture can vividly represent these perils and fears, which are in turn transmitted to popular audiences. Cronenberg uses multiple genres of the fantasy film to articulate contemporary anxieties and to present critical visions of potentially deadly effects resulting from the implosion of sci-ence, technology, capital, and everyday life. His films depict both mind and body (and their mysterious interactions) disintegrating and mutating out of con-trol under the impact of the emergent technoculture, biotechnology, and virtual reality. For Cronenberg, these forces wreak havoc in a hyperrationalized, func-tionalized, and hygienic social order unable to accommodate or deal with fren-zied transmutations of the human mind and body, proliferating disease, and hideous implosions of technology into the human.

Cronenberg's films can thus be read as allegories of a technosociety and cul-ture in which the mutations of science, technology, capital, and the human are producing new species, realities, and organizations of society and culture. Cap-turing the tensions and ambiguities of the new technoculture, Cronenberg tracks the invasion of science, technology, and capital into the inner recesses of the human and depicts the metamorphoses of cultures, minds, and bodies under the impact of new colonizing and transformative powers. Yet he is not a technophobe and shows how the forces of technoscience are producing new pleasures and potentials, as well as dangers and monstrosities.

Cronenberg's early films *Shivers* (1975) and *Rabid* (1976) provide frightening visions of deadly sexual epidemics and psychogenetic bodily mutations, where ordinary individuals are attacked by viral forces and undergo mutations of mind and body. In Cronenberg's films both mind and body, in mysterious interaction, disintegrate or mutate out of control and wreak havoc in a hyperrationalized social order unable to deal with frenzied bodily and social metamorphosis and proliferating disease.

While Cronenberg's early films dealt with fear of sexual disease and viral body invasion, his next cycle, *The Brood* (1979), *Scanners* (1980), and *Videodrome* (1982), present psychotropic and technological powers invading both the mind and the body, putting in question their nature and mutual interaction.[7] *Scanners*, for instance, presents new drugs creating destructive psychic powers while *Video-drome* shows technological invasion conquering mind and body at once in the creation of a new species that synthesizes the technological with the human. Going beyond McLuhan's vision of the media as the exteriorization of mind and body, Cronenberg explores ramifications of media interiorization in an era when media and new technologies are said to produce a implosion of truth, meaning, the masses, and the socio-political system which obliterates boundaries between truth and falsity, and reality and fantasy.

Cronenberg's subsequent films *The Dead Zone* (1983) and *The Fly* (1986) focus more obsessively on the specific roles of politics, science and technology in a new technocapitalist political economy. Most of his films, in different ways, present technology out of control, intersecting with the imperatives of capital accumulation to produce catastrophes for individuals and society. Consequently, Cronenberg naturally comes to make use of the horror, disaster, conspiracy, dystopic, and other fantasy genres that have become highly influential and popular.

Although Cronenberg sometimes presents himself as a Cartesian dualist in interviews, his films deconstruct the opposition between mind and body. Cronenberg's films represent the mind as subject to control by both psychic and material forces, while portraying the body as vulnerable to assault by cultural and technological forces, causing humans to mutate to horrific excess. *Scanners*, for instance, depicts new drugs creating destructive psychic powers, while *Videodrome* shows media culture and particularly television entering and conquering mind and body in the creation of a new techno-posthuman species. Cronenberg concretizes McLuhan's vision of the media as the exteriorization of mind and body that in turn collapse into the human, creating new configurations of experience and culture. He explores ramifications of technological interiorization in an era when media and technology are claimed to produce an implosion of meaning, the masses, and society, obliterating the boundaries between reality and unreality (see Baudrillard 1983a; 1983b, 1993, and the discussion in Kellner 1989b).

Although there is a technophobic element in his depictions of technologies and experiments, for Cronenberg the cataclysms of our era are the product of the conflation of nature, science, technology, the media, capital, and humanity, and thus cannot be blamed on any one factor. In this multiperspectival optic, it is the peculiar conjunction of *all* these ingredients that brings on the human catastrophe rather than just, say, technology run amok, or science surpassing its "natural" limits. In a 1999 interview, Cronenberg claimed:

> I've never been pessimistic about technology – this is a mistaken perception. It's probably the audience's fears that are being tapped, but I think that I look at the situation fairly coldly – in the sense of neutral. I'm

saying that we are doing some extreme things, but they are things that we are compelled to do. It is part of the essence of being human to create technology, that's one of the main creative acts. We've never been satisfied with the world as it is, we've messed with it from the beginning. Most technology can be seen as an extension of the human body, in one way or another, and ... I think that there is a much positive and exciting about it as there is dangerous and negative.[8]

Cronenberg thus resists an explicitly technophobic reading of his work, preferring to explore possible consequences of technology out of control in particular contexts. His films often depict technology and media culture as the product of specific relations of production, generated in distinctive institutions by individuals pursuing economic, political, technological, and perhaps psychological imperatives. This complex and materialist contextualization of technology and the media characterizes Cronenberg's films and distinguishes them from technophobic films, such as *2001, Colossus, Demon Seed,* or *Gattaca,* which blame technology itself for social calamity.

Moreover, Cronenberg depicts the possibility of resistance and struggle against technocratic domination. His 1975 film *Scanners (They Came from Within* in its initial U.S. release),[9] for instance, suggests that new mental powers generated by corporate/scientific excess can be used for power and domination, or for empathy and sociality. *Shivers,* has been aptly described as a "venereal horror" film.[10] The plot depicts a scientist who believes that the contemporary individual is "an over-rational animal that's lost touch with his body," who has produced a parasite that is a combination aphrodisiac and venereal disease. This parasite will both stimulate sexual activity and infect its partner with similar intense desire, and the contagious virus will be passed on to further hosts.

Scanners' plot suggests that the virus is transmitted through blood and sexual activity. Early scenes show blood dripping through windows, being smeared on bodies, intermingling with sweat, in sexual tableaux that mix Eros with Thanatos, passion with blood, in a polymorphic perverse transgression of sexual taboos profuse enough to arouse the most jaded Sadean. The virus takes the form of phallic excrement: the perfect symbol of the wastes and excesses of excremental culture.

The parasite violently transforms the body and mind of its host, and relentlessly passes from one individual to another; like sex itself, it is impossible to avoid or resist. The mise-en-scène frames the Sadean orgies and sexual excess within the ultramodern architecture of a highly controlled and surveilled apartment complex, and against the cold, sterile urban cityscape, all of which represent a hyperrationalized and overly functionalized urban techomodernity. Moreover Cronenberg periodically withdraws his camera from jerky, disjointed images of his characters' hysterical sexual panic within the apartment, to classical, well-framed and centered shots of the apartment complex against the calm Montreal night.

Yet Canadian tidiness and cleanliness is befouled by filthy parasites who excrete noxious fecal matter and tiny droppings of blood – as if the excremental waste of a techno-utopia refused repression and the nasty elements of human and social life, and vomited up its material underside to remind the ultramodern denizens what decay and horror they were at once fleeing and engendering in their sanitized techno-environment.

The body invaders in the film obviously anticipate AIDS, though the parasites do not seem to kill the hosts but rather transform them into hyperactive sex machines recalling the frenetic sexual experimentation of the era. The film ends on an ironic note as the infected viral bodies drive off gaily into the night, ready to invade Montreal and take on its citizens who seem destined to assume the role of the sexual avant-garde.

Critics attacked *Scanners* as a manifestation of "sexual disgust," and the film was savaged in the Canadian magazine *Saturday Night* for its scandalous use of state funds provided by the Canadian Film Development Corporation.[11] Yet the final scene is highly ambiguous, and can be read either as an horrific vision of sexual apocalypse (the destruction of civilization through sexual excess), or as a missionary attempt to share new-found sexual liberation with others.

In *Scanners*, a new drug, Ephemerol, which was intended to tranquillize mothers during pregnancy, propagated paranormal psychic powers, which enable the recipients to scan (i.e. read) other minds, much as one scans a computer system for information. The scanners are also able to externalize their mental powers into physical forces capable of exploding heads, causing fires, and evoking other spectacular cinematic effects. While Darryl Revok, one of the most powerful scanners, wants to organize the scanners into a corporate-political force who will be able to use their powers to take over the world, a small underground wants to use their powers for human empathy, solidarity, and creativity. Cronenberg is thus not anti-technology and tries to represent the new technoscape as both one of the great cataclysms of the present *and* a potentially higher and better stage of history.

To his figures of the viral body in *Shivers* and *Rabid*, and the carcinogenic body and mind in *The Brood* and *Scanners*, Cronenberg adds viral images and a telematic body in *Videodrome* (1982). In this film, a video-machine produces images that create brain tumors that generate hallucinations, and a "new flesh" that is able to assimilate and generate technologies. Thematizing the implosion of mind, body, media culture, and technology, Cronenberg pictures a world where video is at the center of social life and proliferates images that, like viruses, invade the human mind/body and construct new subjects and mutant humans. Cathode Ray Missions provide free video showings to derelicts to help socialize misfits and outcasts so that they can again "mix in" with social life. The shelter is run by Prof. Brian O'Blivion's daughter whose father (an obvious McLuhan figure) had evidently been the first victim of Videodrome; his daughter preserves thousands of tapes of him and pretends that he is alive by releasing his tapes to TV stations.

For O'Blivion, "Public life on television was more real than private life in the flesh," thus his death had no sting – as long as his videotapes and video images circulate. The body invaders pictured in *Videodrome* induce psychic mutations that give rise to a new mode of perception where there is no distinction between video hallucinations and reality, between fantasy and sense impressions. The "Videodrome" is presented as the next phase of human evolution "as technological animal." The film suggests that its viral images might originate a new stage of perception and reality and a "new flesh" that are potentially positive for human experience and evolution, as well as potentially destructive. Such a figure is compelling in our current technoculture as we merge with media, computer, and genetic technologies that are creating new bodies and mutations in culture, identities, and experience with powerful but uncharted effects.

On the one hand, Videodrome is a powerful hallucinatory virus/drug/meme implanted in the minds of citizens. It symbolizes the insidious control media culture and entertainment industries have over the public with their "giant hallucination machines," which in Cronenberg's allegory could be a force of a virulent global technoculture. As made vividly clear in the film, these industries and their media elites have complete contempt for people and democracy. *Videodrome* implies a devolution where the tentacles of the media destroy the higher potentialities of the human brain, nature's most (known) intricate product, and renders subjects unfit for self-organization. Yet the film also suggests an evolutionary process, whereby human perception and the body are reorganized at a higher level, within a technoscape that greatly enhances our existing powers and surpasses the limitations of embodied existence.

Interestingly, while the metamorphoses of Cronenberg's earlier films were primarily products of well-meaning scientists whose experiments contained both great dangers and positive potential, the inventors of Videodrome are more diabolical. The Spectacular Optical Corporation that intends to use Videodrome to manufacture a populace "tough" enough for the "savage times" envisaged in the techno-future. In the words of one of its employees: "North America's getting soft … and the rest of the world is getting tough, very, very, tough." To survive, North America must become "pure, direct, and strong." To reverse the trend toward "rotting away from the inside," the inventors of Videodrome want to create technologies that will generate a tougher and more powerful species which merges technology and mind, video and body. With regards *Videodrome*'s vision, in order to preserve white male hegemony in North America and in the exorbitantly competitive and violent neo-Darwinian world of the global society, it is crucial to shift evolution to the next level of the cyborg, thus merging the human with technology.

Hence, *Videodrome* captures the ruthless competitive ethos of a global capitalism organized around competing hegemonic blocs such as the North American Free Trade Association (NAFTA), the European Union (EU), The Asian-Pacific Economic Cooperation Zone (ASEC) and other groupings. Through the mouthpiece of the techno-elite, Cronenberg critically presents rightwing fears of immigration, multiculturalism, and liberalism, which in the conservative imaginary are responsible for the emasculation of North American (Anglo-Saxon-White) power. Only a revival of rugged competitiveness and more masculine values can preserve the established society and maintain the position of the power elite.

Cronenberg's subsequent 1980s films *The Dead Zone* (1983) and *The Fly* (1986) focus more obsessively on the specific roles of politics, science and technology in a new technocapitalist society. Most of his films, in different ways, present scenes where new forms of technology intersect with the imperatives of capital accumulation, hubris, and psychopathology to spawn catastrophe. Consequently, Cronenberg naturally evolves from fantasy and horror film cineaste to work with the disaster, conspiracy, and dystopic genres which have become key forms of the contemporary Hollywood (international) cinema. While in some ways his unconventional and thematically obsessive films position him as an auteur of modernism, he can also be interpreted as a representative of a specific version of Canadian/North American postmodernism who anticipates many of the central themes of the postmodern adventure, providing cinematic analogues of implosions of humans and technology and the emergence of a posthuman "new flesh."

Cronenberg's works of the later 1980s and 1990s bring to the fore a tragic dimension hitherto submerged, but visible, in his earlier films. Johnny Smith in *The Dead Zone*, Seth Brundle in *The Fly*, the twins in *Dead Ringer* (1988), the junkies in *Naked Lunch* (1991), the hermaphrodite in *Madame B* (1993), the car fetishists in *Crash* (1997), and the video game producer in *eXistenZ* (1999) are victims as much as agents as they cope (unsuccessfully) with their obsessions and mutant minds and bodies. Many of his characters tragically expire as sacrificial victims of the new technologies and science. Some of these figures embody, however, a utopian fantasy of transcendence, of the evolution to higher forms of life with novel potentialities in altered bodies with new pleasures and powers. Unlike the one-dimensional advocates of posthumanism, these films show the risks and dangers involved in evolution to the posthuman; they display how the conventional world threatens and resists unimpeded technological mutation and development. Like Max Renn in *Videodrome*, many of Cronenberg's characters journey to the end of their experiments and perish along the way.[12]

Such is the fate of scientist Seth Brundle (Jeff Goldblum) in Cronenberg's *The Fly*. The film presents a startling evolution into a new species, providing frightening representations of the perils of posthumanism, transgenic species, and the fifth discontinuity. While the original *Fly* (1958) safely anchored the scientist's experiments within the bosom of the family and centered on his devoted wife, Cronenberg's version takes place in the post-familial singles scene. And where the earlier 1950s version was set in a suburban home and garden that looked like a Disneyesque small-town America, Cronenberg's film takes place in an urban loft filled with junk-food, computers, and other detritus of ultramodernity. The metamorphosis machine merging the human with the fly in the earlier film looked clumsily mechanical, whereas Cronenberg's teleportation apparatus is controlled by computers and operates according to the principles of genetic engineering and information theory. Embodying Baudrillard's postmodern molecular model of life as a code, of genetic miniaturization (DNA) being the ultimate constituent of human life (1983a: 103ff.), Cronenberg's teleportation machine breaks down the mind and body into its primary constituents and encodes the molecular structure into one telepod while decoding it into another, showing the interchangeability of matter, energy, and information.

Whereas the 1958 version of *The Fly* presented the experiment as a means to serve humanity (i.e. to instantly bring food to the starving), Cronenberg's remake portrays the invention as an exigency of postmodern life to overcome obstacles of space and time, to move the body instantly from one place to another in order to transcend inertia, entropy, and physical limitation. The transporter also enables the transgression of "laws" of modern science to cross over into a new age of unlimited transposability of information.

Cronenberg's *The Fly* also depicts mutation of the body as itself an evolution-ary/devolutionary fate for the human species as it enters a new era and world. Although Brundle/Fly is destroyed in a paroxysm of special effects, his trans-formation is presented as a synthesis of wonderful new powers alongside destruc-tive ones. Brundle/Fly is in touch with his body to an unparalleled degree, discovers new physical and sexual energies, and is aware that he is the bearer of a new species being. Through the powers of technoscience he exceeds the limi-tations of the merely human for the transhuman. Yet he is unable to synthesize the new and the old, and eventually destroys himself. The victim of unantici-pated consequences, Seth fuses his DNA with a fly that entered the chamber at the key moment of genetic reconstruction. Exuviating from his human shell into the grotesque form of a fly, his now useless ears and teeth falling away, Seth writhes in the spasms of a failed journey into the posthuman, seeking to evolve into a higher state, but instead devolving into a monstrous (Brundle)fly.

Cronenberg's horror over shocking implosions between technology and the human and the emergence of new species previewing a fifth discontinuity are again vividly portrayed in *eXistenZ* (1999). The film is a saga of a renowned game inventor, Allegra Geller, on the run from an ironically named terrorist group, the "Reality Liberation Brigade," who decry virtual reality (VR) as a dangerous narcotic. In a bizarre vision of a near future, Cronenberg presents a coevolutionary scene where mass media and entertainment industries, com-puters and virtual reality devices, and genetic engineering of animals all combine to produce an unprecedently powerful spectacle. Like the film *Strange Days* (1995), Cronenberg portrays media culture and VR devices as addictive narcot-ics, ones so powerful that growing numbers of people have jacks installed in their bodies in order to revel in the artificial world. *eXistenZ* brings to life a social scene of radical implosion with bizarre technological devices serving as hybrids of the organic and inorganic and creating a new species of technohu-mans. The "gristle gun" used by Luddite-realists to shoot Geller is a deadly weapon concocted from bone, gristle, and sinews, and shoots teeth for bullets. Anything but a plastic joystick, the slimy game pod resembles a liver with nipples. It is attached to a fleshy umbilical cord that plugs directly into a player's nervous system through an anus-like bioport inserted into the lower spine, providing a gruesome allegory of the invasion of technology into the human in an era of media spectacle, digitization, biotechnology, and virtual reality.

Cronenberg's startling vision depicts media culture and technology fusing with biology in a new advance of the spectacle, which all but obliterates the distinction between the real and virtual. Parallel to the film's characters, viewers have a hard time discerning which reality they inhabit since Cronenberg opens a proliferating number of ontological drawers in his Chinese box. Thus, the film's end is but a pseudo-stop in the journey of an ever-spiraling confusion as to who is who and what is what, showing our sense of the real perilously undermined in the emerging virtual technoculture. Yet technoculture is not just fun and innocent, and Cronenberg also underscores the dark side to the spectacle of VR, one that numbs the spectator's sense of social reality and inures his or her sensibilities to violence and the consequences of one's actions. After blowing someone away in a VR game, Geller shrugs off her action with: "He's just a game character." But an incessant involvement in an ever more realistic and immersive spectacle of simulated violence is enough for young people today to adopt the same jaded and nihilistic outlook.

In Cronenberg's epics of posthumanism, the feared concepts of carcinogenics and metastasis signify growth and development, but of a sort that careen out of control and destroy their host. Cronenberg's characters try to accept and live with the viral and carcinogenic body invaders, and hope that their technobodies will be able to evolve to a higher state of being, to a new mode of existence. These Nietzschean would-be-*Übermenschen* generally fail, but their attempts to overcome the limitations of body and self, and to cross over to the posthuman exert a certain fascination and a utopian desire for novel sexualities, transcendence of boundaries, and bodily resurrection. There are several intimations, in fact, that Cronenberg's technomutants escape from, or relativize death, transgressing the barrier between life and death as a new adventure, as a new possibility for physical and psychic experience. At the conclusion of *Scanners* the "good" and "bad" brother have merged into one being, opening the door for new scanner evolution. The possibility of a new kind of immortality is a strong undercurrent of *Videodrome* and his later films depict the new passions and pleasures of the mind and body in an age of cryogenics, cloning, stem cell technology, teleomerase therapy, and other technoscientific wonders.

Hence, Cronenberg's notion of the "new flesh" suggests the eruption of novel forms of experience, sexuality, society, and technology in a postmodern adventure of radical transgression of laws and boundaries. Such a construction of the body would be a site of loss and danger, as well as new possibilities and pleasures. It could embody some of the most emancipatory insights into a non-repressive civilization and the resurrection of the body, set out by Herbert

Marcuse (1955) and Norman O. Brown (1985[1955]) in the 1950s, and could concretize Michel Foucault's call for "new passions and new pleasures" (1992 [1984]). Once the viral and technobody has been able to assimilate and live with all the viruses and prostheses in the postmodern scene (from AIDS to television, from cancer to computer and bio-viruses), a rebirth of the flesh and transmutation of the body may be possible. Sexuality will have to be reinvented and the body refunctioned (*Umfunktioniert*) in Brecht's sense in the restructuring of the cultural apparatus. We must transcend sexual panic and cynical sex, and learn once again how secretions can be fused with eroticism, how pleasure can overcome anxiety, how satisfaction can replace panic. This will require a cure for AIDS and other sexually transmitted diseases, and a return to the sexual body and its re-eroticization. Creating new polymorphically eroticized bodies would take the experiments and explorations of the sexual utopias of the 1960s and 1970s to a higher and novel state of existence.

The evolved body must also be emancipated from the performance principle and erotic discipline for the pleasure principle and polymorphic play (Marcuse 1955). Freed from the restrictions of sexuality as we now know it, an evolved body may be able to invent a new sensibility and new pleasures. The technobody may be able to overcome the scandal of sexual difference and discover three sexes, or six, or perhaps just one. Released from the tyranny of sexual difference and the norms of bourgeois performance, the postmodern body and new sensibility could then mutate into a new synthesis of mindbody. In addition, we should explore ways to enhance our senses, increase health and longevity, and expand our powers of perception through all available techniques, ranging from yoga and meditation to smart drugs and mind machines. Such a bodily utopia is, of course, impossible in the present situation of expanding work, stupefying leisure, disease-threatened sex, deadly virus pandemics, and commercialization of the human genome. But critical theory and cultural studies should contain a "dreaming forward" (Ernst Bloch), as well as an illusionless diagnosis and critique of the present scene rooted in historical comprehension of the past. Otherwise, it's unlikely that we'll have either a nice day, or a better one to look forward to tomorrow.

In the next section I shall interrogate the writings of another master of fantasy, the science fiction master Philip K. Dick, and will interrogate the *Blade Runner* films (1982) and (2017) based on his novels. Dick's writing and the *Blade Runner* films provide a more dystopic vision of the contemporary era and a more highly evolved technological nightmare dystopia than even Cronenberg's films, while engaging key philosophical and existential issues of the contemporary era.

Blade runners, dystopia, and social apocalypse

Our present social continuum is disintegrating rapidly; if war doesn't burst it apart, it obviously will corrode away ... to avoid the topic of war and cultural regression is unrealistic and downright irresponsible.

(*Philip K. Dick*)

> Since science fiction concerns the future of human society, the worldwide
> loss of faith in science and in scientific progress is bound to cause convul-
> sions in the SF field. This loss of faith in the idea of progress, in
> a "brighter tomorrow," extends over our whole cultural milieu; the dour
> tone of recent science fiction is an effect, not a cause.
>
> *(Philip K. Dick)*

An apocalyptic imagination emerged after World War II, which accompanied
the genesis of postwar science fiction, politics, and culture. After Hiroshima,
people were haunted by fears of nuclear annihilation, as visible in popular literature and media culture of the day. In particular, science fiction writers like
Philip K. Dick, Bernard Wolfe, J.G. Ballard, and others attempted to imagine
and represent the aftermath of nuclear holocaust, the greatest conceivable catastrophic event ever unleashed by and upon the human species.

Nightmare visions of futuristic societies, or dystopias, are a major 1970s science fiction genre and stand as signs of a crisis in U.S. society and culture. Dystopias are negative utopias, negative images of future worlds. Instead of being
places where people might dream of living because everything is so perfect
there, dystopias represent places from which, given a chance, people would
prefer to flee because everything is so imperfect. Many dystopic post-1970s
Hollywood films about the future portray worlds that contain extreme environmental pollution, overpopulation, violent cities, bureaucratic administration, and
economic exploitation. Conservative dystopias project fears of breakdown of law
and order, the disintegration of the family, and the curtailment of individual
freedom by centralized governments (*THX 1138*, *Logan's Run*, *Divergent*, *The
Hunger Games*, etc.). These films frequently valorize escape to nature (e.g., *THX
1138*, *Logan's Run*) and yearn for the past. In sum, conservative dystopias present individualism, the couple, the family, and other contemporary institutions
and ideologies as more "natural" and desirable than their debased future forms.

In contrast, liberal and radical dystopia films focus on the dangers of increased
pollution, nuclear war, and economic exploitation. Some contain veiled allegorical critiques of advanced capitalism (e.g., *Alien*, *Outland*, *Blade Runner*). They
therefore make a critical commentary on current forms of life and social organization with images of what intensified corporate capitalism, political repression,
and contemporary forms of dehumanization might produce in the future. However, not all dystopias can be easily categorized ideologically. Some articulate
complex and often contradictory attitudes toward, and anxieties about, increasing mechanization and commodification of life in advanced capitalism, and
reveal possible ideological conflicts in such societies. I suggest that *Blade Runner*
provides such a case of an ideologically ambivalent dystopia. It is open to
a diagnostic critique that analyzes its forms of ideology, the film's critique of
traditional and contemporary dominant ideologies, and the limitations of the
film's critique. For a diagnostic critique can provide insight into contemporary
society and ideology, and indicate areas for radical political intervention.

The apocalyptic vision of Philip K. Dick

It is perhaps Philip K. Dick's novel *Do Androids Dream of Electric Sheep?* (1968) that provides his most compelling apocalyptic vision, which also exemplifies the prototypically Dickian themes of the implosion between the real and the artificial, humans and technology, and natural reality and simulation in a high-tech world. In the plot of the novel, which is significantly different from the film *Blade Runner* (1982) that is loosely based on it, Rick Deckard, a bounty hunter who targets androids, craves above all else to own real animals, instead of his electric artificial ones. The novel's narrative suggests a future in which one animal species after another has disappeared after a nuclear war and animals are highly prized as a cherished and vanishing form of life. Deckard is ordered to exterminate a group of highly advanced android Nexus-6 models who have escaped from the "off-colonies," where they were slaves, in order to prolong their short preprogrammed lives. The bounty hunter increasingly sympathizes and empathizes with the androids, one of whom, Rachael, he becomes sexually involved with. Consequently, Deckard is ever more troubled by the killing or "retiring" required by his job, as he comes to recognize the android others as akin to human subjects and forms of life, just as he recognizes humans are becoming more mechanical and reified.

Dick frames his story within the political economy of an interplanetary global capitalism, set in a bombscape of human ruination and massive species extinction in 2021, after World War Terminus. The androids were originally produced to help colonize Mars, when capitalist corporations, having devastated their home base, began inhabiting other planets. In a competitive race between two global giants, the Rosen Association and the Grozzi Corporation vie to market the most advanced androids. This war of technology has produced increasingly complex creatures who are seemingly identical with humans, sharing capacities such as memory, love, empathy, desire, and fear of death. In the form of the Nexus-6 model produced by the Rosen Corporation, androids also have acquired a high level of self-reflexivity, which leads them to repudiate their slave status. Hence, as Marx saw in an earlier industrial context, capitalists created their own gravediggers by manufacturing increasingly complex workers who eventually acquire the class consciousness and will to rebel. Thus, Dick provides a futuristic embodiment of Marx's vision of a rebellious proletariat, while underscoring the contradictory logic of capital.

Dick presents a universe of total commodification, such that nothing escapes the nihilistic reduction of market logic and the profit imperative. Colonists who agree to leave earth are given an android as a reward, a bonus that reveals intensification of the commodification of human beings and other forms of life. After the destruction of nature and animals by nuclear holocaust, animals also are commodified, revered as a token of prestige whose market value is closely documented and watched by investors who crave purchase and ownership of animals. Dick thus presents penetrating portraits of a society ruled by obsessive consumption and the fetishism of commodities.

As in many of Dick's novels and stories, the text interrogates what is real and poses the question "What is human"? Rejecting the classic equation of the human being with language and rationality, Dick instead chooses empathy to characterize the human. In the novel, humans are able to enter into empathetic fusion with Mercer, a religious figure who appears when individuals interact with an "empathy box," which creates a quasi-hallucinatory oneness with Mercer and others participating in the experience. A major theme of the story concerns the difficulty in trying to distinguish between what is real and what is a simulation, what is organic and natural, and what is constructed and artificial. The collapse of clear distinctions between the fake and the authentic applies to both animals and human beings in *Androids*: is it a real animal or an electric model, is it a human being or an android? Even the androids do not really know, since they have simulated lives through implanted memories, and at one point Deckard and his partner Phil Resch, another bounty hunter, begin to doubt whether they too are human or not, as the readers are also left to wonder.

The bounty hunters administer a test to detect whether an entity is a human or an android, thereby updating the old Turing test to detect artificial from human intelligence. The examination is based, interestingly, on empathy; apparently, human beings are capable of sympathy and compassion for animals and other human beings, while androids lack this capacity.[13] Yet Dick's *Androids* portrays humans drained of all natural feeling, becoming more controlled by media and society, thus questioning what is left of humanity in a high-tech world and whether the distinctive features of the human will survive. Likewise, Deckard is attracted to the android Rachael and has sex with her, an episode that can be read allegorically as one way of negotiating new relations with technology in a posthuman world. Indeed, the androids are superior in some ways to humans, they are hyperreal humans, realer-than real, better-than-real, thus providing, Dick implies, superior warriors, lovers, workers, intellects, and the like.

In a subplot, John Isidore, a "special," a "chickenhead," retarded by the nuclear fallout, lives alone in an abandoned apartment; most inhabitants of earth have left for the colonies and only the poorest and most desperate remain on earth. Isidore hears another inhabitant play a television in the apartment, shyly goes down to meet her, bringing her a pat of margarine as a present. It is Pris, one of the escaped androids whose leaders, Roy and Irmina Batty, join her the next day, setting up the eventual showdown with Deckard. The plot structure is typical of Dick's novels that introduce one protagonist, usually an ordinary person thrown into an extraordinary situation, followed by introduction of other, often subhuman, or underclass characters. Then characters in the Dick narrative machine typically encounter extraordinary humans or aliens, like the androids, who often threaten the human race. The characters finally come together in a crisis situation and the resolution of the plot unfolds – a literary structure taken over by William Gibson and other cyberpunk writers, who, rightly, see Dick as their Godfather.

Yet there is a conservative dimension to the narrative resolution in *Androids* in which Dick affirms the superiority of humans over other forms of life in their capacity for empathy, and Deckard's white, male, and professional subjectivity is valorized over other participants in the story. Moreover, Deckard returns to his wife and accepts the conventions of heterosexual marriage, consumerism, and bourgeois normality, as Deckard comes to accept his former life and returns to his normal routine. Thus, the boundaries that the novel so powerfully deconstructed are resurrected and conservative values and identities are ultimately affirmed.

Androids, humans, and entropy in the Blade Runner films

> My grand theme – who is human and who only appears (masquerades) as human? Unless we can individually and collectively be certain of the answer to this question, we face what is, in my view, the most serious problem possible. Without answering it adequately, we cannot even be certain of our own selves. I cannot even know myself, let alone you. So I keep working on this theme; to me nothing is as important a question. And the answer comes very hard.
>
> *(Philip K. Dick)*

> The greatest change growing across our world these days is probably the momentum of the living towards reification, and at the same time a reciprocal entry into animation by the mechanical.
>
> *(Philip K. Dick)*

The 1982 film *Blade Runner* by contrast, directed by Ridley Scott, perhaps even more radically contests the boundaries between the natural, the artificial, and the human.[14] Portraying a society controlled by an advanced technocapitalism, the Tyrell corporation produces "replicants" to work and serve humans. Replicants look exactly like humans and even have memory functions. But because they progressively become more and more "human" by acquiring feelings, they are programmed to live only four years. Some have rebelled against their subjection, so a special police, Blade Runners, exists to "retire" unwilling replicants. The story concerns four such replicant rebels who have returned to earth to get their "maker," the Tyrell Corporation, to reprogram them so they can live longer. A Blade Runner, Deckard (Harrison Ford), is called out of semi-retirement to "retire" them. Deckard falls in love with Rachael (Sean Young), one of Tyrell's most advanced replicants. Deckard manages to kill three of the rebel replicants, and fights a climactic battle with the fourth, Roy (Rutger Hauer). At the end, a police colleague allows Deckard and Rachael to escape from the city and flee into nature.[15]

The film presents Deckard as the film noir individualist detective (whereas he is married and returns to his wife in the novel), and pairs him romantically in an ambiguous relationship with the android Rachael. The bounty hunter is called a "blade runner" in the movie (a term derived from William Burroughs), and Harrison Ford plays the character with world-weary aplomb. In the film, the androids are called "replicants," or "skin jobs," and are described as "more human than human." Whereas Dicks presents his androids as models of inhuman and mechanical beings opposed to the human, in the film the replicants seem to have more fully developed sensibilities and passion for life, as well as strength, cunning, and loyalty to each other, than the human characters.[16]

Blade Runner stylized aesthetic throughout is neo-expressionist with dark shadows, hazy lighting, and odd camera angles. Thematically, too, the film contains marked expressionist elements.[17] The android chief Roy's poetic speeches seem like abbreviated versions of the ideologically ambiguous, rhapsodic monologue found in much expressionist theater. And Roy's conversion from poet-warrior to Christ-like savoir recalls expressionist "transformation drama." Moreover, *Blade Runner* borrows entire sequences from German expressionist films. In addition to the parallels with Fritz Lang's *Metropolis* (1927), where the rich live in lavish dwellings high above the street, while the poor live in squalor below, the sleazy bar where Deckard finds the android Zhora is reminiscent of Mrs. Greifer's party in Pabst's film *The Joyless Street*, even down to the insect-like hats on the women. An image of Deckard, silhouetted on the stairway, parallels a similar moment in *Nosferatu*. Overall, *Blade Runner*'s emphasis on the degraded, alienating city parallels that of expressionist "street films." Thus one could read *Blade Runner* as a reprise of Lang's vision of a futuristic city, featuring a final combat that conspicuously does not repeat *Metropolis*' appeal for class collaboration.[18] *Blade Runner* concludes by promoting the myth of transcendent romantic love in as desperate a way as another expressionist film, *Destiny*.

The stunning visual environment of *Blade Runner* provides startling images of the postmodern metropolis, drenched in radiation-saturated rain, the debris and refuse of the modern industrial city, and the detritus of a global and multicultural capitalist society. The mis-en-scène is populated with several layers of dense imagery. The sky is filled with high-rise apartments, flaming industrial smokestacks, and hovercraft vehicles, surrounded with neon billboards for global corporations and ads for a new life in the out-colonies. Scott's film deploys the postmodern strategy of pastiche, combining the signs of Dick's science fiction genre with the voice-over narrative of Deckard, presented in the style of a film noir detective and variations of the stock characters of the urban crime film appear in the film.[19] The replicant Rachael is portrayed as a noir femme fatale who, however, helps Deckard destroy the androids and even leaves with him in a highly ambiguous romance – a sharp departure from the novel where Deckard returns home to his wife and an uneasy reconciliation.

The representations of technology in *Blade Runner* are extremely interesting. Unlike conservative technophobic films, there is no privileging of nature and the human over technology,[20] and Deckard states at one point: "Replicants are like any other machine. They can be a benefit or a hazard." In the film, Deckard comes to sympathize with the replicants and even falls in love with Rachael, while Roy Batty is presented as the most articulate and philosophical figure in the film, expressing a profound love of life, loyalty toward his fellow replicants, and ultimately saves Deckard with whom he comes to respect and empathize, even though the bounty hunter is sent to "retire" him.

Blade Runner points to the oppressive core of capitalism, which creates technology to exploit human beings and presents figures of rebellion in the form of the replicants who reject their status as pure instruments of commodified labor with limited life spans. The Tyrell Corporation explicitly produces replicants as a pliable work force, including women who are constructed alternately as love-slaves and castrators, pointing to the socially constructed role of women in capitalist patriarchy. Tyrell lives in a high-rise apartment whose neo-Mayan architecture suggests human sacrifice for the entrepreneurial deity and Tyrell is portrayed as a sinister and warped capitalist patriarch.

Most significantly, the film presents humans, machines, institutions, and "reality" itself as socially constructed and thus amenable to reconstruction. Unlike conservative narratives that contrast fixed and unchanging humans with reified technology, Scott's film foregrounds the constructedness of humans and technology, blurs the distinctions, and shows both capable of reconstruction for more socially benevolent purposes. The major protagonists – Deckard and Roy – ultimately renounce violence and come to empathize with their supposed opposites and enemies.

Proliferating entropy is a major theme of Dick's key works like *Androids*, which portray the incessant movement from birth to death, adolescence to senescence, order to disorder, and heterogeneity to homogeneity. As the second law of thermodynamics, "entropy" is a natural process; the cosmos, in Dick's terms, inexorably winds down to a state of "kipple." "No one can win against kipple … except temporarily and maybe in one spot. It's a universal principle operating throughout the universe; the entire universe is moving toward a final state of total, absolute kippleization" (1968: 58).

Entropy is indeed the prototypical condition for Dick's futuristic world: cities are decaying; the natural environment is disappearing; the androids' short life spans are winding down; and the unfortunates stranded on earth are deteriorating in mind and body. Entropy is also evident in the "waning of affect," a symptom of postmodern subjectivity for theorists like J.G. Ballard and Fredric Jameson. In advanced stages of "civilization," individuals are so affectless that they have to rely on mechanical supplementation – via technologies such as a "mood organ" or Dick's "empathy box" – in order to feel. Dick portrays an exhausted human species drained of all feeling and connections with others, and shows androids gaining empathy. He thereby signals a fusion between humans and machines, questions what is left of humanity in a high-tech world, and calls into doubt the long-term survivability of a human species whose members are losing positive emotional bonds with one another.

Dick's texts suggest that just as individuals can hasten the entropy of their own bodies, social systems can quicken their own decay and that of the natural world. As an energy-devouring, resource-depleting, waste-producing, nonstop-guzzling megamachine of growth and accumulation, advanced capitalism rapidly accelerates entropic breakdown. While *Blade Runner* changed much in Dick's novel and omitted the themes of the manipulative effects of media culture and religion, it brilliantly captured the look and feel of a hyperintensive global system of production drowning in its own waste. The incessant downpour of toxic rain, the fire-belching smokestacks, the filthy refuse of the ultramodern metropolis, the densely overpopulated city streets and high-rise apartments, the glowing neon-billboards and crisscrossing traffic of hovercraft vehicles, and the detritus of a multicultural society where even language breaks down into kippled fragments underscore the presence of a dying, nihilistic, technocapitalism.

Blade Runner also adds the ironic touch of metallic blimps moving ponderously across the nuclear-red skies, broadcasting advertisements for the good life in the out-colonies. The underclass denizens – mostly Asian and hybridized – live in crowded ghettolike conditions on the ground level, while the remaining upper class dwells in luxurious high-rise apartments, reproducing the class-structure portrayed in Fritz Lang's *Metropolis*. This futuristic city – which became the prototype for the universe of cyberpunk – was recognizably Los Angeles, where the film was shot, but it could stand for any global and multicultural city of a postholocaust future, or the aftermath of a collapse of the global economy.

Blade Runner quickly became a cult classic and the release of the Director's Cut DVD in 1992, which is significantly different from the movie, started another round of discussions, reviews, and debates about the *Blade Runner* phenomenon. Since then, there has been much buzz over the release of a new *Blade Runner* film and indeed in 2017 *Blade Runner 2049* appeared, directed by Denis Villeneuve and written by Hampton Fancher and Michael Green. The film is a sequel to the 1982 film *Blade Runner* that is set 30 years after the original. The film stars Ryan Gosling as K, a Nexus-9 replicant "blade runner" and reprises Harrison Ford, playing an aging and grizzled version of his character in the original. The name "K" may be a reference to Franz Kafka's fictional character and the setting, plot, and vibe of the film is arguably Kafkaesque, mysterious, menacing and dark.

The cinematography and set design produces a *Blade Runner* that is darker and more polluted than the original. Moreover, the city where the plot unfolds is more run down with fewer people, and the surrounding area and countryside appears to be a wasteland, suggesting a social devolution and regression. The movie begins with K tracking down and "retiring" a rebel replicant, Sapper Morton, who was reputed to be an active soldier in colonial wars and very dangerous. After discovering and killing Sapper, following the mandatory generic fight with the replicant soldier, K finds a box buried under a tree, which contains the remains of a female replicant who died during a caesarean section, perhaps demonstrating that replicants can reproduce biologically, previously thought impossible. K's superior, Lt. Joshi, orders K to find and retire the replicant child, if one exists, setting up a quest narrative whereby K will learn some startling truths about himself.

K visits the headquarters of the Wallace Corporation, which is now the major supplier in the manufacturing of replicants, following the demise of the now defunct Tyrell Corporation, which produced the replicants in the earlier film. K asks Wallace staff members to identify the deceased female from their DNA archives who they identify as Rachael, who was designed as a romantic partner replicant by the Tyrell corporation, and who was Deckard's love interest in the earlier film. Learning of Rachael's romantic ties with Deckard, K sets out to find Deckard, while CEO Niander Wallace wants to discover the secret to replicant reproduction for business purposes and assigns one of his replicant employees, Luv, to follow K to find Rachael and her supposed child.

K goes to the farm where he "retired" soldier Sapper Morton, and sees the date 6-10-21 carved into the tree trunk, a date he recognizes from a childhood memory of a wooden toy horse. In a convoluted plot, K finds the imagined replicant child in an orphanage, discovers the toy horse in a place where he hid it, leading K to wonder if he had a connection to Rachael and the replicant child.

K's holographic AI girlfriend Joi, who lives with him in his apartment and sometimes accompanies him on his outside assignments, believes that because replicant memories are artificially produced, this suggests that K was born, not created. Searching LAPD records, K discovers twins born on that date with identical DNA aside from the sex chromosome, but only the boy is listed as alive. After another trek to the orphanage, K meets Dr. Ana Stelline, a designer of replicant memories, who confirms that K's memory of the orphanage is real, leading him to conclude that he is Rachael's son. After more tortuous plot twists, K is led to Las Vegas, where he finds Deckard, who reveals that he is the father of Rachael's child, that he scrambled the birth records to protect the child's identity, and that he left the child in the custody of the replicant freedom movement.

After killing Joshi, Luv tracks K's LAPD vehicle to Deckard's hiding place in Las Vegas. She kidnaps Deckard, destroys Joi, and leaves K to die. The replicant freedom movement rescues K. When their leader, Freysa, informs him that she helped deliver Rachael's daughter, K understands he is not Rachael's child and deduces Stelline is her daughter and that the memory of the toy horse is hers, which she implanted amongst those of other replicants whose memories she designed. To prevent Deckard from leading Wallace to Stelline or the freedom movement, Freysa asks K to kill Deckard for the greater good of all replicants.

Luv takes Deckard to Wallace Co. headquarters to meet Niander Wallace. Wallace offers Deckard a clone of Rachael in exchange for revealing what he knows. Deckard refuses, and the clone is killed. As Luv is transporting Deckard to a ship to take him off-world to be interrogated, K intercepts and mercilessly kills Luv but is mortally wounded in the fight. He stages Deckard's death to protect him from Wallace and the replicant freedom movement before taking Deckard to Stelline's office and handing him her toy horse. As K lies motionless on the steps, looking up at the snowing sky, an emotional Deckard enters the building and meets his daughter for the first time.

Hence, the 2018 version of *Blade Runner* continues the futuristic vision of the earlier novel and film and provides warnings against how out-of-control technology can provide challenges and perhaps destruction to human beings. Fantasy and science fiction films can thus provide prescient warnings against out of control technology, ecological crisis, political authoritarianism and other dangers of the contemporary era and is thus an important component of media culture.

Let us now turn to some reflections on contemporary tasks and futures for a critical media–cultural studies and sketch out some conclusions to these studies of contemporary media culture.

Notes

1 On allegory, see Benjamin 1977; Jameson 1981. I am not offering one privileged allegorical reading for *LOTR*, but am arguing that a plurality of allegorical readings are possible of the novels and film cycle. While some critics scorn allegorical interpretations because they allegedly build on one-to-one schematic readings of texts, I am using a model of allegory, based on a reconstruction of the positions of Walter Benjamin and Jameson cited above, that posits different levels of allegory in texts ranging from existential and moral to political and philosophical. I am also interpreting *LOTR* as a polysemic text that has multiple readings and effects so that multiple allegorical dimensions and readings are possible; hence, I am articulating certain possible readings that are well grounded in the text, reception, and historical context and am not reducing the *LOTR* phenomenon to a single reading.

2 On the *Bildungsroman*, see Herbert Marcuse's study of the German artist novel (1978 [1922]) and the commentary in Kellner 1984: 22–22.

3 On the classical monomyth formula, see Campbell 1956; Lawrence and Jewett 2002.

4 For my views of the Bush/Cheney administration and account of the contemporary socio-political system that provides a background to the release and reception of *LOTR* films, see Kellner 2001, 2003a, 2003b, 2005. I should probably note here that I am not arguing that *LOTR* cycle is a fascist film event, but that it has fascist motifs.

5 On the *Bruderbunden* and male-bonding in German Nazi groups, see Theweleit 1987, 1989.

6 Images of Trump as Sauron are a popular Internet meme (see www.google.com/search?source=hp&ei=MXE8XbrqEuKc0gK75LzACQ&q=Trump+as+the+Evil+Lord+Sauron&oq=Trump+as+the+Evil+Lord+Sauron&gs_l=psy-ab.12..2543.2543.3608..0.0.0.505.605.0j1j5-1...0..2j1.gwswiz...0.H5GoGG67gRM&ved=0ahUKEwj6xrqxuNXjAhVijlQKHTsyD5gQ4dUDC (accessed July 27, 2019), as was the case with memes of George W. Bush as Sauron in the era in which the films were released see www.google.com/search?source=hp&ei=K7fFXajzOIGe-gS7w7yACQ&q=George+W.+Bush+as+Sauron+&oq=George+W.+Bush+as+Sauron+&gs_l=psyab.12..2471.2471.5507..0.0.0.117.117.0j1...0..2j1.gws-wiz.l_NDZiv6E0I&ved=0ahUKEwjotOixotvlAhUBj54KHbshD5AQ4dUDCAs#spf=1573238576395 (accessed November 8, 2019).

7 For an earlier and more extensive discussion of Cronenberg's films upon which I draw here, see Kellner 1989d and on Cronenberg's life and films, (see Rodley 1992; Beard 2006).

8 In Richard Porton, "The Film Director as Philosopher: An Interview with David Cronenberg." *Cineaste*, Vol. XXIV, No. 4 (1999): 6.

9 David Chute, "He Came from Within," *Film Comment*, March–April 1980: 36. The original title was *Orgy of the Blood Parasites*, followed by the title *The Parasite Murders* for English Canadian release and *Frissons* for French release. When the French version was more successful, the film title was changed to *Shivers*, though it was first released in the U.S. as *They Came From Within*.

10 Nathanael Arnold, "7 of Horror Director David Cronenberg's Most Twisted Movies," *Cheatsheet*, October 23, 2016 at www.cheatsheet.com/entertainment/7-mind-bending-cronenberg-films-every-fan-should-see.html/ (accessed September 7, 2019).

11 "David Cronenberg. "Article and Interview by Paul M. Sammon," *Cinefantastique* 10.4 (Spring, 1981: 6).

12 Is it an accident that cult TV series *Max Headroom* (1987–1988) takes on Max Renn's first name, and that Renn's Channel 83 becomes Headroom's Channel 83 in the TV series? Someone who plays with words and names as creatively and intertextually as Cronenberg would certainly appreciate such a gesture.

13 Jurgen Habermas tells of how in his last talk with Herbert Marcuse, Herbert stated, "I know wherein our most basic value judgments are rooted – in compassion, in our sense for the suffering of others." "Psychic Thermidor and the Rebirth of Rebellious Subjectivity," *Berkeley Journal of Sociology*, 25 (1980), pp. 11–12. In *L'écran fantastique*, the screenwriter Hampton Fancher states that for him, "Empathy is the key to the entire story" (p. 26).

14 The French film journal *L'écran fantastique*, 26 (1982) contains a full dossier of interviews with Dick, Scott, and various other members of the film's production team that I shall draw on in the course of this reading. I am also drawing on an earlier article by Douglas Kellner, Flo Leibowitz and Michael Ryan, "BLADE RUNNER– A Diagnostic Critique," *Jump Cut* (1984), 6–8.

15 In an earlier script, after Roy kills Tyrell, he discovers that Tyrell is a replicant too and that Sebastian is really his creator! Roy then becomes furious that "God is Dead," and kills Sebastian! See *L'écran fantastique*, 36.

16 The *L'écran fantastique* dossier reveals that screenwriter Hampton Fancher saw *Blade Runner* as primarily a tale about empathy (p. 26), while scenarist David People said he considered it essentially a police story (p. 31). Sean Young, who played Rachael, said she treated the film as "a romantic thriller, like *Casablanca*" (p. 48). Harrison Ford (Deckard) perceived it as a detective story in the tradition of Philip Marlowe (p. 47). Ridley Scott interpreted it both as a "philosophical work" and as a futuristic police thriller (pp. 34ff.). The producer of *Blade Runner*, Michael Deeley, who earlier produced *The Deer Hunter*, speaks of the importance of Syd Mead, the visual futurist and concept artist and his futurist design. Finally, Paul M. Sammon, author of *Future Noir Revised & Updated Edition: The Making of Blade Runner* tells of the conflicts on the set of the film between Ridley Scott, Harrison Ford, and other members of the team, which all suggests the heterogeneity of input into the film, and the quite diverse ideological positions embodied in *Blade Runner* itself have produced a contradictory ideological amalgam, requiring multivalent readings that unpack the contradictory aesthetic and ideological components.

17 On the styles, themes, and historical origins and context of German Expressionism, see Stephen Bronner and Douglas Kellner, editors, *Passion and Rebellion: The Expressionist Heritage* (South Hadley, Mass.: Bergin Press, 1983).

18 There are other cinematic parallels to Lang's *Metropolis*. For example, the tycoon Tyrell has a marked physical resemblance to *Metropolis* boss, John Frederson, and Deckard's final duel with Roy copies in some respects the confrontation between Freder, the capitalist's son turned revolutionary, and *Metropolis'* evil Dr. Rotwang, who like the Tyrell Corporation created robots to serve as laborers.

19 Interestingly, the voice-over was not utilized in the Director's Cut of *Blade Runner*, thus creating a more ambiguous and modernist science fiction text and decentering the joining of noir detective fiction with science fiction motifs. The voice-over also tends to create sympathy and identification with the noir detective Deckard whereas the Director's Cut makes Batty more central and perhaps attractive. On the differences between the versions, see the studies in Kerman 1991.

20 For an elaboration of this argument, see Kellner and Ryan 1988: 251ff.; on representations of the city in *Blade Runner* that uses Jameson's postmodern theory to interpret the film, see Bruno 1990; and for a wide range of essays on the film, see Kerman 1997.

CONCLUSION

Technologies, literacies, and the future of media culture

The previous chapters of the second edition of *Media Culture* have attempted to provide readings of some of the major films, television shows, popular music, news and information in the U.S. from the 1980s up to 2020. I have argued that reading media culture in the context of the culture and history of a specific culture in a particular era illuminates the cultural forms, messages, values, ideologies, and impact of media culture and have tried to illustrate this approach with concrete studies. For a diagnostic critique, media culture also provides insights into the politics, society, culture, and psychology of a specific era and illuminates the central conflicts, hopes, fears, and crises of a particular historical epoch. In this sense, *Media Culture* has attempted to provide history lessons concerning major events, moments, struggles, and crises of the past decades. In the conclusion, I will first speculate on some future tasks and possibilities for a media/cultural studies and then will return to the present with some suggestions of how a media/cultural studies can contribute to a critical media pedagogy, media activism, and cultural policy and politics in the contemporary era.

From the future back to the present

The contemporary U.S. society, polity, and culture that have been the topic of these studies are in a situation of seemingly permanent crisis with deteriorating social conditions, political divisions and turmoil, and increasing human suffering. When I published the first edition of *Media Culture* in 1995, in the United States, more than 34 million people lived below the poverty level; over 3 million were homeless; over 10 million were out of work; and millions lacked basic health insurance and guaranteed medical care (Hoffman 1987). Today in 2020, the situation is not much better with growing inequality and poverty, social and political divisions, and crises in U.S. society, polity, culture, and the environment.

Divisions in the U.S. continue to intensify. According to a 2017 Institute for Policy Studies report, three men – Bill Gates, Warren Buffett, and Jeff Bezos – have more wealth (over $240 billion) than around 160 million people, almost half of the U.S. population.[1] Moreover, as the Occupy Movement has publicized, 1% of the U.S. public own more wealth than those in the 90 percentile.[2]

Furthermore, in 1988, "the nations of the world spent over $110 for each man, woman, and child on military expenses – overwhelmingly more than on food, water, shelter, health, education, or protecting the ecosystem" (French 1992: 37). As I conclude the second edition of *Media Culture* in 2020, militarism continues to ravage the earth, and military spending is at the highest level in human history. *Defense News* reports that:

> Overall military expenditures rose 2.6 percent between 2017 and 2018, to hit a total of $1.82 trillion, according to new research from the Stockholm International Peace Research Institute. The total from 2018 is 5.4 percent higher than 2009, and represents a 76 percent increase over 1998, a 20-year period.[3]

In this conjuncture, militarist forms of media culture like *Game of Thrones* are problematic. On the one hand, I would argue that the popular novels of George R. R. Martin and TV series *Game of Thrones* can be read as a critical reflection of the power politics of the contemporary era that itself reveals ideological bias of patriarchal and militarist ideologies. The globally popular TV series was created by David Benioff and D. B. Weiss for HBO as an adaptation of *A Song of Ice and Fire*, George R. R. Martin's series of fantasy novels, the first of which is *A Game of Thrones*. The series premiered on HBO in the United States on April 17, 2011, and concluded on May 19, 2019, with 73 episodes broadcast over eight seasons and produced allegories of power politics.

Game of Thrones is set in a prehistoric era at a time when the dangers of climate change and global warming and the forces in the modern world that are producing them are reaching crisis proportions, and in this context such spectacles of premodern struggles for power can be read as escapist. As we saw in the last chapter, many fantasy and apocalypse films are dealing allegorically with climate changes and present dystopic extrapolations of present ecological conditions leading to environmental devastation in the future. Indeed, scientists are predicting dangers of growing extinction of species,[4] global warming is melting icecaps, causing floods, droughts, and biblical devastation of the environment. Pollutants and industrial-technological production continue to threaten the fate of the earth and human life and scientists warn that if immediate action is not taken to reverse these trends, the effects will be catastrophic.

Meanwhile, the conditions of everyday life, even in the metropoles of the United States, continue to deteriorate dramatically. Numbers of homeless and underemployed continue to grow; epidemics of cancer, AIDS, and other deadly diseases proliferate with no cure in sight; crime and violence are on the rise with an out of control gun culture producing deaths each and every day; tobacco, drugs, alcohol, and opioids, are responsible for millions of casualties yearly; drinking water continues to be contaminated by toxic chemicals and basic foods are adulterated with chemicals, additives, and pesticides, many of which contribute to deadly diseases. Further, global pandemics like the COVID-19 virus sweeping the globe as I edit this text, wreak havoc, killing millions and totally disrupt contemporary life, causing major societal shut-downs. Accidents and deaths in the workplace grow, while people are subject to increased surveillance, insecurity, and cutbacks on social benefits. And the infrastructure continues to deteriorate while Congress seems unable to address problems that most people agree on.

As compensation for decaying social conditions, those who can afford it are offered an always increasing dose of media culture and consumption, as well as proliferating forms of social media. The numbers of channels on cable television continue to multiply, with a previous generation's estimates of more than 500 channels vastly surpassed on many cable systems, to say nothing of the wealth of material on the Internet, social media, and streaming services. The hours of tele-vision watching continue to grow, the amount of advertising continues to increase, and the colonization of leisure and society by myriad forms of media and digital culture continues apace. "Influencers" on social media can become wealthy by promoting products that most people cannot buy. Yet those who are most exploited and oppressed by the social order can often afford little more than the "free" entertainment provided by broadcasting, especially television.

As an escape from social misery, or distraction from the cares and woes of everyday existence, people turn to media culture to produce some meaning and value in their lives. Films glamorize the "American way of life" and provide unreal models of identification, while images of violence constantly increase. Sports offer identification with glamour, power, and success, empowering those who identify with winning teams and stars. TV soap operas and situation com-edies provide education for coping in the contemporary social order, while action entertainment demonstrates who has power and who doesn't, who can and cannot exercise violence, and who does and does not get awarded with the benefits of the "good life" in the media and consumer society. Advertising dem-onstrates how to solve problems and how to be happy, successful, and popular – through proper purchases of commodities, goods, and services. And "gaming" trains young people to compete in the digital economy and other realms of life.

Many individuals practicing cultural studies celebrate this culture and way of life and thus contribute to the perpetuation of an unjust and oppressive social order. I have attempted to develop critical perspectives on contemporary society and culture in this book and believe that surrender of criticism and oppositional resistance is nothing more than capitulation to a way of life that produces incredible misery and suffering for people throughout the world.

People in the future may well look back at this era of political and media culture with disbelief. Perhaps denizens of an age of interactive technologies will look back at the passive couch potatoes of the era in which television was the dominant form of entertainment in wonder. Perhaps those able to access information from a wealth of sources from computer databases will be astonished that in an earlier era the vast majority of people depended on television for their prime source of information. Perhaps later generations who have accessible a vast array of significantly different and better modes of culture, entertainment, and information at their fingertips will be amazed that people actually consumed the programs of commercial television, radio, and film during the present era.

It is conceivable that the society of the future will look back at earlier eras of media culture as an astonishing period of cultural banality, in which commercially driven culture industries pandered to the lowest common denominator, pouring out films, TV shows, novels, and other artifacts that depicted violence as the way to solve problems, that debased women and people of color, and that repeated the same old tired genre formulas over and over. The endless sequels of popular film and eternal recurrence of the same in the fields of television, popular music, and other forms of media culture might strike a future age as highly primitive and mediocre.

A future age might look at an era that idolized Sylvester Stallone, Madonna, Michael Jackson, mediocre TV stars, fashion models, social media "stars," "influencers," and other celebrities as highly peculiar. Future generations may look at our advertising-saturated culture as the crudest and crassest commercialism, as the one of the most amazing wastes of time and resources in the history of civilization. Future ages might look back on the incredible concentration of wealth and striking class differences, the phenomenal amount of world hunger and poverty, the deadly diseases, the violence and social disorder, the lack of humane and egalitarian social institutions, and the continued degradation of the environment, and perceive this society as truly astonishing. Our time might one day be looked upon as a dark age of incredible ignorance and backwardness where life is much more nasty, brutish, and short than it needs to be. Perhaps our time will be looked at as an especially retrograde period when individuals had not yet adjusted to new technologies, when they were overwhelmed by new media, and not yet well enough educated to govern themselves and control the technologies and media.

Yet perhaps younger and future generations are coming to terms with the new media and technologies and are using them to enhance their individual lives and create a more humane and democratic society. Perhaps the growing choice of media programming and explosion of new media is empowering individuals to increase their realm of choice and control over their culture, and thus to increase their autonomy and sovereignty. Robert McChesney (2018) points out that

> on YouTube alone the amount of video being uploaded is roughly the equivalent of 180,000 feature length movies a week. Meaning that YouTube now generates more content on average in a single week, than all of the film and television programs Hollywood has produced in its entire history.

This is, however, a contradictory phenomenon. On the one hand, it is salutary that young people are using advanced forms of cultural communication, but without critical media literacy (CML) education, there are dangers that the explosion of YouTube and social media will increase racism, sexism, classism, or homophobia, although these modes of communication can be used to fight bigotry and oppression. The students of Parkland High School in Florida that experienced a horrific school shooting showed how social media could be used to advance rational gun control and mobilize citizens for voting on a range of progressive issues (see Hogg and Hogg 2018), so there is hope that the youth of the future can use new media as instruments of progressive social change. Yet educators and activists of the present need to continue teaching and advocating for critical media literacy and making media education a standard part of schooling from grade school on up to the universities and beyond (Kellner-Share 2019).

Hence, it is a positive development that individuals are learning to use the new technologies to communicate with each other, to produce their own media creations, which are circulated and distributed throughout society, so that previously marginalized voices are able to speak, so that the full range and diversity of cultures find expression, so that individuals and groups can speak to others, be creative, and participate in the production of society and culture. Indeed, perhaps the present and future generation will discern the importance of diverse forms of culture and voices and drive governments and citizens to subsidize a wide range of cultural groups and individuals to actively participate in cultural production, freeing cultural expression from the tyranny of the market and the iron yoke of advertising. Perhaps the works of the five major media conglomerates – Comcast (via NBC/Universal), Disney, Viacom and CBS (both controlled by National Amusements), and AT&T (via WarnerMedia) – will be shunned and abhorred by audiences who will find many of their products debased, insulting, and boring, and these conglomerates will wither away, to be replaced by a vibrant spectrum of media cultural expression and a wide range of visions and voices.

On the other hand, perhaps people in the future will spend more time watching more and ever stupider products and the lowest common denominator will sink ever lower, to an era of cultural barbarism impossible to envisage in the present. Perhaps the early decades of the twenty-first century will appear as a golden age of individualism, freedom, and democracy to future inhabitants of dystopic societies, much as the post-holocaust, apocalyptic science fiction films represent life in the twentieth century present as utopian compared to the dismal dystopic future depicted in novels and films like *Blade Runner, The Hunger Games* or *The Handmaid's Tale* and other dystopic novels, television, and films.

Media/cultural studies can play some role, however modest, in the struggle for a better future. Progressive science fiction and fantasy, critical utopian thought, and a future-oriented media/cultural studies can articulate imagined and possible futures and help to guide our present and future choices and action. Reflection on possible media and socio-political futures calls attention to the urgency of impending tasks for media/cultural studies that have been neglected or suppressed in the tumult and confusion of the present and that I will delineate in the concluding sections.

On the positive side, we are living in exciting times in which emergent media and technologies are producing new possibilities for communication, cultural expression, and ways of living everyday life – at least for privileged individuals. We should not forget, however, growing inequalities and the misery of vast numbers of individuals, and should struggle so that they can attain the same opportunities as those more fortunate with better and more education, improved job possibilities, better healthcare, and a more humane society. Moreover, we need to consciously come to terms with our new technologies and culture and devise ways to use them to enhance our lives and to make them available to all. This requires reflection on media and technology and the challenges and problems of living in an ever-mutating media/technological society. With these concerns in mind, I would suggest that media/cultural studies needs to engage several topics that have been addressed within some forms of media and cultural studies, but have often not really been incorporated into its projects and problematics.

Critical media pedagogy

Cultural studies has often underplayed the importance of developing pedagogies for promoting critical media literacy. While the Frankfurt School believed that the culture industries were overwhelmingly manipulative and overwhelmingly ideological, some versions of cultural studies argue that the media merely provide resources for audience use and pleasure. Avoidance of its images and messages seems to be the upshot of the Frankfurt School critique, while some cultural studies simply celebrate sports, film and TV, fandom, and other media phenomena. The Frankfurt School's total rejection of mass culture seems inappropriate, as media culture is here to stay and, if anything, its products are becoming increasingly popular and powerful. Yet mindless celebration of media culture, without cultivation of methods to promote critical media literacy, is equally pernicious.

Thus, it is important to pursue a project of developing a critical media pedagogy and to teach ourselves and others how to critically decode media messages and to trace their complex range of effects. It is important to be able to perceive the various ideological voices and codes in the artifacts of our common culture and to distinguish between hegemonic ideologies and those images, discourses, and texts that subvert the dominant ideologies. It is also important to promote critical media literacy in and out of schools, so that individuals can critically read and discuss the products of media culture, along with parents consuming media culture with their children and discussing the meaning, values, and messages being promoted.

You are what you see and hear every bit as much as what you eat, and it is therefore important to impress upon individuals the need to avoid media culture junk food and to choose healthier and more nourishing products. This requires learning discrimination and cultivating tastes for the better products of media culture, as well as alternative forms of culture ranging from poetry, literature, painting, to alternative music, film, and television. Marshall McLuhan (1964) argued that young people of the time were naturally media literate and I argue that critical media literacy is a skill that must be cultivated and developed. Thus, developing critical media literacy requires developing explicit strategies of cultural pedagogy and many dominant schools of contemporary theory – such as the Frankfurt School, cultural studies, and most postmodern theory – have failed to develop a critical media pedagogy.[5]

Within educational circles, there is a debate over what constitutes the field of media pedagogy with different agendas and programs. A traditionalist "protectionist" approach would attempt to "inoculate" young people against the effects of media addiction and manipulation by cultivating a taste for book literacy, high culture, and the values of truth, beauty, and justice. Neil Postman in his books *Amusing Ourselves to Death* (1985) and *Technopolis* (1992) exemplifies this approach, attacking media culture and championing print media. A "media literacy" movement, by contrast, attempts to teach students to read, analyze, and decode media texts, in a fashion parallel to the cultivation of print literacy. Media arts education in turn teaches students to appreciate the aesthetic qualities of media and to use various media technologies as tools of self-expression and creation. Critical media literacy, finally, builds on these approaches, teaching students to be critical of media representations and discourses, but also stressing the importance of learning to use the media as modes of self-expression and social activism (Kellner-Share 2019).

A critical media literacy approach, such as I would advocate, engages the politics of representation and how media culture presents representations and narratives of class, gender, race, sexuality, as well as political ideologies. CML is intrinsically political presenting critique of media culture that promotes racism, sexism, classism, homophobia, or other forms of oppression while valorizing media that presents critical representation of these forms of bias and oppression and presents representations, narratives, and texts that represent more progressive representations of gender, race, class, sexuality, and human and social relations – while recognizing that many media texts contain contradictions and ambiguities.

For example, Quentin Tarantino's *Once Upon a Time ... in Hollywood* (2019), which is one of the most popular and hotly debated films of 2019 as I conclude this second edition, is highly contradictory in its narrative, representations, and reception. Tarantino is an auteur with many fans and detractors with a deep personal investment in film and media culture. He presents the story of an aging actor, Rick Dalton (Leonardo DiCaprio), previously the star of a 1950s Western television series *Bounty Law*, who laments to his best friend and stunt double, Cliff Booth (Brad Pitt), that his career is over, that times have changed and his kind of TV Western is no longer popular. The narrative deals with the challenges of these two white men coming to terms with the end of their previous careers and ways of life, while confronting the changes and craziness of the

1960s, represented by the Charles Mansion family with whom the two men by chance come into contact with.

For a diagnostic critique that engages what the film tells us about men in the contemporary era, it depicts the plight of two guys who are out of time and place and nostalgic for an earlier era. The *LA Times* film critic Mary McNamara calls the film "nostalgia porn" for a time when men were men and they ruled the economy, media, and social world.[6] The "Once Upon a Time" in the title thus refers to a fairy tale of a world where white men ruled, but where evil hippies, women, social forces, and change threaten their position and power. Many of Tarantino's films are nostalgic for genres where men were men and ruled, and yet women are challenging, subverting, and over-throwing this world, presenting a panorama of sexual politics that have been highly contested and debated.[7]

While Tarantino's film encodes nostalgia for the old Hollywood and unchallenged male power, the film can be decoded and interpreted in multiple ways. It depicts a period in the late 1960s when youth culture and a counter culture was emerging and established institutions and hierarchies were being challenged. The Manson family represented the most deranged representatives of the counterculture in grotesque ways and *Once Upton a Time* presents a fantasy that heroic men could step up and defend women and the innocent against hippie scum and countercultural forces, thus keeping alive a white male fantasy that was being steadily eclipsed from the 1960s until the present.

Critical media literacy also sees media as a form of power and looks at political economy and ownership of media, its political effects, and how certain texts of media promote interests of oppression and domination, while others promote liberation, freedom, democracy, and positive values. CML thus takes a contextual and comprehensive approach to media that would teach critical skills concerning how to read media critically, how to understand media in specific historical contexts, how to understand how media is produced and works, and how to use media as instruments of social change.

Media and digital technologies of communication are becoming more and more accessible to young people and average citizens and they should be used to promote democratic self-expression and social change, as well as pleasure and potential enlightenment. Thus, technologies that could help produce the end of participatory democracy, by transforming politics into media spectacles and the battle of images, could help in invigorating democratic debate and participation, a theme I take up in the following section.

Media and cultural activism

Most works in cultural studies have been negligent of developing strategies and practices for media intervention and the production of alternative media. There has been little discussion within cultural studies circles concerning how radio, television, film, computers, and other media technologies could be transformed and used as instruments of social enlightenment and progress. Likewise, the

Frankfurt School seemed inherently skeptical of media technologies and viewed them as totally controlled by capitalist corporations.[8] Although it is understandable that Frankfurt School critical theorists could see the media largely as instruments of social control and domination in the era when German, Italian and Japanese fascism controlled the media of their empires, while the Soviet Union and communist party-controlled governments dominated the media in communist regions, and in the U.S. three major broadcasting corporations controlled the media, whereas in most European countries the state controlled major media in many eras of broadcasting and television, the failure of those active in cultural studies from the 1990s to the present today to engage the issue of alternative media and cultural activism is more puzzling and less excusable. For today, there are a variety of venues for alternative film and video production, community radio, Internet and social media activism, and other forms of communications in which citizens and activists can readily intervene.

To be sure, since the rise in particular of the Internet and social media, there are more efforts within cultural studies to promote cultural activism, yet relating cultural studies to oppositional and transformative practice has not been common. In my view, media/cultural studies today should discuss *how* the media and culture can be transformed into instruments of social change, and should promote activist projects. This requires more focus on alternative media and cultural activism than has previously been evident in cultural studies, and calls for reflections on how media technology can be reconfigured and used to empower individuals and social movements.[9] It requires developing activist strategies to intervene in public access television, community radio, all forms of social media, and other domains currently emerging.

To genuinely empower individuals requires giving them knowledge of media production and allowing them to produce artifacts that are then disseminated to the public. Increasing media activism could significantly enhance democracy, making possible the proliferation of voices and allowing those voices that have been silenced or marginalized to speak. Critical media pedagogy and activism require new roles and functions for intellectuals. Media and computer culture is producing new cyberspaces to explore and map, and new terrains of political struggle and intervention. The new cyber-intellectuals of the present may not be the organic intellectuals of the working class that Gramsci envisaged, but we can become technointellectuals of new technologies, social media, and the media ecologies of the future, charting and navigating through the brave new worlds of media culture and technoculture.

To be sure, current and emergent media technologies can be used as instruments of domination or liberation, of manipulation or social enlightenment, and it is up to the cultural producers and activist intellectuals of the present and future to determine which way the new media and technologies will be used and developed and whose interests they serve.

A democratic media politics will accordingly be concerned that the new media and computer technologies will be used to serve the interests of the people and not corporate or political elites. A democratic and transformative media politics will strive to see that media are used to inform and enlighten individuals rather than to manipulate them. A democratic media politics will teach individuals how to use the new media and technologies, to articulate their own experiences and interests, and to promote democratic debate, diversity, and social justice, allowing a full range of voices and ideas to become part of the cyberdemocracy of the future.

Media, cultural policy, and cultural politics

There has also been a failure in Cultural Studies to discern the importance of media and cultural politics. The question of *who* will control the media of the future and debates over the public's access to media, media accountability and responsibility, media funding and regulation, and what kind of cultures, technologies, and institutions are best for cultivating individual freedom, democracy, and human happiness and well-being will become increasingly important in the future.

The proliferation of media culture and technologies focuses attention on the importance of media politics and the need for public intervention in debates over the future of media culture and communications in the information and social media highways and entertainment byways of the future. One of the key issues of the future will concern whether communications and culture are increasingly commodified or are decommodified. Defenders of commercial television in the United States are always praising "free television," a dubious product, however, only made possible at the expense of allowing advertising to clutter the airwaves and giving advertisers and commercial interests significant power over programming, while making advertised commodities more expensive to consumers.

There is an increasing trend, however, to charge for network and even individual TV programs that were once free, as with cable channels that charge stiff monthly fees such as the Disney channels, CBS All Access, Apple TV, and other programming controlled by media-technology behemoths, or cable TV pay channels like HBO, Showtime, Hulu, and other channels. These pay TV channels were once part of a standard cable TV package, but increasingly one must pay extra for new channels and programming like sports, concerts, or pay-per-view events.

Hence, even mainstream television may be increasingly commodified, owned by corporations that will charge for everything. Likewise, today computer Internet access and social media are free to those who have business, university, or government accounts, whereas all computer communication may be commodified in the future, as is much telephone communication. The struggle confronting us is therefore to decommodify computer communication and information, to make the Internet and other information highways of the future open to everyone, free of charge, to expand public access television and community radio, and to develop alternative cultural institutions and practices that are funded by the community or state and made available to the people.

In France, the government carried out an experiment, providing free Minitel computers to all telephone customers (see Feenberg 2001). These computers were initially to be used for getting information, like time, weather, train and airplane schedules, and the like. But they were soon used for public computer communications, with discussion groups, bulletin boards, and other uses quickly developing. The point is that computers and digital devices are part of the standard package of every household, much like television, and efforts must be made so that everyone who does not currently own or have access to a computer can get one and become part of the new culture and society that they will make possible, rather than restricting use of the new technologies to those privileged groups able to purchase them.

Indeed, the very concept of "information superhighways" contains a democratic core that could provide a terrain and discourse of struggle. While the notion that information superhighways will automatically guarantee a free flow of useful and abundant information to all is obviously ideological, a flimflam promotional discourse to sell the agenda of powerful corporations, the superhighway metaphor has some significance for democratic struggles. For our national highway space is that of a public domain, part of a public space open and accessible to all, free of charge. The danger of the corporate information and entertainment scenarios of the future is that megacorporations will own and control these resources, charging fees for entry and use, transforming freeways into tollways.

Thus, while the Internet, social media, and new media sites like Google are currently free, there have long been plans to monetize them, charging for use and access. Against such plans, one should utilize the discourse of the public sphere and public domain and struggle to keep these information highways open and accessible to all, free of charge and free from corporate control. Likewise, a democratic media politics will struggle for community television and radio, providing public access for all citizens so that the entire community can take part in democratic discussion and debate. The free flow of information and communications is essential to a democratic society and thus democracy requires that powerful instruments of information and communication be accessible to all. Keeping the information superhighways open to all, protecting current highways like the Internet, and struggling to open it to more people is thus a key element of a contemporary democratic media politics.

Without a *free* flow of information, citizens cannot be adequately informed and without access to forums of public discussion and debate, citizens are excluded from the dialogue that constitutes the very heart of participatory democracy. In fact, there are currently powerful struggles going on within and between government, business, and the public concerning who will control the new technologies of the future, who will profit from them, and what role the public will play in determining the future of our new technologies and media culture. Individuals need to get involved in these debates and become informed concerning the importance of the issues involved. For instance, there are recurrent attempts to censor communication on the

Internet, to commodify communication on it, charging for what is now free, to allow commercial uses of it, and to open it to corporate domination. And there is growing concern about what Google, Facebook, and other tech/ comm Behemoths are doing with their information and using it for surveillance, manipulation, and monetization (see Noble 2018).

Other groups and individuals are struggling to preserve free communication, to guarantee democratic access and participation, and to make the resources of the new technologies open and accessible to everyone, thus promoting, rather than restricting, democracy. Yet the rise of violent white supremacist, Nazi, and other anti-democratic movements require public debates about hate speech and movements, and the limits to First Amendment Free Speech rights, just as there is an ongoing debate about the Second Amendment and gun rights with constitutional scholars, activists, and theorists arguing that both in the constitution and in numerous court decisions through American history, limits on speech and use and ownership of guns are necessary in certain locations (Kellner 2008). Such discussions are extremely complicated, but a media/cultural studies must engage these issues to be relevant to the challenge of the present age.

These media/political struggles will determine the future of our culture and society and are therefore of prime importance to those concerned with the future of democracy. It is possible that failures to address political economy and to adequately develop media politics within cultural studies is a main source of the avoidance of public policy concerns within cultural studies that Tony Bennett has criticized (1992, in Grossberg et al.). Without a sense of how the larger social forces (i.e., the nature of the broadcasting industry, state policy towards communications, etc.) impinge on everyday life, it is impossible to grasp the relevance of public policy and media politics on the nature of the system of communications and culture in a given society.

Yet in a context in which new technologies of communications are creating dramatic changes in culture, leisure activity, and everyday life, one should perceive the importance of media politics and the ways that the system and framework of communications in a given society help determine what sort of programming and effects are produced. But without situating discussions of public policy within the context of social theory and political economy that analyzes existing configurations of power and domination, discussions of public policy are hopelessly abstract and beside the point. In the United States, during the era of Reagan and Bush (1980–92), Bush Jr. and Cheney (2000–2008), and Trump (2017–?) there really were not many openings for progressive public policy interventions on the national level. Instead, the political urgency at the time was defending liberal gains of the past against conservative onslaughts (I would imagine that something like this was also the case in other countries ruled by conservative or outright right-wing governments).

On the other hand, the era of conservative rule saw many exciting local interventions, with lively alternative and oppositional cultures proliferating and intense political struggles, often cultural in focus, taking part on the local level.

This was true of the Occupy movements in the U.S. and throughout the world, Black Lives Matter, the Trump resistance, the #MeToo movement, and other resistance movements throughout the world. The experience of opposition and resistance has produced myriad forms of politics, which emphasized local, national, and global struggles, like the environmental movement, which is crucial to human survival in the contemporary era. Hence, it is important to see that local, national, and global struggles and issues are important and that these struggles are interconnected.

On the local level, one can often more visibly make a difference, though even rearguard defensive operations on the national level are important, as are public policy interventions that advocate genuine reform on any level. The neglect of cultural politics by critical media cultural and communications studies is distressing and is a sign of the depoliticalization of intellectual life in the present moment.

Thus media/cultural studies can be of importance for the radical democratic project. A critical media pedagogy can cultivate citizenship by helping form individuals free from media manipulation, capable of criticizing media culture and of obtaining information from diverse sources, allowing an informed citizenry to make intelligent political judgements, as well as promoting alternative media production.

Critical media pedagogy can thus serve as part of a process of social enlightenment, producing new roles for critical and public intellectuals. Media culture itself is producing new public spheres and the need for intervention in new arenas of public debate, such as community radio, public access television, always proliferating social media sites, and on and on into the technofuture. Media culture is producing new forms of digital texts with virtual reality on the horizon, and we need to cultivate a critical media literacy able to read and decode images, discourse, narratives and spectacles of the sort central to media culture, as well as the new texts of social media.

Yet media culture also presents the challenge to cultivate new spaces for political discussion and interaction, to produce alternative forms of media and culture, to use the media to promote social enlightenment and to think how media culture can be used for democratization. The challenge of media culture thus produces new vocations for the critical and public intellectual. The ubiquity and complexity of media and digital cultures require critical intellectuals to subvert disciplinary boundaries and to draw on a range of disciplines to understand media culture. It challenges public intellectuals to use media culture to promote democratization and to produce new spaces and alternatives alongside and within media culture. In other words, it is both a mistake to turn one's back on and to ignore media culture as it is and to totally uncritically embrace it. Media culture must be thoroughly analyzed, and possibilities should be explored to intervene within mainstream culture as well as to provide alternative modes of culture and discourse outside of its conventional forms and genres. Media culture is perhaps our fate and cultural ambience as we rush toward the future and we must therefore chart this new terrain and see how we can make it work for the goals of increasing freedom, happiness, democracy, and other values that we wish to preserve and enhance.

Thus, media/cultural studies has many important tasks for the future and can become part of a process of empowerment and enlightenment. On the other hand, it can easily degenerate into just another academic niche, with its canonized texts, stars, and comfortable institutional homes. It is up to us and to future generations to determine the future of our media and technological society and it is to be hoped that they will use media/cultural studies as a weapon of social critique, enlightenment, and progressive social transformation, rather than just as another source of cultural capital.

Notes

1 Rupert Neate, "Bill Gates, Jeff Bezos and Warren Buffett Are Wealthier than Poorest Half of US," *The Guardian*, November 8, 2017 at www.theguardian.com/business/ 2017/nov/08/bill-gates-jeff-bezos-warren-buffett-wealthier-than-poorest-half-of-us (accessed July 25, 2019). For a systematic analysis of the new pluocrats in the U.S. see Freeland 2012.

2 Christopher Ingraham, "Nation's Top 1 Percent Now Have Greater Wealth than the Bottom 90 Percent," *The Seattle Times*, December 8, 2017 at www.seattletimes.com/ business/economy/nations-top-1-percent-now-have-greater-wealth-than-the-bottom-90-percent/ (accessed July 25, 2019).

3 Aaron Mehta, "Here's How Much Global Military Spending Rose in 2018," *Defense News*, April 28, 2019 at www.defensenews.com/global/2019/04/28/heres-how-much-global-military-spending-rose-in-2018/ (accessed July 23, 2019).

4 Thomas, C.D., Cameron, A., Green, R.E. et al. (16 more authors) (2004) "Extinction Risk from Climate Change," *Nature*, 427 (69–70), pp. 145–148 at http://eprints.white rose.ac.uk/83/1/thomascd1.pdf8 (accessed July 23, 2019).

5 On critical media pedagogy, see Giroux 1992; 1994; Sholle and Denski 1994; Hammer and Kellner 2009; Kellner and Share 2019.

6 Mary McNamara, "'Once Upon a Time … in Hollywood' is Quentin Tarantino's 'Make America Great Again'", *Los Angeles Times,* July 31, 2019 at www.latimes.com/ entertainment-arts/movies/story/2019-07-31/once-upon-a-time-in-hollywood-nostal gia-make-america-great-again (accessed August 23, 2019).

7 Notoriously, Tarantino has his fervent male (and female) fan base, but also armies of critics and haters, as once again the reception of *Once Upon a Time in Hollywood* makes clear. The film has his strong defenders and critics, and recent articles that I have read that allows readers' comments puts on display the contradictions and ambiguities concerning his films as well as heated debates about his representations of men, women, and race in particular. For an excellent overview of the controversy over Tarantino's films throughout his career, see Alison Willmore, "A History of Women in Quentin Tarantino Movies," *Buzz Feed News*, July 21, 2019 at www.buzzfeednews.com/art icle/alisonwillmore/quentin-tarantino-women-margot-robbie-once-upon-time (accessed August 7, 2019).

8 The exception in the Frankfurt School was Walter Benjamin (1969), who like his friend Bertolt Brecht took a more activist stance in using contemporary media and forms of culture as instruments of progressive social transformation.

9 This project has been the life-work of critical theorist Andrew Feenberg, see, among his other works, Feenberg 2017, and my appreciation of Feenberg's work in Kellner 2001.

BIBLIOGRAPHY

In the following reference list, I cite books referenced in the text, or that were useful in developing some of my positions and interpretations. Newspaper and magazine articles cited in notes are not reproduced here.

Abercrombie, N. et al. (1980) *The Dominant Ideology Thesis*. London: Routledge & Kegan Paul.
Adorno, Theodor W. (1941) "'On Popular Music,' (with G. Simpson)," *Studies in Philosophy and Social Science*, Vol. 9, No. 1: 17–48.
———— (1974) *Minima Moralia*. London: New Left Books.
———— (1978) "On the Social Situation of Music," *Telos*, Vol. 35 (Spring): 128–164.
Agger, Ben (1991) *Cultural Studies*. London: Falmer Press.
Alterman, Eric (1992) *Sound and Fury*. New York: HarperCollins.
Althusser, Louis (1971) *Lenin and Philosophy*. London: New Left Books.
Anderson, Benedict (1983) *Imaginary Communities*. London: Verso.
Anderson, Perry (1969) "Components of the National Culture," in Alexander Cockburn and Robin Blackburn, editors, *Student Power*. Harmondsworth: Penguin.
———— (1980) *Arguments within English Marxism*. London: New Left Books.
Ang, Ien (1985) *Watching Dallas*. New York: Methuen.
Antonio, Robert J. and Douglas Kellner (1992) "Communication, Democratization, and Modernity: Critical Reflections on Habermas and Dewey," *Habermas, Pragmatism, and Critical Theory*, special section of *Symbolic Interaction*, Vol. 15, No. 3 (Fall 1992), 277–298.
———— (1994a) "Postmodern Social Theory: Contributions and Limitations," in David Dickens and Andrea Fontana, editors, *Postmodernism and Social Inquiry*. New York: Guilford Press, 127–152.
Antonio, Robert and Douglas Kellner (1994b) "Modern Social Theory and the Postmodern Critique," in David Dickens and Andy Fontana, editors, *Postmodernism and Social Inquiry*. New York: Guilford Press, 127–152.
———— with Robert J. Antonio (1992) "Metatheorizing Historical Rupture: Classical Theory and Modernity," Metatheorizing, edited by George Ritzer. New York: Sage, 88–106.

Aronowitz, Stanley (1993) *Roll over Beethoven*. Hanover, NH: University Press of New England.

Baker, Houston A. (1993a) "Spike Lee and the Commerce of Culture," in Manthia Diawara, editor, *Black Cinema: History, Authorship, Spectatorship*. New York: Routledge, 154–176.

———— (1993b) *Black Studies, Rap and the Academy*. Chicago, IL: University of Chicago Press.

Baraka, Amiri (1993) "Spike Lee at the Movies," in Manthia Diawara, editor, *Black American Cinema*. op. cit., New York: Routledge, 145–153.

Barrett, Michele (1980) *Women's Oppression Today*. London: Verso.

Barthes, Roland (1956) *Mythologies*. New York: Hill and Wang.

———— (1975) *Pleasures of the Text*. New York: Oxford University Press.

Baudrillard, Jean (1976) *L'echange symbolique et la mort*. Paris: Gallimard, Translation: Symbolic Exchange and Death. London: Sage, 1993.

———— (1981 [1975]) *Toward a Critique of the Political Economy of the Sign*. St. Louis: Telos Press.

———— (1983a) *Simulations*. New York: Semiotext.

———— (1983b) *In the Shadow of the Silent Majorities*. New York: Semiotext.

———— (1983c) The Ecstasy of Communication, in *Foster, Anti-Aesthetic*, op. cit., 126–134.

———— (1984) "Interview: Game with Vestiges," *On the Beach*, Vol. 5 (Winter): 19–25.

———— (1988) *America*. London: Verso.

———— (1990) *Fatal Strategies*. New York: Semiotext(e).

———— (1993) *The Transparence of Evil*. London: Verso.

Beck, Ulrich (1992) *Risk Society*. London: Sage Publications.

Bell, Daniel (1960) *The End of Ideology*. New York: The Free Press.

———— (1973) *The Coming of Post-industrial Society*. New York: Basic Books.

———— (1976) *The Cultural Contradictions of Capitalism*. New York: Harper and Row.

Benedict, Michael (1991) *Cyberspace. First Steps*. Cambridge, MA: MIT Press.

Bennett, Tony (1990) *Outside Literature*. London: Routledge.

———— (1992) "Putting Policy into Cultural Studies," in Lawrence Grossberg, Cary Nelson and Paula Treichler, editors, *Cultural Studies*. New York: Routledge, 23–34.

Benshoff, H. M. and S. Griffin (2009) *America on Film*. Wiley-Blackwell.

Berland, Jody (1992) "Angels Dancing: Cultural Technologies and the Production of Space," in Lawrence Grossberg, Cary Nelson and Paula Treichler, editors, *Cultural Studies*. New York: Routledge, 51–66.

Berman, Marshall (1982) *All that Is Solid Melts into Air*. New York: Simon and Schuster.

Berman, Russell (1984) "Modern Art and Desublimation," *Telos*, Vol. 62: 31–58.

Best, Steven (1992) "The Apocalyptic Imagination: Pychon's Gravity's Rainbow," *Centennial Review*, Vol. XXVI, No. 1 (Winter): 59–88.

Best, Steven and Douglas Kellner (1987) "'(re)watching Television: Notes toward a Political Criticism," *Diacritics* Vol. 17, No. 2, (Summer, 1987): 97–113.

———— (1991) *Postmodern Theory: Critical Interrogations*. London and New York: Macmillan and Guilford.

———— (1997) *The Postmodern Turn*. London and New York: Routledge and Guilford Press.

———— (2001) *The Postmodern Adventure. Science Technology, and Cultural Studies at the Third Millennium*. New York and London: Guilford and Routledge.

Biskind, Peter (1983) *Seeing Is Believing*. New York: Pantheon.

Bloch, Ernst (1986) *The Principle of Hope*. Cambridge: MIT Press.

———— (1991 [1935]) *Heritage of Our Time*. Berkeley, CA: University of California Press.

Blundell, Valda et al. (1993) *Relocating Cultural Studies*. New York: Routledge.

Boggs, Carl (1984) *The Two Revolutions: Gramsci and the Dilemmas of Western Marxism*. Boston, MA: South End Press.

—— (1991) "Social Movements and Political Strategy in the Aftermath of the Gulf War" (unpublished MS).

Bono, Paola and Sandra Hemp, editors (1991) *Italian Feminist Thought*. Oxford: Basil Blackwell.

Bordo, Susan (1992) *The Madonna Connection: Representational Politics, Subcultural Identities, and Cultural Theory* (Cultural Studies) (Ramona Liera Schwichtenberg, Deidre Pribram, Dave Tetzlaff, Ron Scott and Laurie Schulze, editors). Boudler, CO: Westview Press, 272–290.

Brantlinger, Patrick (1990) *Crusoe's Footprints*. London and New York: Routledge.

Britton, Andrew, Richard Lippe, Tony Williams, and Robin Wood (1979) *American Nightmare: Essays on the Horror Film*. Toronto: Festival of Festivals.

Bronner, Stephen and Douglas Kellner (1989) "Critical Theory and Society," in Stephen Eric Bronner and Douglas Kellner, editors, *A Reader*. London and New York: Metheun/Routledge.

Brown, Norman O. (1985 [1955]) *Life Against Death: The Psychoanalytical Meaning of History*. Wesleyan University Press, 2nd edition.

Bürger, Peter (1984 [1974]) *Theory of the Avant-Garde*. Minneapolis, MN: University of Minnesota Press.

Burroughs, William (1959) *Naked Lunch*. New York: Grove Press.

Butler, Jeremy G. (1985) "Miami Vice and the Legacy of Film Noir," *Journal of Popular Film and Television*, Vol. 13, No. 3: 132–143.

Cahoone, Lawrence E. (1988) *The Dilemma of Modernity*. Albany, NY: State University of New York Press.

Caldwell, John (2008) *Production Culture: Industrial Reflexivity and Critical Practice in Film/ Television*. Durham, NC: Duke University Press, 2nd edition, 2013.

Campbell, Joseph (1956) *The Hero with a Thousand Faces*. New York: Meridian.

Canadian Journal of Political and Social Theory (1983) *Special Issue on Ideology*, Vol. 7, No. 1–2 (Winter–Spring).

Cannon, Lou (1992) *President Reagan: The Role of a Lifetime*. Washington, DC: PublicAffairs.

Centre for Contemporary Cultural Studies (1979) *On Ideology*. London: Hutchinson.

—— (1980) *Culture, Media, Language*. London: Hutchinson.

—— (1981) *Unpopular Education: Schooling and Social Democracy in England since 1944*. London: Hutchinson.

—— (1982) *The Empire Strikes Back: Race and Racism in 70s Britain*. London: Hutchinson.

Chodorow, Nancy (1978) *The Reproduction of Mothering*. Berkeley, CA: University of California Press.

Chomsky, Noam (1989) *Necessary Illusions*. Boston, MA: South End Press.

Clark, Ramsey (1992) *The Fire This Time*. New York: Thunder Mouth Press.

Clover, Carol (1992) *Men, Women, and Chain Saws. Gender in the Modern Horror Film*. Princeton, NJ: Princeton University Press.

Collins, Jim, Hilary Radner, and Ava Preacher Collins, editors (1993) *Film Theory Goes to the Movies*. New York and London: Routledge.

Connor, Steven (1989) *Postmodernist Culture*. London and New York: Blackwell.

Coward, Rosalind and John Ellis (1977) *Language and Materialism*. London: Routledge & Kegan Paul.

Cox, Oliver (1948) *Caste, Class & Race*. New York: Doubleday, Reprinted 1970, Monthly Review paperback.

Crawford, Alan (1980) *Thunder on the Right*. New York: Pantheon.

Crenshaw, Kimberly (1991) "Mapping the Margins: Intersectionality, Identity Politics, and Violence against Women of Color," *Stanford Law Review*, Vol. 43, No. 6 (Jul., 1991): 1241–1299.

Cross, Brian (1993) *It's Not about a Salary. Rap, Race, and Resistance in Los Angeles*. London: Verso.

Csicery-Ronay, Istvan (1991) "Cyberpunk and Neuromanticism," in McCaffery, editor, op. cit.

——— (1992) "The Sentimental Futurist: Cybernetics and Art in William Gibson's *Neuromancer*," *Critique* Vol. 33, No. 3, (Spring, 1992): 221–240.

Curtis, Neil and Valentina Cardo (2018) "Superheroes and third-wave feminism," *Feminist Media Studies*, Vol. 18, No. 3, Published online: 24 Jul 2017 at www.tandfonline.com/doi/abs/10.1080/14680777.2017.1351387 (accessed February 17, 2020)

D'Antonio, Michael (2015) *Never Enough: Donald Trump and the Pursuit of Success*. New York: MacMillan.

Davies, Ioan (1995) *Cultural Studies and Beyond: Fragments of Empire*. London: Routledge.

Davis, Mike (1986) *Prisoners of the American Dream*. New York: Verso.

de Beauvoir, Simone (1952) *The Second Sex*. New York: Knopf.

de Certeau, Michel (1984) *The Practice of Everyday Life*. Berkeley, CA: University of California Press.

Decker, Jeffrey Louis (1993) "The State of Rap: Time and Place in Hip Hop Nationalism," *Social Text*, Vol. 34: 53–84.

Deleuze, Gilles and Felix Guattari (1977) *Anti-Oedipus*. New York: Viking.

Denton, Robert E. (1993) *The Media and the Persian Gulf War*. Westport, CT: Praeger.

Denzin, Norman (1991) *Images of Postmodern Society*. Newbury Park and London: Sage Press.

Derrida, Jacques (1976) *Of Grammatology*. Baltimore, MD: John Hopkins University Press.

——— (1978) *Writing and Difference*. Chicago, IL: University of Chicago Press.

Dylan, Bob (2004) *Chronicles: Volume 1*. New York: Simon and Schuster.

Dyson, Michael (1993a) *Reflecting Black*. Minneapolis, MN: University of Minnesota Press.

——— (1993b) "Between Apocalypse and Redemption: John Singleton's Boyz N the Hood," in Jim Collins, Hilary Radner and Ava Preacher Collins, editors, *Film Theory Goes to the Movies*. New York and London: Routledge, 209–226.

Eisenstein, Zillah (1979) *Capitalist Patriarchy and the Case for Socialist Feminism*. New York: Monthly Review Press.

Emery, Michael (1991) *How Mr. Bush Got His War: Deceptions, Double-Standards & Disinformation*. Westfield, NJ: Open Magazine Pamphlet Series, originally published in the Village Voice, March 5, 1991, pp. 22–27.

Ewen, Stuart (1988) *All Consuming Images*. New York: Basic Books.

Ewen, Stuart and Elizabeth Ewen (1982) *Channels of Desire*. New York: McGraw-Hill.

Exoo, Fred, editor (1987) *Democracy Upside Down*. New York: Praeger.

Faludi, Susan (1991) *Backlash*. New York: Crown Publishers.

——— (1999) *Stiffed: The Betrayal of the American Man*. New York: William Morrow.

Fanon, Frantz (1965) *The Wretched of the Earth*. New York: Grove Press.

Featherstone, Mike (1991) *Consumer Culture and Postmodernism*. London: Sage.

Ferguson, Tom and Joel Rogers (1986) *Right Turn*. New York: Will and Wang.

Fiske, John (1986a) "Television: Polysemy and Popularity," *Critical Studies in Mass Communication*, Vol. 3, No. 4: 391–408.

———— (1986b) "British Cultural Studies and Television," in R. C. Allen, editor, *Channels of Discourse*. Chapel Hill: University of North Carolina Press, 254–289.

———— (1987a) *Television Culture*. New York and London: Routledge.

———— (1987b) "Miami Vice, Miami Pleasure," *Cultural Studies*, Vol. 1, No. 1: 113–119.

———— (1989a) *Reading the Popular*. Boston, MA: Unwin Hyman.

———— (1989b) *Understanding Popular Culture*. Boston, MA: Unwin Hyman.

———— (1993) *Power Works*. New York and London: Verso.

Fitting, Peter (1991) "The Lessons of Cyberpunk," in Constance Penley and Andrew Ross, editors, *Technoculture*. Minneapolis: University of Minnesota Press, 295–296.

Flew, Terry (2014) *New Media: An Introduction*. Oxford, UK: Oxford University Press.

Foster, Hal, editor (1983) *The Anti-Aesthetic*. Seattle, WA: Bay Press.

Foucault, Michel (1970) *The Order of Things*. New York: Pantheon.

———— (1977) *Language, Counter-Memory, Practice*. Ithaca, NY: Cornell University Press.

———— (1979) *Discipline and Punish*. New York: Vintage Books.

———— (1992 [1984]) *The History of Sexuality Volume 2: The Use of Pleasure*. London: Penguin Books.

Frank, Lisa and Paul Smith (1993). *Madonnarama*. Pittsburgh, PA: Cleis Press.

Fraser, Nancy (1989) *Unruly Practices*. Minneapolis, MN: University of Minnesota Press.

Fregoso, Rosa Linda (1993) *The Bronze Screen*. Minneapolis: University of Minnesota Press.

French, Marilyn (1992) *The War Against Women*. New York: Ballantine Books.

Friedman, Alan (1993) *Spider's Web*. New York: Bantam Books.

Friere, Paolo (1972) *The Pedagogy of the Oppressed*. New York: Herder and Herder.

Frisby, David (1985) *Fragments of Modernity*. Cambridge: Polity Press.

Frith, Simon, Andrew Goodwin, and Lawrence Grossberg (1993) *The Music Video Reader*. London and New York: Routledge.

Fromm, Erich (1941) *Escape From Freedom*. New York: Holt, Rinehart and Winston.

Galloway, Scott (2017) *The Four: The Hidden DNA of Amazon, Apple, Facebook, and Google*. London: Portfolio; First Edition.

Gane, Mike (1991a) *Baudrillard. Critical and Fatal Theory*. London: Routledge.

———— (1991b) *Baudrillard's Bestiary*. London: Routledge.

George, Nelson (1988) *The Death of Rhythm & Blues*. New York: Pantheon.

Gerbner, George (1992) "Persian Gulf War: The Movie," in Hamid Mowlana, George Berbner, Herbert I. Schiller, editors, *Triumph of the Image: The Media's War in the Persian Gulf - A Global Perspective*. Westview Press, 243–265.

Gerbner, George and Larry Gross (1976) "Living with Television: The Violence Profile," *Journal of Communication* Vol. 26, No 2 (Spring): 173–199.

Gibson, William (1984) *Neuromancer*. New York: Dell Books.

———— (1986) *Burning Chrome*. New York: Arbor Books.

Gibson, William and Bruce Sterling (1991) *The Difference Engine*. New York: Bantam.

Gilroy, Paul (1991) *There Ain't No Black in the Union Jack*. Chicago, IL: University of Chicago Press.

———— (1993) *The Black Atlantic: Modernity and Double Consciousness*, London: Verso Books.

Giroux, Henry (1992) *Border Crossing*. New York: Routledge.

———— (1993) "The Era of Insurgent Multiculturalism in the Era of the Los Angeles Uprising," *The Journal of the Midwest Modern Language Association*, Vol. 26, No. 1 (Spring): 12–30.

———— (1994) *Disturbing Pleasures*. New York: Routledge.

———— (2009) *Youth in a Suspect Society: Democracy or Disposability?*. London: Palgrave Macmillan.

Gitlin, Todd (1978) "Media Sociology: The Dominant Paradigm," *Theory and Society*, Vol. 6: 205–253.

—— (1987) *Watching Television*. New York: Pantheon.

Goldman, Robert (1992) *Reading Ads Socially*. London and New York: Routledge.

Goldman, Robert and Stephen Papson (forthcoming) *Sign Wars*. New York: Guilford Press.

Gorz, Andre (1982) *Farewell to the Working Class*. Boston, MA: South End Press.

—— (1985) *Paths to Paradise*. Boston, MA: South End Press.

Gouldner, Alvin W. (1976) *The Dialectic of Ideology and Technology*. New York: Seabury.

Gramsci, Antonio (1971) *Selections from the Prison Notebooks*. New York: International Publishers.

—— (1987) "The In-Difference of Television," *Journal of Communication Inquiry*, Vol. 10, No. 2: 28–46.

—— (1989) "The Formations of Cultural Studies: An American in Birmingham," *Strategies*, Vol. 22: 114–149.

—— (1992a) *Prison Notebooks*. New York: Columbia University Press, Vol. 1.

—— (1992b) *We Gotta Get Out of This Place*. New York and London: Routledge.

Grossberg, Lawrence (1982) "Ideology of Communication: Post-Structuralism and the Limits of Communication," *Man and World*, Vol. 15: 83–101.

Grossberg, Lawrence, Cary Nelson, and Paula Treichler (1992) *Cultural Studies*. New York: Routledge.

Guerrero, Ed (1993a) "Spike Lee and the Fever in the Racial Jungle," in Collins, Jim, Hilary Radner, and Ava Preacher Collins, editors, *Film Theory Goes to the Movies*. New York and London: Routledge, 170–181.

—— (1993b) *Framing Blackness. The African American Image in Film*. Philadelphia, PA: Temple University Press.

Guralnick, Peter (1995) *Last Train to Memphis: The Rise of Elvis Presley*. Back Bay Books.

—— (2010) *Careless Love: Unmaking of Elvis Presley*. Abacus.

Habermas, Jurgen (1975) *Legitimation Crisis*. Boston, MA: Beacon Press.

—— (1987) *The Philosophical Discourse of Modernity*. Cambridge, MA: MIT Press.

Hafner, Katie and John Markoff (1991) *Cyberpunk. Outlaws and Hackers on the Computer Frontier*. New York: Simon and Schuster.

Haley, Alex and X Malcolm (1965) *The Autobiography of Malcolm X*. Baltimore and London: Penguin.

Hall, Stuart (1980a) "Cultural Studies and the Centre: Some Problematics and Problems," in Hall, et al., editors, *Culture, Media, Language*. London: Hutchinson, 15–47.

—— (1980b) "Encoding/Decoding," in Hall, et al., editors. 128–138.

—— (1980c) "Cultural Studies: Two Paradigms," *Media, Culture, & Society*, Vol. 2: 57–72.

—— (1981) "Notes on Deconstructing 'The Popular'," in R. Samuel, editor *People's History and Socialist Theory*. London: Routledge, 227–239.

—— (1986) "The Problem of Ideology – Marxism without Guarantees," *Journal of Communication Inquiry*, Vol. 10, No. 2 (Summer): 28–44.

—— (1987) "On Postmodernism and Articulation: An Interview," *Journal of Communication Inquiry*, Vol. 10, No. 2: 45–60.

—— (1990) *The Road to Renewal*. London: Verso.

—— (1992) "What Is This 'Black' in Black Popular Culture?" in Gina Dent, editor *Black Popular Culture*. Seattle, WA: Bay Press, 21–33.

Hall, Stuart and Martin Jacques, editors (1983) *The Politics of Thatcherism*. London: Lawrence & Wishart.

Hall, Stuart and T. Jefferson (1976) *Resistance Through Rituals, Youth Subcultures in Post-War Britain*. London: HarperCollinsAcademic.

Hall, Stuart and Paddy Whannel (1964) *The Popular Arts*. London: Hutchinson.

Hall, Stuart et al. (1980) *Culture, Media, Language*. London: Hutchinson.

Hammer, Rhonda (2001) *Antifeminism and Family Terrorism: A Critical Feminist Perspective*. New York: Peter Lang.

Harms, John and Douglas Kellner (1991) "Towards a Critical Theory of Advertising," *Critical Perspectives in Social Theory*, Vol. 11: 41–67.

Hartmann, Heidi (1981) "The Unhappy Marriage of Marxism and Feminism," in *Sargent, Women and Revolution*, op. cit.

Harvey, David (1989) *The Condition of Postmodernity*. Oxford: Blackwell.

Hebdige, Dick (1979) *Subculture*. London: Methuen.

———— (1988) *Hiding in the Light*. London and New York: Routledge.

Herman, Edward and Noam Chomsky (1988) *Manufacturing Consent*. New York: Pantheon.

Hertsgaard, Mark (1988) *On Bended Knee: The Press and the Reagan Presidency*. New York: Farrar Straus & Giroux.

Hoffman, Abie (1987) *Steal This Urine Test*. New York: Viking/Penguin.

Hogg, David and Lauren Hogg (2018). *#NeverAgain: A New Generation Draws the Line*. New York: Random House.

Hoggart, Richard (1958) *The Uses of Literacy*. New York: Oxford University Press.

hooks, bell (1984) *Feminist Theory: From Margin to Center*. Boston, MA: South End Press.

———— (1990) *Yearning: Race, Gender, and Cultural Politics*. Boston, MA: South End Press.

———— (1992) *Black Looks. Race and Representation*. Toronto: Between the Lines.

———— (1993) "Malcolm X: Consumed by Images," *Z Magazine* (March): 36–39.

hooks, bell and Cornel West (1991) *Breaking Bread. Insurgent Black Intellectual Life*. Toronto: Between the Lines.

Horkheimer, Max and Theodor W. Adorno (1972) *Dialectic of Enlightenment*. New York: Seabury.

Howard, Dick and Karl E. Klare (1972) *The Unknown Dimension*. New York: Basic Books.

Hunt, Darnell, et al. (2018) Hollywood Diversity Report 2018. UCLA College Social Sciences at https://socialsciences.ucla.edu/wp-content/uploads/2018/02/UCLA-Hollywood-Diversity-Report-2018-2-27-18.pdf (accessed on February 17, 2020).

Hunter, James and Davison (1991) *Culture Wars*. New York: Basic Books.

Hutcheon, Linda (1989) *The Politics of Postmodernism*. New York: Routledge.

Isikoff, Michael and David Corn (2018) *Russian Roulette: The Inside Story of Putin's War on America and the Election of Donald Trump*. New York: Twelve Books.

Jackson, John A. (1991). *Big Beat Heat: Alan Freed and the Early Years of Rock & Roll*. Schirmer.

Jameson, Fredric (1979) "Reification and Utopia in Mass Culture," *Social Text*, Vol. 1 (Winter): 130–148.

———— (1981) *The Political Unconscious*. Ithaca, NY: Cornell University Press.

———— (1983) "Postmodernism and the Consumer Society," in *Foster, The Anti-Aesthetic*, op. cit.

———— (1984) "Postmodernism, or the Cultural Logic of Late Capitalism," *New Left Review*, Vol. 146: 53–93.

———— (1990) *Signatures of the Visible*. New York and London: Routledge.

———— (1991) *Postmodernism, or the Cultural Logic of Late Capitalism*. Durham: Duke University Press.

———— (1993) "On 'Cultural Studies'," *Social Text*, Vol. 34: 17.

———— (2000 [1977]) "Class and Allegory in Mass Culture: Dog Day Afternoon as Political Film," in Michael Hardt and Kathi Weeks, editors, *The Jameson Reader*. London and Malden, MA: Blackwell, 288–307.

Jeffords, Susan (1989) *The Remasculinization of America*. Bloomington, IN: Indiana University Press.

———— (1994) *Hard Bodies*. New Brunswick, NY: Rutgers University Press.

Jeffords, Susan and Lauren Rabinovitz (1994) *Seeing through the Media. The Persian Gulf War*. New Brunswick, NJ: Rutgers University Press.

Jenkins, Henry (2012) *Textual Poachers*. London and New York: Routledge, 2nd Edition.

Jewett, Robert and John Lawrence (1988) *The American Monomyth*. Lanham, MD: University Press of America, 2nd edition.

Johnson, Richard (1985 [1986]) "What Is Cultural Studies Anyway?" *Social Text*, Vol. 16: 38–80.

Johnson, Sam and Chris Marcil (1993) *Beavis and Butt-Head. This Book Sucks*. New York: Pocket Books.

Kaplan, Ann (1987) *Rocking around the Clock: Music Television, Postmodernism, and Consumer Culture*. London and New York: Methuen.

Katz, Elihu and Paul F. Lazarsfeld (1955) *Personal Influence*. New York: The Free Press.

Kellner, Douglas (1973) *Heidegger's Concept of Authenticity*. Ann Arbor, Mich.: University Microfilms.

———— (1978) "Ideology, Marxism, and Advanced Capitalism," *Socialist Review*, Vol. 42 (November–December): 37–65.

———— (1979) "TV, Ideology, and Emancipatory Popular Culture," *Socialist Review*, Vol. 45 (May–June): 13–53.

———— (1980) *Television Images, Codes, and Messages, Televisions*, Vol. 7, No. 4: 2–19.

———— (1981) "Brecht's Marxist Aesthetic: The Korsch Connection," in Betty Weber and Herbert Heinin, editors, *Bertolt Brecht: Political Theory and Literary Practice*. Athens, GA: University of George Press, 29–42.

———— (1982a) "Television Myth and Ritual," *Praxis*, Vol. 6: 133–155.

———— (1982b) "Kulturindustrie Und Massenkommunikation. Die Kritische Theorie Und Ihre Folgen," in Wolfgang Bonss and Axel Honneth, editors, *Sozialforschung als Kritik*. Frankfurt: Suhrkamp, 482–514.

———— (1984) *Herbert Marcuse and the Crisis of Marxism*. London and Berkeley, CA: Macmillan and University of California Press.

———— (1985) "Public Access Television: Alternative Views," *Radical Science Journal*, Vol. 16: 79–92, Making Waves.

———— (1987) "Baudrillard, Semiurgy and Death," *Theory, Culture & Society*, Vol. 4, No. 1: 125–146.

———— (1988) "Postmodernism as Social Theory: Some Challenges and Problems," *Theory, Culture & Society*, Vol. 5, No. 2–3: 239–270.

———— (1989a) *Critical Theory, Marxism, and Modernity*. Cambridge and Baltimore, MD: Polity and John Hopkins University Press.

———— (1989b) *From Marxism to Postmodernism and Beyond: Critical Studies of Jean Baudrillard*. Cambridge and Palto Alto: Polity Press and Stanford University Press.

Kellner, Douglas, editor (1989c) *Jameson/Postmodernism/Critique*. Washington, DC: Maisoneuve.

———— (1989d) "Reading Images Critically: Toward a Postmodern Pedagogy," *Journal of Education*, Vol. 170, No. 3: 31–52.

———— (1990a) *Television and the Crisis of Democracy*. Boulder, CO: Westview.

———— (1990b) "Fashion, Advertising, and the Consumer Society," in John D. H. Downing and Ali Mohammadi, editors, *Questioning the Media*. Beverley Hills and London: Sage, 242–254.

———— (1991) "Reading Film Politically: Reflections on Hollywood Film in the Age of Reagan," *The Velvet Light Trap*, Vol. 27 (Spring): 9–24.

———— (1992a) "Toward a Multiperspectival Cultural Studies," *Centennial Review*, Vol. XXVI, No. 1: 5–41.

———— (1992b) *The Persian Gulf TV War*. Boulder, CO: Westview.

———— (1994a) *A Baudrillard Reader*. Oxford: Blackwell.

———— (1994b) "Ideology, Culture and Utopia in Ernst Bloch," in Tom Moylan and Jaime Owen Daniel, editors, *Ernst Bloch Revisited*. London: Verso, 80–95.

———— (1995) *Media Culture*. London and New York: Routledge.

———— (1997) "Political Economy and Cultural Studies: Overcoming the Divide," in Marjorie Ferguson and Peter Golding, editors, *Cultural Studies in Question*. London: Sage Publications, 102–120.

———— (2002) "Presidential Politics: The Movie," *American Behavioral Scientist*, Vol. 46, No. 4 (December 2002): 467–486.

———— (2003a) *Media Spectacle*. London and New York: Routledge.

———— (2003b) *From September 11 to Terror War: The Dangers of the Bush Legacy*. Lanham, MD: Rowman and Littlefield.

———— (2003c) *From September 11 to Terror War: The Dangers of the Bush Legacy*. Lanham, MD: Rowman and Littlefield.

———— (2005) *Media Spectacle and the Crisis of Democracy*. Boulder, CO: Paradigm Press.

———— (2007) "The Elvis Spectacle and the Culture Industry," in Gerry Bloustien, Margaret Peters and Susan Luckman, editors, *Sonic Synergies: Music, Technology, Community, Identity*. Hampshire, England and Burlington, VT: Ashgate Publishing Company, 59–69.

———— (2008) *Guys and Guns Amok: Domestic Terrorism and School Shootings from the Oklahoma City Bombings to the Virginia Tech Massacre*. Boulder, CO: Paradigm Press.

———— (2010) *Cinema Wars: Hollywood Film and Politics in the Bush/Cheney Era*. Malden, MA and UK: Blackwell.

———— (2012) *Media Spectacle and Insurrection, 2011: From the Arab Uprisings to Occupy Everywhere*. London and New York: Continuum/Bloomsbury.

———— (2016) *American Nightmare: Donald Trump, Media Spectacle, and Authoritarian Populism*. Rotterdam, The Netherlands: Sense Publishers.

———— (2017) *American Horror Show: Election 2016 and the Ascent of Donald J. Trump*. Rotterdam: Sense Publishers.

Kellner, Douglas and Michael Ryan (1988) *Camera Politica: The Politics and Ideology of Contemporary Hollywood Film*. Bloomington, IN: Indiana University Press.

Kellner, Douglas and Jeff Share (2019) *The Critical Media Literacy Guide: Engaging Media and Transforming Education*. Rotterdam: Brill-Sense Publishers.

Kerswell, J.L. (2012) *The Slasher Movie Book by J. A. Kerswell*. Chicago: Chicago Review Press.

King, Stephen (1981) *Danse Macabre*. New York: Everett.

Kolb, David (1986) *The Critique of Pure Modernity*. Chicago, IL: University of Chicago Press.

Kolko, Gabriel (1991) "Obsessed with Military 'Credibility'," *Progressive* (March): 24–26.

Kracauer, Siegfried (1947 [1074]) *From Caligari to Hitler*. Princeton, NJ: Princeton University Press.

Kroker, Arthur and David Cook (1986) *The Postmodern Scene*. New York: Saint Martin's Press.

LaMay, Craig et al. (1991) *The Media at War*. New York: Gannett Foundation Media Center.

Lash, Scott (1988) "Discourse or Figure? Postmodernism as a 'Regime of Signification'," *Theory, Culture & Society*, Vol. 5, No. 2–3 (June): 58–102.

Lash, Scott and John Urry (1987) *The End of Organized Capitalism*. Cambridge: Polity Press.

Lavery, David (2002) "Emotional Resonance and Rocket Launchers": Joss Whedon's Commentaries on the *Buffy the Vampire Slayer* DVDs, Slayage Six (November) at www.slayage.tv/.

Lavery, David and Rhonda Wilcox, editors (2002) *Fighting the Forces: What's at Stake in Buffy the Vampire Slayer*. Lanham, MD: Rowman and Littlefield.

Lazarsfeld, Paul (1941) "Remarks on Administrative and Critical Communications Research," *Studies in Philosophy and Social Science*, Vol. IX: 2–16.

Leary, Timothy (1990) "Quark of the Decade," *Mondo*, Vol. 2000 No. 7: 53–56.

Lee, Spike, (with Lisa Jones) (1988) *Uplift the Race. The Construction of School Daze*. New York: Simon and Schuster.

Lee, Spike (1989) *Do the Right Thing*. New York: Simon and Schuster.

Lee, Spike, (with Ralph Wiley) (1992) *By Any Means Necessary. The Trials and Tribulations of the Making of Malcolm X*. New York: Hyperion.

Lepenies, Wolf (1988) *Between Literature and Science: The Rise of Sociology*. Cambridge: Cambridge University Press.

Lewis, Lisa (1993) "Emergence of Female Address on MTV," in *Frith, Goodwin, and Grossberg*, op. cit.

Livingstone, Sonia (2017) *The Class: Living and Learning in the Digital Age (Connected Youth and Digital Futures)*. New York: NYU Press.

Lohmann, Georg (1980) "Gesellschaftskritik Und Normativer Massstab," in A. Honneth and U. Jaeggi, editors, *Arbeit, Handlung, Normatativität*. Frankfurt: Suhrkamp, 270–272

Lorde, Audre (1984) *Sister Outsider*. CA: The Crossing Press.

Lyotard, Jean-Francois (1984) *The Postmodern Condition*. Minneapolis, MN: University of Minnesota Press.

Macdonald, Dwight (1944) "A Theory of Popular Culture," *Politics*, Vol, 1, No. 1: 20–23.

———— (1957) "A Theory of Mass Culture," in Rosenberg and White, editors, op. cit.

———— (1962) *Against the American Grain*. New York: Random House.

Macherey, Pierre (1978) *A Theory of Literary Production*. London: Routledge & Kegan Paul.

Malcolm X (1992) *The Final Speeches*. New York: Pathfinder Press.

Males, Mike (1996a) *The Scapegoat Generation: America's War On Adolescents*. Boston, MA: Common Courage Press.

———— (1996b) *The Scapegoat Generation: America's War On Adolescents*. Monroe, Maine: Common Courage Press.

Marable, Manning (1982) *How Capitalism Underdeveloped Black America*. Boston, MA: South End Press.

Marcus, Greil (1989) *Lipstick Traces*. Cambridge, MA: Harvard University Press.

Marcuse, Herbert (1955) *Eros and Civilization*. Boston, MA: Beacon Press.

———— (1964) *One-Dimensional Man*. Boston, MA: Beacon Press.

———— (1968) *Negations*. Boston, MA: Beacon Press.

———— (1973) *Grundrisse*. London: Penguin Books.

———— (1977) *The German Ideology*. New York: International Publishers.

———— (1978 [1922]) "Bd. 1: Der Deutsche Kunstlerroman," in Peter-Erwin Jansen, editor, *Schriften 1*. Frankfurt: Suhrkamp.

Marx, Karl (1906) *Capital*. New York: The Modern Library.

———— (1978) in Robert C. Tucker, editor, *The Marx-Engels Reader*. New York: Norton, 2nd edition.

Marx-Engels (1978) *The Marx-Engels Reader*, edited by Robert Tucker. New York: W.W. Norton.

McAllister, Matthew P. and Robert E Denton, Jr. (1993) "'What Did You Advertise with the War, Daddy?': Using the Persian Gulf War as a Referent in Advertising," in Robert E. Denton, editors, *The Media and the Persian Gulf War*, 213–234. Westport, CT: Preager.

McCaffery, Larry (1991) Editor *Storming the Reality Studio*. Durham: Duke University Press.

McChesney, Robert W. (2013) *Digital Disconnect: How Capitalism is Turning the Internet Against Democracy*. New York: New Press.

McGuigan, Jim (1992) *Cultural Populism*. London: Routledge.

McHale, Brian (1991) POSTcyberMODERNpunkISM, in McCaffery, editor, *Storming the Reality Studio*, op. cit., 308–323.

———— (1992) "Elements of a Poetics of Cyberpunk," *Critique*, Vol. XXXIII, No. 3 (Spring): 149–176.

McLaren, Peter (1993) "White Terror and Oppositional Agency," *Strategies*, Vol. 7: 1–37.

———— (1996) *The Predatory Society*. London and New York: Routledge.

McLaren, Peter, Rhonda Hammer, David Sholle, and Susan Reilly (1995) *Rethinking Media Literacy. A Critical Pedagogy of Representation*. New York: Peter Lang.

McLuhan, Marshall (1964) *Understanding Media*. New York: McGraw Hill.

McQuaig, Linda (1993) *The Wealthy Banker's Wife*. London and Toronto: Penguin Books.

McRobbie, Angela (1994) *Postmodernism and Popular Culture*. London: Routledge.

Mead, David (1991) "Technological Transfiguration in William Gibson's Sprawl Novels," *Extrapolation*, Vol. 32, No. 4: 350–360.

Mitchell, Juliet (1974) *Psychoanalysis and Feminism*. New York: Pantheon.

Molina-Guzman, Isabel (2010) *Dangerous Curves. Latina Bodies in the Media*. New York: NYU Press.

Morton, Melanie (1992) "Don't Go for Second Sex Baby!," in Cathy Schwichtenberg, editor, *The Madonna Connection: Representational Politics, Subcultural Identities, and Cultural Theory*, 220–243. Boulder, CO: Westview.

Mowlana, Hamid, George Gerbner, and Herbert Schiller (1992) *Triumph of the Image*. Boulder, CO: Westview.

Nance, Malcolm (2016) *The Plot to Hack America. How Putin's Cyberspies and WikiLeaks Tried to Steal the 2016 Election*, New York: Skyhorse.

———— (2019) *The Plot to Betray America: How Team Trump Embraced Our Enemies, Compromised Our Security, and How We Can Fix It*. New York: Hachette.

Nicholson, Linda (1985) *Gender and History*. New York: Columbia University Press.

Nietzsche, Friedrich (1968) *The Will to Power*. New York: Random House.

———— (1969) *The Genealogy of Morals*. New York: Random House.

Nimmo, Dan and Mark Hovind (1993) "Vox Populi: Talk Radio and TV Cover the Gulf War," in Robert E. Denton, editors, *The Media and the Persian Gulf War*, 89–106. Westport, CT: Preager.

Noble, Sofia (2018) *Algorithms of Oppression: How Search Engines Reinforce Racism*. New York: NYU Press.

Noriega, Chon (2000) *Shot in America: Television, the State, and the Rise of Chicano Cinema*. Minneapolis: University of Minnesota Press.

O'Connor, Alan (1989) "The Problem of American Cultural Studies," *Critical Studies in Mass Communication* Vol. 6 (1929): 405–413.

Offe, Claus (1985) *Disorganized Capitalism*. Cambridge: Polity Press.

Ollman, Bertell and Edward Vernoff, editors (1982) *The Left Academy*. New York: McGraw and Hill.

Patterson, Alex (1992) *Spike Lee. A Biography*. London: Abacus.

Pecheux, Michel (1982) *Language, Semantics, and Ideology*. Saint Martin: New York.

Poster, Mark (1991) *Mode of Information*. Cambridge: Polity Press.

Postman, Neil (1985) *Amusing Ourselves to Death*. New York: Viking-Penguin.

——— (1992) *Technopolis: The Surrender of Culture to Technology*. New York: Random House.

Pribram, E. Deidre (1992) "Seduction, Control, & the Search for Authenticity: Madonna's Truth or Dare," *The Madonna Connection: Representational Politics, Subcultural Identities, And Cultural Theory*, 193–219.

Prince, Stephen (1993) "Celluloid Heroes and Smart Bombs: Hollywood at War in the Middle East," *The Media and the Persian Gulf War*, 235–256.

Radaway, Janice A. (1984) *Reading the Romance*. Chapel Hill, NC: University of North Carolinea Press.

Reed, Adolph (1993) "The Trouble with X," *The Progressive* (February): 18–19.

Reid, Mark (1993) *Redefining Black Film*. Berkeley, CA: University of California Press.

——— (1997) *PostNegritude Visual and Literary Culture (SUNY series, Cultural Studies in Cinema/Video) Hardcover*. Buffalo, NY: SUNY University Press.

Rich, Ruby B. (2013) *New Queer Cinema: The Director's Cut*. Durham, NC: Duke University Press Books.

Ricoeur, Paul (1970) *Freud and Philosophy*. New Haven: Yale University Press.

——— (1984) *Time and Narrative*. Chicago, IL: University of Chicago Press.

Riesman, David et al. (1950) *The Lonely Crowd*. Garden City, NY: Anchor Books.

Rifas, Leonard (1994) "Supermarket Tabloids and Persian Gulf War Dissent," in Susan Jeffords and Lauren Rabinowitz, editors, *Seeing through the Media: The Persian Gulf War*. New Brunswick, NJ: Rutgers University Press, c1994. 230–242.

Ritzer, George, editor (1990) *Frontiers of Social Theory*. New York: Columbia University Press.

Robinson, Lillian (1978) *Sex, Class, and Culture*. Bloomington, IN: Indiana University Press.

Rojek, Chris (2004) *Celebrity*. London: Reaktion Books.

Rosenberg, Bernard and David White, editors (1957) *Mass Culture*. Glencoe, IL: The Free Press.

Rosenthal, Michael (1992) "What Was Postmodernism?" *Socialist Review*, Vol. 92, No. 3: 83–106.

Ross, Andrew (1988) *Universal Abandon?* Minneapolis, MN: University of Minnesota Press.

Roszak, Theodor (1968) *The Making of a Counter Culture: Reflections on the Technocratic Society and Its Youthful Opposition*. Berkeley, CA: University of California Press (October 18, 1995).

Rowbotham, Shelia (1972) *Women, Resistance, & Revolution*. New York: Vintage.

Ryan, Michael (1982) *Marxism and Deconstruction*. Baltimore, MD: John Hopkins University Press.

——— (1989) *Marxism and Deconstruction Culture and Politics*. London: Macmillan and Johns Hopkins University Press.

Said, Edward (1978) *Orientalism*. New York: Random House.

Salinger, Pierre and Eric Laurent (1991) *Secret Dossier: The Hidden Agenda behind the Gulf War*. New York: Penguin Books.

Sargent, Lydia (1981) *Women and Revolution*. Boston, MA: South End Press.

Savan, Leslie (1993) "Commercials Go Rock," in Simon Frith, Andrew Goodwin, and Lawrence Grossberg, editors, *Sound and Vision. The Music Video Reader.* London: Routledge, 85–90.

Sayre, Henry M. (1989) *The Object of Performance.* Chicago, IL: University of Chicago Press.

Scatamburlo, Valerie (1994) *Critical Pedagogy, Multiculturalism, and Political Correctness.* Masters Dissertation, Department of Communication, Windsor University, Canada.

Schiller, Herbert (1989) *Culture, Inc.* Oxford, U.K.: Oxford University Press Inc.

Schorr, Juliet (1992) *The Overworked American.* New York: Basic Books.

Schudson, Michael (1984) *Advertising, the Uneasy Persuasion.* New York: Basic Books.

Schwichtenberg, Cathy, editor (1992) *The Madonna Connection.* Boulder, CO: Westview.

Segal, Lynne (1991) "Feminism and the Future," *New Left Review*, Vol. 185: 81–91.

Sexton, Adam (1993) *Desperately Seeking Madonna.* New York: Delta Books.

Shaheen, Jack (1984) *The TV Arab.* Bowling Green, Ohio: The Popular Press.

Shaw, Martin and Roy Carr-Hill (1991) "Mass Media and Attitudes to the Gulf War in Britain," *The Electronic Journal of Communication*, Vol. 2, No. 2 (Fall). www.cios.org/EJC PUBLIC/002/1/00212.HTML

Shiner, Lewis (1991) "Confessions of an Ex-Cyberpunk," *New York Times*, January 7: A19.

Sholle, David and Stan Denski (1994) *Media Education and the (Re)production of Culture.* Westport, CT: Bergin & Garvey.

Showalter, Elaine (1985) *The New Feminist Criticism.* New York: Pantheon.

Shusterman, Richard (1992) *Pragmatist Aesthetics, Living Beauty, Rethinking Art.* Cambridge, MA: Blackwell.

Simons, Herbert W., editor (1990) *The Rhetorical Turn: Invention and Persuasion in the Conduct of Inquiry.* Chicago, IL: University of Chicago Press.

Solop, F.I. and N.A. Wonders (1991) "Reaction to the Persian Gulf Crisis: Gender, Race, and Generational Differences." Paper presented at American Association of Public Opinion Research.

Sontag, Susan (1969) *Against Interpretation.* New York: Dell.

Spivak, Gayatri (1988) *In Other Worlds.* New York and London: Methuen.

Sterling, Bruce, editor (1986) *Mirrorshades.* New York: Ace.

——— (1992) *The Hacker Crackdown.* New York: Bantam Books.

Storey, John (2015) *Cultural Theory and Popular Culture, An Introduction.* London and New York: Routledge.

Theweleit, Klaus (1987) *Male Fantasies.* Minneapolis, MN: University of Minnesota Press.

Thompson, David (1981) *Overexposures: A Crisis in American Filmmaking* New York: Morrow.

Thompson, Edward Palmer (1963) *The Making of the English Working Class.* New York: Vintage.

Thompson, John (1984) *Studies in the Theory of Ideology.* Cambridge: Polity Press.

——— (1990) *Ideology and Modern Culture.* Cambridge and Stanford, CA: Polity and Stanford University Press.

Toobin, Jeffrey (2000) *Vast Conspiracy.* New York: Simon and Schuster.

Toop, David (1984) *The Rap Attack: African Jive to New York Hip-Hop.* Boston, MA: South End Press.

Turnbull, Sue and Vyvyan Stranieri (2003) *Bite Me.* Victoria, Australia: The Australian Centre for the Moving Images.

Turner, Graeme (1990) *British Cultural Studies: An Introduction.* New York: Unwin Hyman.

Veblen, Thorstein (2009) *The Theory of the Leisure Class.* Oxford, UK: Oxford University Press

Venturi, Robert (1972) *Learning from Las Vegas*. Cambridge, MA: MIT Press.

Wallace, Michelle (1992) "Boyz N the Hood and Jungle Fever," in Gina Dent, editor, *Black Popular Culture*. Seattle, WA: Bay Press, 123–131.

Warner, William (1992) "Spectator Aesthetics," in Lawrence Grossberg, Cary Nelson and Paula Treichler, editors, *Cultural Studies*. New York: Routledge, 672–688.

Warshow, Robert (1962) *The Immediate Experience*. New York: Garden City.

Waxman, Chaim (1968) *The End of Ideology Debate*. New York: Simon and Schuster.

West, Cornel (1992a) "A Matter of Life and Death," October 61 (Summer), 20–27.

——— (1992b) "Nihilism in Black America," in Gina Dent, editor, *Black Popular Culture*. Seattle, WA: Bay Press, 37–47.

Wexler, Philip (1992) *Becoming Somebody*. London and Washington, DC: The Falmer Press, Turnball.

Wilcox, Rhonda V. (2002) "'Who Died and Made Her the Boss?': Patterns of Mortality in Buffy the Vampire Slayer," in David Lavery, editor, *Fighting the Forces: What's at Stake in Buffy the Vampire Slayer*. Lanham, MD: Rowman & Littlefield Publishers, 3–17.

Williams, Raymond (1958) *Culture and Society*. New York: Harper and Row.

——— (1976) *Keywords: A Vocabulary of Culture and Society*. London: Fontana.

——— (1977) *Marxism and Literature*. New York: Oxford University Press.

——— (1981) *Culture*. London: Fontana.

Williamson, Judith (1978) *Decoding Advertisements*. London: Marion Boyers.

Willis, Ellen (1984) "Radical Feminism," in Sohnya Sayres, editor, *The Sixties Without Apology*. Minneapolis, MN: University of Minnesota Press, 91–118.

Wilson, Elizabeth (1985) *Adorned in Dreams: Fashion and Modernity*. London: Virago.

Winter, James (1992) *Common Cents*. Montreal and New York: Black Rose Books.

Wolin, Richard (1984) "Modernism versus Postmodernism," *Telos*, Vol. 62: 9–30.

Wood, Robin (1986) *Hollywood from Vietnam to Reagan*. New York: Columbia University Press.

——— (2018) *Robin Wood on the Horror Film: Collected Essays and Reviews*. Detroit, MI: Wayne State University Press.

Woodward, Bob (1991) *The Commanders*. New York: Simon and Schuster.

Zavarzadeh, Mas'ud (1991) *Seeing Films Politically*. Albanym N.Y.: State University of New York Press.

INDEX

13th 122–123, 158
27 Dresses 150–151
The 40-Year-Old Virgin 168–169

Abolition Democracy 158
Active Measures 244
activism, media and cultural 296–298
advertising 291, 292, 293, 298
African American films 107–108; *13th*
  122–123; audience for 108–109;
  BlacKkKlansman 118–120; *Do the Right
  Thing* 108, 109–116; *The Hate U Give*
  124–126; *Malcolm X* 116–118; *Selma*
  120–122; Spike Lee 108–109; *When
  They see Us* 123–124
AIDS 173–174
Ailes, Roger 215
Amer, Karim 244
American Bandstand 182
American Horror Story 89–91
American nightmares: crisis of family and
  patriarchy 89–91; extreme horror,
  violence and 91–92; middle-class
  anxieties 84–89; racial and class angst
  98–104
The Amityville Horror 86
anticipatory dimension to media culture 46
Apatow, Judd 168, 169
apocalypse, social 101, 278; Dick's vision of
  279–281
The Apprentice 237–239
Arita-Howard, Maria 231
Arriaga, Guillermo 131

Atwood, Margaret 62, 63, 65
audience reception and uses of media
  culture 41–47
auteurs 80–81, 110, 183
Avatar 39–40, 68
The Aviator 160–162

Babel 131–134
*Barack Obama – The Man and History
  Journey* 231
Barack Obama: People's President 233
Barker, Greg 235
Barry 235
Batman, social corruption and 6–8
Batman Begins 6–7
Beavis and Butt-Head 187–190,
  208n5–208n8, 209n9
Beyoncé 205–207
Beyond the Sea 162–164
The Big Beat 181
Bildungsroman 194, 256
biopics, major male 160–167; *Beyond the
  Sea* 162–164; *The Hoax* 162; *I Walk the
  Line* 164; *I'm Not There* 164–165; *Ray*
  162; *Straight Outta Compton* 165–167
Birmingham Centre for Contemporary
  Cultural Studies 31, 33, 35, 54, 179
Black culture 108; appropriation of 182;
  spectacle of 206 *see also* African
  American films
Black nationalism 109
Black Panther 70, 71, 73–76, 78n15, 78n16,
  79n20, 79n22

BlacKkKlansman 118–120
Blade Runner 278, 281–284
Blade Runner 2049 284–286
Bloch, Ernst 66, 77n8
Bonnie and Clyde 40
Bordertown 137–138
Bowling for Columbine 245
Brecht, Bertolt 109–110, 117, 143n5,
    144n21
British cultural studies 31–33; encoding/
    decoding 46; focus on youth culture 179;
    ideology and media culture 21; political
    struggles and 35–36; terminology 34
Brokeback Mountain 170
Bryan, Jack 244
Buffy the Vampire Slayer 192–200, 209n14,
    210n19; allegorical level 196–198,
    210n18; film 194–195; television series
    192–194, 195–200
Buñuel, Luis 186
Burns, Ken 159
Burnett, Mark 238
Bush/Cheney era: *Batman* films a critical
    allegory of 6–8; *Lord of the Rings*
    resonating with mood of 261, 264, 265,
    268; patriarchal conservatism of 256
Bush, George H.W. 32, 215–218; death
    222, 250n10; Horton advertisements
    215; Persian Gulf TV war 216–217;
    presidency 216–217; presidential election
    campaign 1988 215–216; presidential
    election campaign 1992 217–218; sons
    223, 250n11
Bush, George W. 221–227, 251n14; as
    Batman 7; family scandals 222–224; as
    Governor of Texas 221, 224; *Grand Theft
    2000* 221–222, 223; September 11 terror
    attacks 222 *see also* Bush/Cheney era
Bush, Jeb 223
Bush, Prescott 222
*By the People: The Election of Barack
    Obama* 233

cable television 63, 291, 298
Caldwell, John 37
Cambridge Analytica 244–245
Camera Politica 20
Cameron, James 39
Capitalism: A Love Story 246
capitalism, critique of 101–104, 114,
    283–284
Capote 170–171
Carol 174
Carpenter, John 91

Cash, Johnny 164
Cecile B. Demented 171
celebrity: ascribed, attributed or achieved
    230; culture of 218, 229–230;
    intersection of politics and 213, 218–219
The Celebrity Apprentice 238
Charles, Ray 162
Cheney, Dick 224–226 *see also* Bush/
    Cheney era
"chick flicks" 150, 168
Clark, Dick 182
class: *Buffy the Vampire Slayer* and
    representations of 198–199; *Poltergeist* and
    anxieties of middle- 84–89; and racial
    angst 98–104; and re-distribution of
    wealth 82, 105n5; social anxiety of
    young working- 187–192; *Us* and
    blocks to mobility 100–101 *see also*
    working-class
Clemente 140
Clinton, Bill 218–221, 233, 243; blending
    of information and entertainment 218;
    Monica Lewinsky scandal 219–220;
    presidency, first term 218–219;
    presidency, second term 219–220;
    presidential election campaign
    217, 218
Clinton, Hillary 218, 248
Close Encounters of the Third Kind 88
Clover, Carl 81
Columbus, Chris 173
Comey, James 243, 244
commodification: of communications 298,
    300; of culture 15; Philip K. Dick's
    dystopia of total 279–280
communication: culture and 31, 33–34,
    49n20, 50n26; policy 298–300
conservative hegemony 36, 61, 82, 184
contested terrain of media culture 3, 17,
    20–21, 38, 54, 55, 120; news and
    infotainment as 227–229
Coogler, Ryan 73, 79n20
corporate: America 191–192, 245–249;
    control of information highways
    299–300; media 38, 70, 219, 229, 230
Craven, Wes 92
Crenshaw, Kimberly 22, 40, 55, 153
crime and violence, fear of 97
critical intersectional multiculturalism
    53–58
critical media literacy 2, 8–10, 293; need
    for new types of 13, 15–16, 301;
    pedagogies for developing 294–296
critical race theory 22, 40, 53

critical social theory 8, 30, 31, 54–55, 60, 61
Cronenberg, David 269–277; *The Dead Zone* 270, 274; *eXistenZ* 275–276; *The Fly* 270, 274–275; "new flesh" 272, 273, 274, 276–277; *Rabid* 269; *Scanners* 270, 271–272, 276; *Shivers* 269, 271; *Videodrome* 269, 270, 272–274, 276
Crossing Over 140–141
cultural: activism, media and 296–298; identity 111, 112–113; industry 29; policy 300; politics, media and 298–301; production and political economy 36–39, 50–51n30

Daldry, Stephen 174
Daniels, Greg 190
Darin, Bobby 162–164
The Dark Knight 6, 7–8
Davis, Angela 158
Dazed and Confused 187
The Dead Zone 270, 274
The Deer Hunter 67
Defense News 290
Destiny's Child 205
The Devil Wears Prada 149–150, 176n1
diagnostic critique 69, 80; *Buffy the Vampire Slayer* a 192–200; of superheroes 69–76
Dick, Philip K. 277, 278; *Do Androids Dream of Electric Sheep?* 279–281; entropy 283–284
digital culture: new literacies for 13, 15–16, 301; Trump and 38, 236, 239, 240, 241, 244–245
A Dirty Shame 171–172
Do Androids Dream of Electric Sheep? 279–281
Do the Right Thing 108, 109–116; characters 111–112; color-coding symbolism 111–112; criticism of 115; cultural identity 112–113; influencing fashion trends 112; as a modernist film 110; as a postmodern film 111, 115, 143n8, 143n9; question of political and social morality 110–111; racial slurs 114; violence in the ghettoes 114–115, 144n16
Dole, Bob 219
Dr. Dre 165–166, 167
"dude flicks" 167–169; *The 40 Year Old Virgin* 168–169; *Forgetting Sarah Marshall* 169
Dukakis, Michael 215–216
DuVernay, Ava 120–124; *13th* 122–123, 158; *Middle of Nowhere* 120; *Selma* 120–122; *When They see Us* 120, 123–124
Dylan, Bob 164–165
dystopias 278; *Blade Runner* 278, 281–284; *Blade Runner 2049* 284–286; *The Handmaid's Tale* 62–65

Easy Rider 20
Eazy-E 165–166, 167
ecological/political critique: *The Handmaid's Tale* 62–65; *Lord of the Rings* 263
El Cantante 135
El Norte 136–137
encoding/decoding 41–42, 46, 60
English, Diane 152
entropy 283–284
Epstein, Rob 175
E.T. 84, 87, 88–89, 105n11
ethnographic research 42–43
eXistenZ 275–276
Extract 191

Facebook 38, 42, 239, 244, 245, 300
Fahrenheit 9/11 245
Fahrenheit 11/9 67, 248–249
Falchuk, Brad 89
Fall of the Republic 233
Faludi, Susan 159–160, 176–177n9
families: depiction in *Buffy the Vampire Slayer* 193–194; horror films and crisis of 89–91, 95; as source of monsters 84; in Spielberg's work 88–89
fan cultures 42–43
Fancher, Hampton 284
fantasy entertainment: as political allegory 256–257 *see also Lord of the Rings (LOTR)*
fashion: and identity 200–203; Madonna, identity and 202, 203–205; mass cultural images pervading 112; -subversion 201–202
The Fellowship of the Ring 257–261
femininity 147, 149
feminism 18, 22, 40; *Buffy the Vampire Slayer* and 198; multiperspectival informing of 59–60
Ferguson, Tom 105n5, 203
The Final Year 235–236
Fletcher, Anne 150
Flint, Michigan 248
The Fly 270, 274–275
Forgetting Sarah Marshall 169
Fox & Friends 239

Fox News 38, 219, 229, 253n39
France 299
Frankel, David 149
Frankfurt School 21, 28, 29–31, 54, 67–68, 294, 297
Freed, Alan 181–182
Frida 127–129
The Front Runner 227–229
Fukunaga, Cary 141–142
future generations looking back to present 289–292

Gaga: Five Foot Two 207
Game of Thrones 41–42, 58, 290
Gance, Abel 266
Gandhi, Vikram 235
Gathara, Patrick 75–76
Gemeinschaft 258, 261
genre criticism 39
German Expressionism 197, 282
Get Out 98–100
global popular 9, 44
globalization 38–39, 130–131; *Babel* in world of 131–134
Godard, Jean-Luc 186
Gore, Al 221
Gramsci, Antonio 31
Grand Theft 2000 221–222, 223
The Great Hack 244–245
The Green Berets 25–26
Green Book 119
Green, Michael 284
Gulf war, 1991 32, 216–217
gun violence 75, 97, 248–249, 293

Hairspray 171
Halestrom, Lars 162
Hall, Stuart 41
Halliburton 225, 226
Halloween 91–92, 92–95, 93, 106n15
The Handmaid's Tale 62–65
Harken Energy Corporation 224
Hart, Gary 227–229
The Hate U Give 124–126
Haynes, Todd 164, 170, 174
hegemony: conservative 36, 61, 82, 184; contesting dominant 67–68; theory 31–32
Hell's Angels 161
Heroes of Rock 201
high culture and low culture 30, 32–33
Hitler, Adolf 249
The Hoax 162
Hoggart, Richard 35

home, fear of losing one's 85–86
Homecoming 205–207
Hooper, Tobe 84, 92, 98, 105n7
horror films: allegories 81, 82, 83–84, 84–85, 86, 87, 101, 196–197; *American Horror Story* 89–91; earnings from 93, 104–105n4; in Germany 83; *Get Out* 98–100; *Halloween* 91–92, 92–95, 106n15; Hollywood and 81–84; *Poltergeist* 83, 84–89, 105n7; racial and class angst 98–104; *Sorry to Bother You* 101–104; stalk and slash 91–98; *Us* 98, 100–101
Horton, Willie 215
The Hours 174
Hughes, Howard 160–162
Hunter, Duncan 172
Hype: The Obama Effect 232

I Spit on Your Grave 92, 96
I Walk the Line 164
Ice Cube 165–166, 167
Icebox 142
Ichaso, Leon 134; *El Cantante* 135; *Pinero* 134–135
icons, pop culture *see* pop culture icons
identity: fashion and 200–203; Madonna, fashion and 202, 203–205; mass-produced images and mediation of 112–113
ideology critique 19, 21–23, 65–66, 68
I'm Not There 164–165
immanent critique 67–68
immigration, issue of 130, 139–142; *Clemente* 140; *Crossing Over* 140–141; *El Norte* 136–137; *Icebox* 142; *La Tragedia de Macario* 140; *Orange is the New Black* 156–157; *Sangre de mi Sangre* 139; *Sin Nombre* 141–142; in Trump era 142, 245; *Under the Same Moon* 139–140
Inarritu, Alejandro Gonzalez 131
Infamous 170–171
information superhighways 299
infotainment and news as contested terrain 227–229
Instagram 230, 239–240
intersectional multiculturalism, critical 53–58
intersectionality 22, 40, 55; *Orange is the New Black* 153–158
Iran-Contra Affair 214
Iraq War 224, 226, 231
irrationalism, resurgence of 82–83
Irving, Clifford 162

J'Accuse 266
Jackson, Michael 203, 243
Jackson, Peter 255, 258, 263–264
Jaws 66
Jeffords, Susan 25
Jenkins, Patty 71, 73
Jones, Alex 233–234, 252n30
Judge, Mike: *Beavis and Butt-Head* 187–190, 208n5–208n8, 209n9; *Extract* 191; *King of the Hill* 190; *Office Space* 190–191; *Silicon Valley* 191–192
The Justice League 44

Kahlo, Frida 127–129
Kellner, Douglas 222, 246, 251n15, 252n31; and Michael Ryan 20 Kerman, Piper 153
King, Martin Luther, Jr. 111, 115, 120–122, 231, 232
King of the Hill 190
King, Stephen 85–86
Kohan, Jenji 153
Kramer, Wayne 140–141
Kubrick, Stanley 167
Kuzui, Fran Rubel 194

La Bamba 126–127
La La Land 67
La Tragedia de Macario 140
Lady Gaga 207
Lang, Fritz 282
last girl standing, theme of 81, 92, 96
The Last House on the Left 92
Latino films 126–138; *Babel* 131–134; *Bordertown* 137–138; *Clemente* 140; *Crossing Over* 140–141; *El Cantante* 135; *El Norte* 136–137; *Frida* 127–129; *La Bamba* 126–127; *La Tragedia de Macario* 140; *Pinero* 134–135; *Sangre de mi Sangre* 139; *Selena* 129–130; *Sin Nombre* 141–142; *Under the Same Moon* 139–140; *Zoot Suit* 126
Latinos' underrepresentation in Hollywood films 126, 145n27
Lavoe, Hector 135
Lavoe, Puchi 135
Lee, Spike 107, 108–109; *BlacKkKlansman* 118–120; body of work 118; *Do the Right Thing* 108, 109–116; *Malcolm X* 116–118, 144n22, 145n24; parallels with Brecht 109–110, 117, 143n5; profitability of films 109, 142n2
lesbian-centric films 174
Lewinsky, Monica 219–220

LGBTQ+ movement and Hollywood 169–176; *Capote* 170–171; *Carol* 174; *Cecile B. Demented* 171; *A Dirty Shame* 171–172; *Hairspray* 171; *The Hours* 174; *Infamous* 170–171; *Milk* 170, 174–176, 178n21; *Rent* 173–174; *Transamerica* 170, 172–173, 177n19
Linklater, Richard 183; *Dazed and Confused* 187; *Slacker* 184–187
Lipstick 96
Livingston, Jennie 170
Lopez, Jennifer 130, 135, 137
Lord of the Rings (LOTR) 256–269; critique of industrial and technological modernity 258, 262, 263; ecology 263; *The Fellowship of the Ring* 257–261; *Gemeinschaft* 258, 261; militarism in 263–265, 267, 268; parallels with War on Terror 256, 261, 264, 265; patriarchal conservatism 256, 261, 267, 268; racism 260, 262, 266; representations of women 261, 262, 267; *The Return of the King* 264, 265–269; *The Two Towers* 261–265; Whiteness 266

Madonna 202, 203–205
Malcolm X 110, 111, 115, 116, 121, 144n22, 145n23, 205–206
Malcolm X (film) 116–118, 144n22, 145n24
Mangold, James 164
Marston, William Moulton 71, 78n12
Martin, George R.R. 42, 58, 290
Marxism 18, 21, 22, 32, 40, 247; Bloch's critique of 66; multiperspectival informing of 59–60
masculinity 147; crisis of 159–160; "dude flicks" and renegotiation of 167–169; men's films and crises of 159–167; of *Rambo* 25; Vietnam a blow to White 25
mass culture, terminology 33
mass shootings 75, 97, 248–249, 293
McCarty, John 92, 106n15
McChesney, Robert 292
McGarth, Douglas 170
McKay, Adam 225
McKenna, Aline Brosh 150
McQueen, Steve 153
"mean world" syndrome 97
media/cultural studies 5, 8–10; approaches to 28–36; components of critical 36–47; politics of 35–36; terminology 5, 33–35; transdisciplinary 28–29
media spectacle of presidential politics: Bush I 215–218; Bush II 221–227;

Clinton 217, 218–221, 233, 243; contested terrain of news and infotainment 227–229; corporate media and 230; Obama 211, 231–236, 239, 247–248; Reagan 212–215; Trump 211, 236–245
MeToo movement 148, 301
Metropolis 282
Mexican American identity 126–127
Michael Moore in TrumpLand 248
middle-class, *Poltergeist* and anxieties of 84–89
Middle of Nowhere 120
military spending 290
Milk 170, 174–176, 178n21
The Milky Way 186
Miller, Bennett 170
Miller, Bruce 63
Missing in Action 24, 25
Moore, Michael 245–249; *Bowling for Columbine* 245; *Capitalism: A Love Story* 246; *Fahrenheit 9/11* 245; *Fahrenheit 11/9* 67, 248–249; *Michael Moore in TrumpLand* 248
multicultural ideological critique 23
multiculturalism, critical intersectional 53–58
multiperspectival, cultural studies as 46–47, 57; towards 58–62
Murphy, Ryan 89
mythic redemption 27

nationalism: Black 109; media culture and 113; opposition to Trump's agenda of White 55–56
Native Americans 85, 105n8
Nava, Gregory 129, 135–136; *Bordertown* 137–138; *El Norte* 136–137; *Selena* 129–130
"new flesh" 272, 273, 274, 276–277
New Jack City 45
New Queer Cinema 170
news media 38; corporate 38, 70, 219, 229, 230; highly ideological and partisan 219, 229; infotainment and 212, 219, 227–229; Trump's presidential campaign's domination of 241
Nietzsche, Friedrich 58
Nolan, Christopher 6, 7
Norris, Chuck 24, 25
Nosferatu 197, 282
Noujaim, Jehane 244
N.W.A. 165–166

Obama, Barack 122, 211, 231–236; anticipation of election of 46; digital age presidential campaign 231–232, 239; documentaries 231–234, 235–236; fictional films on early life 234–235; in Flint 248; Moore's critique of 247–248
The Obama Deception 233
occult: *Poltergeist* 83, 84–89, 105n7; resurgence of 82–83
Office Space 190–191
Once Upon a Time In Hollywood 295–296
One Plus One 186
Orange is the New Black 153–158

paleosymbols 45–46
Pandemonium 95
Paris is Burning 170
Parkland High School, Florida 248–249, 293
patriarchy: *American Horror Story* and crisis of 89–91; *Babel* and crisis of 132–134, 146n34; *Buffy the Vampire Slayer* and 198; *Lord of the Rings* and 256, 261, 267, 268; men's films and crises of 159–167
Peele, Jordan 98, 100
Pennies From Heaven 67
Perot, Ross 218, 250n11
personality, presidential culture of 220–221
Petersen, Alan 232
Pinero 134–135
Platoon 67
police violence 123, 124–126, 145n26
political allegory, fantasy entertainment as 256–257
political documentary 245–249
political economy, cultural production and 36–39, 50–51n30
political reading of media culture 19–21
political spectacle: Bush I 215–218; Bush II 221–227; Clinton 217, 218–220, 233, 243; contested terrain 227–229; culture of personality 220–221; as entertainment 212, 242; Obama 211, 231–236, 239, 247–248; Reagan 212–215; Trump 211, 236–245
Poltergeist 83, 84–89, 105n7
pop culture icons 200, 203–208; Beyoncé 205–207; Britney Spears 205; Lady Gaga 207; Madonna 202, 203–205
popular culture, terminology 33
Postman, Neil 295
postmodernism 111, 115, 143n8, 143n9, 185, 208n3
President Barack Obama: The Man and His Journey 231

Presley, Elvis 182–183
prison-industrial complex 123
prisoners: *13th* 122–123, 158; *Abolition Democracy* 158; *Orange is the New Black* 153–158
production and political economy 36–39
psychoanalysis 40, 60, 69

Quintanilla-Pérez, Selena 129–130

Rabid 269
race: absence from films in 1980s 107; *Buffy the Vampire Slayer* and representations of 199; *Rambo* films and 25–26 *see also* African American films; Latino films
racial and class angst 98–104; *Get Out* 98–100; *Sorry to Bother You* 101–104; *Us* 100–101
racial Other, *Poltergeist* and fear of 86–87
racism: *13th* and intersection of mass incarceration and 122; *Black Panther* in opposition to culture of 70, 71, 73–76; *BlacKkKlansman* and investigation of 118–120; in *Do the Right Thing* 111, 114; *Green Book* and 119; *The Hate U Give* and resistance to 124–126; hierarchy of 114, 144n15; *Lord of the Rings* and 260, 262, 266; *Selma* and 120–122; *When They see Us* and victims of 123–124
Rambo: as global media spectacle 23–28; multicultural ideological critique 23; paleosymbolic scenes 45
rap singers/groups 165–167
Ray 162
Reagan, Ronald 212–215; *E.T.* and American consciousness in age of 87; *The Handmaid's Tale* a critique of era of 62; Iran-Contra Affair 214; mythic redemption 27; *Poltergeist* and middle-class anxieties in era of 84–89; Star Wars program 214; television networks and support for 38; wealth re-distribution under 105n5; youth culture in era of 203
Reitman, Ivan 227–228
religion, *Buffy the Vampire Slayer* and 199, 210n19
Rent 173–174
resistance movements 243, 301
resonant images 44–45
The Return of the King 264, 265–269
revenge fantasies 81, 92, 96
Rice, Amy 233
Rice, Donna 228
Riefenstahl, Leni 261

Riggen, Patricia 139
Riley, Boots 101, 103–104
Riviera, Diego 127, 128, 129
rock and roll culture 181–183; exploitation and cultural appropriation of Black artists 182; fashion, identity and 202, 203
Rocky–Rambo syndrome 25
Roger and Me 67
Rogers, Joel 105n5, 203
romantic comedies 168–169; *27 Dresses* 150–151
Roosevelt, Franklin D. 246–247
Ross, Herbert 67
Rumsfeld, Donald 214
Russian hacking scandal 243–244
Ryan, Michael 20

Sam, Alice 233
Sangre de mi Sangre 139
Sawka, Daniel 142
Scanners 270, 271–272, 276
Schechter, Danny 233
science fiction 277–278; *Blade Runner* 278, 281–284; *Blade Runner 2049* 284–286; *Do Androids Dream of Electric Sheep?* 279–281
Scorsese, Martin 160
Scott, Ridley 281
Selena 129–130
Selma 120–122
semiotics 39, 60
September 11 terror attacks 222, 256
Sex and the City 151–152
sexual tensions and hostilities 96–97
The Shining 167
Shivers 269, 271
Short Eyes 134, 135
Silicon Valley 188, 191–192
Sin Nombre 141–142
Slacker 184–187
"slasher films" 91–98
The Slumber Party Massacre 95, 96
Smith, Anna Deavere 78n16
social apocalypse 101, 278; Dick's vision of 279–281
social corruption, *Batman* and 6–8
social media 13, 180, 291, 293, 297; access to 298, 299; audiences and 37, 42–43, 44; Cambridge Analytica and data harvesting 38, 244–245; critical media literacy and 293, 301; "influencers" 16, 230, 291; Obama and 231, 239; Trump and 38, 239, 240, 241

society, deep anxieties in U.S. 82–84; crisis of family and patriarchy 89–91; middle-class anxieties 84–89; racial and class angst 98–104; sexual tensions and hostilities 96–97; violence against women 92–98; working-class youth and social anxiety 187–192
society, media culture and 3–6
Sorry to Bother You 101–104
Southside with You 234–235
Spears, Britney 205
Spielberg, Steven 84, 87, 88–89, 105n7, 105n11
stalk and slash films 91–98
A Star is Born 153
Stiffed 159
Stoller, Nicholas 169
Stone, Oliver 27, 67, 81, 224
Storey, John 34
Straight Outta Compton 165–167
Student Bodies 95
Succession 70
superheroes 6, 69–76, 255; *Batman* and social corruption 6–8; *Black Panther* 70, 71, 73–76, 78n15, 78n16, 79n20, 79n22; challenging previous stereotypes in genre 149; *The Justice League* 44; *Wonder Woman* 44, 70, 71–73, 78n12, 79n22
Superman I and *II* 6, 70, 71
surveillance, fears of 87
The Survivor 238

tabloid journalism 219, 227, 229, 230
Tanne, Richard 234
Tarantino, Quentin 295, 302n11
technoculture 269–277
technology: fear of new 87; *Lord of the Rings* and critique of industrial and technological modernity 258, 262, 263; representation in *Blade Runner* 282–283, 284; young people's use of new media and 292–293
television: cable 63, 291, 298; as dominant form of entertainment and information 291; fear of 87, 105n11; increasing commodification of 298; looking back from future at today's 291–292, 293; production and political economy 37, 38; proliferation of production 63; and reality 269; researching programming 209–210n16; rock and roll on 181–182
terminology 5, 33–35
textual analysis 39–41, 47, 60
Thelma and Louise 67

theories of media culture 4–5
theory wars 18–21
Thomas, Angie 124
Thomas, Anna 136; *Bordertown* 137–138; *El Norte* 136–137
Thompson, David 97
Thompson, John 48n9
Tilman, George, Jr. 124
The Times of Harvey Milk 175
Tolkien, J.R. 256, 257–258, 260, 262, 263, 264, 265, 268
Top Gun 66, 67
Transamerica 170, 172–173, 177n19
transcoding 20
Traymor, Julie 127
Trotsky, Leon 128–129
Trump, Donald 211, 236–245; *The Apprentice* 237–239; authoritarian populist 242; background 241–242; *Black Panther* and rebuke to 75, 78n16, 79n20; Cambridge Analytica scandal 38, 244–245; Conway on 119; demonstrations against 71; *Fahrenheit 11/9* 248–249; firing of Comey 243, 244; *Fox & Friends* 239; golf 221; *The Handmaid's Tale* in era of 62, 64–65; Latino experience of immigration in era of 142, 245; master of media spectacle 236; *Michael Moore in TrumpLand* 248; opposition to White nationalist agenda of 55–56; *Orange is the New Black* in era of 155, 157; parallels with Hitler 249; politics as entertainment 242; presidency 242–245; presidential campaign in 'Summer of Trump' 240–241, 242; racial and class angst in era of 98–104, 119; racial injustice under 124; Russian hacking scandal 243–244; Twitter and 239, 240, 241; unleashing of repressed instincts under 101; war on the media 243
Trump, Fred 249
The Twilight Zone 100
Twitter 239, 240, 241
The Two Towers 261–265

Under the Same Moon 139–140
Us 98, 100–101
utopias 66–67; *Beavis and Butt-Head* 190; ideology and 68

Valdez, Luis 67, 126–127
Valens, Ritchie 126–127
vampires, representations of 197

van Peeble, Mario 45
van Sant, Gus 174, 175
Veliz, Pablo 140
Vice 224–226
Videodrome 269, 270, 272–274, 276
Vietnam: a blow to White masculinity 25;
  films with themes of return-to- 24–25;
  mythic redemption of U.S. defeat in 27;
  as Other 26
Villeneuve, Denis 284
Visiting Hours 96

W. 224
Walker, George Herbert 223
War 159
War on Terror: *Lord of the Rings* and
  parallels with 256, 261, 264, 265;
  September 11 terror attacks and 222, 256
The War Room 233
Warhol scene, Andy 171, 177n17
Waters, John 171
WB Network 209n14
wealth distribution 82, 105n5, 290
Weisberger, Lauren 149
Whedon, Joss 194, 195, 209n14, 209n15,
  210n19
When They see Us 120, 123–124
White, Dan 175–176
Widows 153
Wikipedia 206–207
Wiley, Ralph 115, 145n24
Winfrey, Oprah 123
The Women 152, 176n4
women: *Bordertown* and deaths and
  disappearance of 137–138;
  Buffy the Vampire Slayer and
  images of 198; in comedies 149;
  DuVernay and empowerment of
  120–126; *The Handmaid's Tale*
  a dystopian story of oppression of

62–65; Hollywood representations of
  148–149; *Lord of the Rings* and
  representations of 261, 262, 267;
  Rambo films and 25–26; representation
  in *Blade Runner* 283; revenge fantasies
  81, 92, 96; as victims in stalk and slash
  films 95–96; violence against 92–98;
  Wonder Woman in opposition to
  oppression of 70, 71–73
women's films and television series
  148–158; *27 Dresses* 150–151; *The Devil
  Wears Prada* 149–150, 176n1; *Orange is
  the New Black* 153–158; *Sex and the City*
  151–152; *A Star is Born* 153; *Widows* 153;
  The Women 152, 176n4
Wonder Woman 44, 70, 71–73, 78n12,
  79n22
working-class: communities 35; Other,
  Poltergeist and fear of 86–87; social
  anxiety of youth 187–192; victimization
  of 25; youth sub-cultures 179
workplace in high-tech America 191–192

youth culture 179–181; exploitation and
  cultural appropriation of Black artists
  182; fashion, identity and 200–203; pop
  culture icons 203–208; rock and roll
  181–183
youth films: Alan Freed 181–182; *Beavis
  and Butt-Head* 187–190, 208n5–208n8,
  209n9; *Buffy the Vampire Slayer* 192–200,
  209n14, 210n18, 210n19; *Dazed and
  Confused* 187; Elvis Presley 183; *King of
  the Hill* 190; *Silicon Valley* 191–192;
  Slacker 184–187
YouTube 292–293

Zalla, Christopher 139
Zoot Suit 67, 126